Grounds of Comparison

Grounds of Comparison
Around the Work of Benedict Anderson

Edited by Pheng Cheah and Jonathan Culler

ROUTLEDGE
NEW YORK AND LONDON

Published in 2003 by
Routledge
29 West 35th Street
New York, NY 10001
www.routledge-ny.com

Published in Great Britain by
Routledge
11 New Fetter Lane
London EC4P 4EE
www.routledge.co.uk

Routledge is an imprint of the Taylor & Francis Group.

Library of Congress Cataloging-in-Publication Data

Grounds of comparison : around the work of Benedict Anderson / edited by Pheng Cheah and Jonathan Culler.
    p.   cm.
Includes bibliographical references and index.
ISBN 0-415-94335-3 (HB : alk. paper)—ISBN 0-415-94336-1 (PB : alk. paper)
    1. Anderson, Benedict R. O'G. (Benedict Richard O'Gorman), 1936–   2. Nationalism.
3. Nationalism in literature.   4. Politics and literature.   I. Cheah, Pheng.   II. Culler, Jonathan D.

JC311.G76   2003
329.54'01—dc21   2003013604

Contents

Preface   vii

1. Grounds of Comparison   1
   Pheng Cheah

2. On Imagined Communities   21
   Ernesto Laclau

3. Anderson and the Novel   29
   Jonathan Culler

4. Bogeyman: Benedict Anderson's "Derivative" Discourse   53
   Andrew Parker

5. Imagi-Nation: The Imagined Community and the
   Aesthetics of Mourning   75
   Marc Redfield

6. Be-Longing and Bi-Lingual States   107
   Doris Sommer

7. Authority, Solidarity, and the Political Economy of
   Identity: The Case of the United States   145
   David A. Hollinger

8. Anderson's Utopia   161
   Partha Chatterjee

9. Ghostly Comparisons: Anderson's Telescope   171
    H. D. Harootunian

10. Desire and Sovereign Thinking   191
    Lydia H. Liu

11. Responses   225
    Benedict Anderson

Contributors   247

Index   249

Preface

Among the many books written in the unprecedented growth of academic theorizing on nationalism during the past two decades, Benedict Anderson's *Imagined Communities: Reflections on the Origin and Spread of Nationalism* is probably the most widely cited. Oddly enough, however, Anderson's ideas are rarely discussed in thorough detail and most of his generalist readers remain unaware of his origins in and contribution to Southeast Asian studies. This book is devoted to a critical exploration of Anderson's substantive theoretical contributions and their methodological implications for comparative studies (such as comparative literature and the comparative study of cultures). The recent publication of his new book, *The Spectre of Comparisons: Nationalism, Southeast Asia and the World* (Verso, 1998), offers a timely occasion for such an exploration because it foregrounds the Southeast Asian roots of his theoretical reflections. *The Spectre of Comparisons* attempts to bridge area studies and theory by viewing contemporary events in the world such as the rise of identity politics and long-distance nationalism from the cartographical vantage point of Southeast Asia. At the same time, it also focuses the attention of the outside world on Southeast Asia by foregrounding the fact that the culture, economics, and politics of "Southeast Asia," for instance the current financial crisis, are part of, influenced by, and in turn have an impact on the larger world. Hence, Anderson also broaches through example the issues of the enduring importance of comparison for the production of knowledge and the appropriate methodological approach to a comparative study of cultures: what did Hitler's Third Reich look like in the eyes of Indonesia's Sukarno? What does Peru look like when viewed alongside the Philippines, also a former Spanish colony? More generally, how can "universal" theoretical generalizations about the nation-form and its future, the nationalist novel and its future, the fate of tribal minorities, etc. be legitimately pieced together from such locally rooted comparative glances without leading to relativism?

Anderson implies that one can bridge the gap between universal ideals and concepts and particular examples—or, which is not quite the same thing, theoretical speculation and empirical evidence—by means of a comparative perspectivalism. This suggestion deserves to be further debated because it addresses urgent questions that threaten to cripple the production of knowledge at the beginning of a new millenium. On the one hand, disciplines in the humanities that have traditionally generated universalistic claims about human existence such as philosophy and the comparative study of world literature have been put into crisis by the critique of Eurocentrism. On the other hand, however, the world of the late twentieth century is a globalized world where transnationalism has purportedly rendered obsolete the traditionally bounded areas of area studies. But how can we avoid at one and the same time unquestioning universalism and complacent particularism? Can comparison lead to the formulation of genuine universals, that is to say, universals that are always in principle open to the infinite testing of every particular example? Conversely, if comparison has always presupposed geographical areas that are *a priori* distinct, how must comparative studies be reconfigured?

This book explores these broader issues about reinventing comparison by ranging across Anderson's work. This is the first book devoted to Anderson's work with contributions from leading scholars from various disciplines (philosophy, comparative literature, Spanish literature, history, political theory) and various areas of specialization (Europe, USA, Latin America, India, Japan). It originated as a special issue of *Diacritics*, augmented here by an additional essay and, most important, a response by Benedict Anderson. Taking up each essay in turn, he reveals both remarkable scholarly and personal generosity, as he acknowledges and accepts criticism and reflects on where it might lead, after which he always has something extremely shrewd and telling to add in response. One comes away with a greater appreciation than ever of his modesty about his extraordinary contributions and his eagerness to continue discussion of the most important issues of political and intellectual history.

We are grateful to Johns Hopkins University Press and to *Diacritics* (Department of Romance Studies, Cornell University), for permission to reprint the essays from the special issue of the journal and to William P. Germano of Routledge, for his enthusiasm for this project and his determination to pursue it. But above all we are grateful to Benedict Anderson himself for the writings that have inspired the contributors and a very real as well as imagined community of readers around the world.

Jonathan Culler and Pheng Cheah
Ithaca and Berkeley, 2003

CHAPTER 1

Grounds of Comparison

PHENG CHEAH

Reflection is born of the comparison of ideas, and it is their variety that leads us to compare them. Whoever sees only a single object has no occasion to make comparisons. Whoever sees only a small number and always the same ones from childhood on still does not compare them, because the habit of seeing them deprives him of the attention required to examine them: but as a new object strikes us, we want to know it, we look for relations between it and the objects we do know; this is how we learn to observe what we see before us, and how what is foreign to us leads us to examine what touches us.

Apply these ideas to the first men, you will see the reason for their barbarism. Never having seen anything other than what was around them, they did not know even it; they did not know themselves. They had the idea of a Father, a son, a brother, but not of man.

—Jean-Jacques Rousseau

In recent years, the comparative study of cultural formations has undergone critical reinvigoration. The quasi-exponential globalization of all aspects of human existence, which has brought territorially divided or geographically bounded units such as states, national economies, and cultures to an unprecedented and jarring proximity to one another, is, no doubt, an important material condition of possibility for this heightened interest in the cultural branch of comparative studies. For comparison is today no longer a matter of intentional choice. The gradual defamiliarization of our daily lives by globalizing processes has made comparison an inevitable and even unconscious perspective.

Indeed, the grounds of comparison have changed. Comparative work is generally understood as a mode of analysis that begins from one given national or cultural case of a subject of legitimate interest, X, which is the basis for forming a provisional hypothesis or working idea about this subject that serves as the *tertium comparationis.* One then proceeds to examine a range of other cases of X. Discovered similarities confirm or amplify the various essential features of X that were initially posited, and recognized differences serve to modify our working idea about X. A ground of comparison is therefore both the empirical or objective basis from which comparison begins as well as the interest or principle of reason that motivates each particular activity of comparison.

In the past, the grounds of comparison were undeniably Eurocentric. Not only was the material starting point of comparison always from Europe or the North Atlantic. Comparison also had a teleological aim. Whether explicitly or implicitly, the interests of comparison in canonical texts such as Hegel's *Aesthetics,* his *Lectures on the Philosophy of History,* and *Lectures on the Philosophy of Religion* or Max Weber's sociology of world religions served to affirm a certain idea of Europe as a world historical model. For Hegel and Weber, other cases merely provided the *mise-en-scène* for the appearance and *Bildung* of this idealized, universalized figure of Europe. Today, in the humanities and interpretive social sciences, this old framework for comparison has been challenged by critiques of Eurocentrism and Orientalism, by postcolonial studies, and also from the more parochial perspective of multiculturalism. One can no longer nonchalantly or dogmatically start a comparative endeavour from Europe or the North Atlantic. But the problem goes deeper. Many theoreticians and some funding bodies, including the Social Sciences Research Council (SSRC) of the United States, have recently suggested that post–Cold War transnationalism has rendered obsolete the traditionally bounded areas of area studies. If this is so, the claim to begin from any area outside the North Atlantic has also become problematic. In other words, if comparison has always presupposed geographical or cultural areas that are *a priori* distinct and to be compared, how must the grounds of comparison be re-envisioned?

The work of Benedict Anderson stands in an oblique relation to such recent trends in humanistic studies. Although Anderson is an area-specialist, a Southeast Asianist trained in political studies, his *Imagined Communities: Reflections on the Origin and Spread of Nationalism* is one of the most widely cited works in the humanities. Anderson's conceptualization of the nation as an "imagined community", his argument about the importance of "print capitalism" to the rise of the national public sphere, and his suggestion that the novel and the nation-form are contemporaneous analogues of each other have become accepted ideas in contemporary political-theoretical discourse about nationalism. They have also exerted an enormous influence on a whole range of issues that reach across the humanities and the social sciences such as the role of literature and culture in the formation of the national public sphere; the connections between nation-ness and ethnic and racial violence; and the relationship between modernity and colonialism and postcoloniality in the Third World.

However, Anderson's ideas are rarely thoroughly discussed. His influence in literary theory and criticism primarily consists of the oft-quoted but much travestied dictum that the nation is an imagined community, the imagining of which is tied to the novel. Even in the sub-field of postcolonial studies, where one might reasonably expect more informed engagement with Anderson's scholarship on colonial and postcolonial Southeast Asia, awareness of his work is similarly limited. Many postcolonial theorists take the idea of the nation as imagined community to imply that the nation is an ideological fiction and proceed to amalgamate Anderson's ideas with their own denunciations of the pathological nature of Third World nationalism. More generally, many of his readers in the humanities remain oblivious to the Southeast Asian "roots" of his theoretical reflections and his contribution to the study of Southeast Asian societies even though he, together with Clifford Geertz, is regarded by scholars in Asian studies as the foremost authority on Indonesia in the English-speaking world today.[1]

The publication of his most recent book, *The Spectre of Comparisons: Nationalism, Southeast Asia and the World,* offers a timely occasion for a critical exploration of both Anderson's substantive theoretical contributions as well as their methodological implications for comparative studies. These essays offer elaborations on the futures of nationalism and the nationalist novel and provocative theoretical elaborations of the rise of identity politics and the phenomenon of long-distance nationalism, the absentee nationalist sentiment of expatriates that a globalized condition makes more potent. *The Spectre of Comparisons* is also profoundly marked by a humbling polyglossia—Latin, French, German, Spanish, Dutch, Indonesian, Javanese, Thai, Tagalog, and English—and an impressive comparative and interdisciplinary reach that characterizes the best work in area studies.

In Anderson's words, the book "is intended to show the relationship between country studies, area studies in the strict sense of the word, and "theory," as well as their collective embedment in our portion of homogeneous, empty time. . . . The idea is to invite the reader to reflect first on some theoretical considerations [on the origin, nature, and prospects of nationalism in general], then move downwards to the empirical studies [of

Indonesia, Siam and the Philippines] out of which they grew, and finally to return to the initial more rarefied atmosphere" (*SC*, 20). Anderson's general aim, in other words, is to demonstrate how theoretical reflection is gradually constructed from careful comparative analyses that are in turn rooted or grounded in the solidity of empirical studies of specific areas. Insofar as these areas that supply the empirical ground of comparison and theory lie "outside" the North Atlantic, Anderson attempts to bridge the study of non-Western areas and theory by viewing contemporary events in the world such as the rise of identity politics and long-distance nationalism, from the cartographical vantage point of Southeast Asia.

But at the same time, Anderson also problematizes any clear demarcation of areas in at least three ways. More generally, he points to the essentially fictive nature of Southeast Asia, how it became bounded as an imaginary entity by means of the Mercatorian map. More specifically, he foregrounds how this imaginary entity became invested with meaning as a result of imperialist intervention; how Southeast Asia became imbricated with and haunted by the outside world by virtue of "the strange history of mottled imperialism in the region" that spanned the sixteenth to twentieth centuries and included players such as "the British in Burma, Malaya, Singapore and northern Borneo, the Dutch in the Indies, Portugal in eastern Timor, the Spaniards and Americans in the Philippines, and the French in Laos, Cambodia, and Vietnam" (*SC*, 4–5). Finally, he points out that the culture, economics, and politics of contemporary Southeast Asia, for instance, the current financial crisis or the treatment of tribal minorities, are part of, influenced by, and in turn can have an impact on larger global processes.

The spectral nature of "Southeast Asia" as an empirical ground of comparison and the complications of re-envisioning grounds of comparison in general become even clearer if we examine the metaphors that Anderson uses to describe his own aims more carefully. To say that it is salutary to move downwards from the rarefied heights of theory to something more empirical clearly suggests that theory is ethereal and needs to be grounded in something that is more solid or substantial. Yet, curiously enough, both theory and the more empirically grounded area studies are themselves embedded in something that is far from being substantial in the colloquial sense. For like the nation, both theory and the areas of area studies subsist in a common medium that is abstract: homogeneous empty time. Indeed, Anderson describes the substance of nationalism (substance in the Greek sense of *hypokeimenon*—the substrate that lies before everything, the medium in which everything is gathered together) not as a stable solidity but as "a universal grammar," which in "our portion of homogeneous empty time" is characterized by the incessant movement and restless energy of "contemporary mass migrations and revolutions in communications and technology" (*SC*, 20, 26). Thus, it turns out that the fundamental substrate or condition of possibility of individual nations, a ground that should serve as a fundamental principle of comparison and that should inform all theorizing about nationalism, is a form of entropy. This entropy is not easily arrestable as an empirical thing or presence because "it" is nothing other than the spectralizing processes of capital, forces of upheaval and change that destabilize what is at rest and break down what is organically whole. These forces are sometimes associated with the more general term, "modernity." In Marx's famous words:

> Constant revolutionizing of production, uninterrupted disturbance of all social conditions, everlasting uncertainty and agitation distinguish the bourgeois epoch from all earlier ones. All fixed, fast-frozen relations, with their train of ancient and venerable prejudices and opinions, are swept away, all new-formed ones become antiquated before they can ossify. All that is solid melts into air[.]
> [*Manifesto of the Communist Party*, 70]

For Anderson, this entropy and its various technological by-products provide the fermentative conditions for the genesis of the nation-form and its ensuing modulations. Conjured up by these conditions, the nation is constitutively linked to imagination and comparison. These are two key themes that run through Anderson's writings and the main points of engagement for the chapters in this book.

Nation and Imagination

The connection Anderson posits between the nation-form and imagination is so axiomatic to contemporary academic discourse by now that it scarcely needs to be mentioned. Nevertheless, it may be worthwhile to emphasize two provocative features in his argument that are often overlooked. First, Anderson is not primarily interested in the specific ideational or thematic contents of the imagining of particular nations. He is concerned with the paradigmatic style of how the nation in general as a unique form of community is imagined and the material conditions that give rise to this new paradigm of imagining community. As he puts it, he is concerned with "the framework of a new consciousness—the scarcely-seen periphery of its vision—as opposed to the centre-field objects of its admiration or disgust" (*IC*, 65). This an argument about the genesis of a new *form* of consciousness; a formal argument about *how* nations are imagined rather than *what* they imagine themselves as. This is why Anderson often employs an analogy with grammar *qua* systematic mechanics of signification.

But what creates or sets into place the grammar of nations and what are the elements of this grammar?

> What, in a positive sense, made the new communities imaginable was a half-fortuitous, but explosive, interaction between a system of production and productive relations (capitalism), a technology of communications (print), and the fatality of human linguistic diversity. . . . The essential thing is the *interplay* between fatality, technology and capitalism. [*IC*, 42–43]

Anderson's formal argument is clearly allied with a certain materialism. What makes possible the formal structure of national consciousness is a constellation of economic and technological forces. However, unlike Marx's historical materialism, this materialism is non-teleological. For this constellation of forces that Anderson calls "print capitalism" is not the result of the dialectical process of creative labor's alienation but of chance and accident. This fortuitous coupling engenders a form of community that frustrates the relentless dehumanizing logic of capitalism as well as the cosmopolitan proletarian revolution Marx envisaged. The nation-form may be a product of capitalism. But it is a product of *print* capitalism, which Anderson repeatedly links to *pre-industrial mercantile* capitalism and not *industrial* capitalism. This is a form of capitalism that is more "communal," capitalism with a more sociable face, if you will. For instead of shattering and vaporizing all communal bonds, the upheavals of print capitalism, which destroyed the transnational religious communities of the pre-modern era, also led to the creation of new imagined solidarities from below through the spectrality of vernacular print. The characterization of the nation-form as the chance product of print capitalism is significant because it allows Anderson to suggest that the nation is originally neither a means of social organization nor an ideological superstructure emanating from the state *qua* tool of industrial capitalism.[2]

The second important feature of Anderson's argument is that he locates the initial workings of print capitalism and the first imaginings of the nation in the Creole Americas and not in mid-nineteenth century Europe.[3] The belatedness of Europe in the history of nationalism is a constant theme, and part of Anderson's persistent attempt at undoing a teleological vision of Europe. (I will return to this later when I touch on the issue of comparison.)

Anderson's interest in the novel form and his more general fascination with literary and aesthetic issues ought to be situated within the framework of his account of print capitalism. His main concern is the *synchronic mode of temporality,* or the simultaneity that allows one to imagine a limited sovereign community beyond face-to-face relations as well as to envision other limited sovereignties besides one's own as equivalent. He suggests that this synchronicity, which he calls "homogeneous empty time" following Benjamin, is a fundamental characteristic of both the nation and the narrative form of the old-fashioned novel. The connection between the novel form and the imagining of nations is therefore one of isomorphism or original affinity, wherein the novel supplies an analogue or even a heuristic device for understanding the simultaneity of the nation.[4] In other words, print capitalism creates a mode of temporality that is the formal condition of possibility for the genesis of the kind of consciousness that will later become the modern nation, and the novel obeys and enacts the same mode of temporality in its formal functioning.[5]

Anderson's understanding of the affinity between novel and nation can be schematized as follows: technological innovations such as the clock, the calendar, and print enable the formal apprehension of a sociological organism moving up and down homogeneous empty time.[6] The old-fashioned novel is spawned in the same conjuncture. Its formal structure, especially its omniscient style of narration, supplies a paradigmatic representation of the totality of society as a determinable form. For Anderson, the "causal" or "formative" power the novel possesses in relation to the nation largely rests on its structure of address, its ability to interpellate the reader as a national and to create a symbolic mapping of external social space. As individual readers are held in the embrace of its omniscient narrative, the world inside the novel becomes fused with the external real world, and they are enabled to "see" or represent their external surroundings as part of the larger proto-national or national community to which they belong as members. At this point, the novel merely allows us to picture the form of the community in general. However, at a later historical stage, once the nation has been born, more determinate and even ideological uses can be made of the novel. Here, "representation" is more than the picturing/figuration of the form of the community. It is "thematization." A particular nation and its characteristics can be made the referent and theme of the novel's plot and characters. Conversely, nations can also use the novel to represent themselves as in activist nationalist literature or official nationalist propaganda.

The chapters by Ernesto Laclau, Jonathan Culler, Andrew Parker, and Marc Redfield critically question various aspects of Anderson's views on the role of imagination/images, the novel, literature, and aesthetics in the nation's genesis. Fastening onto Anderson's definition of the nation as an imagined community, Laclau incisively points out that because the nation is the bearer of a potential infinitude (since it has to include an unlimited number of members who are not given in advance), images of national communion must be images of a totality that is infinitely open, symbols of an always receding horizon. The symbols governing nationalist discourse are, therefore, empty signifiers. Drawing on his influential work on hegemony, Laclau argues provocatively that nationalism is not, as Anderson insists, the dominant framework of collective life, nor is it always separable from racism. While a universalistic assertion of national diversity is an important possibility, the empty symbols of nationalism can also be articulated in various ways and directions, which have recently included global Islamism and xenophobic particularisms. In a rigorous examination of Anderson's propositions about the novel's relationship to the nation, Culler argues that many literary critics who either rely on Anderson's authority or criticize him in their work on nationalist novels have misread him. They have transformed his formal argument about the novel *qua* structural condition for imagining the nation into a claim about how novels can historically shape and legitimate nations through their themes, content, characters, or plot. But Culler also points out that at times, Anderson himself veers toward a thematic approach, especially when he describes the novel as a representational mapping of the nation's social world. He also points out that Anderson's suggestion that nineteenth century novels stimulate the imagination of national community through addressing readers as nationals needs to be heavily qualified by studying a range of cases.

Parker's essay interrogates the tension between the political power that Anderson grants to the novel and fiction (broadly defined to include the newspaper) in their capacity to enable us to imagine the national community and his frequent descriptions of literature as having a mimetic function and a derivative status vis-à-vis sociopolitical reality. Commenting on Anderson's reading of Mario Vargas Llosa's *El Hablador,* Parker notes that when Anderson tries to answer the question of how the modern Peruvian nation can represent its displaced indigenous tribal minorities without silencing them through ventriloquism, he fixes on the non-derived nature of the storyteller in the novel, someone who is at the same time neither authentic nor a translator. For Parker, Vargas Llosa's storyteller personifies the enigmatic power and ontological primacy of fiction in Anderson's work because like the nation, fiction is a replica without an original. Redfield likewise points to the unstable and destabilizing nature of imagination in his exploration of the connection between Anderson's account of the nation as an imagined community and aesthetic discourse as this term has been defined by Paul de Man's writings on Romanticism. Anderson, Redfield notes, points to the nation's fundamentally fractious nature and its susceptibility to self-loss by linking it to language and technological change. However, Redfield also argues that Anderson is a "late Romantic" thinker, who papers over this instability by resorting to an aesthetic discourse. Because aesthetic discourse is also the hallmark of the state's pedagogical project, he suggests that it undermines the distinction Anderson tries to make between the nation and the state.

Nation and Comparison

Anderson's interest in literary and aesthetic issues helps him to elucidate the temporal element of nationalism's underlying grammar. His subsequent focus on the importance of the comparative moment in nationalism derives from his investigation of its grammar's spatial aspect. For the nation is also imagined in spatial coordinates and its boundaries bring to mind contiguity to *other* national bodies, but within the *same* world. This makes comparison an inevitable component of nationalism.

Anderson's interest in nationalism's spatiality was introduced in the revised edition of *Imagined Communities* in a study of how the census, the map, and the museum, three institutions of colonial governmentality, were crucial to the imaginings of popular and official nationalism in Asia and Africa. Anderson used two terms to describe the legacy of these institutions: "classification," the establishment of state control over its bounded dominions through a grid that enabled categorization and enumeration, and "serialization," the assumption that the abstract categories of classification were universal series, categories that had ontological truth and existential validity throughout the world because they were indefinitely replicated by sensible particulars (*IC,* 184–85). Whereas the novel's temporality enabled the imagining of the nation as a synchronic whole, classification and serialization gave the barest and most general content to this bounded form: every nation in the world would contain ethnicities, races, people of different religious faiths, a cultural heritage, and so on. Although Anderson does not yet use the word explicitly, it is obvious that these series enable comparison between nations. They are the basis of comparability, the *tertium comparationis,* precisely because they are part of the grammar of every nation.

In *The Spectre of Comparisons,* Anderson elaborates on this by modifying his earlier thoughts on serialization in a way that leads to a comparative method. Where he had earlier associated serialization with the colonial state's apparatuses, he now sees this grammar of representation as operating in newspapers also. Newspapers, Anderson argues, presuppose natural universality. They have the entire world as their domain even if their readership is linguistically and territorially confined. Moreover, the vocabulary used to describe local and foreign events needs to be standardized so that foreign events can be made locally comprehensible and vice versa. This standardized vocabulary reinforces the natural universality presupposed by newspapers. As a result, print serialization supplies two further requisite principles of coherence for imagining nations: each nation is necessarily imagined as part of a common world, and they are imagined as *equivalent* co-inhabitants of this continuous global domain through the use of similar categories to describe their internal features. Thus, Anderson observes that "series of this kind were quotidian universals that seeped through and across all print-languages, by no means uni-directionally.... This does not mean that [the local and the foreign terms for the series] meant exactly the same thing, but rather that from Bangkok and Birmingham two parallel series were stretching out across, and seamlessly mapping, a singular world" (*SC*, 33–34).

The immediate implication of this extension of the idea of serialization is the suggestion that imagining the nation is essentially a comparative process in which the nation is always haunted by something that is at one and the same time both spatially other or exterior to it but also similar to it in the sense that it is part of it and inhabits the same frame of consciousness. For Anderson, the typecase of the irreducible comparative moment in nationalism as it is personified in a representative individual consciousness comes from a passage in José Rizal's *Noli me tangere*, where "the young mestizo hero [Ibarra], recently returned to the colonial Manila of the 1880s from a long sojourn in Europe, looks out of his carriage window at the municipal botanical gardens, and finds that ... [t]hese gardens are shadowed automatically ... and inescapably by images of their sister gardens in Europe. He can no longer matter-of-factly experience them, but sees them simultaneously close up and from afar" (*SC*, 2). Rizal's novel was, of course, central to Anderson's initial discussion of homogeneous empty time. Here, he reads this passage from the novel, which supplies the title of his later book, as thematizing Rizal's own experience as a gifted European-educated polyglot mestizo in the Spanish Philippines:

> [Rizal] encountered what he later described as "el demonio de las comparaciones," a memorable phrase that could be translated as "the spectre of comparisons." What he meant by this was a new, restless double-consciousness which made it impossible ever after to experience Berlin without once thinking of Manila, or Manila without thinking of Berlin. Here indeed is the origin of nationalism, which lives by making comparisons. [*SC*, 229]

The theme of internalized estrangement and exile as the nursery of national consciousness is certainly interesting in itself. It has obvious points of intersection with both W. E. B. Du Bois's account of the "two-ness" of the American Negro's consciousness (as this has been popularized in African-American and diaspora studies by Paul Gilroy) and Frantz Fanon's account of the belatedness of the African in a colonial world as this has been taken up in postcolonial studies.[7] But Anderson's "spectre of comparisons" is perhaps more provocative and broader in its implications because it refers to much more than the existential angst generated by the mental shackles imposed upon the victims of colonialism and slavery. Double-consciousness is basically a psychological, psychical, or phenomenological fetish, the gift/curse of the educated colonized or hyphenated minority that can sometimes be turned back in critical reproach at Europe and North America. In contradistinction, "the spectre of comparisons," which Anderson also characterizes as "the *agent* of this incurable doubled vision" (*SC*, 2, emphasis added) rather than double-consciousness itself, is, like Adam Smith's "invisible hand," a catachresis for the material conditions that have brought double-consciousness into being—innovations in communications and technology, more precisely, newspaper-print language and long-distance transportation, which have caused the world to shrink for everyone and not just the intelligentsia. These material developments have created quotidian universals that make everything comparable for everyone, and cause everyone to compare everything.

In this regard, there may be a tension between Anderson's own characterization of the spectre of comparison as a double-consciousness and his unwavering interest in the entropy of capitalism and its material-technological forces. The former attenuates the comparative moment into the gift/curse of the educated. It would perhaps be more in keeping with Anderson's fascination with material-technological forces to speak as Pramoedya Ananta Toer (another important novelist for Anderson) does in *Jejak Langkah* (Footsteps), the third volume of his Buru quartet, of the *world of comparison* (*alam perbandingan*) as the midwife of national consciousness.

The phrase, "world of comparison," appears in an episode of Pramoedya's novel where the protagonist, Minke, a scion of the Javanese aristocracy who has been educated in the exclusive Dutch colonial school system, becomes possessed by an anxious restlessness as a result of his awareness that his people have been subjected to a foreign people because of their comparative backwardness. He contrasts this restlessness to the stagnant tranquillity and childlike ignorance of "traditional" communal life in the villages and points out that they remain stagnant because they are not part of the world of comparison. This is the catalyst for Minke's organizational activity as a radical nationalist:

> Remembering what my friend the painter had said to me [about the importance of understanding my people], I began to observe more closely the life of the village. I clearly could not ask its inhabitants to discuss the issue of modern organisation. They did not possess any knowledge of their own country. Most probably, they rarely left their own village. . . .
>
> A large number of [the small village children playing] will die due to a parasitical disease. . . . And if they survive, if they manage to overcome the parasitical diseases, is their condition any better than the time of their childhood? They will

continue to live within their narrow destiny. Without ever having any comparison. Happy are those who know nothing. Knowledge, comparison, makes people
aware of their own situation, and the situation of others, there is dissatisfied restlessness in the world of comparison [*gelisah dalam alam perbandingan*]. . . .

The people around me have never known what I know. . . . They do not know
anything except how to make a living and reproduce themselves. Oh, creatures
like herded cattle! They do not even know how lowly their lives are. Nor do
they know of the monstrous forces [*kekuatan raksasa*] in the wider world, which
grow and expand, gradually swallowing everything in their way, without being
satiated. Even if they knew, they would not pay any heed.

Within these surroundings, I felt like an All-Knowing god, who also knew
their fate. They would become the prey of both criminals and imperialists.
Something had to be done [*Sesuatu memang harus dikerjakan*].[8]

Minke is the counterpart of Rizal's Ibarra in the Dutch East Indies. What is
significant is that for Minke/Pramoedya, comparison stems from the disqui-
eting knowledge of material forces at work in the wider world as it disrupts
the non-reflective intimate relationship we have with the social surroundings in which we find ourselves immersed. As in Rousseau, comparison is
here the progenitor of a reflective understanding of the self, but with the
crucial qualification that comparison is something that comes upon and
constitutes the reflective self rather than something that it decides to do.
Comparison is a spectre precisely because it is a form of inhuman automa-
tism conjured up by capitalism's eternal restlessness. The crucial point of
contrast with the figure of double-consciousness is that the colonized intelligentsia does not possess a monopoly over the comparative moment. It is
not solely *their* gift/curse. Instead, they are possessed by comparison. They
are the earliest recipients of its visitations merely by virtue of the acciden-
tal fact that their social situation enables them to be the first members of
their society able to perceive these material-technological forces at work and
to recognize how these forces can radically destabilize and change human
consciousness by bringing what is alien up close and defamiliarizing the
complacent immediacy of everyday life that we take for granted.

In any event, Anderson's account of quotidian universals yields the out-
lines of a comparative method that differs from conventional accounts of
comparison based on the idea of Europe as the telos of all comparative activity. In *The Spectre of Comparisons,* comparison signifies various things.
As we have seen, at a theoretical level, the serial logic of the newspaper is
characterized as enabling multidirectional comparison across various reading publics. At the most pragmatic level, Anderson observes that following
his ban from his main field of research in 1972, "Siam and the Philippines
appeared as the 'natural' comparisons with Indonesia" because they are regional neighbours (*SC*, 20). In between, there are many other modalities
of comparison: the comparison between a colony and its metropolis that is

part of the colonized subject's self-imaginings;[9] the comparative mindset of the practitioner of non-Western area-studies who in addition to indigenous sources, must also take into account the influence of the culture and politics of the former colonizer on the previously colonized area and archival records about the area in the colonizer's language; comparison between different societies previously governed by the same colonizer, for instance, Peru from the vantage point of the Philippines; and finally, the intraregional comparative study of the various colonialisms and postcolonial political cultures in Southeast Asia, sometimes by indigenous scholars.

What is common to most of these modalities of comparison is the recurrent use of the related perspectival metaphors of the inverted telescope and lighting effects. In the opening pages of the introduction to *Spectre*, Anderson describes how Sukarno's characterization of Hitler as a great nationalist leader had a dizzying effect on him as a European: "For myself, I felt a kind of vertigo. For the first time in my young life I had been invited to see my Europe as through an inverted telescope. . . . It was going to be difficult from now on to think of 'my' Hitler in the old way" (*SC*, 2). When one looks through an inverted telescope, i.e. staring through the large end, one views a distanced and, therefore, miniaturized object. Hearing Sukarno speak of Hitler from the perspective of Indonesian nationalism, the young Anderson sees a distanced, miniaturized Europe, a Europe mapped by series that begin in Indonesia: Hitler is understood through the series, "great nationalist leader," with the connotations it has in Indonesia. The Europe that he is habitually accustomed to has been rendered alien or estranged from him. The telescope metaphor is used again in the next paragraph where Anderson comments on the passage from Rizal about the specter of comparisons. The additional gloss that he makes is that the object of present visual experience in the colonies—botanical gardens—is shadowed, surrounded by the phantomatic aura of a Europe that is far away. Thus, Anderson implies that Europe is estranged in the eyes of Rizal and his protagonist, just as his conventional understanding of Hitler had become alien for him.

The inverted telescope therefore works to place the privileged status of Europe as the primary ground of comparison and main point of reference for theoretical work *en abîme*. Commenting on how his general theoretical reflections about nationalism were inflected through the lenses of his earlier work on nationalism in Indonesia and the 1978–79 war between China, Vietnam, and Cambodia, Anderson observes that "the telescopic view of Hitler from Jakarta . . . had made it forever impossible to take Europe for granted" (*SC*, 20).[10] Moreover, Europe has been rendered abyssal by relocating the ground of comparison and theory in Southeast Asia. Anderson writes on a Peru that is shadowed by the Philippines as a co-colony under Spain, a Philippines "which, in a certain stage-lighting, can seem to have floated away to the distant west from the littoral of the Hispanic Andes" (*SC*, 20). Similarly, he reminds his reader that his theoretical reflections about nationalism and national identity in the age of contemporary mass migrations and revolutions in communications and transportation began "with the big end of my telescope in 'South East Asia': the sugar belt of colonial Java, the monument to Rizal in downtown contemporary Manila, and the airport in Bangkok, where frail migrants set off every day to all quarters of their unseen employers' world" (*SC*, 26).

What are the implications of this comparative method which problematizes Europe as ground of comparison? At least two important issues need to be raised here: first, if the inverted telescope metaphor from which the comparative method is drawn is identical to the figure of the double-consciousness of the colonized subject as Anderson seems to suggest, is Europe really distanced? Or is Europe instead brought closer and made larger as an objective ideality, an ideal presence or a world-historical model that is either positive and to be emulated—the historical repository of enlightenment, freedom and modern political institutions—or as something negative—the metropolitan origins of the tyranny and despotism of colonial rule which betrays Europe's own claim to be the bearer of modern ideals—that needs to be sublated through anti-colonial critique and revolution according to the same universalist logic? Second, if Europe is rendered remote and miniaturized, does not the relocating of the grounds of comparison in another bounded region (Southeast Asia) repeat the same problem of privileging any given region as ground of comparison insofar as this will always exclude other grounds or only include them by subordinating them? These and other issues are broached in various essays from scholars who are experts in the study of other "areas"—India, Japan, the Americas, and China.

The contribution by Partha Chatterjee, the subaltern studies scholar, is partly a concise and trenchant critique of Anderson's comparative vision that develops his earlier criticism that the account of nationalism in *Imagined Communities* is a sociological-determinist theory that fails to respect the specificity of third world nationalism. He argues that the tacit site of enunciation of the comparative vision Anderson deploys to uphold nationalism's ethical legitimacy is the North Atlantic. Anderson's defense of the universalism of classical nationalism, Chatterjee suggests, stems from an understanding of politics in which the utopian time of capital (homogeneous empty time) governs the organization of social space and is conflated with real time, although the latter is in fact heterogeneous. He contends that Anderson overlooks the fact that universalism is a legacy of European history and is unavailable to people from postcolonial nations. For peoples from the postcolonial world, social space is more heterogeneous, and, hence, forms of political organization other than the nation may be more feasible.

Harry Harootunian, a prominent figure in Japanese studies, is of a different persuasion. He views Chatterjee's attempt to find sites that are outside the homogeneous empty time of capitalism and colonialism as a romantic endeavor. Anderson's theory of seriality, Harootunian suggests, is more realistically attuned to the historical fact that capitalism, which has set up systematic relations of social interdependence that encompass non-capitalist societies, has created a single global space of co-existence in which differences are still allowed to subsist. However, Harootunian also criticizes Anderson's comparative method. In his view, it ends up magnifying the West at the expense of the non-West. Anderson, he suggests, sees the West as a larger copy of political modernization and the non-West as a smaller copy of the same processes. Harootunian also argues that Anderson's employment of the trope of double-consciousness conflates haunting as such with comparison between Europe and its (former) colonies. Since Anderson's account of haunting is limited to how these other sites are shadowed by Europe, he does not take into account other kinds of specters. The precolonial past is one such specter. Destroyed by colonialism and modernization, it can no longer be recovered as a fully present intact tradition within the homogeneous empty time of Euro-American modernity and its exported social forms. But the precolonial past lives on as a ghost that returns from outside time to disrupt the singular temporality of modern social space.

In evaluating the comparative method extracted from Anderson's inverted telescope metaphor, the precise relationship between this metaphor and the figure of double-consciousness appears to be crucial. Put another way, is the telescope metaphor reducible to this figure? What is the frame of the comparative vision? Is it colonialism or the institutions and processes spread by capitalism's restless energy?

A comparative method based on the figure of double-consciousness and the colonial experience will inevitably lead to the magnification of Europe as an ideal presence. Anderson's identification of the figure of double-consciousness with comparison is misleading because it suggests that the fundamental basis of comparability is colonialism. This is not easily reconciled with his repeated insistence that the basis of comparison is the "remarkable planetary spread not merely of nationalism but of a profoundly standardized conception of politics [as this is manifested in] . . . every day practices, rooted in industrial material civilization, that have displaced the cosmos to make way for the world[]" (*SC*, 29).

From a historical point of view, it is of course a truism to say that colonialism was the efficient means by which capitalism remade the world in the image of its institutions and processes or, to follow Lenin, that imperialism is the highest stage of capitalism. However, the fact that these by-products of capitalism were introduced to other parts of the world by colonialism does not necessarily mean that they are stamped in perpetuity by colonial and neocolonial designs and that any comparison which utilizes this material culture as the *tertium comparationis* ends up privileging Europe as the telos. When the telescope metaphor is dissociated from the figure of double-consciousness, it becomes clear that the focus falls on Southeast Asia: Anderson's general methodological presupposition is that Southeast Asia is the exemplary ground of comparison that can help us understand Europe in a new light because these general processes of change—which we fail to foreground when we think of Europe because they unfolded in the *longue duree* there—were greatly accelerated in Southeast Asia and, therefore, are more easily recognized.[11]

The overall impression given by Anderson's theoretical writing is the temporal belatedness of Europe vis-à-vis the Americas with regard to the emergence of nationalism, and the heuristico-strategical priority of material from Southeast Asia over the North Atlantic with regard to theoretical issues such as the connections between the census, identity politics, and diasporic nationalism, and the political relationships between majorities and minorities. For instance, the earliest model of nationalism is Creole-American; the colonial census in Southeast Asia is the point of departure for a discussion of the proportional-distributive logic of the welfare state and its effects on minority identity politics in the North (*SC*, 43–45); the fate of national monuments of mourning in the Philippines is said to offer instructive examples of how late official nationalism can be politically resisted (*SC*, 54–55); radical writers in Indonesia and Thailand are said to offer a different trajectory of post-Communist history than the one propounded by Francis Fukuyama (*SC*, 295); the experiences of the dispossessed indigenous tribal minorities in Southeast Asia leads to a discussion of Vargas Llosa's portrayal of how the tragic fate of Machiguenga is inscribed in Peruvian nationalism, and so forth. But Southeast Asia is not intrinsically "reverse-telescopic." Because its exemplarity as a ground of comparison stems from the view that it is merely the regional localization of capital's spectral processes, this new ground of comparison is also an abyssal site of haunting. There is, in principle, no reason why the same method cannot be used when the focus is on grounds of comparison outside Southeast Asia.

The translatability of the comparative method, however, does not mean that the substantive theoretical conclusions Anderson arrives at are universally translatable and uncontestable. This is especially true with regard to his claims about diasporic identity politics and long-distance ethnonationalism. Anderson's thoughts on these issues stem from a second important modification of his earlier account of seriality, a modification that has more directly political consequences. Whereas in *Imagined Communities,* serialization was a function of the colonial state, a principle of representation imposed from above, Anderson now distinguishes between unbound and bound modes of seriality: the popular forms of serialization that originate from print and market performances vs. the regulatory series of the colonial census. The first, he argues, leads to a kind of political practice based on committed action—the practice of revolutionary nationalists and patriots. The second leads to a reactionary and essentialist ethnic politics based on entitlement. In a world of mass migrations where collective subjectivities are no longer territorialized or bound by the borders of nation-states, the logic of bounded seriality also governs diasporic or long-distance nationalism. Long-distance nationalism is "a probably menacing portent for the future" partly because "it creates a serious politics that is at the same time radically unaccountable" (*SC*, 74).

It is important to remember that for Anderson, the classical nationalist project, which first took shape in the era of print capitalism, has now become the enduring legacy of nation-states in the former Second and Third Worlds. In contradistinction, he defines long-distance nationalism as a variant form of nationalism conjured up by the current conjuncture of global capitalism, a fundamental characteristic of which is mass migration to wealthy post-industrial states. For him, what is troubling about the ethno-nationalism of the diaspora is that it supplements the classical nationalist project in such a way that threatens its very existence as a universalistic project. Long-distance nationalism is a form of nationalism in which a particularistic ethnicity-in-exile tries to remake the nation-state into an ethnic state. It is a form of imagined community in which the nation, which Anderson had emphatically distinguished from ethnicity and race, becomes cannibalized by ethnicity.

The contributions by Chatterjee, Sommer, Hollinger, and Liu challenge Anderson's views on long-distance nationalism and multicultural/diasporic identity politics from very different perspectives. Chatterjee suggests that from the point of view of those living in postcolonial nations born during the Bandung era, the patriotic absurdities of diasporic communities may be examples of a failed cosmopolitanism rather than a perverse variant of nationalism.

Doris Sommer, a specialist in the Latin American novel, directly takes issue with Anderson's reading of Vargas Llosa's *El hablador* and indirectly questions his views on diasporic communities. She argues that Anderson's sanguine view of the future of nationalism in his chapter entitled "The Goodness of Nations" does not translate into Peruvian for Vargas Llosa's narrator. Where Anderson had celebrated the egalitarian nature of Creole nationalism (a nationalism based on a common language) but also cautioned against its ventriloquism in the Peruvian case as something that violently silences the voices of tribal groups, Sommer counters with the argument that translation and a bilingual aesthetics are especially important to establish ethically legitimate forms of group solidarity in multicultural liberal societies such as North America. She proceeds to offer an outline of such an aesthetics through critical readings of Freud and Wittgenstein. In a similar vein, David Hollinger, an Americanist who is an authority on liberal multiculturalism, takes issue with Anderson's association of bound seriality with the United States census. Anderson's distinction between bound and unbound seriality, he suggests, can be seen as reproducing the classical distinction between voluntary and ascribed identities. He argues that identity is a complex term in the United States, a vibrant site for multiple identities and the celebration of voluntary identity. Anderson's linking of bound seriality with the U.S. census ironically participates in the general neglect of the United States shown by most theorists of nationalism.

Lydia Liu's contribution contests Anderson's account of long-distance nationalism by returning to his own turf—Southeast Asia in its historical connection with China. She explores the case of Ku Hung-ming, a diasporic Chinese born in the British colony of the Straits Settlement, what is today Malaysia, and the peculiar patriotic attachment he felt for the imperial Qing dynasty rather than the republican movement of Sun Yat-sen. Liu argues that Ku's case indicates that long-distance nationalism is not primarily the product of the census and the ethnicization of politics that follows from its logic of bound seriality. The desire for sovereignty in international relations also plays a part in the production of Ku's long-distance nationalism and nationalism in general. This desire for sovereign right, which is inherited from positivist jurisprudence, she contends, is an unexamined axiom in Anderson's theory of nationalism. It imposes constraints on the capacity of the national community as a vehicle of freedom.

The essays collected here engage with different parts of Anderson's work written over a period of twenty-five years. Their different approaches demonstrate the fecundity of his thought for research on the most intractable problems of our time. Through active dispute, they attest to Anderson's ongoing development of his seminal work on nationalism, the historical factors involved in the imagining of communities in modernity and in the contemporary globalization, as well as the political consequences of such imaginings. This collection also foregrounds Anderson's contribution to the methodological problem of how to think about these matters comparatively, without dogmatically privileging the North Atlantic as the main point of theoretical reference or taking it for granted as a world-historical *telos*. This has also been a fundamental problem of the comparative study of culture in general and postcolonial studies in particular, which have also called for the decentering of Europe. If attempts at rectifying the problem in those fields have thus far not succeeded, it may be because their theoretical articulations and attempted resolutions of the problem have focused on critiques of Eurocentrism and pronouncements about hybrid conditions and postcolonial counter-modernities—when what is needed is work of genuine comparative reach, detailed and empirically grounded research on particular regions outside the North Atlantic, and a theoretically sophisticated understanding of the complexity of material culture and social-scientific evidence. In contradistinction, Anderson's writings are exemplary instantiations of the productive relationship that can be forged between theory, comparative studies, and interdisciplinary area studies for scholars in a wide range of disciplines and fields of research. The collection concludes with a response chapter from Anderson.

Notes

I am grateful to Jonathan Culler for his helpful comments.

1. Not many literary theorists or practitioners of postcolonial and cultural studies who are interested in the connections between language and political and social formations cite Anderson's collection of essays on Indonesia entitled *Language and Power: Exploring Political Cultures in Indonesia* (1990), even though these essays explore topics such as the politics of literature and the role of languages, cartoons and monuments in Indonesian politics and culture. For a recent statement of Anderson's view of Indonesian nationalism, see his "Indonesian Nationalism Today and in the Future."

2. In their different ways, both Marx and Gellner link the nation to the state. Marx saw the nation as an ideology of an underdeveloped bourgeoisie seeking to industrialize. See Marx, "Draft of an Article on Friedrich List's Book, *Das nationale System der politischen Ökonomie.*" This is the position taken by the subaltern studies scholars within the context of decolonization. For Gellner, nationalism is "the consequence of a new form of social organization [under industrial conditions], based on deeply internalized, education-dependent high cultures, each protected by its own state" (48).

3. Chapter 4 of *IC* is entitled "Creole Pioneers." Cf. *SC*, 60, where in a comment on Bossuet's oration on homeland, Anderson notes that "Bossuet was already an anachronism, for he was born 1627, seven years after the Puritan Pilgrim Fathers had landed at Plymouth Rock and over a century after the Catholic Hernán Cortés had stormed the fabled capital of Moctezuma."

4. See *IC*, 26: "The idea of a sociological organism moving calendrically through homogeneous empty time [which is conveyed by the novel] is a precise analogue of the idea of the nation, which is also conceived as a solid community moving steadily down (or up) history." Anderson's argument about affinity may have been so badly misunderstood because he also characterized the novel as providing "the technical means for 're-presenting' the *kind* of imagined community that is the nation" (25). While he most likely means that the nation could not have been so easily imagined without the novel as a form of *techne*, the phrase could also give rise to a more instrumentalist understanding where the novel is seen as a tool deployed to represent the nation.

5. Placing the novel at the threshold of the epistemic *coupure* between "traditional" and "modern" worldviews is, of course, not peculiar to Anderson. Lukács makes a similar argument in his *Theory of the Novel*, as does Benjamin in "The Storyteller," the latter being an important theoretical source for Anderson's essay on Vargas Llosa in *SC*. Echoing Anderson's focus on the "meanwhile," Lyotard (following Erich Auerbach) links the grand narratives of modernity to "the adoption of a paratactic arrangement of short sentences linked by the most elementary of conjunctions: the *and*" (24).

6. My schematization is a gloss on *IC*, 24–36, and *SC*, 334–35.

7. See Du Bois, 10–11: "After the Egyptian and Indian, the Greek and Roman, the Teuton and Mongolian, the Negro is a sort of seventh son, born with a veil, and gifted with second-sight

in this American world, a world which yields him no true self-consciousness, but only lets him see himself through the revelation of the other world. It is a peculiar sensation, this double-consciousness, this sense of always looking at one's self through the eyes of others, of measuring one's soul by the tape of a world that looks on in amused contempt and pity. One ever feels his two-ness, an American, a Negro; two souls, two thoughts, two unreconciled strivings; two warring ideals in one dark body, whose dogged strength alone keeps it from being torn asunder." Gilroy's discussion of du Bois' idea of double-consciousness is in chapter 4 of *The Black Atlantic*. Cf. Fanon, p. 122: "You come too late, much too late. There will always be a world—a white world—between you and us."

8.   Pramoedya, 170–71, Lane trans., 132–33. The translation is mine.

9.   "Each imperial power, jealous of, and rivalrous with, its competitors, worked to close off its possessions from the rest, so that at the beginning of this century young educated people in Batavia (Jakarta) knew more about Amsterdam than they did about a Cambodia with which their ultimate ancestors had once had close ties, while their cousins in Manila knew more about Madrid and New York than about the Vietnamese littoral a short step across the South China Sea." [*SC*, 5]

10. Sometimes the give and take between "theory" and its "empirical ground" may become blurred so that it becomes unclear which springs from which. On the one hand, Anderson's experience of and research on Indonesian nationalism must have been an important influence on theory of nationalism. On the other hand, in an essay on the state in Indonesian history that is contemporaneous with the first edition of *Imagined Communities*, Anderson characterizes Indonesian political history using the theoretical vocabulary of the nation as imagined community. See "Old State, New Society: Indonesia's New Order in Comparative Historical Perspective," in *Language and Power*, 94–120.

11. See *SC*, 29: "I will draw a good deal of my illustrative material from the *ci-devant* Third World, where the speed and scale of change experienced over the past century has been so rapid as to throw the rise of the two serialities into the highest relief."

Works Cited

Anderson, Benedict. *Imagined Communities: Reflections on the Origin and Spread of Nationalism*. Rev. ed. London and New York: Verso, 1991. [*IC*]

———. *Language and Power: Exploring Political Cultures in Indonesia* . Ithaca: Cornell University Press, 1990.

———. "Indonesian Nationalism Today and in the Future." *New Left Review* 235 (1999): 3–17.

———. *The Spectre of Comparisons: Nationalism, Southeast Asia and the World*. London and New York: Verso, 1998. [*SC*]

Benjamin, Walter. "The Storyteller: Reflections on the Work of Nikolai Leskov." *Illuminations*. Ed. Hannah Arendt and trans. Harry Zohn. New York: Schoken, 1969. 83–109.

Du Bois, W. E. B. *The Souls of Black Folk*. Eds. Henry Louis Gates Jr. and Terri Hulme Oliver. New York: Norton, 1999.

Fanon, Frantz. *Black Skin, White Masks*. Trans. Charles Lam Markmann. New York: Grove Press, 1967.

Gellner, Ernest. *Nations and Nationalism*. Ithaca: Cornell U.P., 1983.

Gilroy, Paul. *The Black Atlantic: Modernity and Double Consciousness*. Cambridge, MA: Harvard UP, 1993.

Lukács, Georg. *The Theory of the Novel*. Trans. Anna Bostock. Cambridge, MA: MIT Press, 1971.

Lyotard, Jean-François. *The Postmodern Explained: Correspondence 1982–1985*. Trans. Don Barry, Julian Pefanis et al. Minneapolis: University of Minnesota Press, 1993.

Marx, Karl. Draft of an Article on Friedrich List's Book, *Das nationale System der politischen Ökonomie*. Marx and Engels, *Collected Works*, vol. 4. New York: International Publishers, 1975. 265–93.

———. *Manifesto of the Communist Party. The Revolutions of 1848*. Ed. and intro. David Fernbach. Harmondsworth: Penguin, 1973. 62–98.

Pramoedya, Ananta Toer. *Footsteps*. Trans. Max Lane. Victoria: Penguin, 1990.

———. *Jejak Langkah*. Kuala Lumpur: Wira Karya: 1986.

CHAPTER **2**

On Imagined Communities

ERNESTO LACLAU

Benedict Anderson's deservedly famous thesis about the origins and nature of modern nationalism turns around the central notion of an "imagined community." This category provides him with a matrix out of which one can apprehend—theoretically and historically—the different variants of nationalist discourse formulated over the last two hundred years. We will refer, in the brief comments that follow, to three basic dimensions structuring the fabric of Anderson's argument: 1) the presuppositions implicit in the notion of an "imagined" community; 2) the kind of substitutability or solidarity which is required to be a member of such a community; 3) the kind of relationship that is established between such a community—which is by definition finite or limited—and its outside. Before that, however, let us describe the main features of Anderson's thesis.

Anderson describes a nation as "an imagined political community—and imagined as both limited and sovereign" (15). It is *imagined* because most of its members never meet yet nonetheless participate in an "image of their communion." It is *limited* because it is not an infinite grouping embracing the totality of humanity—as was the case with the great monotheistic religions—but a definite group of people separated by clear-cut boundaries from other groups. It is *sovereign* because it has transferred to the State the notion of an illimited power that originally belonged only to God. Finally, it is a community because the nation, "regardless of the actual inequality and exploitation that may prevail in each, the nation is always conceived as a deep, horizontal comradeship" (16). *A defines nation.*

The emergence of the nation as an imagined community can only be explained in terms of the occupation by the nation of the place that originally belonged to other—equally imagined—communities. Anderson points to two of them: the religious community and the dynastic realm. Focusing for a moment on the first—which is the most important—Anderson argues that nationalism inherits from religious types of belonging a deep sense of identification: religion is connected with death, with something we should be able to die for. The tombs of the Unknown Soldier are evoked in this connection. So nationalism would not simply be an *ideology*, which we could approach in the same way that we do conservatism or liberalism, but something that goes deeper in the shaping of human identities. With the decline of religion at the beginning of modern times, there was the need for some kind of existential belonging that occupied the void that religion had left. "With the ebbing of religious belief, the suffering which belief in part composed did not disappear. Disintegration of paradise: nothing makes fatality more necessary. What then was required was a secular transformation of fatality into continuity, contingency into meaning . . . few things were (are) better suited to this end than the idea of nation" (19).

If the previous analysis refers to the continuities within which nationalism inscribes itself, equally important are the discontinuities that its emergence presupposes. The most important is the new experience of temporality that modernity brings about. As Anderson points out, the notion of homogeneous time as a unique space of representation, which radically separates past and present and shows a temporal series as an endless succession of cause and effect, is radically absent in traditional, sacredly based communities. He quotes Auerbach on the figural conception of reality in the Middle Ages, based on a notion of *simultaneity* essentially different from our own. It is, on the contrary, the notion of homogeneous time that in modernity makes possible the coexistence of events in such a way that their equivalence presupposes a rupture between cosmology and history. Anderson illustrates the operation of the new notion of temporality with two paradigmatic forms of literary expression: the novel and the newspaper. As for the historical preconditions of this new type of temporality, he stresses the importance of the generalisation of printing and of capitalism.

There are two other key notions in Anderson's analysis: that of *pilgrimage* and that of *the modular*. By pilgrimage he refers to the experience of people whose participation in circuits which break their links with their original, particularistic belongings creates a new fraternity based upon sharing something which necessarily transcends those belongings. He gives many examples—in fact his whole historical narrative is structured around a succession of pilgrimages: functionaries of the new European absolute monarchies whose initial heterogeneity is superseded through their sharing of a vernacular which has become the *lingua franca* of the administration and through a mobility which uproots them from their geographical origins; creole bureaucracies which are the starting points of the new nations; unification through language and education of the colonial new bureaucratic élites of Asia and Africa, etc. In all cases we are faced with a communitarian construction based in the homogeneity of an experience.

As for the *modular,* the argument runs as follows: once a certain original experience of the nation is historically available, it can be imitated and consciously advocated in a process of political construction. This imitation can proceed in many different directions. What Anderson calls "official nationalism" was the symbiosis between the dynastic principle—which preceded the "nation" and did not involve any kind of nationalistic attachment—and a communitarian nationalism which has its origins in the popular upheavals of the mid XIXth Century. The exaltation of German nationalism by Wilhelm II and the policy of Russification advocated by Uvarov are examples mentioned, among others, by Anderson. But the process can also advance in the opposite direction—i.e. there can be attempts at articulating nationalistic symbols to revolutionary ideologies:

> Thus the model of official nationalism assumes its relevance above all at the moment when revolutionaries successfully take control of the state in pursuit of their visions ... [T]he capital of the USSR was moved back to the old Czarist capital of Moscow; and for over 65 years CPSU leaders have made policy in the Kremlin, ancient citadel of Czarist power ... Similarly, the PRC capital is that of the Manchus ... and the CCP leaders congregate in the Forbidden City of the Sons of Heaven. In fact, there are very few, if any, socialist leaderships which have not clambered up into such worn, warm seats ... The more the ancient dynastic state is naturalized, the more its antique finery can be wrapped around revolutionary shoulders. (145–46)

Let us now move to the issues that we want to discuss in connection with Anderson's text. We'll start with the notion of imagined communities. There is a certain ambiguity in Anderson's approach, for many times we don't know whether he is referring to the nation as a *specific* imagined community or whether he is speaking about *any* imagined community, about the category of imagined community in general (unless he is asserting that the only possible imagined community is the nation, which I hardly think could be his position). The discrimination between these two aspects is, however, imperative if we want to put the imaginary ascribable to the nation in connection with other imaginaries which could be crossing the same social space. Let us stick to Anderson's conceptualisation of the imaginary: a community is imagined when, for members who never met each other, "in the minds of each lives the image of their communion." That is, the community is, from the point of view of its extension, infinite (France is eternal, as Anderson says quoting Debray), but this potential infinitude has to crystallise in the image of a certain communion. But if there is an image of the *communion* it must also be an *image* of the communion. That is, the image cannot consist in a chaotic aggregation of contents precisely because it has to represent what Anderson perceptively points out: not an abstract common feature of a *given* group of individuals but, instead, the symbol of a totality which, as such, is *never given*. It is the symbol of an always-receding *horizon* and not the *ground* of a fully graspable reality—or, perhaps, it is a horizon which works as a ground. That is, a community is really an imagined one whenever it only finds its ground in a horizon. The symbols in which the imaginary of that society crystallises have, in that sense, to be tendentially empty, for they have to signify not only the given but also the infinitude of what is not given.

To put it in other terms: Anderson quite rightly opposes primordial villages of face-to-face contact to larger communities only distinguishable from each other "by the style in which they are imagined." This means that the larger a community is, the more it will depend on the imaginary—that is, the more it will have to give some form of representation to its potential infinitude. What is specific in the representation of something to which no determinable referent can be ascribed can better be seen by contrast with those forms of visual representation, belonging to sacred communities, that Anderson describes. We see in these mediaeval or early modern images: the Virgin Mary in the dress of a Tuscan merchant's daughter, or the shepherds around Christ's cradle with the features of Burgundian peasants. The conclusion of Anderson is clear: "While the trans-European Latin-reading clerisy was one essential element in the structuring of the Christian imagination, the mediation of its conceptions to the illiterate masses, by visual and aureal creations, always personal and particular, was no less vital" (29). The important point is not so much the anachronism of the representation; what is crucial is the fact that the universal, eschatological meaning is immersed in an entirely particularistic reality—the incarnating body hegemonises what is incarnated in it. In the national symbols—or in other symbols also giving expression to imagined communities—what is expressed always transcends the particularism of the incarnating material, the latter being systematically deformed and impoverished. I think that here lies the explanation of one of the paradoxes of nationalism alluded to by Anderson: what he calls "[t]he 'political' power of nationalisms vs. their poverty and even incoherence" (14). If the point that I am making is correct, such poverty is not a deficiency: it is the result of a discourse which can only function on the basis of emptying its central signifiers.

This emptiness is also what explains another dimension of the imagined community, to which Anderson also calls our attention: the continuity between the radical ethical investment to be found in religious discourse and that present in nationalism. Anderson very well describes the historical reasons for this passage and there is little I could add to his explanation. What I want to insist on, however, is this dimension of what I have called "ethical investment," which we could also describe as the experience of the unconditioned in a fully conditioned universe—the experience of the sacred, if you will. This experience always requires the contact with a certain "beyond" which we later project in a certain concrete content. At its purest we find it in the mystical experience: the Absolute as a total emptiness incommensurable with anything to be found in the world. But it is possible to project it in certain worldly contents which acquire in this sense a "numinous" dimension. Militancy in its different forms is the expression of this ethical commitment. The only point where I would part company with Anderson is in the almost exclusive character that he attributes to the nation as an object of ethical investment in the modern world. Although I recognize that it has had an undisputable centrality, many other objects have constituted imagined communities helping to shape contemporary societies: devotion to purely secular causes—socialism, for instance—has been nearly as important. I actually think that it is in the interaction between these various social imaginaries that the specificity of our times is to be found.

Let us now move to our second subject: the way Anderson conceives of the relations of solidarity or fraternity existing between members of the imagined community. There is a pathbreaking move that he makes in this respect. He does not simply speak about the ways in which social agents interact between themselves, but he is also and mainly concerned with the emergence of the spaces of representation that make that interaction possible. This is what he describes as the beginning of a homogeneous conception of time without which the simultaneity required by an imagined community could not have arisen. As we said earlier his main examples are taken from the novel and the newspaper. As for the relations of interaction as such, what is crucial is that through a plurality of actions something of an equal nature is established. It is important to realise that the resulting community is the opposite of the organic unity of a hierarchical society: in the latter, time is not homogeneous but essentially discontinuous. The unity among elements of the imagined community that Anderson has in mind is not hierarchical and differential but of an equivalential nature. Now, a relation of equivalence is not a relation of identity. There is nothing mechanical or purely repetitive in an equivalential relation: it is only as far as a space of common representation has emerged (a homogeneous time, for instance, as a condition of the simultaneity just referred to) that actions that are unconnected between themselves become equivalent. To take one of the examples given by Anderson: entrepreneurs geographically separated between themselves are put together by a series of economic mechanisms which do not require their direct interaction. The readers of the same national newspaper would be another example. (One cannot avoid thinking in the notion of "publics" of Gabriel Tarde as an approach at least comparable to Anderson's.)

It is worthwhile remembering that contemporary historiography (the school of *Annales,* for instance) has tended to pluralize the notion of historical time against an intellectual tradition which had asserted its essential homogeneity—and which, as a result, tried to grasp it through the logic of a simple narrative. Anderson does not deny the heterogeneity of historical time but, starting from that heterogeneous terrain, tries to show the homogenising forces operating in modern society. It is in the terrain of this complex dialectic of homogeneity/heterogeneity that the full meaning of his notion of imagined communities is shown. Nationalism would be unthinkable in a universe in which a certain homogenising simultaneity did not operate.

This is the point, however, where I would like to introduce some qualifications regarding Anderson's model. In his analysis of official nationalism—to take one example—Anderson speaks of the way in which popular nationalism was articulated to a dynastic principle which was originally external to it. What to think of this articulation? Let us avoid easy moralistic analysis in terms of manipulation, opportunism, etc. The important point is that certain subject positions which were originally separated from each other, which belonged—to use our previous terminology—to heterogeneous temporalities enter, through their articulation, a homogeneous space of equivalential representations. This process is what in my work I have called "hegemony." We can easily see how the two dimensions that we have explored come together at this point: 1) there is no a priori limitation of the experiences, perceptions, struggles, etc. that can enter into an equivalential chain and, thus, constitute an imagined community; 2) the more the chain is extended, the more empty will be the signifiers, the "images" which represent the totality of the chain, for in order to homogenise heterogeneous elements the hegemonic images could not identify with the particularistic heterogeneity of any of the intervening links. "Hegemony" for Gramsci meant the construction of an imagined community by bringing to a common space of political representation many struggles, demands, etc. which had been so far closed within their particularistic heterogeneity. "Communism," for him, as the name of an imagined community, should become the empty image *naming* that new relatively homogeneous space. As Anderson points out quite well, that process of articulation can move in *any* direction: a proof can be found in the hegemonization of the symbols of official nationalism by various Communist movements that he refers to at the end of his work.

So in what sense am I introducing some qualifications to my broad agreement with Anderson's analysis? Essentially in one point. Because the chain of equivalences constituting the imagined community can advance in many directions, I do not think that the "images" which will stabilise those chains are necessarily attached to the construction of "national" spaces. The experience of the contemporary world certainly does not show the generalisation of any kind of universalism, but it does not show either any uniform pattern leading to the establishment of the national community as the dominant framework of collective life. In some areas of the world such as the Middle East, for instance, the last twenty years have seen the decline of Arab nationalism and the rise of Islamism—which constitutes, no doubt, an imagined community, but one which does not tend to consolidate any national communitarian space. And the European experience since 1989 is, as far as the nation is concerned, rather complex and contradictory, to say the least.

Our last question concerns the outside of the community. Anderson rightly reminds us that, in a difference from other communities—Christianity or Islam, for instance—which claim to be purely universal—the national community is a limited one. Its limits, its difference with other communities, define what a specific national community is. There are, of course, good reasons for doubting that an entirely unmediated universality could exist: the putative universality only exists incarnated in particular institutions which necessarily contaminate its universal claims—and, in many cases, reduce the latter to a mere superstructure of themselves. What is important, however, for our subject is that the same contamination operates in the case of those communities—as the national one—which construct themselves through their limits. Let's put it bluntly: a national community is not one whose particularism excludes all kind of universal reference, but one whose relation between universality and particularity is negotiated in a different way than the communities claiming to be strictly universal. How is this possible?

Everything turns around the notion of limit that we are using. Limits can be discursively constructed in two entirely different ways. As we have said, in the case of the national community—and in other comparable cases—the limits of the community—i.e. its difference from other communities—determine what the community actually is. Without those limits social relations would certainly continue to exist, but we would not have an "imagined community"—the latter presupposing symbols representing it as a totality. In that case, however, one has to assert the differential element and, as a result, the second community as a condition of the constitution of the first. But we can also have a different kind of limit. The limit can also be an antagonistic one: what is outside one's own community is the incarnation of evil and, in that case, the symbols constructing one's own imagined community are the true *names of the good,* of the *universally valuable.* This identification of the universal with the particular values of a certain community is, of course, the source of all forms of xenophobia and chauvinism. The universal reference is not absent, but it is directly identified with a certain particularity. What is important, however, is that the antagonistic dimension is also present—although displaced—in our first kind of limit: to accept the differential element as an ethically valuable one presupposes some kind of discourse such as "the right to cultural diversity," etc., which is necessarily universal and antagonistically opposed to those forces opposing such a right. So the conclusions of this argument are that 1) the dialectic universality/particularity is present in both discourses, although the antagonistic limit is established at different points of the imaginary spectrum; 2) without some kind of antagonistic limit the universal dimension would be impossible.

This allows us to tackle an issue that Anderson discusses towards the end of his book: the relationship between patriotism and racism. I think that Anderson is right in his critique of Nairn and Hobsbawm, who find in nationalism the root of racist and xenophobic leanings. But I also think that his defence of nationalism is rather weak. It is reduced to quoting empirical instances of nationalistic discourses which do not involve a strong rejection of the "other." My line of argument is different. I would contend that a racist or xenophobic turn is *one* of the inherent possibilities of nationalism, but I would immediately add that *that is also the case with universalism.* If universal claims are always incarnated in institutions and practices that are necessarily particular, nothing a priori guarantees that this element of particularity will not prevail and transform the universal dimension in the mere mask of this particularism. Conversely, nothing determines a priori that national identities will create exclusionary limits vis-à-vis anything different from themselves. That depends entirely on how and where the unavoidable antagonistic limit is established. Communities in a globalised world constantly oscillate within this set of contradictory possibilities, where ethnocentric universalisms or particularisms are always possible, but where a universalistic assertion of national and cultural diversity is also a non-excluded alternative.

Work Cited

Anderson, Benedict. *Imagined Communities: Reflections on the Origins and Spread of Nationalism.* 1983. 2nd rev. ed. London: Verso, 1991.

CHAPTER 3

Anderson and the Novel

JONATHAN CULLER

1

Benedict Anderson's *Imagined Communities: Reflections on the Origins and Spread of Nationalism* has, in the past decade, become a classic of the humanities and social sciences. Any theoretically savvy discussion of nations or of societies of any sort must cite it for its fundamental insight that nations and, as Anderson points out, "all communities larger than primordial villages of face-to-face contact (and perhaps even these) are imagined" (6). In retrospect, it seems obvious that nationality, nationness, and nationalism "are cultural artifacts of a particular kind" (4), but this had previously been obscured by intellectuals' sense that nationalism was above all an atavistic passion, an often noxious prejudice of the unenlightened. *Imagined Communities* both argued that we had better seek to understand it, since "nationness is the most universally legitimate value in the political life of our time" (3), and gave us a constructivist way of thinking about the phenomenon of nationalism, which becomes more interesting and intellectually more acceptable when we ask how it is created, what discursive, imaginative activities bring particular nationalisms into being and give them their distinctive form. When nationalism was vulgar passion provoked by empirically occurring nations, it was vulnerable to the objection implicitly or explicitly mounted against it: why should I feel more affinity with people who happen to inhabit the country I live in than with others, more like-minded, who happen to have been born in other nations? Anderson neatly turned the tables on us by taking this as a serious question. Why indeed do we feel such affinities? How to explain the fact that people are more willing to make great sacrifices for others of the same nation whom they have never met (and whom they might dislike if they did) than for worthy and unfortunate people elsewhere?

Read today, the introduction to *Imagined Communities* has the rightness and efficiency of a classic ("why hadn't anyone realized this before?"), as it guides us into the paradoxes of the modern world of nationalism: nations are objectively recent but subjectively antique, even eternal; nations may be messianic, but no nation's citizens imagine that everyone should eventually join their nation. Already here Anderson displays what I take to be the key to his appeal to the nonspecialist: his ability concretely to show us the strangeness of the familiar by judicious comparisons. Try to imagine a "Tomb of the Unknown Marxist or a Cenotaph for fallen Liberals," he suggests. But a Tomb of the Unknown Soldier does not seem risible. Why? "Many different nations have such tombs without feeling any need to specify the nationality of their absent occupants. What else could they be but Germans, American, Argentinians . . . ?" (10). We are in a sentence or two brought to appreciate the necessity of accounting for a social and cultural phenomenon that comparison and humor highlight.

The second edition of *Imagined Communities* demonstrates, in a compelling if serendipitous way, just how much we need Anderson to provide such insights, as it takes up what he and his readers had failed to notice in the first edition. There he had quoted Ernest Renan remarking "in his suavely backhanded way," "Or l'essence d'une nation est que tous les individus aient beaucoup de choses en commun, et aussi que tous aient oubliés bien des choses [in fact the essence of a nation is that all the individuals have many things in common and also that they have all forgotten many things]," with a footnote continuing the quotation: "tout citoyen français doit avoir oublié la Saint-Barthélemy, les massacres du Midi au XIIIe siècle [every French citizen must have forgotten Saint Bartholomew's, the Provence massacres in the thirteenth century]" (6). In the preface to the second edition Anderson notes, "I had quoted Renan without the slightest understanding of what he had actually said: I had taken as something easily ironical what was in fact utterly bizarre" (xiv). He calls this a "humiliating recognition" (xiv), which led him to write the (superb) essay for the second edition, "Memory and Forgetting." This is humbling, if not humiliating, for readers as well as for Anderson himself, for we too, I dare say, had taken Renan's observation as a version of an amusing, ironical insight: we could say that what Americans share is that they have all forgotten *The Federalist Papers,* for instance.

But now Anderson puts it in a more estranging perspective: "At first sight," he writes in the second edition, "these two sentences may seem straightforward. Yet a few moments' reflection reveals how bizarre they actually are." First, Renan feels no need to tell his readers what these to-have-been forgotten things are. "Yet who but 'Frenchmen,' as it were, would have at once understood" these elliptical references (200). Frenchmen are identified by their recognition of things they are required to forget. But second and most important, the expression "*la* Saint-Barthélemy" conceals both the killers and those killed in this religious pogrom, whose partic-ipants "did not think of themselves cosily together as 'Frenchmen'" but who (like the Albigensians of the thirteenth century and the followers of Pope Innocent III, who slaughtered them, in the other massacre cited) are now constructed, by the forgotten "memories" of today's nationals, as frat-ricidal fellow Frenchmen. The peremptory syntax of *doit avoir oublié* ("is obliged to have forgotten") casts this forgetting as a civic duty. "Having to 'have already forgotten' tragedies of which one needs unceasingly to be 'reminded' turns out to be a characteristic device in the later construction of national genealogies" [201]. On second encounter, Anderson exposes in Renan's ironic remark the strange processes by which national communities are constructed as ancient despite their modernity, and are thus imagined and sustained in a way that forges links with both the dead and the yet unborn.[1]

Anderson's chapter "Cultural Roots" is another tour de force, succinctly outlining nationalism's links and contrasts with the fundamental modes of organizing experience: with religions and dynasties, which preceded nation-alism, but, above all, with a new conception of time that made the imagining of nations possible, a conception of simultaneity "marked not by prefiguring and fulfillment, but by temporal coincidence, and measured by clock and calendar" (24). "So deep-lying is this new idea that one could argue that every essential modern conception is based upon a conception of 'mean-while'" (24n). The imagined community of a nation involves the simulta-neous existence of large numbers of individuals, and the most vivid figure "for the secular, historically-clocked, imagined community" (35) is the daily ceremony of the simultaneous consumption of the newspaper: "each com-municant is well-aware that the ceremony he performs is being replicated simultaneously by thousands (or millions) of others, of whose existence he is confident, yet of whose identity he has not the slightest notion" (35). More-over, the newspaper itself is constructed on the principle of simultaneity: the only link between the items that appear in it is calendrical coincidence.

The other aspect of "print capitalism"—to use Anderson's key phrase—that "made it possible for rapidly growing numbers of people to think about themselves, and to relate to others, in profoundly new ways" (36) was the novel. The old-fashioned novel, Anderson writes, "is clearly a device for the presentation of simultaneity in 'homogeneous, empty time,' or a complex gloss upon the word 'meanwhile' " (25). The narrative voice, taking a quasi-omniscient view that helps to constitute something like a "society," tells us what different characters—who may never encounter one another—are doing at the same time. This imagined world, "conjured up by the author in his readers' minds," "a sociological organism moving calendrically through homogeneous, empty time, is a precise analogue of the idea of a nation" (26). Through the basic structures of address of novels and newspapers, "fiction seeps quietly and continuously into reality, creating that remarkable confidence of community in anonymity which is the hallmark of modern nations" (36).

Anderson's deft analysis of novels as a force for imagining the communities that are nations is doubtless one reason for the great appeal of his work for people in literary and cultural studies, who have a stake in the cultural and political significance of the literary objects they study. But despite the frequency with which Anderson's general claims are cited and deployed, there has been surprisingly little discussion of his claims about the novel and of the possible ramifications of its characteristic structures of narration. Yet his later collection, *The Spectre of Comparisons*, makes clear the continuing importance of the novel for his theory of nations.[2] Anderson devotes several essays to José Rizal's novel *Noli me tangere*, a crucial founding text for Filipino nationalism; and he develops his line of thought about novels and the nation further in another essay, "El malhadado país," which takes Mario Vargas Llosa's *El hablador* as an instance of imagining the nation in the novel of our own day, where the issues of the nature of the national community and of the novelist's role in imagining it have acquired new complications.

I want to focus on three elements or aspects of the novel that are particularly relevant to claims about its relation to the imagined communities of nations: the formal structure of narrative point of view, the national content of the fictions (which may include both the plot and the particular nature of the world of the novel), and finally the construction of the reader. If Anderson's insights are to have the value that they should in literary studies, we need to be more precise about what we are claiming when we cite his authority to discuss the role of fiction in the construction of nations.

2

The most important feature of the novel for Anderson's claim seems to be a narrative technique that, through its presentation of simultaneous events, creates a world "embedded in the minds of the omniscient readers. Only they, like God, watch A telephoning, B shopping, and D playing pool all at once" (26). The novel represents a bounded community to readers. What sort of narrative does this? Our narratological terminology is not especially helpful here. This effect is achieved by a broad range of narratives in which the narrator is not limited to what an empirical individual might know or perceive. Omniscient narrative certainly fits the bill, but the narrative needn't be omniscient, for the narrator need not be privy to the thoughts and feelings of the different characters. All that is necessary is that the narrative provide a point of view exterior to and superior to that of any particular character. In other words, this set of novels consists of narratives where the narrator is not a character in the story (or at least is not confined to what a character might know). Most significantly (and this is why Anderson speaks of the "old-fashioned novel") the narrative is not filtered through the consciousness or position of a single observer. What is excluded is the limited point of view that developed in the novel during the course of the nineteenth century.

Though many novels represent a society conceived as national, in Anderson's account what is crucial to the role of fiction in the imagining of nations is not this representation but that the world evoked by the novel include events happening simultaneously, extend beyond the experience of particular individuals, and be conceived as geographically situated or bounded. This involves "homogeneous empty time"—so-called to highlight its difference from an earlier experience of time, the conception of events as instantiating a divine order which is not itself historical. But for thinking about novels (and about which novels do this and which don't), it might be more pertinent to speak of novels that present "the space of a community." There is some ambiguity in Anderson's discussions about whether it is important that the space or community evoked by the novel be that of a nation: does it simply present an *analogue* to the nation, or does it characteristically represent this nation in particular? There is a tension between the explicit claim about the novel as analogue of the nation and Anderson's remarks about the novels he presents in chapter 2 of *Imagined Communities*. He suggests that what is new and striking about Rizal's *Noli me tangere* (from the Philippines), José Joaquín Fernández de Lizardi's *El periquillo sarniento* (Mexico), and Mas Marco Kartodikromo's *Semkarang Hitam* (Indonesia) is that "the national imagination" fuses the world inside the novel with a world outside which is bounded by the potential nation that is the particular colony. The plurals of shops, offices, and prisons "conjure up a social space full of comparable prisons" (30). In other words, this is not an analogue of the nation but a representation of its social space. But Anderson's explicit claims about the role of the novel and homogeneous empty time treat the world of the novel as in principle an *analogue* of the nation—one which would not therefore need to be a representation of that particular nation in order to contribute to the imagining of the nation.

Since Anderson rests his claim on formal structures, some critiques of his views seem misdirected. Thus, David Lloyd claims that the absence of consensus about the meaning of Irish history makes the Irish novel an instrument of imposition rather than a vehicle for imagining a nation. Anderson's emphasis on the anti-imperial thrust of the novel, Lloyd claims, "precludes his acknowledging that the dialogism of the novel is not confined to its production of an anti-imperial national culture but also involves, as the Irish example makes evident, the subordination of alternative narratives within a multi-voiced national culture. For the novel not only gives voice to formerly voiceless national elites, but also disenfranchises other possible voices" (*Anomalous States* 154). Lloyd writes,

> Like Bakhtin, Anderson omits the crucial regulative function of the novel that puts in place a developmental narrative through which the nation apes empire and through which it orders internally a certain hierarchy of belonging, of identity within the nation. Far from being simply an intrinsically benign and democratic form, the novel enacts the violence that underlies the constitution of identity, diffusing it in the eliciting of identification. [154]

One might reply that Anderson's chapter in *Imagined Communities* on what he calls "Official Nationalism" provides ample acknowledgment of the ways in which "nation apes empire," and that in "Census, Map, and Museum" (a chapter of the second edition) Anderson writes shrewdly about the ways in which minorities are constructed as minorities—more by means of such things as the census than by novels. But, above all, Anderson's account does not treat the novel as "an intrinsically benign and democratic form." The novel offers a particular formal structure, involving what can be called "the space of a community," embracing what an individual cannot in fact perceive, but there is nothing intrinsically benign or democratic about this. Timothy Brennan, in an article that appeals to Anderson's authority, extends Anderson's formal argument by suggesting that "It was the novel that historically accompanied the rise of nations by objectifying the 'one, yet many' of national life, and by mimicking the structure of the nation, a clearly-bordered jumble of languages and styles" ("The National Longing for Form" 49). That is, the novel's formal encompassing of different kinds of speech or discourse enacts the possibility of a community larger than any one individual can know: "objectifying the nation's composite nature: a hotch potch of the ostensible separate 'levels of style' corresponding to class" (51).[3] This will be relevant later on to Anderson's discussion of Vargas Llosa.

Some novels, of course, are national narratives with plots that are especially pertinent to the imagining of a nation.[4] The two studies of the novel that, to my knowledge, do most to flesh out Anderson's insight about the novel as a precondition for the nation both focus on novels whose plots symbolically represent the resolution of national differences. Such, for instance, are the "foundational fictions" of Latin America that Doris Sommer has studied in her book of that title. These are historical romances that "became national novels in their respective countries," potboilers that "cooked up the desire for authoritative government from the apparently raw material of erotic love" (*Foundational Fictions* 51). These romances, which illustrate "the inextricability of politics from fiction in the history of nation-building," "are inevitably stories of star-crossed lovers who represent particular regions, races, parties, or economic interests, which should naturally come together" (Sommer, "Irresistible Romance" 75).[5] Erotic and political desires reinforce one another: "one libidinal investment ups the ante for the other. And every obstacle that the lovers encounter heightens more than their mutual desire to (be a) couple, more than our voyeuristic but keenly felt passion; it also heightens their/our love for the possible nation in which the affair could be consummated" (*Foundational Fictions* 48). These novels are very different but share the project of national reconciliation: the coherence of this special genre comes "from their common need to reconcile and amalgamate national constituencies, and from the strategy to cast the previously unreconciled parties, races, classes, or regions as lovers who are 'naturally' attracted and right for each other" ("Irresistible Romance" 81).

In Franco Moretti's *Atlas of the European Novel, 1800–1900,* emphasis falls on ways in which "the novel functions as the symbolic form of the nation state . . . it's a form that (unlike an anthem or a monument) not only does not conceal the nation's internal differences but *manages to turn them into a story*" (20). Abstract and enigmatic, the new nation-state was a problem. Readers "needed a symbolic form capable of making sense of the nation-state," but before Jane Austen "no one had really come up with it" (20). "Well, the nation-state found the novel. And vice-versa: the novel found the nation-state. And being the only form that could represent it, it became an essential component of our modern culture" (17). Jane Austen's novels narrate a national marriage market, taking local gentry and joining them to a national elite (18); historical novels, with their concern for boundaries and differences that are subjects of contention, represent internal unevenness in nations and its erasure (40); picaresque novels, with their roads and inns where strangers meet, drink, and tell stories of their adventures, "define the nation as the new space of 'familiarity,' where human beings re-cognize each other as members of the same wide group" (51); and the *Bildungsroman* provides a new articulation of national space, stressing the contrast between the provinces and the metropolis (old versus young, unfashionable versus fashionable) and the lure of the metropolis for the young of the provinces (64–65). In exploring these different relations, Moretti argues that the meeting of the novel and the nation-state "was far from inevitable. The novel didn't simply find the nation as an obvious, pre-formed fictional space: it had to wrest it from other geographical matrices that were just as capable of generating narrative—and that indeed clashed with each other through-out the eighteenth century" (53). The novel of the nation had to wrest supremacy from *supra*national genres such as the *Robinsonade* and the *conte philosophique,* for example.

While pursuing Anderson's insight, Moretti thus ends up with a different claim from Anderson's, for the *conte philosophique,* for instance, is a genre perfectly suited to the modern "meanwhile" that Anderson sees as crucial. What we seem to find is that the more interested one becomes in the way in which particular sorts of novels, with their plots and their imagined worlds, might advance, sustain, or legitimate the operations of nation-building, the richer and more detailed one's arguments about novel and nation become, but at the cost of losing that general claim about the novelistic organization of time that was alleged to be the condition of possibility of imaging a nation. The more detailed the critical accounts of novels and their possible effects, the less powerful and encompassing the general theory of the novel. I return to this problem below.

3

After the presentation of the space of a community and the representation of the world of a nation, the third aspect of the novel pertinent to Anderson's claim is its address to the reader. His discussion of print capitalism links nov-els and newspapers in a way that is not self-evident but that is fleshed out somewhat by Roddey Reid. Describing a new public discourse, whose effects were feared at the time,[6] he maintains that "prose fiction had a particularly powerful role to play as a social actor in constructing a discourse that rewrote the social body and cast social relations of post-revolutionary France into a language of family and sexuality. Moreover, I argue that it was this language that was to serve as the foundation for what Benedict Anderson has termed modern, discursively based 'imagined communities of national identity'" (*Families in Jeopardy* 3). In France in the 1840s "the new public sphere pro-duced by the commercial print media granted the laboring classes a droit de cité that they had not enjoyed before" (140). "The reading of best sellers and the daily consumption of newspapers by the middle class and workers alike amounted to identical rituals of imagining a national community, however internally differentiated or divided it may be" (139). This is especially true of serial novels, such as Eugène Sue's *Les mystères de Paris* of 1842–43 and *Le juif errant* of 1844, which were initially consumed in newspapers. (The latter helped raise the circulation of *Le constitutionnel* to 25,000 [McPhee 127].)

But as we start to think about audiences for novels and newspapers, and especially about empirical examples, such as serialized novels, in which they are conjoined, it is easy to miss what is most striking and original about

Anderson's claim: that is, "the profound fictiveness of the newspaper," insofar as it depends on the literary convention of novelistic time, of an imagined world where characters go about their business independently of one another. The newspaper represents what is happening in different arenas, and when, say, events in Mali disappear from its pages, "the novelistic format of the newspaper assures [readers] that somewhere out there the character 'Mali' moves along quietly, awaiting his next appearance in the plot" (*Imagined Communities* 33). Newspapers may be thought of as "one-day bestsellers" (35). Through them and novels, joined by the formal structure of a way of representing the space-time of a community, "fiction seeps quietly and continuously into reality, creating that remarkable confidence of community in anonymity that is the hallmark of modern nations" (35).

What is not clear, once we try to take this claim further, beyond the formal *analogy* between the space-time presumed by novels and newspapers to the idea of a national community imagined by readers of novels, as by readers of newspapers, is how far novels or newspapers do indeed lead to imagining a national community of readers. Few newspapers in the period of nation-building are sufficiently dominant to constitute in themselves a national voice or their readers as a national community, and few are genuinely national in their readership. What of provincial newspapers? In nineteenth-century France, for instance, none of the many Parisian papers was dominant. Do readers of *La presse* imagine a national community composed of readers of this journal or of all journals?[7] What is the evidence that readers of a Parisian newspaper imagine a French community of readers performing together the daily ritual? None of this matters if the argument depends upon the fact that the community of readers of a novel or newspaper is the *model* for the imagined community of a nation, but it does matter if the national community is supposed to be that imagined by those simultaneously reading a newspaper.

But, while it is easy to imagine (though hard to demonstrate) that readers of newspapers are brought together as a community (whether regional or national) by the shared daily ritual of reading the same text at the same time, what about readers of novels? For novel readers, the notion of a community of readers who together are consuming the best-seller of the day is accompanied by another possibility: the potential community of all those addressed by the novel, wherever and whenever they should pick it up. Since newspapers are read on the day of publication and thrown away, while novels are characteristically readable at any time, not tied, as newspapers are, to a particular time and place of origination, we cannot assume that they generate the same kind of community of readers, created in the ritual of reading.

We can thus ask about the audience of novels. This is not only a question of who actually reads them but of whom they address. Novels construct a role for readers by positing a reader who knows some things but not everything, needs to have some things explained but not others. But let us look at Anderson's first example of the nation-imagining novel, José Rizal's *Noli me tangere*. Here is the beginning:

> A fines de octubre, don Santiago de los Santos, conocido popularmente bajo el nombre de Capitán Tiago, daba una cena, que, sin embargo de haberlo anunciado aquella tarde tan sólo, contra su costumbre, era ya el tema de todas las conversaciones en Binondo, en otros arrabales y hasta en Intramuros. Capitán Tiago pasaba entonces por el hombre más rumboso y sabíase que su casa, como su país, no cerraba las puertas a nadie, como no sea al comercio o a toda idea nueva o atrevida.
>
> Como una sacudida eléctrica corrió la noticia en el mundo de los parásitos, moscas, o colados, que Dios creó en su infinita bondad, y tan cariñosamente multiplica en Manila....
>
> Dábase esta cena en una casa de la calle de Analoague, y, ya que no recordamos su número, la describiremos de manera que se la reconozca aún, si es que los temblores no la han arruinado. [*Noli* 49–50]

> Towards the end of October, Don Santiago de los Santos, popularly known as Capitan Tiago, was giving a dinner party. Although, contrary to his usual practice, he had announced it only that afternoon, it was already the subject of every conversation in Binondo, in other quarters of the city, and even in Intramuros. In those days Capitan Tiago had the reputation of a lavish host. It was known that his house, like his country, closed its doors to nothing, except to commerce and to any new or daring idea.
>
> So the news coursed like an electric shock through the community of parasites, spongers, and gatecrashers whom God, in His infinite goodness, created and so tenderly multiplies in Manila....
>
> The dinner was being given at a house on Anloague Street. Since we do not recall the street number, we shall describe it in such a way that it may still be recognized—that is, if earthquakes have not yet destroyed it. [*Imagined Communities* 26–27][8]

Anderson comments:

> the image of a dinner party being discussed by hundreds of unnamed people, who do not know each other, in different parts of Manila, ... immediately conjures up an imagined community. And the phrase "a house on Anloague Street" which "we shall describe it in such a way that it may still be recognized," the would-be recognizers are we-Filipino-readers. The casual progression of this house from the "interior" time of the novel to the "exterior" time of the [Manila] reader's everyday life gives a hypnotic confirmation of the solidity of a single community, embracing characters, author and readers, moving onward through calendrical time. [27]

A community within the novel is evoked, and it is subtly extended to the community of those addressed, who might still recognize the house. But the fact that Anderson puts "Manila" in brackets—"the [Manila] reader"—indicates that there is a difficulty here. One can't simply say that the community addressed is the residents of Manila in Rizal's day, nor its residents since Rizal's day, nor simply "we-Filipino-readers." Even the Westerner reading this is drawn in by the narrative address, which assures him or her that if one were there (and the house hadn't been destroyed by earthquakes) one could recognize the house, that there is a continuity between the world of the novel and the reader's own. Indeed, though the novel is replete with place-names from Manila (Binondo, Intramuros), presented as if they needed no explanation and thus presuming a reader who knows Manila, this is a technique by which realistic fiction posits the reality and independence of the world it describes—asserts by presupposing.

Indeed, the mode of address of *Noli me tangere* often suggests that the reader is not a Manileño but someone who needs to be told how things are done there—a stranger, even. The house on Anloague Street, we are told,

> Es un edificio bastante grande, al estilo de muchos del país, situado hacia la parte que da a un brazo de Pásig, llamado por algunos ría de Binondo, y que desempeña, como todos los ríos de Manila, el múltiple papel de baño, alcantarilla, lavadero, pesquería, medio de transporte y comunicación y hasta fuente de agua potable, si lo tiene por conveniente el chino aguador [It was a sizable building in the style of many houses of the country, situated in a spot that gave onto an arm of the Pasig, which some call the river of Binondo, and which, like all the rivers in Manila, plays the multiple role of bath, sewer, washing place, fishing spot, means of transport, and even source of drinking water, if the Chinese water-seller finds it convenient]. [50]

The explanations "like all the rivers in Manila" and "in the style of many buildings of the country" have a quasi-anthropological air, as if telling others about a land not theirs. And there are many similar passages in the novel: "we will immediately find ourselves in a large room, called *caída* in these parts, I don't know why" ("nos encontraremos de golpe en una espaciosa estancia llamada allí caída, no sé por qué" [51]); a beautiful girl "dressed in the picturesque costume of women of the Philippines" ("vestida con el pintoresco traje de las hijas de Filipinas" [81–82]); the door "leads to a little chapel or oratory, which no Filipino house should be without" ("que no debe faltar en ninguna casa filipina" [88]). The effect here is similar to Balzac: offering a veritable anthropology of Manila and its ways, with references that would not have been necessary for Manila readers, who don't need to be told what things are called in their country, or that someone is dressed like a Filipino, or what every Filipino house must have. While it could be argued that this last phrase, for instance, works to satirize, for Manila readers, the empty piety of the land that makes chapels obligatory, whatever the faith of their owners, one can reply that it is by speaking anthropologically, as if to an outsider to whom these things need to be explained, that the narrator achieves this effect.

Another distinctive passage to which Anderson draws our attention contains a direct address to the reader:

> Pues no hay porteros ni criados que pidan o pregunten por el billete de invitación, subiremos, ¡oh tú que me lees, amigo o enemigo! si es que te atraen a ti los acordes de la orquesta, la luz o el significativo clin-clan de la vajilla y de los cubiertos, y quieres ver cómo son las reuniones allá en la Perla del Oriente. [50–51]

> Since there are no porters or servants requesting or asking to see invitation cards, let us proceed upstairs, O reader mine, be you enemy or friend, if you are drawn to the strains of the orchestra, the light(s) or the suggestive clinking of dishes and trays, and if you wish to see how parties are given in the Pearl of the Orient. [*Spectre* 240]

Anderson's translation of "allá en la Perla del Oriente" as simply "in the Pearl of the Orient" rather than, say, "*over there* in the Pearl of the Orient" attenuates the implication of the Spanish original that the readers addressed are not necessarily themselves in Manila (the French renders this "*là-bas* au pays de la Perle d'Orient" [*N'y touchez pas!* 44]). But the main point here is the address, "O you who read me, friend or enemy." In *Imagined Communities* Anderson spoke of these opening pages being addressed to "we-Filipino-readers" (27), but in *The Spectre of Comparisons* he notes that the text "makes its readership marvelously problematic: *amigo ó enemigo?* Who are these *enemigos?* Surely not other Filipinos? Surely not Spaniards? After all, the *Noli* was written to inspire the nationalism of Filipino youth, and for the Filipino people! What on earth would Spanish readers be doing 'inside it'?" (240). But inside it they are, as addressees. A footnote allows, "Rizal certainly expected copies of his novels to fall into the hands of the colonial regime and the hated friars, and doubtless enjoyed the prospect of their squirming at his biting barbs" (240n), and earlier, contrasting Rizal with Tagore, Anderson notes that only three percent of Rizal's countrymen understood Spanish (232). The audience for a novel in Spanish necessarily included many who were not potential Filipinos—whence "you who read me, friend or enemy." "He wrote as much for the enemy as the friend," Anderson concludes here—a point which in my view corresponds with the structures of presupposition and address adopted in the novel.

One might add, further, that in his address to readers Rizal evokes the antagonism, the opposition between friend and enemy, that will prove crucial for building a nationalist movement and a nation, as for politics in general. Far from assuming that the community he addresses consists of like-minded friends, he recognizes that they can band together as friends only against the enemies, whom his work helps to constitute as enemies of the national project.[9] I shall return to this problem later.

In Balzac, whose national situation is quite different, we find a similarity in the structures of presupposition and the role created for the reader. What is common is the novelistic address which creates a community of those who pick up the book and accept the readerly role that it offers. Thus Balzac purveys ethnological information about Parisian habits and types, as if for readers who view them from a distance, but at the same time evokes a community of readers through the presupposition of shared knowledge: "he was one of those Parisians who always manages to look inordinately pleased with himself," for instance, presupposes familiarity with the type, and thus an insider's view, at the same time that it gives us, French or not, the information we need to position ourselves as insiders. The phrase "one of those" marks this as a category readers are presumed already to possess, as if they were already initiated into the mysteries of Paris, but in fact gives them what they need to know, in the Balzacian ethnology of Paris. And, more important perhaps, it makes this sort of "insider information" into an object of readerly desire. For readers of Rizal's novel, who may have never before taken any interest in the inhabitants of Manila, much less in its inhabitants of the late nineteenth century, it becomes desirable to be such an insider, to know about the types that comprise this nation. The presentation of "the Pearl of the Orient" as an object of interest, as something people might or might not know about, gives it a position in the world and makes it something to which one might feel allegiance. In short, novels like Rizal's and Balzac's, in their evocation of a world of diverse characters, adventures, and national or regional ways of being, may do much to encourage the imagining of those communities that are or that become nations, but they do not do so, I submit, by addressing readers *as nationals.* At the very least, this is an issue that needs to be examined more closely for a range of cases.

4

Anderson's essay on Mario Vargas Llosa's *El hablador* in *The Spectre of Comparisons* offers an opportunity to pursue the problem of the community of readers addressed. First, though, we need to consider its credentials as a novel of the nation. Anderson notes that "our century's hard times have made some at least of the utopian elements of nineteenth-century nationalism, for which universal progress was the foundation, decreasingly plausible," so that novelists today are "faced with aporiae with which the great novelists of the last century did not feel compelled to contend" (335).[10] If nineteenth-century novels of the nation enacted the overcoming of national divisions or inequalities, today we are more prepared to appreciate the obduracy of the problems and obstacles. In the Americas, as elsewhere, we are today all too aware that the triumph of the nation involves the conquest or oppression of indigenous peoples; but dramatizing their situation in a novel of the nation is a matter of some difficulty, since "we are living in a time when ventriloquizing persecuted and oppressed minorities has become (and not only ethically) intolerable" (335). Vargas Llosa's novel might be said to take as an implied point of reference San Martín's 1821 proclamation that "in the future the aborigines shall not be called Indians or natives; they are children and citizens of Peru and they shall be known as Peruvians" (qtd. in *Spectre* 193). It has not yet happened, but could it, and if so, at what cost? In dramatizing debates about the future of the Indians of Peru and the impossibility of satisfactory solutions, *El hablador* does not pretend to resolve national differences, as earlier novels did. Yet, Anderson writes, that it is "a nationalist novel is beyond doubt . . . the interesting question is how its nationalism is 'performed'" (*Spectre* 356).

The narrator of *El hablador* is a cosmopolitan Peruvian writer, living in Italy, trying to escape his "malhadado país"—his "unfortunate" or "accursed" nation. He comes upon an exhibition of photographs of a tribe of Amazonian Indians of Peru, the Machiguenga, who had obsessed a friend from his student days, Saúl Zuratas. He and Saúl had debated the moral and political issues concerning the status of the Indians, and he himself had come to be haunted by the idea of this tribe. The narrator speaks of this in chapters that alternate with chapters presenting the world of the Machiguenga in the voice of a tribal storyteller who is not identified but whom readers eventually come to take as Saúl Zuratas himself.

The novel does not account for the presence of these Machiguenga chapters in any way: the narrator has not seen Saúl for two decades, and while he himself had tried to write about the Machiguenga, each time he was blocked by

> the difficulty of inventing, in Spanish and within a logically consistent intellectual framework, a literary form that would suggest, with any reasonable degree of credibility, how a primitive man with a magico-religious mentality would go about telling a story. All my attempts led each time to the impasse of a style that struck me as glaringly false, as implausible as the various ways in which philosophers and novelists of the Enlightenment had put words into the mouths of their exotic characters in the eighteenth century when the theme of the "noble savage" was fashionable in Europe. [*Storyteller* 157–58]

The narrator's chapters tell of his debates with Saúl about the Indians, his own investigations, his failure to write about them, and his growing conviction that his friend Saúl had, in a process he claims to be unable to imagine, become the storyteller he is convinced he sees in a photograph of the tribe, displayed with others at the spot in Florence where Dante first glimpsed Beatrice. The other chapters—in a language whose grammar suggests a different way of thinking, a different perception of time, space, and individuals—present the lore of the Machiguengas and, at the end, tales recognizable in their links to Kafka or the history of the Jews (Saúl was "an ex-Jew" who knew much of Kafka by heart). The novel presents no warrant for these chapters. As Anderson remarks, Vargas Llosa has set himself the arduous task of "inventing a persuasive voice for the *hablador* which is as remote as possible from that of any self-imagined Peruvian, yet which at the same time radically undermines its own authenticity" (*Spectre* 355). The storyteller is supposed to be the voice of the community, the source of its knowledge and its traditions, whose storytelling is "Something primordial, something that the very existence of a people may depend on" (Vargas Llosa, *Storyteller* 94). Yet in the Americas tales of indigenous communities have had to emerge through translations of the missionaries, anthropologists, or other contaminating intermediaries, and here Saúl Zuratas is positioned to be the dubious imagined intermediary. One of the distinctive devices of the Machiguenga chapters—the way tales usually conclude with "That, at any rate, is what I have learned" ("Eso es, al menos, lo que yo he sabido")— works to undermine any narrative authority, if we think of the storyteller as an individual, such as Saúl, but it works also, or alternatively, to situate this discourse in a web of discourse, which it repeats.[11]

As is clear from the way the novel boldly does what the narrator finds impossible—invents a language for a people with a radically different worldview—this is a novel that takes risks in approaching the problem of the nation and those who, it seems, cannot be included without losing their identity. The impossible relation between the novel's parts dramatizes the unsolvable problem of the position of the Indians in Peru, where inclusion means assimilation, transformation, and destruction of their world, just as surely as exclusion will bring their destruction. In his debates with Saúl, the narrator argues for integrating and modernizing, but the story puts his position in doubt (shouldn't they, on the contrary, be left alone in their own world?), and his research obsession, which seems disinterested by comparison with that of missionaries, makes more plausible Saúl's position. Yet if the *hablador* is Saúl and not just a fantasy of the narrator's, preservation occurs through the intervention of an outsider; culture is preserved through imitation, repetition, and adulteration (for instance, the assimilation to Machiguenga culture of tales from Kafka and from the history of the Jews). Moreover, and this is especially pertinent to the novel's performance, from the point of view of the reader, it is precisely the "dubious," "compromised" representation, in Spanish, of the Machiguenga world that earns support for the idea of preserving this world in its purity and autonomy.

In juxtaposing these two sets of chapters (as if to fulfill Bakhtin's dubious claim that the novel is a dialogistic form which cites all forms of discourse without any one dominating) and in offering no explanation or claim about the authenticity of the Machiguenga lore, the novel stages the national project articulated by San Martín, in his claim, before the existence of Peru, that the Indians were "children of Peru." Or rather, as Anderson claims, *El hablador* considers the truth of Walter Benjamin's paradox, that every document of civilization is at the same time a document of barbarism: "considers the truth of Benjamin's paradox, taking all its terms together. One could say that it 'performs' the impossibility of transcending it, as well as of escaping from it. This is, perhaps, the only way in our time in which the national novel, the narrative of the nation, can be written, and rewritten, and rewritten" (359).

One might say that unlike the "old-fashioned novel," whose narrative voice easily encompassed characters unknown to each other and created "in the mind of the omniscient reader" the community to which they could belong, which was or was like that of the nation, here there is no all-encompassing narrator, no possibility of inventing a voice that can include all those who might be claimed by the nation. That impossibility may be read, as Anderson does, as a bringing "the timbre of tragedy as well as the semantics of shame" to the nation (359), but it may also be read as an attempt to imagine a community without unity, or what Jean-Luc Nancy calls a "communauté désoeuvrée": community as spacing rather than fusion, sublation, or transcendence. "Communauté *désoeuvrée*" because it is based on the fact that "there can be no singular being without another singular being" (71), and that what beings share "is not a common work that exceeds them but the differential experience of the other as finite being" (Melas, chap. three).[12] One does not recognize the Other but "éprouve son semblable"—experiences one's counterpart, who is similar in being singular [82].

Anderson reads *El hablador* in the register of tragedy and shame in part because he reads it not just as a novel of Peru but as a novel *for* Peruvians about the problem of their nation; he speaks of "the Peruvian Spanish-reading public which is the writer's first audience" (355). But one might wonder. Vargas Llosa is a novelist of international fame, whose non-Peruvian Spanish readers far outnumber his Peruvian ones. In "The National Longing for Form" Tim Brennan describes the way in which the novel—especially for a group of eminent writers from the Third World—functions today above all in an international market. Today the novel is "the form through which a thin foreign-educated stratum (however sensitive or committed to domestic political interests), has communicated to metropolitan reading publics, often in translation. It has been, in short, a naturally cosmopolitan form that empire has *allowed to play a national role, as it were, only in an international arena*" (56, my emphasis). In particular, there has emerged an important strain of Third-World writing: "the lament for the necessary and regrettable insistence of nation-forming, in which the writer proclaims his identity with a country whose artificiality and exclusiveness have driven him into a kind of exile—a simultaneous recognition of nationhood and alienation from it" (63).

Though this is not exactly true of Vargas Llosa (Brennan is thinking of writers such as Rushdie and Naipaul), it helps prevent us from taking it for granted that the community of readers addressed by *El hablador* is a national one. Read its opening lines:

> I came to Firenze to escape Peru and Peruvians for a while, and suddenly my unfortunate country [*malhadado país*] forced itself on me this morning in an unexpected way. I had visited Dante's restored house, the little Church of San Martino del Véscovo, and the lane where, so legend has it, he first saw Beatrice, when in the little Via Santa Margherita, a window display stopped me short: bows, arrows, a carved oar, a pot with a geometric design, a mannequin bundled into a wild cotton cushma. [*Storyteller* 3]

What sort of narrative audience is addressed here? It is first of all one that does not need explanation of the easy references to Firenze and to Dante's glimpse of Beatrice. Proper names, taken for granted, delineate the European scene, but when the narrator turns to the materials from the jungle in the window display and then to the photographs that "suddenly brought back for me the flavor of the Peruvian jungle," he does not use proper names or technical terms, such as the objects might be known by in Peru, but "bows, arrows, a carved oar." If one had to describe the reader whom this opening page appears to imagine and address, it would not be the Peruvian national but rather an international cosmopolitan reader, one likely to be struck by the unexpected contrast between the archetypal literary site and reminders of the unmarked scene identified with Peru: "The wide rivers, the enormous trees, the fragile canoes, the frail huts raised on pilings, and the knots of men and women, naked to the waist and daubed with paint, looking at me unblinkingly from the glossy print" (3).

El hablador may not be addressed to Peruvians, and indeed Peruvian readers may be precisely the wrong audience for this novel. Doris Sommer, whose "About-Face: The Talker Turns" is a brilliant, conflicted critical study of the novel,[13] reports that educated Peruvians dislike it: "One simplified version of the impatience Vargas Llosa's novel, along with his fiction in general, elicits among educated Peruvian readers, is presented by Mirko Lauer.... His fundamental objection, it seems, is that the novelist fails to maintain an ethical and coherent position" (129n). Peruvians may be in a particularly bad position to read it as a novel, for as inhabitants of a country where the status of the Indians has been a burning political question for some time and where Vargas Llosa is also a political figure with a record of actions, pronouncements, and essays on political and cultural topics, they are likely to take the novel, as Sommer herself does for most of her essay, as primarily a political statement, which can then be faulted for quietism or evasiveness. Sommer herself, as a critic responsible to the cultural context, interprets the novel in the light of Vargas Llosa's essays and political activities, where she reads insensitivity to the Indians, "readiness to sacrifice the Indian cultures, since they interfere with modernity's fight against hunger and need" ("About-Face" 126).[14] In a passage early in her essay, where she poses the question well, she suggests that the novel is his attempt to give himself an alibi. Vargas Llosa, she argues, does not see himself as internally divided, doesn't presume to contain the two sides of Peru:

> Either this reluctance to contain Peru is a facile admission of limits, based on rigid notions of difference between Indian tradition and modern projects, or the lack of presumption can be an ethical caution against containment and control of the incommensurable cultures in a multifarious nation. On the one hand, Vargas Llosa could be absolving himself from the moral obligation of inclusiveness and tolerance, a likely hand, given his impatient prescriptions for neutralizing and nationalizing specifically Indian cultures. But on the other hand, more promisingly, the refusal could be read against his politics, as a defense of difference. [94]

She makes it clear that his countrymen take the first, "more likely" view, which she resourcefully pursues for most of her essay. The duality the novel presents "can lead to dismissing indigenous otherness as inassimilable and inessential to the Peruvian body politic, a dismissal that countrymen read in Vargas Llosa's consistent carelessness about Indian cultures and lives" ("About-Face" 128). But at the end, putting Peruvian contexts behind her, Sommer turns to Levinas, who provides warrant for the second, unlikely possibility that the novel is a defense of difference: presuming to contain or "to understand the Other willfully ignores the mystery of his Saying." The structure of the novel, by allowing that saying, "holds out a hope: the possibility of recognition—on a reading from this geographic remove—even if the promise is betrayed by the man called Vargas Llosa" (130).

How striking that to permit a reading of this book as a novel rather than the political statement of the man Vargas Llosa, Doris Sommer requires what she suddenly names as a "geographic remove," the move with which the novel begins! All the more reason to think, as the opening of the novel itself suggests, that the reader the book addresses is not, perhaps, the educated Peruvian intent on evaluating the political statement or reading it like a newspaper, but the reader at some geographic remove, who picks up a new novel by a well-known novelist.

5

In the chapter on Vargas Llosa in *The Spectre of Comparisons,* Anderson summarizes his original hypothesis about the historic role of the novel:

> In *Imagined Communities* I argued that the historical appearance of the novel-as-popular-commodity and the rise of nation-ness were intimately related. Both nation and novel were spawned by the simultaneity made possible by clock-derived, man-made "homogeneous empty time," and thereafter, of Society understood as a bounded intrahistorical entity. All this opened the way for the human beings to imagine large, cross-generational, sharply delineated communities, composed of people mostly unknown to one another, and to understand these communities as gliding endlessly towards a limitless future. The novelty of the novel as a literary form lay in its capacity to represent synchronically this bounded, intrahistorical society-with-a-future. [334]

His basic claim, he reminds us, was based on the form of the novel. But this linking of novel and nation led to the assumption "that the novel would always be capable of representing, at different levels, the reality and truth of the nation"—an easy assumption since, for instance, "Balzac's *La Comédie humaine* (which is really, if the expression be excused, *La Comédie française*), the huge oeuvre of Zola, and even that of Proust, provide us with incomparable accounts of the France of their time" (334). He then lists various reasons why, in the second half of the twentieth century, the affinities between novel and nation become strained, including the division of the novel into subgenres—gothic, crime novel, and so on—"each with its own conventions and audiences which are by no means necessarily the fellow nationals of the author" (335). Anderson is scrupulous in distinguishing between the formal argument about the formal representation of time and space in the novel and the fact that, at "different levels," *particular* traditional novels provide a convincing representation of the society of a nation. But his own choice of examples, Rizal and Balzac, with their national *content,* has encouraged critics to assume that the decisive factor is the novel's representation of the nation, without being as scrupulous as Anderson here in making the distinction.

Anderson's own remark about subgenres and national audiences shows how easy it is to pass without noticing it from one sort of argument to another—to a different argument which may be highly contestable. It is only from the vantage point of a twentieth-century reader that the nineteenth-century novel looks "unified" in a national way, without subgenres and without international audiences. Just by way of indication—but this is a subject that requires much fuller discussion and documentation—Franco Moretti's lively, brief chapter on "Narrative Markets" notes the dominance in nineteenth-century Europe of the subgenres of the historical novel, the sensation novel and the sentimental novel, whose audiences were international:

> the great successes of the nineteenth century: Scott, Bulwer-Lytton, most of Dickens, and sensation novels from the British sample; sentimental novels, Dumas, Sue and Hugo from the French one. It is a regular and monotonous pattern: all of Europe reading the same books, with the same enthusiasm, and roughly in the same years (when not months). All of Europe unified by a desire, not for "realism" (the mediocre fortune of Stendhal and Balzac leaves no doubts on this point)—not for realism but for... "the melodramatic imagination": a rhetoric of stark contrasts that is present a bit everywhere and is perfected by Dumas and Sue (and Verdi), who are the most popular writers of the day. [176–77][15]

When we are discussing the audience for novels, we need to avoid unwarranted presumptions about both their address—the readerly role they construct—and their actual audiences. It seems to me very likely that in both cases the link between novel and nation will prove less strong than those who cite Anderson's authority are inclined to assume.

The power of Anderson's thesis about the novel is that it makes it a formal condition of imagining the nation—a structural condition of possibility. Critics, who are interested in the plots, themes, and imaginative worlds of particular novels, have tended to transform that thesis into a claim about the way some novels, by their contents, help to encourage, shape, justify, or legitimate the nation—a different claim, though one of considerable interest. The fact that Anderson's own examples involve some slippage from one claim to the other helps to explain the critical reception but does not excuse it. Literary critics in particular ought to be skilled at distinguishing an argument about the implications and consequences of a literary form from claims about particular sorts of plots and thematic representations.

The distinction between the novel as a condition of possibility of imagining the nation and the novel as a force in shaping or legitimating the nation needs to be maintained, not only for greater theoretical rigor and perspicacity but also for the force of the argument. When there is slippage from an argument about conditions of possibility to one about the effects of certain novelistic representations, the argument may become richer and more specific in some respects but also considerably weaker, vastly more dubious. If, for instance, we ask what made Britons "Britons," it is more plausible to answer "war with France" than "Jane Austen." The historian Linda Colley writes, "we can plausibly regard Great Britain as an invented nation." "It was an invention forged above all by war" (5). "Imagining the French as their vile opposites" (367), Britons "defined themselves against the French as they imagined them to be: superstitious, militarist, decadent, and unfree" (5). The differential construction of identity makes the oppositions Protestant versus Catholic and British versus French into the principal generators of this identity, even though Austen's marriage plots help to show that there is a large space in southern England where heroines can be at home. In a similar vein, Gopal Balakrishnan in "The National Imagination" argues that "the cultural affinities shaped by print capitalism do not themselves seem sufficiently resonant to generate the colossal sacrifices that modern peoples are at times willing to make for their nation" (208). It is in wartime and in relation to enemies that the culture of sacrifice takes over and feeds national feeling.

If we try to argue that the novel, through its representations of nationhood, made the nation, we will find ourselves on shaky ground, but if we argue that the novel was a condition of possibility for imagining something like a nation, for imagining a community that could be opposed to another, as friend to foe, and thus a condition of possibility of a community organized around a political distinction between friend and enemy, then we are on less dubious ground. We have considerable warrant for maintaining its importance in the face of the historian's insistence on socioeconomic and political factors, from markets to wars. Notice that the work of novels envisioned here is not that of propagandistically opposing the wicked and decadent French to the stalwart Britons (though some novels do this). On the contrary, the novel can be a condition of possibility of imagining communities that may become nations because it addresses readers in a distinctively open way, offering the possibility of adhering to a community, as an insider, without laying down particular criteria that have to be met. If a national community is to come into being, there must be the possibility for large numbers of people to come to feel a part of it, and the novel, in offering the insider's view to those who might have been deemed outsiders, creates that possibility. When José Rizal's *Noli me tangere* addresses the reader, "O you who read me, friend or enemy," the distinction between friend and enemy, on which the political events that make the nation will come to depend, is exposed as not external to the novel but as a possibility that arises within the novel. The community of readers that arises from a novel is one in which readers may be both friend and enemy, at once insider and outsider. If politics depends upon the distinction between friend and enemy, deciding who is which or ranging oneself on one side or the other, the novel provides a space within which the distinction can arise, prior to those decisions.

This is a complex matter because there are radically different ways in which readers of the novel may be both insiders and outsiders. In colonies or former colonies in particular, readers' idea of a national identity may arise from a vision from outside, when they see how they are placed on the map. In the case of Rizal's *Noli me tangere*, the readers as insiders/outsiders might be European-educated Filipinos who observe the inhabitants of the colony through the book's anthropological gaze, and who thus come to see themselves as Filipinos through this vision. The insider/outsider might also be the nineteenth-century Spaniard or the twentieth-century cosmopolitan reader who comes to share the narrative's commitment to a Filipino community. Anderson calls this double or comparative vision, with its oscillation between inside and outside, "the spectre of comparisons," and it is a spectre that haunts the novel, that makes it possible.

Anderson's work can lead us to realize that what is distinctive about the novel, about its formal adumbration of the space of a community, is its open invitation to readers of different conditions to become insiders, even while the novel raises as a possibility the distinction between insider and outsider, friend and foe, that becomes the basis of political developments.[16] This gives the novel a richer role as condition of possibility of the nation than it is likely to retain if we shift, as readers of Anderson seem inclined to do, from the form of the novel as condition of possibility of imagining the nation to the content of novels as representations of the nation.

Notes

1. Homi Bhabha, in his critique of Anderson in his *Nation and Narration,* uses the Renan quotation as a primary piece of evidence for Anderson's neglect of "the alienating and iterative time of the sign" [309]. Renan shows us that forgetting constitutes the beginning, writes Bhabha: "Listen to the complexity of this form of forgetting which is the moment in which the national will is articulated" [310]. "To be obliged to forget—in the construction of the national present—is not a question of historical memory; it is the construction of a discourse on society that performs the problematic totalization of the national will" [311]. Bhabha's reading of Renan depends upon Anderson's new account of Renan's obligatory forgetting, published as "Narrating the Nation" in the *Times Literary Supplement* before being taken up in the revised edition of *Imagined Communities.*

2. One might also note the place of novels—Cooper's *The Pathfinder,* Melville's *Moby Dick,* and Twain's *Huckleberry Finn*—in the new chapter of *Imagined Communities* (1991), "Memory and Forgetting" [202–03].

3. Franco Moretti argues, on the contrary, "In general, the novel has not stimulated social polyphony (as Bakhtin would have it), but rather reduced it (as I have tried to show here and there in *The Way of the World* and *Modern Epic*). The undeniable polyphony of the Russian novel of ideas is in this respect the exception, not the rule, of novelistic evolution: not by chance generated . . . by a European, not a national frame" (*Atlas of the European Novel* 45n26). State-building requires streamlining, as various jargons and dialects are reduced to a national language.

    In fact, Brennan might not disagree with this. The question may be how far the novel represents the social polyphony that by its embrace or containment it in effect works to reduce. Critics' eagerness to embrace the Bakhtinian thesis of the dialogistic nature of the novel may have led them to neglect the novel's contribution to national homogenization.

4. Fredric Jameson notoriously claims, "All third-world texts are necessarily, I want to argue, allegorical in a very specific way: they are to be read as what I will call national allegories" (69). The relation of this claim about all third-world texts to claims about the "old-fashioned novel" in general is scarcely clear.

5. The central argument of *Foundational Fictions* is nicely summarized by Doris Sommer in "Irresistible Romance: The Foundational Fictions of Latin America."

6. Especially piquant evidence for the "invention of a national community based on new norms for the family" comes from a contemporary complaint (by Alfred Nettement), that journalism had created "an invisible man seated in the home, between husband and wife, who returns every morning with the newspaper, seizes hold of the thoughts of a young woman, and creates for her a new ideal" (Reid 145). Even more frequently, though, the ideas disturbing young women were attributed to novels.

7. For discussion, see Bellanger et al., vol. 2, and McPhee.

8. Since Anderson convincingly analyzes the inadequacies of the English translation, I quote the English from Anderson's version, where he provides it. I have also consulted the excellent French translation, *N'y touchez pas!*

9. For the constitutive role of "antagonism" in the construction of hegemony and in politics generally, see Laclau and Mouffe. For the crucial role of the distinction between friend and enemy, see Derrida's discussion of Blake, Nietzsche, and especially Carl Schmitt in *Politiques de l'amitié* [91–157 and 272–80]. Schmitt's *Der Begriff des Politischen* (1932) treats the discrimination of friend from enemy as constitutive for politics; and the essence of a people's political existence is its determining for itself who is friend and who enemy [qtd. in Derrida 276]. Derrida stresses that in this distinction "one concept bears the ghost of the other: the enemy the friend and the friend the enemy" [92].

10. For discussion of the novels of two contemporary writers of nationalist projects, the Indonesian Pramoedya Ananta Toer, to whom Anderson alludes [*Spectre* 337–38,] and the Kenyan Ngugi wa Thiong'o, see Cheah.

11. In addition, assertions frequently close with "perhaps" ("quizá," or "talvez") ("Everything was going very well, perhaps")—another device that is likely to strike the reader as undermining narrative authority, as traditionally conceived. Efrain Krystal, discussing the language of these chapters, writes, "the most salient feature of this stylized language for the reader is a recursive pattern of ungrammatical conventions, suggestive of a different way of thinking" (165).

12. I am indebted to Melas's discussion of the usefulness of Nancy's concept for conceiving community in the postcolonial world and breaking away from the Hegelian model of mutual recognition as a dialectical model of community based on identity. She herself develops a notion of *dissimilation* to set against the model of assimilation.

13. In addition to Doris Sommer's "About Face," see the fine treatment by Lucille Kerr in *Reclaiming the Author: Figures and Fictions from Spanish America* and the discussion by Efrain Kristal in *Temptation of the Word: The Novels of Mario Vargas Llosa*. Jean O'Bryan-Knight, in *The Story of the Storyteller*, maintains, wrongly in my view, that this is a novel about the novelist writing this novel. I think that the narrator's inability to write the part of the storyteller is crucial.

14. In what might be a key point, Sommer suggests that in constructing the Machiguenga chapters Vargas Llosa has been influenced by the better-known native language, Quechua, spoken in the mountains of Peru, and that he there deploys what she calls "Quechua-inflected Spanish": "The Andean sounds are so improbable in the jungle that the effect is to suggest the writer's indifference to Indians" [97]. If this were true, it would be a pertinent critique of the artistic realization of these chapters and their failure to imagine a plausible language of otherness. I myself am not competent to judge this point and can note only that other critics I have consulted do not see the Machiguenga chapters in this way, including Efrain Kristal, who has the most convincing discussion of the style of these chapters, and especially of the grammatical and other devices by which Vargas Llosa has created the effect of a non-Western mode of thinking.

15. In fact, this quotation ("all of Europe reading the same books") exaggerates what Moretti's data show, for he goes on to describe the uneven diffusion of British and French novels, for example. But the central points remain: niche markets are not a twentieth-century invention, and the audiences are international, not simply national.

16. I am grateful to Pheng Cheah for incisive comments on a draft of this paper and especially on the point developed here.

Works Cited

Anderson, Benedict. *Imagined Communities: Reflections on the Origins and Spread of Nationalism.* 1983. 2nd rev. ed. London: Verso, 1991.
———. "Narrating the Nation." *Times Literary Supplement.* 13 June 1986: 659.
———. *The Spectre of Comparisons: Nationalism, Southeast Asia, and the World.* London: Verso, 1998.
Balakrishnan, Gopal. "The National Imagination." *Mapping the Nation.* Ed. Balakrishnan. London: Verso, 1996: 198–213.
Bellanger, Claude, et al. *Histoire générale de la presse française.* Paris: Presses universitaires de France, 1969.
Bhabha, Homi. "DisseminNation: Time, Narrative, and the Margins of the Modern Nation." *Nation and Narration.* Ed. Homi Bhabha. London: Routledge, 1990: 291–322.
Brennan, Tim. "The National Longing for Form." *Nation and Narration.* Ed. Homi Bhabha. London: Routledge, 1990. 44–70.
Cheah, Pheng. "Spectral Nationality: The Idea of Freedom in Modern Philosophy and the Experience of Freedom in Postcoloniality." PhD diss. Cornell U, 1998.
Derrida, Jacques. *Politiques de l'amitié.* Paris: Galilée, 1994.
Castro-Klaren, Sara. *Understanding Mario Vargas Llosa.* Columbia, SC: U of South Carolina Press, 1990.
Colley, Linda. *Britons: Forging the Nation 1707–1837.* New Haven, CT: Yale UP, 1992.
Jameson, Fredric. "Third-World Literature in the Era of Multi-National Capitalism." *Social Text* 15 (Fall 1986): 65–88.
Kerr, Lucille. *Reclaiming the Author: Figures and Fictions from Spanish America.* Durham: Duke UP, 1992.
Kristal, Efrain. *Temptation of the Word: The Novels of Mario Vargas Llosa.* Nashville, TN: Vanderbilt UP, 1988.
Laclau, Ernesto, and Chantal Mouffe. *Hegemony and Socialist Strategy: Toward a Radical Democratic Politics.* London: New Left Books, 1985.
Lloyd, David. *Anomalous States: Irish Writing and the Post-Colonial Movement.* Durham, NC: Duke UP, 1993.
McPhee, Peter. *A Social History of France, 1780–1880.* London: Routledge, 1992.
Melas, Natalie. *All the Difference in the World: Postcoloniality and the Ends of Comparison.* Stanford: Stanford UP, 2004.
Moretti, Franco. *Atlas of the European Novel, 1800–1900.* London: Verso, 1998.
Nancy, Jean-Luc. *La communauté désoeuvrée.* Paris: Christian Bourgois, 1986.
O'Bryan-Knight, Jane. *The Story of the Storyteller.* Amsterdam: Rodopi, 1995.
Reid, Roddey. *Families in Jeopardy: Regulating the Social Body in France, 1750–1910.* Stanford: Stanford UP, 1993.
Rizal, José. *Noli me tangere.* 1887. Madrid: Ediciones de Cultural Hispánica, 1992. French: *N'y touchez pas!* Trans. Jovita Ventura Castro. Paris: Gallimard, 1980.
Sommer, Doris. "About-Face: The Talker Turns." *boundary 2* 23.1 (Spring 1996): 91–133.
———. *Foundational Fictions: The National Romances of Latin America.* Berkeley: University of California Press, 1991.
———. "Irresistible Romance: The Foundational Fictions of Latin America." *Nation and Narration.* Ed. Homi Bhabha. London: Routledge, 1990. 71–98.
Vargas Llosa, Mario. *The Storyteller.* Trans. Helen Lane. New York: Penguin, 1990. Trans. of *El hablador.* 1987. Barcelona: Biblioteca de Bolsillo. 1991.

CHAPTER **4**

Bogeyman

Benedict Anderson's "Derivative" Discourse

ANDREW PARKER

> Between life and death, nationalism has as its own proper space the
> experience of haunting. There is no nationalism without some ghost.
> —Jacques Derrida, "Onto-Theology of National-Humanism"

Writing a mere decade ago about Benedict Anderson's *Imagined Communities,* Timothy Brennan noted that "with the exception of some recent
sociological works which use literary theories, it is rare in English to see
'nation-ness' talked about as an imaginative vision—as a topic worthy of
full fictional realization. . . . Even in the underrepresented branch of Third
World English studies, one is likely to find discussions of race and colonialism, but not the 'nation' as such" (47). If these sentences appear astonishing
today—if over the past ten years we seem to have done little else but regard
the nation as an imaginative construction—our sense of surprise may help
to register how rapidly and profoundly Anderson's work has transformed the
nature of literary and cultural studies. Viewing the modern nation primarily
as an anthropological rather than political category, one that has less inherently to do with ideologies than with kinship, gender, and religion, Anderson
argues in *Imagined Communities* for the irreducibility of material-cultural
practices (what he memorably termed "print capitalism") in creating and
sustaining the "imagined community" of a nation whose citizens maintain
"deep attachments" to each other in the absence of face-to-face contact: "the

members of even the smallest nation will never know most of their fellow-members, meet them, or even hear of them, yet in the minds of each lives the image of their communion" (6). Part of what makes such communities *national,* Anderson suggests, is a shared experience of simultaneity modeled on the spatio-temporal organization of newspapers and novels, for "these forms provided the technical means for 're-presenting' the *kind* of imagined community that is the nation" by furnishing their reader-consumers with a "complex gloss on the word 'meanwhile'" (25). The "old-fashioned novel" especially, through its distinctive structures of address and omniscient point of view, becomes in this schema a "device" for generating a sociologically complex world populated by characters who, even though they "may be largely unaware of each other," nevertheless move together "calendrically through homogeneous, empty time"—a world, in short, that may be considered "a precise analogue of the idea of the nation, which also is conceived as a solid community moving steadily up (or down) history" (25–26). As Jonathan Culler aptly summarizes in his contribution to this issue, Anderson thus takes the novel to be "a precondition for the nation" (24), "a formal condition of imagining the nation—a structural condition of possibility" (37). Such strong emphasis on the novel as "a force for imagining the communities that are nations" certainly helps to explain why *Imagined Communities* so swiftly and pervasively became doxa in literary study—even if, as Culler elaborates, some of Anderson's readers have mistaken his argument for a stronger if less defensible version that sees the novel as "a force in shaping or legitimating the nation" (37).

While Anderson's analogy between novel and nation has been put by literary critics to a multitude of creative uses, what has been acknowledged much less commonly is that his literary interests are by no means exhausted by the paradigm for which he is best known.[1] The very title of his most recent book is, significantly as we shall see, a translated quotation from a novel, and he returns repeatedly for insights into the politics of literary form not only to Walter Benjamin but to certain exemplary "nationalist" novelists, José Rizal and Pramoedya Ananta Toer first and foremost. Where *The Spectre of Comparisons* is unusual in containing chapter-length readings of literary works (several of them reprinted from the earlier *Language and Power*), *Imagined Communities* was no stranger to detailed discussions of fiction. We may be struck, in fact, by the extent to which Anderson's theoretical and historical studies locate themselves persistently over time with reference to "literature" and its various cognate terms. Much though not all of this work will seem traditional in the status it accords the literary: fiction often is presented as an ontologically derivative discourse, one whose characteristic secondariness may be offset in part by an indirection that provides a kind of bonus truth-effect. I stress *though not all* of Anderson's work, since "literature" cannot stay derivative for long when "imagining" and "creation" resist being cast as "fabrication" and "falsity": "Communities are to be distinguished," he famously puts it, "not by their falsity/genuineness, but by the style in which they are imagined" (*IC* 6). If "style" here will have more to do with notions of phantasm or performativity than with belletristic norms, it is because Anderson's most challenging thinking about nation and novel tends to efface received distinctions between origin and derivation, distinctions it at other times upholds. By focusing below on some critical places in his writings about literature—places where aporiae associated with writing and translation make secondariness, as it were, come first—we may find that Anderson's is indeed "a derivative discourse," though not at all in the spirit in which Partha Chatterjee initially intended this phrase.

"A Derivative Discourse?" is the subtitle to *Nationalist Thought and the Colonial World*, where Chatterjee began an argument with Anderson, developed more fully in *The Nation and Its Fragments*, over the nature and function of nationalist thought in the decolonizing world. Chatterjee objects to the way Anderson traces the origins of modern nationalism to the creole republics of the New World, which began to think of their own populations as nationals "*well before most of Europe*" (*IC* 50; Anderson's emphasis). For Chatterjee, the Americas attain in this story of origins an unwarranted privilege in relation to which the subsequent nationalisms of Asia and Africa can only be secondary. But if the precedence Anderson grants to the Americas does indeed seem peculiar, this will have less to do with their supposed ontological primacy than with the way that they portrayed themselves as imitative from the start:

> The independence movements in the Americas became, as soon as they were printed about, "concepts," "models," and indeed "blueprints." . . . Furthermore, the validity and generalizability of the blueprint were undoubtedly confirmed by the plurality of the independent states. . . . In effect, by the second decade of the nineteenth century, if not earlier, a "model" of "the" independent national state was available for pirating. . . . But precisely because it was by then a known model, it imposed certain "standards" from which too-marked deviations were impermissible. [*IC* 81]

"As soon as they were printed about": at their origin, in other words, the new republics conform already to a generalized model of nationness, to a pattern that originates in an elsewhere that in turn never rests in a proper self-identity. Although Chatterjee reads Anderson as a kind of Hegel in reverse (the national idea completing itself as it passes eastward through European ethno-nationalisms to Asia and Africa [*NT* 20]), it is striking how much Anderson's account of the nation's modularity recalls Derrida's description of the play of difference and identity that underwrites the structure of the sign: as a "signifying form" intrinsically open to piracy, the nation "only constitutes itself by virtue of its iterability" (Derrida, *SEC* 10). No wonder, then, that the nation for Anderson "proved an invention on which it was impossible to secure a patent": already derivative at its origin, "the 'American' model" will have earned its set of scare quotes from the outset (*IC* 67, 113).

For Chatterjee, however, Anderson's modular nationalism clearly has been patented, for if even anticolonialists have to imitate "models of nation, nation-ness, and nationalism distilled from the turbulent, chaotic experiences of more than a century of American and European history" (*IC* 140), then the nation will have always been a Western invention:

> I have one central objection to Anderson's argument. If nationalisms in the rest of the world have to choose their imagined community from certain "modular" forms already made available to them by Europe and the Americas, what do they have left to imagine? History, it would seem, has decreed that we in the postcolonial world shall only be perpetual consumers of modernity. Europe and the Americas, the only true subjects of history, have thought out on our behalf not only the script of colonial enlightenment and exploitation, but also that of our anticolonial resistance and postcolonial misery. Even our imaginations must remain forever colonized. [*NF* 5][2]

As far as I know, Anderson has never replied directly to Chatterjee's complaint, though part of a response may be discerned in the intention of a recent essay "to dispose of such bogeys as 'derivative discourses,' and 'imitation' in understanding the remarkable planetary spread, not merely of nationalisms, but of a profoundly standardized conception of politics" (*SC* 29). If the issue of derivativeness can be dismissed here as a "bogey," it is because Anderson has rejected in principle the ontologized distinction between origin and derivation on which Chatterjee's criticism depends: for Anderson there can be nothing authentic—West or East—with which to oppose the nation's constitutive secondariness. Anderson in his later work restates this point strongly in language that has since absorbed the inflections of post-structuralism: he speaks of "the peculiarity of nationalist images as replicas without originals" (*SC* 26); of national monuments that "can never, as such, be singular" and "do not have auras" (48–49); of "the paradoxical question of the origin of what one can only call originlessness" (56); of the mediated immediacy of "real print-encounters" (62) and the similarly oxymoronic "pure mix" (259). There is no better description of *Nachträglichkeit* than Anderson's gloss on the "reverse teleology" that "transformed the Great War into World War I, and made the state of Israel the ancestor of the Warsaw uprising": "Hence there is no Originator of the nation, or rather the Originator is a ceaselessly changing, here-and-now, 'Us'" (57n19). These theoretical commitments underlie as well Anderson's interest in technologies of the iterable like the census, whose "'weft' was what one could call serialization: the assumption that the world was made up of replicable plurals" (*IC* 184). Clearly we are *not* discussing "copying in any simple manner" (*SC* 32).

Even so, however, Chatterjee is not entirely mistaken in finding residual ontologies in *Imagined Communities:* if, on the one hand, Anderson is a thinker of models-without-origins, he is also on the other a theorist of the Fall. As Pheng Cheah has demonstrated in a remarkable recent essay, Anderson's genealogy of nationalism depends for its coherence on "a strict demarcation between organic spontaneity and technical manipulation: between the nation-people and the state," a distinction that moreover retraces "the line between the organic and the artificial, between life and death" (234). What contaminates the vital nation is the self-legitimating apparatus of "official nationalism," the artificial creation of "dynastic states and archaic nobilities" that "developed *after,* and *in reaction to,* the popular national movements proliferating in Europe since the 1820s" (*IC* 86 and *SC* 47n2; Anderson's emphasis). "As an emanation and armature of the state," official nationalism conjures up scenes of mass ritual that are transparently empty and yet, somehow, especially dangerous for children: "It manifests itself, not merely in official ceremonies of commemoration, but in a systematic programme, directed primarily, if not exclusively, through the state's school system, to create and disseminate an official nationalist history, an official nationalist pantheon of heroes, and an official nationalist culture, through the ranks of its younger, incipient citizens—naturally, in the state's own interests" (*SC* 253). Anderson obviously much prefers to the imposed *technē* of the state a "genuine, popular nationalist enthusiasm," but recognizes that this ideal always may fall prey in time to a "systematic, even Machiavellian, instilling of nationalist ideology" (*IC* 113–14).[3] The problem, of course, is how to tell the good and bad versions apart when, by definition, both are derivative. Although Anderson showed nationalism to have been modular already at its "origin," he proceeds here as if this hadn't been the case—as if at one time nations *were* self-present and modularity something into which, regrettably, they might on occasion tumble. This revision allows Anderson to deprecate official nationalism for its "reactionary and secondary modelling" of "the largely spontaneous popular nationalisms that preceded them"—to reproach it, in other words, simply for being imitative: "If these nationalisms were modelled on American and French histories, so now they became modular in turn. It was only that a certain inventive legerdemain was required to permit the empire to appear attractive in national drag" (86–87, 110). If this is a story of the empire's new clothes, these may be styles—*pace* Anderson—that never have gone out of fashion anywhere.

These two different versions of the derivative—the one ontologically secondary, the other paradoxically "constitutive"—both make their presence felt in Anderson's remarkably allusive, cantfree discussions of literature. The variety of his literary references is as astonishing as are the number of different roles that they play in his work. He tosses off aperçus contrasting, for example, the novel's polyphonic portrayal of social life with Petronius's *Satyricon*, whose "narrative proceeds in single file" (*IC* 25); he uses extracts from Musil's *Posthumous Papers of a Living Author* to launch an inquiry into the vapidity of public monuments (*SC* 46–47); he quotes stanzas from Rizal's *Último Adiós* to remind us that nations inspire love (*IC* 142–43); he reads two very long (and sexually adventurous) classics of Javanese literature, the *Serat Centhini* and the *Suluk Gatholoco*, as compendia of kinds of knowledge prized by an emerging professional class (*SC* 105–30); he devotes a chapter to Mario Vargas Llosa's *The Storyteller*, an "extraordinary, aporetic, nationalist novel about modern Peru and its Amazonian 'tribal minorities'" (*SC* 26), about which I will say much more below. Anderson's encyclopedic command over literary and cultural materials from widely diverse linguistic traditions rivals even that of Erich Auerbach, whose own affecting writing on the limits of nationalism Anderson prominently acknowledges.

To date, Anderson's most influential treatment of literature remains his discussion in *Imagined Communities* of "four fictions from different cultures and different epochs"—the first two Filipino, the others Mexican and Indonesian—"all but one of which, nonetheless, are inextricably bound to nationalist movements" (26). In showing, first, how Rizal's *Noli me tangere* evokes in its opening description of an anticipated dinner party "the solidity of a single community, embracing characters, authors and readers, moving onward through calendrical time" (27), Anderson suggests that this novel provides its readers an experience of simultaneity that is a sine qua non of national consciousness—an experience that Francisco Balagtas's earlier *Florante at Laura* (set in an invented medieval Albania!) had not yet been able to achieve formally and ideologically. If this is a residually Hegelian argument, it is one with the great merit of imagining an entirely new way that works of fiction can be said to perform politically. But Anderson's argument changes subtly as he turns to his next two examples, José Joaquín Fernández de Lizardi's *El periquillo sarniento* and Mas Marco Kartodikromo's *Semarang Hitam*, each of which offers its readers a national-typical "world of plurals"—prisons in the one case, newspaper readers in the other. As Jonathan Culler notes, Anderson no longer reads these works as analogues of the nation but as "a representation of its social space" (23), each novel reproducing faithfully the classification systems it imports from the outer social world. We see this different emphasis as well in Anderson's later discussion of a tale by Pramoedya Ananta Toer in which a character comes to a sense of her identity generically in occupying "a defined position in that

society: as a woman, as a typist in a government office, as a free individual"
(*SC* 41). Anderson presents the entire scene to us as part of an effort to
"show how basic to the modern imagining of collectivity seriality is" (40),
and although this notion of series replaces the earlier language of plurals
what hasn't changed in Anderson's reading is the novel's secondariness with
respect to the social categories it incorporates and reflects.

What is in question here is the status of the literary example, or better, the
status of literature *as* an example: departing from the terms of his analysis
of *Noli* (where the novel forms the nation's possibility condition), Anderson
seeks more commonly from literature a confirmation of its mimetic power—
and indeed, *In the Mirror* is the title of a collection of stories he translated
from Thai. Culture's very purpose is reflection: if, for example, "nations
inspire love, and often profoundly self-sacrificing love," this is what "the
cultural products of nationalism—poetry, prose fiction, music, plastic arts—
show . . . very clearly in thousands of different forms and styles" (*IC* 141). We
look to writers, accordingly, for the ways their language provides insight into
a social world that preexists its fictional representation: "No one has found
a better metaphor for this frame of mind [about seriality] than the great
Indonesian novelist Pramoedya Ananta Toer" (*IC* 184). To his own immense
credit, Anderson worries about making literature play such ontologically diminished roles: "So far, so clear. Probably too clear. For I have treated the
Centhini as if it were a mirror of society or a quasi-ethnological treatise,
permitting us to infer that its pages more or less directly transcribed the
life of late eighteenth-century Java." And yet he continues to inquire after
"the social basis for the peculiarities" he detects in the *Centhini,* a poem that
"shows that something new is in the air" at a particular moment in Javanese
society (*SC* 109, 119–20). Here, as elsewhere, literature assumes a mimetic
function in conforming to what Derrida describes as a metaphysics of illustration: "through fiction truth properly declares itself. Fiction manifests
the truth: the manifestation that illustrates itself through evasion. . . . Truth
governs this element from its origin or its telos, which finally coordinates
this concept of literary fiction with a highly classical conception of *mimesis:*
a detour toward the truth, more truth in the fictive representation than in
reality, increased fidelity, 'superior realism' " (*PC* 467–68).

What is striking by contrast is that Anderson seldom thinks "classically"
about fiction when it oversteps the boundaries of the literary text. Indeed,
this is one of the chief reasons that *Imagined Communities* has proven indis-
pensable to literary and cultural theorists. In speaking, for example, about
the "profound fictiveness" of the newspaper (33), Anderson never simply
opposes to this quality an ontologically prior social world. On the contrary,
"fiction seeps quietly and continuously into reality, creating that remarkable
confidence of community in anonymity which is the hallmark of modern
nations" (36). Unlike Ernest Gellner, who wants to submit the self-invention

of nations to the model of false consciousness (and thereby be done with it), Anderson thinks it inappropriate to impose constative criteria for nationness, claiming instead with J. L. Austin that the invention of nations has more to do with conditions of felicity than truth. Where Gellner "implies that 'true' communities exist which can be advantageously juxtaposed to nations," Anderson recognizes that "all communities larger than primordial villages of face-to-face contact (and perhaps even these) are imagined" (6). Nations therefore differ from one another not by their "falsity/genuineness" but by the performative "style" of their imagining—which makes such style into something other than a calculable deviation from the truth. Marilyn Ivy usefully defines this something other as a phantasm, "an epistemological object whose presence or absence cannot be definitively located" (22) and which disturbs, as a consequence, the kinds of opposition (before/after and outside/inside) on which the orderly declension of derivations from origins depends. In the following pages I turn again to several of Anderson's literary analyses, seeking to discern in them traces of such phantasms—specters that, in haunting such "secondary" processes as writing and translation, will trouble imputed distinctions between the fictions of nation and novel.

It may seem surprising at first that Anderson devotes his most sustained treatment of a literary work to Mario Vargas Llosa's novel *The Storyteller*—surprising, above all, given Vargas Llosa's inexorable drift to the right over the past three decades (see Martin; Rowe; Sommer). Where Anderson acknowledges that "we are living in a time in which ventriloquizing persecuted and oppressed minorities has become (and not only ethically) intolerable" (*SC* 359), Vargas Llosa has shown no such reticence whether in his public voice (he was the principal author of the report of a commission investigating the murder of a group of journalists in the Andean community of Uchuraccay) or in fictional works like *The Storyteller* (which purports to render directly the cosmogonic myths of a beleaguered Amazonian tribe).[4] One can hardly think of a figure more uncongenial to Anderson's political values than the Vargas Llosa who rewrites Jorge Basadre's contrast between the Peruvian state and nation—*el país legal* and *el país profundo*—as a racialized distinction between a modern and an archaic Peru (*UA* 200–11; see Mayer 192–95). For Vargas Llosa, Peru *profundo* is exclusively Indian:

> Two cultures, one Western and modern, the other aboriginal and archaic, hardly coexist, separated from each other because of the exploitation and discrimination that the former exercises over the latter. . . . Important as integration is, the obstacle to achieving it lies in the huge economic gap between these two communities. Indian peasants live in such a primitive way that communication is practically impossible. It is only when they move to the cities that they have the opportunity to mingle with the other Peru. The price they must pay for their integration is high—renunciation of their culture, their language, their beliefs,

their traditions and customs, and the adoption of the culture of their ancient masters. After one generation they become mestizos. They are no longer Indians.

Perhaps there is no realistic way to integrate our societies other than by asking the Indians to pay that price. Perhaps the ideal—that is, the preservation of the primitive cultures of America—is a utopia incompatible with this other and more urgent goal—the establishment of societies in which social and economic inequalities among citizens be reduced to human, reasonable limits and where everybody can enjoy at least a decent and free life.

Vargas Llosa's unflinching conclusion: "If forced to choose between the preservation of Indian cultures and their complete assimilation, with great sadness I would choose modernization of the Indian population, because there are priorities; and the first priority is, of course, to fight hunger and misery. . . . Where there is such an economic and social gap, modernization is possible only with the sacrifice of the Indian cultures" (*CIII* 377; *QC* 52–53).

This argument is amplified in *The Storyteller,* in which the narrations of an unnamed cosmopolitan writer very much like Vargas Llosa alternate with those of an Amazonian tribal storyteller who, over the course of the novel, is revealed gradually to be the narrator's old college friend, Saúl Zuratas. Nicknamed Mascarita, a half-Jew whose face is half-covered with a birthmark (Vargas Llosa does nothing here if not by halves), Zuratas joins the tribe he formerly studied and, in "bringing stories from one group of Machiguengas to another," reminds "each member of the tribe that the others were alive, that despite the great distances that separated them, they still formed a community" (93). Zuratas travels, however, in the opposite direction (both temporally and spatially) from the majority of the Machiguengas, who have had little choice but to relinquish their traditional culture—a process the narrator seems to endorse in criticizing his friend's *indigenismo:*

> What did he suggest, when all was said and done? That, in order not to change the way of life and the beliefs of a handful of tribes still living, many of them, in the Stone Age, the rest of Peru should abstain from developing the Amazon region? Should sixteen million Peruvians renounce the natural resources of three-quarters of their national territory so that seventy or eighty thousand Indians could quietly go on shooting at each other with bows and arrows, shrinking heads and worshiping boa constrictors? [21–22]

The narrator continues more provocatively, and with even more pointed sarcasm:

> No, Mascarita, the country had to move forward. Hadn't Marx said that progress would come dripping blood? Sad though it was, it had to be accepted. We had no alternative. If the price to be paid for development and industrialization for the sixteen million Peruvians meant that those few thousand naked Indians would have to cut their hair, wash off their tattoos, and become mestizos—or to use the ethnologists' most detested word, become acculturated—well, there was no way around it. [22–23]

These passages match so closely Vargas Llosa's own published views that critics easily have taken *The Storyteller* to be "a vindication of national integration by other means; the obvious impossibility of integrating with the Machiguenga is used to lend weight to the idea that they can only integrate with us, the central and stable implicit *nosotros* of the text. Fiction has ceased to be a complex figuration of multiplicities in conversational space-time, to become administration of opinion" (Rowe 60).

One problem with this reading, however, is that the novel's dramatized argument for the national assimilation of the tribes is far from the exclusive property of the right. Indeed, we find among others the late Marxist critic (and antagonist to Vargas Llosa) Angel Rama defending this position as well: today one can hope no longer "for the survival of indigenous culture, rather for mestizo culture, because Indian culture no longer made sense. What [the Peruvian novelist and anthropologist José María] Arguedas understood is that for all practical purposes the solution was the muddy road of mestizaje. That torturous, and often dirty, road, like life itself, but that was richer in possibilities" (*sic;* qtd. in Beverley 46).[5]

If left and right thereby surrender some of their distinctiveness around this issue, we then have every reason to ask, "What Is Left?"—the question Anderson poses as the title of the final section of *The Spectre of Comparisons*, in which his essay on Vargas Llosa, "El Malhadado País," appears. Anderson's is not primarily an ideological analysis of *The Storyteller* (he will not be playing Marx to Vargas Llosa's Balzac), and he disclaims in fact any special knowledge of or interest in the author's life and works more generally (338). Though he is attracted to this novel in particular for the light it sheds on the diminished capacity of late twentieth-century narratives to model the imagined nation, *The Storyteller* may have proven irresistible to Anderson in any case, its own themes haunted by the epigraph from San Martín that lies close to the origin of *Imagined Communities:* "In the future, the aborigines shall not be called Indians and natives; they are children and citizens of Peru and they shall be known as Peruvians" (*SC* 333; see *IC* 49, 81). Vargas Llosa returns the favor of his own attention in "Nations, Fictions," an essay that refers explicitly and positively to Anderson's work (*MW* 301). As cosmopolitan intellectuals most at home in the borderlands between culture and politics, both writers share a number of affinities, among them, as it turns out, the mimetic conception of literary truth we encountered above: "In effect, novels lie—they can do nothing else," writes Vargas Llosa, "—but that is only part of the story. The other part is that, by lying, they express a curious truth that can only be expressed in a furtive and veiled fashion, disguised as something that it is not" (*MW* 320).

Anderson's and Vargas Llosa's greatest affinity would consist, however, in their shared fascination with figurations of community from the zero-degree of the tribe to the contemporary nation, a continuum *The Storyteller* assumes as its palette. The novel depicts the Machiguengas as historically so primitive as to be *just* this side of the nature/culture divide:

> The strength and the solitude of Nature—the tall trees, the mirror-smooth lagoons, the immutable rivers—brought to mind a newly created world, untouched by man, a paradise of plants and animals. When we reached the tribes, by contrast, there before us was prehistory, the elemental, primeval existence of our distant ancestors: hunters, gatherers, bowmen, nomads, shamans, irrational and animistic. This, too, was Peru, and only then did I become fully aware of it: a world still untamed, the Stone Age, magico-religious cultures, polygamy, head-shrinking . . . that is to say, the dawn of human history. [*S* 72–73]

Although they recently "had begun to accept the idea of forming villages, of coming together in places suitable for working the soil, breeding animals, and developing trade relations with the rest of Peru" (161), the Machiguengas traditionally lack all social organization beyond the nuclear family—"one of the distinctive features of the tribe [had] been the absence of any sort of hierarchical political organization, with leaders and subordinates" (162)— and even the notion of stable proper names was alien to them: "Their names were always temporary, related to a passing phenomenon and subject to change: the one who arrives, or the one who leaves, the husband of the woman who has just died, or the one who is climbing out of his canoe, the one just born, or the one who shot the arrow" (83). Under these circumstances, the narrator wonders, can one even speak of this tribe *as* a community (80)?

That the Machiguengas manage nonetheless to cohere as a group is wholly the result of the efforts of its roving storytellers, "those habladores who—by occupation, out of necessity, to satisfy a human whim—using the simplest, most time-hallowed of expedients, the telling of stories, were the living sap that circulated and made the Machiguengas into a society, a people of interconnected and interdependent beings [*un pueblo de seres solidarios y comunicados*]" (93). While Vargas Llosa leaves open the question of whether the storyteller is a primordial (if secret) component of this community or is instead its belated supplement, the novel is very clear that his oral performances depend upon the kind of face-to-face contact—"I in the middle, you all around me. I talking, you listening [*Yo hablando, ustedes escuchando*]" (40)—dispensed with by modern nations in the collective anonymity of their citizenry. What Derrida writes about Rousseau's fantasies of social origins may apply just as easily to the storyteller, whose function in the novel is to produce an "image of a community immediately present to itself, without difference, a community of speech where all the members are in earshot"—to furnish, in short, all the "classic" predicates of "social authenticity" including "self-presence, transparent proximity in the face-to-face of countenances and the immediate range of the voice" (*OG* 136, 138).[6] Indeed, the audience made into a tribe would conform to the ethnographic ideal of a people without writing even if, as the novel admits, its members wear "red or black tattoos" (167), cover their bodies with "designs" of an "extremely subtle" symbolism (89), and honor taboos on incest (on the latter see González). While *The Storyteller* portrays the Machiguengas as still relatively isolated from the reaches of the modern state, theirs is territory the West has certainly visited often before.[7]

Anderson points out "how moved [the narrator] is by the very idea of the hablador" (*SC* 343), and while Anderson clearly is affected as well this will be for rather different reasons. From the narrator's perspective, to be a storyteller "means being able to feel and live in the very heart of that culture, means having penetrated its essence, reached the marrow of its history and mythology, given body to its taboos, images, ancestral desires, and terrors. It means being, in the most profound way possible [*de la manera más esencial*], a rooted Machiguenga . . ." (244–45). This organic rootedness is precisely what is foreign to the modern novelist, who lacks any such "tangible proof that storytelling can be something more than mere entertainment. . . . Something primordial, something that the very existence of a people may depend on" (94). If the storyteller can become for the narrator "a great stimulus for my own work, a source of inspiration and an example I would have liked to emulate" (157, 174), this is because, as Anderson emphasizes, the possibility of intimate presence in language "is exactly what seems out of the novel's reach" (*SC* 353). Where Lucille Kerr sees in the narrator's identification with the storyteller an attempt to bridge the gap between orality and print (135–37, 147), Anderson, on the contrary—for whom, we remember, even face-to-face contact always may be mediated—finds this gap irreducible and thus a source of anguished pathos: "the novelist's *pueblo* is, in the first instance, the imagined community of the nation, which is not in the least primordial, and whose everyday circulating sap is not the novel but the newspaper, radio, the electronic media, and other purveyors of 'information'" (*SC* 353). This latter distinction between novel and news derives from Walter Benjamin's essay "The Storyteller," and Anderson thinks "there can be little doubt" (351) that Vargas Llosa had in mind throughout his novel Benjamin's meditation on the insuperable difference between the communal mode of oral narrative and the privitive mode of the novel.[8]

Though it is hard to resist construing this difference between speech and writing as yet another version of the Fall, Anderson never loses sight of a curious aspect of *The Storyteller* that defies any such account of ontological decline. As many critics have noted, *hablador* is not the original Machiguenga term for "storyteller" but an imprecise equivalent for what the novel cannot bring itself to represent in writing:

> "Ah, you mean the . . ." Mr. Schneil said, and hesitated. He uttered a long, loud guttural sound full of s's. Remained silent, searching for a word. "How would you translate it?"
>
> She half closed her eyes and bit a knuckle. She was blond, with very blue eyes, extremely thin lips, and a childish smile.
>
> "A talker [*conversador*], perhaps. Or, better yet, a speaker [hablador]," she said at last. And uttered the same sound again: harsh, sibilant, prolonged.
>
> "Yes." He smiled. "I think that's the closest. Hablador: a speaker." [90–91]

Later, Edwin Schneil will allow for even more imprecision (" 'Habladores. *Speakers*. Yes, of course, that's one possible translation'" [173]), but the English-language reader knows already from the title that "speaker" will unlikely be the best of choices. The problem, however, is not simply that the original Machiguenga word resists both transcription and translation, but that the Spanish word itself sounds strangely foreign in this context, as if it were infected by contagion with what in Machiguenga dare not write its name: *hablador* "is something of a neologism that seems neutralized by the common 'storyteller' of the English translation. . . . *Escuchadores* is the equally uncommon, even clumsy, counterpart for those who hear the talk" (Sommer 112–13; see also Kerr 145–47). If the novel's privileging of voice over writing is represented generally as the difference between Machiguenga and Spanish, the text envisions this difference (which, as with *hablador,* may also be *internal* to Spanish) as a loss that writing cannot restore: "An irrepressible sadness came over me at the thought that this society scattered in the depths of the damp and boundless forests, for whom a few tellers of tales acted as circulating sap, was doomed to disappear" (*S* 164). As Anderson recognizes, what gets lost in translation here rather has been stolen: "In the Americas . . . tales of the indigenous communities, where these survived, had to emerge, in print, through dubious processes of translation. Everywhere the hand of the enemy left its imprint, no matter if that enemy took the form of anthropologist, missionary, parish priest, bureaucrat, litterateur, or mestizo broker. No one is more aware of this condition than the novelist, *non-hablador,* Mario Vargas Llosa" (*SC* 354). Indeed, the novel seeks to dramatize translation in its many political dimensions: the Schneils, for example, are Protestant missionaries who run "translation camps" for the Summer Institute of Linguistics ("Translating the Bible into Machiguenga! How about that!" fumes Zuratas [96]), while the narrator, formerly host of the television series *Tower of Babel* (146), is made duly mindful of

> the difficulty of inventing, in Spanish and within a logically consistent intellectual framework, a literary form that would suggest, with any reasonable degree of credibility, how a primitive man with a magico-religious mentality would go about telling a story. All my attempts led each time to the impasse of a style that struck me as glaringly false, as implausible as the various ways in which philosophers and novelists of the Enlightenment had put words into the mouths of their exotic characters in the eighteenth century, when the theme of the "noble savage" was fashionable in Europe. [157–58]

And as we have already noted with Anderson, such ventriloquism is now intolerable.

Not, though, because the tribe has since acquired a national voice, but because the language of the nation has become a mere ghost of itself. Anderson is one of the few readers of the novel to take the full measure of its most peculiar structural features: not only do we not know with certainty the identity of the storyteller, but we do not know in what language the storyteller speaks—or rather, we do not know anymore what translation is if we understand what the storyteller is saying. Other critics dwell more upon the first of these issues, which tries to settle the question whether the storyteller "is" Saúl or the narrator's fantasy of Saúl (this would be, if the latter, another way the narrator identifies with his friend). Posed in this binary fashion, the question simply makes fiction into falsity.[9] As we may anticipate, Anderson is more interested in the second crux:

> Put it this way: if one could imagine that the fleeing Machiguengas had real *habladores,* one could also imagine the open or surreptitious tape-recording of their tales. But these tapes, transcribed, would be unintelligible to the Peruvian Spanish-reading public which is the writers's first audience. As it were, authenticity yes, readability no. This is why, in the first place, the novel needs the bilingual Peruvian, or ex-Peruvian, intermediary who is Saúl Zuratas. But this intermediary is by no means enough. The novelist has set himself a much more arduous task. This task can be described as inventing a persuasive voice for the hablador which is as remote as possible from that of any self-imagining Peruvian, yet which at the same time undermines its own authenticity: the delicate features of inspired pastiche.

Anderson's very syntax (remote *yet* unreliable?) strains in specifying what makes the novelist's problem "arduous." Even bilinguality is inadequate to explain how or why "the tales of the *hablador* are given *without any claim to the status of translation,* in Spanish. . . . When the *hablador* speaks, his tales come out of nowhere. There is no point in the novel at which [the narrator] claims to 'report' what the *hablador* has said. Indeed, the very structure of the novel is designed to rule out such a possibility" (355; Anderson's emphasis).

What the storyteller says in Spanish is therefore something other than Spanish, which is certainly not an act of translation in any conventional sense of the term (and this would be true moreover for any translated versions of the novel). Neither is this speaking of or on behalf of the other in one's own or in a borrowed other's voice, nor giving voice to the "living body" of one's own or an adopted other's culture—the voice is made here as "remote as possible" to the national self, and the body exappropriated by an alien tongue that is also one's very own. One might call this performance an impossible translation, were it not that Derrida has suggested that "translation is another name for the impossible" (*MO* 57). Or again, following Derrida, we might say that the storyteller's discourse is "an absolute translation, a translation without a pole of reference, without an originary language," or that it is "the translation of a language that does not as yet exist, and that will never have existed, in any given target language [*dans une langue à l'arrivée donnée*]" (*MO* 61, 65). However we describe the storyteller's performance in *The Storyteller*'s performance, Anderson's remarkable reading breaks with all mimetic conceptions of literary fiction in making translation an originary derivation—which always produces ghosts: "But to translate the memory of what, precisely, did not take place, of what, having been (the) forbidden, ought, nevertheless, to have left a trace, a specter, the phantomatic body, the phantom member—palpable, painful, but hardly legible—of traces, marks, and scars" (*MO* 61).

Anderson shares with Vargas Llosa one final affinity worth mentioning: both, it seems, have had long experience with these phantoms. Angel Rama took Vargas Llosa to task for using the term *demonios* to describe the sources of his own creativity—a term that carries, for Rama, "an archaic and theological burden that individualizes the process of fiction writing and removes it from the sphere of social acts" (Rowe 45–46; see Rama and Vargas Llosa). For Vargas Llosa, writers necessarily are "under the sway of their personal demons [*bajo el imperio de sus demonios personales*]" (*VM* 19–20), and he defends himself against Rama's charges by explaining that his demons, at any rate, are

> not the sulphurous characters of the Gospels with pitch-forks and pointed tails, but strictly human creations: a certain type of negative obsession—of an individual, social, and cultural nature—that causes so much friction between a person and his reality that it instills in him the ambition of contradicting this reality by remaking it verbally. I accept that my use of the term "demon [*demonio*]" is inexact; I do not use "obsession" since that would have suggested I had adopted an orthodox "psychologistic" explanation of [the writer's] vocation. [*CI* 263]

Anderson, too, is familiar with this type of demon. At the very beginning of *The Spectre of Comparisons,* for example, he owns to having felt once "a kind of vertigo" when, hearing Sukarno praise Hitler as a nationalist, "for the first time in my young life I had been invited to see my Europe as through an inverted telescope." He pondered this experience "till almost a quarter of a century later, when I was in the Philippines and teaching myself to read Spanish by stumbling through José Rizal's extraordinary nationalist novel *Noli Me Tangere*." The sense of vertigo returns, but this time *within* the discourse of the novel:

> There is a dizzying moment early in the narrative when the young mestizo hero, recently returned to the colonial Manila of the 1880s from a long sojourn in Europe, looks out of his carriage window at the municipal botanical gardens, and finds that he too is, so to speak, at the end of an inverted telescope. These gardens are shadowed automatically—Rizal says *maquinalmente—and* inescapably by images of their sister gardens in Europe. He can no longer matter-of-factly experience them, but sees them simultaneously close up and from afar. The novelist arrestingly names the agent of this incurable vision el demonio de las *comparaciones*. So that's what it was in 1963, I said to myself: the spectre of comparisons. [2]

Many pages later Anderson again speaks of a kind of dizziness—"Few countries give the observer a deeper feeling of historical vertigo than the Philippines" (227)—which once more turns out to be connected to the polyglot Rizal, who in his travels had "encountered what he later described as 'el demonio de las comparaciones,' a memorable phrase that could be translated as 'the spectre of comparison'": "What he meant by this was a new, restless double-consciousness which made it impossible ever after to experience Berlin without at once thinking of Manila, or Manila without thinking of Berlin. Here indeed is the origin of nationalism, which lives by making comparison" (229).

We might be tempted to say that here indeed is the origin of *The Spectre of Comparisons,* though its readers may experience their own vertigo in comparing these two different accounts of the book's beginning, let alone in wondering why both were included. Anderson also repeats elsewhere and often the story of teaching himself Spanish by reading Rizal: for example, "Using dictionaries, my residual French and Latin, and a dissembling crib—I taught myself the language in the most enjoyable way imaginable: by reading in the original José Rizal's great incendiary novels *Noli Me Tangere* and *El Filibusterismo*" (23); "But five years ago, having opted to do research on Philippine nationalism, I recognized that I needed to learn to read Spanish, and decided to teach myself by reading the *Noli* and the *Fili* in the original, with Guerrero's translations as cribs" (237). We may grant, of course, that the essays in this collection were written originally for different occasions over a period of many years, which is why it is likely that material will migrate from any one of them to any other. But Rizal's fiction had been on Anderson's mind already for decades—it was the model, we recall, around which *Imagined Communities* developed its thesis about narration and nation—and Anderson is thinking of Rizal even (or especially) when reading Vargas Llosa, whose novel "worked on me like a madeleine, bringing back, powerfully and unexpectedly, remembrances of Southeast Asia's past" (*SC* 26):

> When, a few years ago, on first reading Mario Vargas Llosa's remarkable novel *El Hablador*, I felt immediately that I had run once again into the spectre of comparisons; for it brought immediately to my mind's eye the Buru Quartet of Indonesia's master Pramoedya Ananta Toer, and at a longer, complementary run, the great Spanish novels of the Philippine national hero, José Rizal.... It is, I think, necessary to make this half-digression, before turning to the detailed account of, and reflections on, *El Hablador* that take up the remainder of this chapter. They offer a view of a late-century, Latin American/Spanish/Peruvian nationalist masterpiece seen telescopically from, so to speak, Southeast Asia. It scarcely needs to be said that my command of Spanish is limited (what there is comes from Rizal), and my knowledge of Latin America and Peru still scantier. [337–38]

Anderson confesses in a footnote to the revised edition of *Imagined Communities* that he "had no command of Spanish" when he first discussed Rizal in the "original" edition, "and was thus unwittingly led to rely on the instructively corrupt translation of Leon Maria Guerrero" (26n41).[10] His new preface shows how exacting Anderson can be on his own perceived failings as a translator [xiv]. He is also highly instructive about the politics of others's translations—especially Guerrero's, which was "distorted systematically in the most interesting ways" (237). And he is never more fascinating than when recounting how, with American English supplanting Spanish in the Philippines over the course of the twentieth century, "Rizal's two novels had become inaccessible in the original form" (234): the national literature begins today for most Filipinos in and as an experience of translation, the founding texts having become "sepulchred in Spanish" (233).

But nothing seems more haunting than *The Spectre of Comparisons*'s primal scene: "el demonio de las comparaciones, a memorable phrase that could be translated as 'the spectre of comparisons.'" As every native speaker I've asked has replied, one *could* translate *demonio* as *specter*—but this is hardly a likely or neutral choice. Why not simply use *demon* or *devil*, each wondered, as I did too after looking through a web of Spanish dictionaries, all of which cross-reference *demonio* with *diablo* but never with *espectro*. Even the latest English version of *Noli me tangere* (which Anderson considers largely an improvement over Guerrero's [*SC* 233]) translates "el demonio de las comparaciones" as "the devil of comparisons" (51). Why not give the devil his due? Is it because demons may indeed be theological, and what haunts Europe for Marx is precisely not a devil? Or because specters today have attained a certain *style?* Why not choose instead *bogey,* whose meanings in British English include "specter" or "phantasm"—and which is also a proper name of the devil? In seeking "to dispose of such bogeys as 'derivative discourses,'" would Anderson have been saying all along that derivations (whether novels or nations) cannot themselves be derived?

Notes

1. For Gayatri Chakravorty Spivak, Anderson's emphasis on the "European novelistic tradition" is the least original aspect of his enterprise: "there is surely a degree of question begging in the transformation into scholarly premise of what is otherwise a cliché" [332, 344n8]). We will acknowledge below, however, some of the ways in which the value of originality is neither assured nor assumed in Anderson's writing.

2. Chatterjee proceeds in his critique to defend Asian and African nationalist movements as uniquely authentic since they "are posited not on an identity but rather on a *difference* with the 'modular' forms of the national society propagated by the modern West" (5). He then concedes that Anderson may have been right after all—but only with respect to the political history of anticolonial nationalism, which "cannot but converge with Anderson's formulations. In fact, since it seeks to replicate in its own history the history of the modern state in Europe, nationalism's self-representation will inevitably corroborate Anderson's decoding of the nationalist myth" (5–6). Anderson's modular paradigm thus is applicable only

    > to the domains of the "outside," of the economy and of statecraft, of science and technology, a domain where the West had proved its superiority and the East had succumbed. In this domain, then, Western superiority had to be acknowledged and its accomplishments carefully studied and replicated. The spiritual, on the other hand, is an "inner" domain bearing the "essential" marks of cultural identity. The greater one's success in imitating Western skills in the material domain, therefore, the greater the need to preserve the distinctness of one's spiritual culture. This formula is, I think, a fundamental feature of anticolonial nationalisms in Asia and Africa. [6]

    Whatever its merits in other respects, Chatterjee's criticism stakes itself in these passages on a series of defensive and compensatory contrasts (outside/inside, politics/culture, West/East, material/spiritual) of a kind that Anderson's "print capitalism" works expressly to deconstruct.

3. Thus, where Cannon Schmitt uses *Imagined Communities* to reread the Gothic novel's preoccupation with nationality, we might recognize already in Anderson's genealogy the basic elements of a Gothic plot.

4. As Mayer demonstrates, "the voice of the comuneros of Uchuraccay was never once heard [in the Commission's Report]. Their point of view was always mediated by translators, interpreters, experts. . . . People in Uchuraccay come through to us in the third person plural and in indirect speech" (205). The Report ("Informe sobre Uchuraccay") and related materials are collected in *CIII* (87–215). Sommer notes that *The Storyteller*'s rendering of indigenous myth has been "a cause for concern in a novel that seems to respect culturally specific languages, because the indigenous sounds are familiar from Quechua-inflected Spanish, with its trailing gerunds (*diciendo, hablando*) at the end of sentences, for example. The Andean sounds are so improbable in the jungle that the effect is to suggest the writer's indifference to Indians" (97). For Rowe, the "Machiguenga" chapters of *The Storyteller* "read like a bad *indigenista* novel, where the voice of the native culture is obviously and awkwardly constructed from the acculturating culture" (60–61).

5. See also Nettle and Romaine. Derrida reflects on the form of this predicament in *Monolingualism of the Other:*

    > What if, in order to save some humans lost in their language, in order to deliver the humans themselves, at the expense of their language, it was better to renounce

the language, at least to renounce the best conditions for survival "at all costs" for the idiom? And what if some humans were more worth saving than their language, under circumstances where, alas, one needed to choose between them? For we are living in a period in which the question at times arises. Today, on this earth of humans, certain people must yield to the homo-hegemony of dominant languages. They must learn the language of the masters, of capital and machines; they must lose their idiom in order to survive or live better. A tragic economy, an impossible counsel. I do not know whether salvation for the other presupposes the salvation of the idiom. (30)

6.   The fact that the storyteller incorporates in his narrative "foreign" elements from Kafka and the Bible may do less to challenge this authenticity than to suggest a larger universality of myth.

7.   Moss and Wilder chronicle the ongoing struggles of the Machiguengas against the Peruvian state's alliance with multinational "natural resource extraction companies" [8]. Lévi-Strauss remains the canonical modern instance of the fantasy of a pristine orality undone by the advent of writing:

> We are no longer linked to our past by an oral tradition which implies direct contact with others (storytellers, wise men, or elders), but by books amassed in libraries, books from which we endeavor—with extreme difficulty—to form a picture of their authors. And we communicate with the immense majority of our contemporaries by all kinds of intermediaries—written documents or administrative machinery—which undoubtedly vastly extend our contacts but at the same time make those contacts somewhat "inauthentic." This has become typical of the relationship between the citizen and the public authorities. We should like to avoid describing negatively the tremendous revolution brought about by the invention of writing. But it is essential to realize that writing, while it conferred vast benefits on humanity, did in fact deprive it of something fundamental. [366]

8.   Though Anderson refers jointly to the figure of "the *Erzähler/Hablador*" (353), this reading is somewhat mooted by the fact that Benjamin's storyteller works within an artisan or guild economy rather than that of a tribe (see González 10). There is, however, little doubt that Benjamin's paradigm has been immensely fruitful for Anderson, who returns to it in his recent introduction to a collection of *tales* (not writerly "short stories") by Pram (*TD* 11). In an essay that predates *Imagined Communities,* Anderson suggested that "Pramoedya—a modern writer in the only true sense of the word, condemned never to see the effects of his work on his reader's face or in his voice, separated by print and market—longs for that reader's response. (He can see around him all the old Javanese artists, *dalang,* dancers, *gamelan* players, singers, *batik*-makers and so forth, who still have that opportunity.)" (RR 57).

9.   "Thus, the hablador chapters are not really Saúl's narrations at all but are in fact simulations created by the Western narrator as projections of his own notions of Machiguenga storytelling. . . . In fact, there is no real evidence in the text that Saúl ever becomes an hablador at all. Saúl's entire experience with the Machiguenga is a fiction posited by the modern novelist" (Booker 131).

10.   This lack of Spanish presumably accounts for Anderson's reliance on Jean Franco's plot summary of *El periquillo sarniento;* it is from Franco (rather than directly from the novelist) that Anderson retrieves the pluralized language of "hospitals, prisons, remote villages, monasteries" [*IC* 29–30].

Works Cited

Anderson, Benedict. *Imagined Communities: Reflections on the Origins and Spread of Nationalism.* Rev. ed. London: Verso, 1991. (*IC*)

———. Introduction. *Tales from Djakarta: Caricatures of Circumstances and their Human Beings.* By Pramoedya Ananta Toer. Ithaca, NY: Southeast Asia Program Publ., Cornell University, 1999. (*TD*)

―――. *Language and Power: Exploring Political Cultures in Indonesia*. Ithaca: Cornell UP, 1990.

―――. "Reading 'Revenge' by Pramoedya Ananta Toer (1978–1982)." *Writing on the Tongue*. Ed. A. L. Becker. Michigan Papers in South and Southeast Asia, no. 33. Ann Arbor: Center for South and South-east Asian Studies, University of Michigan, 1989. 13–73. (*RR*)

―――. *The Spectre of Comparisons: Nationalism, Southeast Asia and the World*. London: Verso, 1998. (*SC*)

Anderson, Benedict R. O'G., and Ruchira Mendiones, eds. and trans. *In the Mirror: Literature and Politics in Siam in the American Era*. Bangkok: Duang Kamol, 1985. (*IM*)

Benjamin, Walter. "The Storyteller: Reflections on the Work of Nikolai Leskov." *Illuminations*. Ed. and intro. Hannah Arendt. Trans. Harry Zohn. New York: Schocken, 1969. 83–109.

Beverley, John. *Subalternity and Representation: Arguments in Cultural Theory*. Durham: Duke UP, 1999.

Booker, M. Keith. *Vargas Llosa among the Postmodernists*. Gainesville: University of Florida Press, 1994.

Brennan, Timothy. "The National Longing for Form." *Nation and Narration*. Ed. Homi K. Bhabha. London: Routledge, 1990. 44–70.

Chatterjee, Partha. *Nationalist Thought and the Colonial World: A Derivative Discourse?* London: Zed, 1983. Rpt. Minneapolis: U of Minnesota P, 1998. (*NT*)

―――. *The Nation and Its Fragments: Colonial and Postcolonial Histories*. Princeton: Princeton UP, 1993. (*NF*)

Cheah, Pheng. "Spectral Nationality: The Living On [*sur-vie*] of the Postcolonial Nation in Neo-colonial Globalization." *boundary 2* 26.3 (1999): 225–52.

Culler, Jonathan. "Benedict Anderson and the Novel." *diacritics* 29.4 (1999): 20–39.

Derrida, Jacques. *Monolingualism of the Other; or, The Prosthesis of Origin*. Trans. Patrick Mensah. Stanford, CA: Stanford University Press, 1998. [*MO*]

―――. *Of Grammatology*. Trans. Gayatri Chakravorty Spivak. Baltimore: Johns Hopkins UP, 1976. (*OG*)

―――. "Onto-Theology of National-Humanism (Prolegomena to a Hypothesis)." Trans. Geoffrey Bennington. *Oxford Literary Review* 14.1–2 (1992): 3–23.

―――. *The Post Card: From Socrates to Freud and Beyond*. Trans. Alan Bass. Chicago: University of Chicago Press, 1987. (*PC*)

―――. "Signature Event Context." Trans. Samuel Weber and Jeffrey Mehlman. *Limited Inc.* Evanston, IL: Northwestern UP, 1988. 1–23. [*SEC*]

González, Eduardo. *The Monstered Self: Narratives of Death and Performance in Latin American Fiction*. Durham: Duke UP, 1992.

Ivy, Marilyn. *Discourses of the Vanishing: Modernity, Phantasm, Japan*. Chicago: University of Chicago Press, 1995.

Kerr, Lucille. *Reclaiming the Author: Figures and Fictions from Spanish America*. Durham: Duke UP, 1992.

Lévi-Strauss, Claude. *Structural Anthropology*. Trans. Claire Jacobson and Brooke Grundfest Schoepf. New York: Basic, 1963.

Martin, Gerald. "Mario Vargas Llosa: Errant Knight of the Liberal Imagination." *On Modern Latin American Fiction*. Ed. John King. New York: Hill and Wang, 1987. 205–33.

Mayer, Enrique. "Peru in Deep Trouble: Mario Vargas Llosa's 'Inquest in the Andes' Reexamined." *Rereading Cultural Anthropology*. Ed. George E. Marcus. Durham: Duke UP, 1992. 181–219.

Moss, Daniel, and Jennifer Wilder. "A Clash of Cultures—An Imbalance of Power in Peru." *Oxfam America Viewpoint* (Winter 1999–2000): 8–9.

Nettle, Daniel, and Suzanne Romaine. *Vanishing Voices: The Extinction of the World's Languages*. Oxford: Oxford UP, 2000.

Rama, Angel, and Mario Vargas Llosa. *García Márquez y la problemática de la novela*. Buenos Aires: Corregidor, 1973.

Rizal, José. *Noli me tangere*. Trans. Ma. Soledad Lacson-Locsin. Ed. Raul L. Locsin. Honolulu: University of Hawaii Press, 1997.

Rowe, William. "Liberalism and Authority: The Case of Mario Vargas Llosa." *On Edge: The Crisis of Contemporary Latin American Culture*. Ed. George Yúdice, Jean Franco, and Juan Flores. Minneapolis: University of Minnesota Press, 1992. 45–64.

Schmitt, Cannon. *Alien Nation: Nineteenth-Century Gothic Fictions and English Nationality*. Philadelphia: University of Pennsylvania Press, 1997.

Sommer, Doris. "About-Face: The Talker Turns." *boundary 2* 23.1 (1996): 91–133.

Spivak, Gayatri Chakravorty. "Cultural Talks in the Hot Peace: Revisiting the 'Global Village.'" *Cosmopolitics: Thinking and Feeling beyond the Nation.* Ed. Pheng Cheah and Bruce Robbins. Minneapolis: University of Minnesota Press, 1998. 329–48.

Vargas Llosa, Mario. *Contra viento y marea, I (1962–1972).* Barcelona: Seix Barral, 1983. (*CI*)

———. *Contra viento y marea, III (1964–1988).* Barcelona: Seix Barral, 1990. (*CIII*)

———. *Making Waves.* Ed. and trans. John King. New York: Farrar, Straus and Giroux, 1996. (*MW*)

———. "Questions of Conquest." *Harper's Magazine.* Dec. 1990: 45–53. (*QC*)

———. *The Storyteller.* Trans. Helen Lane. New York: Penguin, 1990. (*S*) Trans. of *El hablador.* Barcelona: Seix Barral, 1987.

———. *La utopía arcaica: José María Arguedas y las ficciones del indigenismo.* México, DF: Fondo de Cultura Económica, 1996. (*UA*)

———. *La verdad de las mentiras: Ensayos sobre literatura.* Barcelona: Seix Barral, 1990. (*VM*)

CHAPTER 5

Imagi–Nation

The Imagined Community and the Aesthetics of Mourning

MARC REDFIELD

Of the many relics of the Romantic era that continue to shape our (post)modernity, the nation-state surely ranks among the most significant. Two decades ago Benedict Anderson commented that "'the end of the era of nationalism,' so long prophesied, is not remotely in sight" (*IC* 3), and the intervening years have made it increasingly clear that the developments and processes we summarize as "globalization" operate in mingled synchrony and tension with the political form of the nation-state.[1] That the nation-state should remain the premier vehicle of political and economic legitimation in an era dominated by American imperialism and international capital—forces that, of course, regularly and flagrantly violate the sovereignty of disadvantaged nations—is unsurprising if one accepts the continuing pertinency and power of a Western master-narrative of modernity, according to which the nation represents the emergence of a people into history and prefigures the global achievement of universal human concord. As the proper subject of history, the nation-state can prefigure history's end because, as David Lloyd writes, "the particularism of [nationalism's] contents, potentially in contradiction with the universalism of modernity, is subsumed in the *formal* congruence between its own narratives of identity, directed at one people, and the narrative of identity that universal history represents for humanity in general" ("Nationalisms" 178). Lloyd goes on to note that the nation's intermediate status in this narrative—halfway between primitive tribalism and modernity's ever-deferred perpetual peace—accounts for nationalism's irreducibly double association with modernization and atavism. In consequence, the modernist paradigm continues to rule many skeptical or hostile accounts of nationalism, for so long as the nation-state is taken to supersede other political or social formations, the cosmopolitan critique fails to challenge "the fundamental philosophy of universal history that underwrites nationalism's inscription in modernity" ("Nationalisms" 177). Indeed, both in the corporate media and in mainstream Western political discourse generally, nations and nationalisms are commonly treated as atavistic or progressive depending on the degree to which their behavior harmonizes with globalizing imperatives. That these imperatives emanate quite blatantly from Wall Street in no way seriously troubles the effectiveness of modernity as a narrative paradigm.[2]

Seeking to discredit universalizing narrative, much cultural criticism in recent years has exchanged cosmopolitanism and the abstract question of "nationalism" for an emphasis on the contextual construction of national movements or identities.[3] This valuable body of work has sought to recover the particularity of cultural and socioeconomic circumstance, stressed the fundamental role of racism in colonialist contexts, and noted ways in which nationalist movements draw on or unleash forms of resistance that challenge representationalist politics. The pages that follow, however, remain focused on the nationalist fantasy proper to the discourse of modernity. Cultural critique can only profit from knowing as much as possible about the favored turns of the universal-historicist model, particularly since, as Lloyd and others have emphasized, this model is an aesthetic one that grants a world-historical role to "culture." The state, in a tradition that in its main lines runs from Schiller through Hegel and Matthew Arnold and is still very much alive today, *represents* the community to itself, thereby giving the community form and in a certain sense giving it an ethical imperative and a future: the state represents "our best self" (Arnold 99, passim), "the archetype of a human being" (Schiller 17), because it signifies the formal unification both of the citizen with the community and of the community with universal humanity. Because this unification is ideal rather than actual, it can be projected as the ethical terminus of history (that is, as the ideal of an accomplished modernity). The state's core mission thus becomes pedagogical: its job is to acculturate its subjects into citizens. The production of a docile citizenry thereby obtains an ethical aura and an aesthetic character, insofar as the artwork and the domain of aesthetic or "cultural" experience generally become imaginable as disinterested spaces in which the subject of aesthetic education achieves a proleptic, formal moment of identification with humanity per se. The retooling of liberal education that resulted in the creation of national literature departments in universities at the end of the nineteenth century would have been inconceivable in the absence of this aesthetic model of culture.[4]

The aesthetic substratum of state-oriented nationalism helps account, perhaps, for the fact that the title of Benedict Anderson's *Imagined Communities* has become a tag phrase—almost a mantra—in academic and para-academic discussions of nationalism. Particularly within that amorphous field we call cultural studies, a powerful set of expectations seems to hold sway: no matter what the critic's agenda or methodology, she or he can usually be counted on to affirm—usually more or less in passing, with a bare nod at Anderson's actual arguments—that nations are "imagined communities." The affinity between nation and imagination is incessantly noted and rarely interrogated; it has about it, in other words, something of the force of the "imaginary" in Lacan's sense as well as Anderson's.[5] No less than that of the nation, the notion of the imagination maintains a tenacious purchase on "our models of culture, interpretation, and evaluation" (Pyle vii).[6] And the roots of the association between these two Romantic inventions—imagination and nation—run very deep indeed, at least if one credits Philippe Lacoue-Labarthe's archaeology of "the fiction of the political" in the Western tradition:

> The political (the City) belongs to a form of plastic art, formation and information, *fiction* in the strict sense. This is a deep theme which derives from Plato's politico-pedagogical writings (especially *The Republic*) and reappears in the guise of such concepts as *Gestaltung* (configuration, fashioning) or *Bildung*, a term with a revealingly polysemic character (formation, constitution, organization, education, culture, etc.). The fact that the political is a form of plastic art in no way means that the *polis* is an artificial or conventional formation, but that the political belongs to the sphere of *techne* in the highest sense of the term, that is to say in the sense in which *techne* is conceived as the accomplishment and revelation of *physis* itself. This is why the *polis* is also "natural": it is the "beautiful formation" that has spontaneously sprung from the "genius of a people" (the Greek genius) according to the modern—but in fact very ancient—interpretation of Aristotelian mimetology. [66]

Our itinerary will be more circumscribed than that recommended by Lacoue-Labarthe, but we shall be engaging a similar cluster of themes. I propose first to recall a few passages from Anderson's *Imagined Communities* in order to remark ways in which this text both opens up and veers away from a critique of aesthetic nationalism. Anderson makes legible the nation's inseparability from questions of language and technics; furthermore, without necessarily meaning to, he allows us to locate the possibility of aesthetic formalization—the engine of modernity's aesthetic narrative—in a "prior" condition of anonymity, contamination, and loss: a predicament

78 · Marc Redfield

that aesthetic narrative both forecloses and records. Anderson's text suggests that the "imagined community" of the nation develops in productive tension with the conditions of mechanical reproduction that make it possible, and that imagining the nation entails fantasies about communication and technology and the production of gendered and irretrievably mournful scenes of pedagogy.

In the second part of this essay I turn to a text authored by one of the Romantic era's great theorists of the imagination, Fichte's *Addresses to the German Nation*. Bizarre though it may seem, such a trajectory holds unexpected advantages. In a rather broad sense it might be said that Anderson writes as a late Romantic, not just because he invokes the creative imagination but because, in doing so, he sets out to rescue nationalism from the condescension of an enlightened cosmopolitanism. Identifying nationalism, particularly in the wake of the Indochinese conflicts of the late 1970s, as "an uncomfortable *anomaly* for Marxist theory" (*IC* 3), Anderson proposes to reclassify it "with 'kinship' and 'religion' rather than with 'liberalism' or 'fascism'" (*IC* 5)—to understand nationalism, that is, as an expression of fundamental human needs (for continuity, for affective bonds) in an age of mechanical reproduction. Anderson thus positions nationalism at a remove from the state: its roots are different from the state's and run deeper, tapping, ultimately, into the substratum of the imagination itself. That no doubt sounds like a Romantic preoccupation, as does Anderson's interest in drawing sharp distinctions between authentic, popular nationalism and the mass-produced icons and manipulative strategizing of "official" nationalisms. But it is an equally "Romantic" characteristic of Anderson's text that, to some extent despite itself, it also suggests the impossibility of keeping nation and state from blurring into each other, precisely because the nation, *as* "imagined," inevitably becomes the object of aesthetic pedagogy. For a dramatic instance of this slippage between nation and state one can scarcely do better than consult Fichte's *Addresses:* a work so famous for its ethnolinguistic celebration of "Germanness" that readers routinely underestimate its central theme of mass national (state) education, and often overlook entirely the fact that Fichte's ethnolinguistic nation is also, fundamentally and crucially, an *imagined* community. My point throughout will not be to suggest that we can or ought to do without the notion of the imagination in thinking about nationalism; as Anderson so brilliantly shows, that would be tantamount to not thinking about nationalism at all. I am rather proposing that we understand both imagination and nation as figures inextricable from aesthetic discourse, which is another way of saying that they are fictions possessed of great referential force and chronic referential instability—fictions of an impossible, ineradicable mourning.

1

All communities, as Anderson points out, are in some sense "imagined." Even the members of a hamlet or a family (and we shall be returning to the family) relate to each other with "an element of fond imagining," as Anderson rather optimistically puts it (*IC* 154); and any political unit larger than a hamlet or possessed of a sense of history longer than a generation necessarily requires its constituents to partake of a collective identity irreducible to a face-to-face encounter. But the nation is *radically* imagined: it cannot be experienced immediately as a perception. The subject of a kingdom can at least in principle perceive the monarch, and willy-nilly has face-to-face encounters with the monarch's bureaucratic or feudal representatives; but a nation-state is fundamentally and irretrievably faceless, even when a king or a charismatic dictator rules it. Elaborating with his own inimitable brio on this Andersonian theme, Franco Moretti remarks that one can imagine or visualize a town, valley, or city, even the universe itself ("a starry sky, after all, is not a bad image of it"). "But the nation-state? 'Where' is it? What does it look like? How can one *see* it?" (Moretti 17). The nation can only be visualized—imagined—through the mediation of a catachresis, an arbitrary sign. It is no coincidence that in Hegel's famous account of the difference between signs and symbols in his *Encyclopedia of the Philosophical Sciences,* one of his three exemplary examples of the sign is the flag (the two others are the cockade and the gravestone; we shall shortly reencounter the matter of gravestones), or that his discussion of the sign occurs as part of a section of the *Encyclopedia* devoted to "imagination" (*Einbildungskraft*). As Paul de Man comments, "although it would not be correct to say that Hegel valorizes the sign over the symbol, the reverse would be even less true"—for, precisely because it is arbitrary, "the sign illustrates the capacity of the intellect to 'use' the perceived world for its own purposes" (de Man 96).[7] The sign results from the imagination's ability to posit what cannot simply be perceived. Hence the abstract forms and solid colors favored by the flags of modern nation-states; unlike the detailed fretwork of heraldry, these aggressively simple bars and stars testify to the arbitrariness of a sign that has been posited, not inherited or found. The nation, like one's own death, cannot be imagined and can only be imagined; inevitably, if often in banal and prefabricated ways, it partakes of the discourse of the sublime.[8]

Anderson's great Benjaminian argument in *Imagined Communities* derives the possibility of this imaginative act out of developments in reproductive and communication technologies. The modernity of the nation is that of the Gutenberg revolution: as language becomes mechanically reproducible in Walter Benjamin's sense and print capitalism begins to create markets, the fundamentally anonymous community of the nation-state becomes imaginable. Anderson hypothesizes that novels and newspapers "provided the technical means for 're-presenting' the *kind* of imagined community that is the nation" because they exploited and reinforced a perception of time as "homogenous, empty time"—a temporal field "in which simultaneity is, as it were, transverse, cross-time, marked not by prefiguration and fulfilment, but by temporal coincidence, and measured by clock and calendar" (*IC* 24). Homogenous, empty time opens the possibility of the anonymous community ("An American will never meet, or even know the names of more than a handful of his 240,000,000-odd fellow Americans. . . . But he has complete confidence in their steady, anonymous, simultaneous activity" [*IC* 26].) Far more than the novel, the newspaper is Anderson's exemplary cultural form ("What more vivid figure for the secular, historically-clocked, imagined community can be envisioned?" [*IC* 35]).[9] A commodity that expires within twenty-four hours or less, the newspaper summons its reader to a "mass ceremony" predicated on the simultaneous participation of uncountable other readers elsewhere. Furthermore, "the newspaper reader, observing exact replicas of his own paper being consumed by his subway, barbershop, or residential neighbors, is continually reassured that the imagined world is visibly rooted in everyday life." Thus "fiction seeps quietly and continuously into reality, creating that remarkable confidence of community in anonymity which is the hallmark of modern nations" (*IC* 36).

Anderson's argument retains a cagily respectful relation to Marxist etiological narrative. Claiming that the book is "the first modern-style mass-produced, industrial commodity" (*IC* 34), he suggests that print capitalism laid "the bases for national consciousness" in three ways: it produced "unified fields of exchange and communication below Latin and above the spoken vernaculars"; it gave "a new fixity to language, which in the long run helped to build that image of antiquity so central to the subjective idea of the nation"; and it created new "languages of power" as certain dialects, closer to the print-language, gained prestige and ground over others. Anderson goes so far as to credit print capitalism with contributing fundamentally to the emergence of the bourgeoisie as a self-conscious class:

> Here was a class which, figuratively speaking, came into being as a class only in so many replications. Factory-owner in Lille was connected to factory-owner in Lyon only by reverberation. They had no necessary reason to know of one another's existence; they did not typically marry each other's daughters or inherit each other's property. But they did come to visualize in a general way the existence of thousands and thousands like themselves through print-language. For an illiterate bourgeoisie is scarcely imaginable. Thus in world-historical terms bourgeoisies were the first classes to achieve solidarities on an essentially imagined basis. [*IC* 77]

The material production of class consciousness and national consciousness, here, remains inseparable from capitalism as a mode of production, but is equally inseparable from the shock of print technology. Anderson does not write about shock, preferring to allow Benjamin's phrase "homogenous, empty time" to float free of complication; but in his own British-commonsensical way he subtly defamiliarizes and repositions the question of technology. Without ever becoming personified as an independently determining force, technics nonetheless ceases to be conceivable simply as congealed labor—that is, as an externalization of an originating, self-producing human identity—and becomes a version of the question of "language," a question that then in its turn undergoes complications. The nation's material base is language; and language, for Anderson, means neither this or that so-called natural language (the modern ones, in any case, being products of print capitalism's intervention into a heterogenous field of vernaculars) nor a formal interplay of *langue* and *parole*. Rather (though Anderson certainly never puts it this way) language appears here as what Jacques Derrida calls a tele-technics, bound up with and in excess of the materiality and historicity of its occurrence.[10] "Print-language," Anderson emphasizes, "is what invents nationalism, not *a* particular language per se" (*IC* 134). Indeed, he notes, twentieth-century communication technologies "made it possible and practical to 'represent' the imagined community in ways that did not require linguistic uniformity" (*IC* 139). If nationalism is inherently an affair of language, language is a question of technics, and technics a matter of inscription, communication, dissemination, reserve.[11]

It is at this point, however, that we may begin to remark Anderson's resistance to his own insight; and as a first step toward getting myself back to the topic of the imagination let me return to Anderson's homogenizing presentation of "homogenous, empty time." If *Imagined Communities* makes legible a tele-technics of language, it nonetheless labors to efface its own accomplishment by characterizing the homogeneity and emptiness of the time of capitalism, modern technology, and modernity as *fundamentally* homogenous. Hence, perhaps, Anderson's elision of Benjamin's account of the shock experience, the shattering of the aura, and all the other dislocations proper to "the age of mechanical reproduction." For surely "homogenous, empty time" is always also fracture and rupture; it is capitalism's inhuman accumulative rhythms; modernity's unnerving acceleration; "the virtualization of space and time, the possibility of virtual events whose movement and speed prohibit us more than ever . . . from opposing presence to its representation, 'real time' to 'deferred time,' effectivity to its simulacrum, the living to the non-living, in short, the living to the living-dead of its ghosts" (Derrida, *Specters* 169). We may briefly recall that Benjamin defined the shock experience by drawing on Freud's counterintuitive proposal that one of consciousness's functions is to ward off stimuli, and that, consequently, becoming conscious works against the formation of a memory trace: "The greater the share of the shock factor in particular impressions, the more consciousness has to be on alert as a screen against stimuli; the more efficiently it does so, the less do these impressions enter experience (*Erfahrung*), tending to remain in the sphere of a certain hour of one's life (*Erlebnis*)" (Benjamin 163). Anderson, in his essay "Memory and Forgetting," which he appended to the revised edition of *Imagined Communities*, touches on this Benjaminian theme but leaves unstated the ways in which it might complicate time's homogeneity:

> How strange it is to need another's help to learn that this naked baby in the yellowed photograph, sprawled happily on rug or cot, is you. The photograph, fine child of the age of mechanical reproduction, is only the most peremptory of a huge modern accumulation of documentary evidence (birth certificates, diaries, report cards, letters, medical records, and the like) which simultaneously records a certain apparent continuity and emphasizes its loss from memory. Out of this estrangement comes a conception of personhood, identity (yes, you and that naked baby are identical) which, because it cannot be "remembered," must be narrated.... These narratives, like the novels and newspapers discussed in Chapter 2, are set in homogenous, empty time. [*IC* 204]

Yet what bears emphasis is that the amnesia conditioning these narratives, these everyday identity-effects, is structurally irreducible to the subject's biological or psychological existence. Even the photograph taken yesterday, at my behest, captures me in a way irreducible to perception or recollection; it can circulate beyond my knowledge or lifespan and can be altered, spliced, remade; as in Ridley Scott's *Blade Runner*, it and the identity-narrative it generates can always possibly be fakes, because technical reproduction captures its referent thanks to procedures that are inherently and essentially iterable, alien to the identity they construct and document. An irreducible anonymity laces our technonarratives of self-formation; and the impact of this anonymity is precisely what Benjamin calls shock. The homogenous empty time in which these narratives unfold corrodes the identities it enables. Benjamin consistently emphasizes that the disruption of *Erfahrung* goes hand in hand with the "homogenizing" force of capitalist and mechanical reproduction: the shock experience of the crowd, the photograph, the film, and so on "corresponds to what the worker 'experiences' at his machine"—the numbing drill of a reiterated present tense, "sealed off from experience" (Benjamin 176). Homogenous, empty time's field of the "meanwhile" generates not just the imagined certainties of Balzacian or scientific or nationalist narrative, but also Emma Bovary's shattering boredom—her inability to live in time.[12] It is possible that the time of modernity necessitates "imaginative" operations such as, for instance, the production of the sort of containerlike trope that undergirds Anderson's account of homogenous temporality. Yet Anderson's own narrative of nationalism's origins deconstructs that trope, suggesting the inextricability of homogenous, empty time from the operations of print capitalism, which is to say from the mechanical exploitation of the iterability of the sign. The newspaper can always in principle be read *elsewhere:* the community of its readers is irretrievably exposed to an alterity that is never unreservedly "outside" the community, but labors at its heart, constituting its intimacy. This predicament names the condition of possibility of any linguistic event, as Jacques Derrida has shown; Derrida's most famous name for this fundamental tele-technics of the sign is, of course, "writing." The homogenous time of modernity emerges out of print capitalism's exploitation of writing as *différance.*[13]

Anderson's narrative about nationalism thus encourages us to understand the experience of the nation as grounded in and produced by a systematic misrecognition of its origins. The nation is a hallucinated limit to iterability. Made possible by difference, deferral, and technological shock, the nation homogenizes time and space, draws and polices borders, historicizes itself as the continuous arc of an unfolding identity. (Furthermore, since every border presupposes an outside, outside the nation lies more space, occupied by other nations and by atavistic entities that ought to become nations. The globe—as in "globalization"—figures the totality of nation-space as imagined community.) Originating in an anonymity "prior" to any identity—an anonymity constitutive of the possibility of imagining an identity—the nation imagines anonymity *as* identity: as an essentialized formal abstraction. The nature of this imaginative act becomes correspondingly complex. It is frequently characterized in nationalist discourse as an act of will—of a will capable of willing itself, as national will, into existence.[14] Anderson's phrase "imagined community" draws on this tradition: he intends it to capture the Romantic theme of the "creative" imagination (*IC* 6); and this notion of the imagination goes along with his running emphasis on the positive aspects of nationalism—so long as nationalism is understood as an authentic impulse toward continuity and meaning, rather than as the instrumentalism and bad faith of "all those nationalisms which, by the late twentieth century, have got married to states" (*S* 47). Yet if the nation as "imagined community" is always fundamentally irreducible to the state, the difference between spontaneous and "official" nationalism nonetheless becomes, under the impact of Anderson's narrative of nationalism's origins, as unstable as it is necessary. Enabled, even in its most affirmative manifestations, by the dislocations of technical reproduction, the "imagination" ceases to be a psychological faculty and becomes an aesthetic, unstable figure that tropes anonymity as identity, and difference as homogeneity. The signs of nationhood—the flags and emblems that, according to Hegel, in their sheer arbitrariness demonstrate the mind's creative power—serve the cause of misrecognition insofar as they transform a semiotic function (linguistic arbitrariness) into an *image:* an image of the nation as will, or, better, of the nation as imagi-nation. The arbitrariness of the sign and the radical anonymity that marks the possibility of the sign's apprehension are thus figured as a sensuous experience, and become a sublime intuition of the nation as *this* flag, anthem, building, cultural monument. Sensuous tokens of lack, mechanically produced substitutes for what Benjamin calls *Erfahrung,* these signs are in a quite precise sense the fetishes of an imagined nation.

They are aesthetic fetishes not just because they transform the supersensuous into the perceivable, but because they interpellate the national subject as the subject of a national culture. In his most extended discussion of how nations "transform fatality into continuity," and "turn chance into destiny" (*IC* 11, 12), Anderson—facing the challenge of explaining why people should be willing to die for the sake of a community composed of mutually anonymous readers of the same newspaper—inevitably slips into an aesthetic terminology:

> [I]n everything "natural" there is always something unchosen. In this way, nation-ness is assimilated to skin-colour, gender, parentage, and birth-era— all those things one cannot help. And in these "natural ties" one senses what one might call "the beauty of gemeinschaft." To put it another way, precisely because such ties are not chosen, they have about them a halo of disinterestedness. [*IC* 143]

I would suggest that "disinterestedness" bears its full Arnoldian burden in that last sentence, and would also stress that here, as in his account of nationalism's origins, Anderson willy-nilly blurs the difference between popular, affective nationalism, on the one hand, and the "official" nationalism associable with a state's educational apparatus, on the other. For as his subsequent discussion shows, the natural is naturalized by way of a culture that manifests itself as canonical texts, symbols, and touchstones—a culture that is in fact, once again, "language," language as a naturalized technics, humanized and homogenized as voice:

> No one can give the date of birth of any language. Each looms up imperceptibly out of a horizonless past. (Insofar as *homo sapiens* is *homo dicens,* it can seem difficult to imagine an origin of language newer than the species itself.) Languages thus appear rooted beyond almost anything else in contemporary societies. At the same time, nothing connects us affectively to the dead more than language. If English-speakers hear the words "Earth to earth, ashes to ashes, dust to dust"— created almost four and a half centuries ago—they get a ghostly intimation of simultaneity across homogenous, empty time. [*IC* 144–45]

The words of the Anglican burial service occasion here the diachronic equivalent of the "unisonance" that, according to Anderson, singers of national anthems experience as they imagine a nation of anonymous others singing along. Unisonance (or "imagined sound") is nothing less than "the echoed physical realization of the imagined community. . . . How selfless this unisonance feels!" (*IC* 145). Anderson rightly describes these English speakers as "hearing" (rather than, say, "reading") the burial service. Like the anthem singers, they are hearing imagined voices; in this hallucinated moment of unisonance they identify with the totality of a nation and, at the globe's horizon, with the universality of *homo dicens.* These instances of logocentric interpellation constitute the national subject's properly *aesthetic* education. Culture, that is, names the subject's identification with anonymity as "disinterestedness"—with anonymity as the formal, abstract identity of the nation and the human, as mediated by the national state. Anderson's account of the "eerie splendor" that characterizes these moments—as anonymity is aestheticized as voice and image—appropriately strings together scraps of canonical and subcanonical national culture, which is to say, school texts: lines from the *Book of Common Prayer,* a sentence of Thomas Browne's; Charles Wolfe's patriotic elegy "The Burial of Sir John Moore" (*IC* 145–46).

Without exception all of these exemplary scraps are about death; in one case about death in war. No doubt it is hardly occasion for surprise that imagined communities—many sorts, if not all sorts, of imagined communities for that matter, not just the nation per se—should foster their sense of themselves by invoking death's universality, and by representing death as enemy action. But in what is perhaps his text's most resonant paragraph, Anderson suggests that imagining the nation entails a scene of mourning unlike those of earlier societies:

> No more arresting emblems of the modern culture of nationalism exist than cenotaphs and tombs of Unknown Soldiers. The public ceremonial reverence accorded these monuments precisely *because* they are either deliberately empty or no one knows who lies inside them, has no true precedents in earlier times. To feel the force of this modernity one has only to imagine the general reaction to the busy-body who "discovered" the Unknown Soldier's name or insisted on filling the cenotaph with some real bones. Sacrilege of a strange, contemporary kind! Yet void as these tombs are of identifiable mortal remains or immortal souls, they are nonetheless saturated with ghostly national imaginings. [*IC* 9]

The funereal and thanophilic character of much official Western national culture has often been noted, but Anderson's brilliant commentary on the cenotaph reveals nationalism's peculiarly absolute *abstraction* of death. The abstraction is, or pretends to be, "at the origin": no corpse ever was or ever could be buried under this gravestone—indeed, as Anderson suggests, burying a corpse under the monument would pollute it as perhaps no other act of sacrilege would. The corpse, then, may be read as the remainder, the excess that nationalism's official scene of mourning excludes. The corpse marks death's resistance to its own universality, recalling the inassimilable particularity and finitude of *this* death, the absoluteness of an irrecuperable loss. In the terminology we have been working with, the corpse marks the resistance of anonymity to abstraction or formalization. From a national perspective, it is the *unimaginable.* Yet without it—without, that is, the possibility of the radically other death that it represents—the Tomb could not exist. And if we understand the irrecuperability of loss as a restatement of the essential drift of "writing" in a Derridean sense, we may say that the nation itself as imagined community comes into existence thanks to a death it cannot mourn, a corpse it cannot bury—a corpse that must be foreclosed, expelled from the nation's abstracted, aestheticized anonymity.

But if we interpret the Tomb of the Unknown Soldier's exclusion of the *identifiable* corpse as a symptom of the fundamental instability of an identity predicated on anonymity, we also need to underscore the ideological power of such monuments.[15] The Tomb's scene of interpellation can have very powerful effects, for it permits the mourning subject to transform a particular loss—real or imagined—into the general loss suffered by the nation. Because the absolute singularity and irreparability of loss is thereby foreclosed, a sheen of hypocrisy inevitably clings to official acts of mourning, however passionately felt or well intended. Yet this halo of bad faith, which registers the ontological instability of official nationalism, does not necessarily impede the production of nationalistic pathos. It is no coincidence, I think, that the most memorable paragraph in *Imagined Communities* should invoke the Tomb of the Unknown Soldier—an invention of "official nationalism" if ever there was one, and the exemplary emblem of the aesthetic culture of nationalism, insofar as it stages the subject's identification with the nation as formalized anonymity. Official nationalism constantly infiltrates Anderson's account of the "imagined community," because the state's aesthetic-pedagogic project, or work of mourning, exploits the same processes of technical reproduction that make the imagining of the nation possible in the first place.

In closing we may remark one final complication: the Unknown Soldier's tomb commemorates a death that is not, after all, entirely abstract. The death it remembers, mourns, and celebrates is a male death, suffered in war—war with some other, anonymous, abstract nation. From the perspective of nationalism per se, only male citizens can die, and they can only die in war. All other kinds of loss or damage are to be sublated into this death, to the extent that national identity succeeds in trumping all other forms of identity.[16] The mourners are thus in principle both male and female, for they are the entire people of the nation; but the feminine position in this scene is immutable, for all a woman will ever be able to do is mourn. She mourns, furthermore, above all as a mother, as Anderson hints at the end

of his penultimate chapter as he rapidly and tacitly sets another scene of
mourning:

> It may indeed appear paradoxical that the objects of all these attachments are
> "imagined." . . . But *amor patriae* does not differ in this respect from the other
> affections, in which there is always an element of fond imagining. (This is why
> looking at the photo-albums of strangers' weddings is like studying the archae-
> ologist's ground plan of the Hanging Gardens of Babylon.) What the eye is to the
> lover—that particular, ordinary eye he or she is born with—language—whatever
> language history has made his or her mother-tongue—is to the patriot. Through
> that language, encountered at mother's knee and parted with only at the grave,
> pasts are restored, fellowships are imagined, and futures dreamed. [*IC* 154]

Throughout his discussion of the role of aesthetic culture in national consciousness, Anderson tends to drift somewhat leeward of his historicist argument. In the passage I quoted earlier, for instance, he writes of nationalism's
seeming "disinterestedness" without noting that, historically speaking, aesthetic disinterestedness is a rather recent notion—a notion more or less
coeval with that of the nation-state, uncoincidentally. And his supple blend
of distance from and sympathy with aesthetic nationalism yields to a more
pressing rhetoric of pathos as he discovers similarities between nationalism
and familial sentiment, identifies *amor patriae* with a heterosexual passion
that leads straight to a wedding (albeit that of strangers), and finally inscribes it within a domestic scene, figuring language as a "mother-tongue"
that accompanies the male nationalist in his itinerary from "mother's knee"
to "the grave." We know, of course, that this grave cannot be that of the Unknown Soldier, for no mother's son can be buried there. But the mother can
mourn there; mourning is her destiny, as Anderson's sentence suggests (the
patriot was first at her knee, then in the grave), and this because continuity
is her function.[17] Sheltered within her domestic space, anonymity becomes
familiarity. She provides a "natural" origin not just for the male patriot but
for language itself, and thus for the (imagi)nation itself.[18] Summarizing a
good deal of feminist work on nationalism, the editors of the recent collection *Between Woman and Nation* comment that "the 'essential woman'
(raced or not) becomes the national iconic signifier for the material, the
passive, and the corporeal, to be worshipped, protected, and controlled by
those with the power to remember and to forget, to guard, to define, and
redefine" (Alarcón, Kaplan, and Moallem 10). It is part of the achievement
of *Imagined Communities* to have shown how poorly grounded, yet also how
insistent, that patriarchal fantasy is.[19]

2

The foregoing pages have argued two principal points: that the imagination of the nation responds to and to some extent cushions or wards off

the shock of modernity, and that in doing so it constructs an imagined community at once irreducible to the state and fundamentally tangled up with the state's aesthetic-cultural project. These two points are interrelated: because processes of mechanical replication constitute the material condition of possibility of imagining the nation, this imagination's spontaneous force is haunted by a technically enhanced iterability that also serves—and exceeds, and at times destabilizes—state power. The imaginative transformation of this iterability into sensuous tokens of abstract anonymity and unisonance generates a sense of the collective which no state can embody or entirely control, yet which also animates the movement of aesthetic education. The "crisis of the hyphen," Anderson's witty phrase for the morphings of the late twentieth-century nation-state ("Introduction" 8) originates in tensions that the nation-state has to some degree always known. I should perhaps reemphasize that I am not proposing that we ignore the difference between nation and state or between popular and official nationalisms; a great deal, both hermeneutically and politically, frequently hangs on that difference. But it will never be an absolute or stable difference. Anderson hesitates between a keen awareness of this dilemma and a reluctance to confront it: he writes powerfully of the role of the "replica" in official nationalism, a replica for which *"there is no original"* (S 48, Anderson's emphasis), but he overforcefully associates such originary replication with an "imaginative impasse" and a lack of what Walter Benjamin called aura, the better to contrast official nationalism with more genuine expressions of national feeling (S 47, 49). We would rather insist, with Samuel Weber, that *"aura thrives in its decline,* and that the reproductive media are particularly conducive to this thriving" (101, Weber's emphasis). The national flag, as Anderson says, is the ultimate model of a replica without original [S 48n6]; it is always ready to become sheer kitsch, yet it cannot be entirely dissociated from the stranger movement of what Weber would call "mediauratic" effects: "auratic flashes and shadows that are not just produced and reproduced by the media but which *are* themselves the media, since they come to pass in places that are literally inter-mediary, in the interstices of a process of reproduction and recording . . . that is above all a mass movement of collection and dispersion, of banding together and disbanding" (Weber 106).[20] The (national) imagination caught up in that mediation is perhaps best thought of neither as a simple victim of state manipulation nor as Hegel's pure act of mind, but rather as a figure for the ambivalence at the heart of nationalism's relation to the state and to modernity. Imagining difference as unisonance, the imagination presents itself both as a spontaneous force and as a faculty to be tended, disciplined, and trained—in other words, as a faculty dependent for its realization on those exemplary imaginative acts that, since the Romantic era, we have called aesthetic culture.

It will be interesting at this point to return to a text written quite early in the history of nationalist discourse and test the reach of some of these generalizations within an aesthetic-nationalist tradition. Johann Gottlieb Fichte gave his *Addresses to the German Nation* at the Academy of Sciences in Berlin during the winter of 1807–08, in the wake of Napoleon's crushing defeat of Prussia. Throughout that winter, French troops continuted to patrol Berlin; the era of the Holy Roman Empire was over, and Prussia's future in the new world order was by no means assured. Modernity had arrived with a shock: Fichte, opening his lectures, speaks of the giant steps, the *Riesenschritte,* with which time had begun to move (11/2).[21] In this exigency, addressing himself to a "German nation" that did not yet exist, vacillating between prudence and pugnacity as he walked a fine line between sedition and patriotism, fighting the censor (the Prussian authorities, not the French, who seem to have ignored him entirely) for the right to publish each lecture in the series, Fichte provided a text that eventually became a classic within the German tradition, and in its own time knew a degree of influence: old-fashioned histories of Germany often characterize the *Addresses* as the first significant and fully developed expression of German nationalism, and as an event that helped prepare, in some small and hard-to-define fashion, for the "war of national liberation" in 1813–15, and the development of more properly nationalist movements in subsequent decades.[22] What "influence" means, however, is complicated by the fact that Fichte's text was misread, or read selectively, from the start. Even today his text is still often assimilated to "Romantic" celebrations of *Volk, Vaterland,* and the German language: themes that unquestionably loom large in the *Addresses,* but that undergo fundamental reorientation under the pressure of Fichte's theories of imagination and will.[23] A close reading of the *Addresses*—and they deserve a far closer and fuller reading than I shall be able to offer here—uncovers a complex, conflicted text: one that, for present purposes, I shall represent as forcefully replaying some of the tensions we have remarked in Anderson's *Imagined Communities.* Basking in "the devouring flame of a higher patriotism [*Vaterlandsliebe*]" that transcends loyalty to the state(135/141), Fichte's text nonetheless takes as its main theme the necessity of a state-run educational program, a proposal that I shall suggest we understand as the Fichtean version of aesthetic pedagogy.

One can hardly blame Fichte's readers for having tended to privilege his ethnolinguistic theme: language, in the *Addresses,* plays so leading a role that its story is that of modernity itself. According to Fichte, language, in its essence, is "in no way dependent on arbitrary decisions and agreements," but is rather governed by "a fundamental law, in accordance with which every idea becomes in the human organs of speech one particular sound and no other" (61/56). All languages are thus originally one language, though

Fichte's version of this Adamic fantasy understands the original unity as a transcendental model that may never have existed in reality: from the beginning different environments and experiences would have influenced the original language, deflecting it into particular phonetic and semantic channels.[24] Nevertheless, such deviations from "the one pure human language" are to be understood as governed by "strict law" (62/56). As languages change over time, they remain organically continuous and in conformity with their particular and proper deviation, so long as the people (*Volk*) continues to speak the language. Even though "after some centuries have passed the descendants do not understand the language of their ancestors," their language remains fundamentally the same language, because at any one time its speakers never cease understanding each other, and "their eternal go-between and interpreter always was, and continues to be, the common power of nature speaking through all" (63/57).

In the modern world, however, only the Germans can claim to be in touch with this natural power. Fichte's argument here relies on an implicit limitation of the modern world to Northern Europe, and an explicit affirmation of the common origin of all northern European peoples: "The German [*der Deutsche*] is in the first instance a branch of the Teutons [*ein Stamm der Germanier*]. Of the Teutons it suffices here to define them as those who were to unite the social order of ancient Europe with the true religion of ancient Asia, and thereby develop in and out of themselves a new age, opposed to the fallen ancient world" (58/52). Yet in the struggle to produce this new age, certain Teutons fell away from the source. In conquering Rome, they gained the ancient world and lost their Teutonic soul precisely to the extent that they lost their language. Because all abstractions, concepts, or ideas, according to Fichte, are produced as figurative displacements of sensuous perceptions, the meanings of a culture's language are all ultimately rooted in concrete experience. So long as a people retains its original language, it remains connected to "the root where concepts [*Begriffe*] stream forth from spiritual nature herself" (86/86). When a people forgets its language and adopts a foreign one, it inherits meanings irreducibly foreign to its experience. The aesthetic link between perception and cognition breaks, and with it the natural continuity of a language and thus of a people. Despite their appearance of being alive, Romance languages and cultures (including post-Norman-Invasion English, presumably, though Fichte, obsessed with France, rather surprisingly says nothing at all about Britain) bear within them "a dead element deeper down" (68/64). Indeed, Romance cultures "are entirely without a mother tongue [*Muttersprache*]" (71/67).

It follows that the Germans are the only people who are genuinely a *people:* they are "quite simply *the* people [*das Volk schlechtweg*]" (106/108), having remained "in the stream of original culture [*ursprunglicher Bildung*]"

(87/87). The task of modernity itself—the destiny proper to the Teutons—belongs to them. Defeated in war, the Germans now have the chance to rise above selfishness, assume the mantle of nationality, and achieve a genuine, spiritual rather than martial, conquest of history. Fichte points out that it is in the world's interest that Germany should fulfill its destiny. For, in that happy event, even the Franks' self-loss in their encounter with Rome becomes a fortunate fall: the Romance cultures will then have achieved their proper historical role of serving as mediators or buffers between Germany and antiquity. The Franks, overwhelmed by Roman culture, allow the Germans, secure in their Teutonic modernity, to absorb antiquity "after their own nature . . . as an element in their own life" (88/88). "In this way both parts of the common nation [*gemeinsamen Nation:* that is, the original Teutons] remained one, and only in this simultaneous separation and unity do they form a graft on the stem of the culture of antiquity, which otherwise would have been broken off by the new age, and so humanity would have begun again from the beginning" (88/88). With Germany's emergence as a nation, history itself will be healed. On the other hand, if Germany is destroyed, Europe will fall into "spiritual death" (89/89), its last living cultural-historical-linguistic root having been severed. And Europe's fate is the world's fate: "If you perish in this your essential nature," Fichte tells his audience (that is, the "German nation") at the end of the *Addresses,* "then there perishes with you every hope of the whole human race for salvation from the depths of its miseries. . . . [I]f you go under, all humanity goes under with you, without hope of future restoration" (246/269).

Such, in its main lines, is Fichte's version of a narrative one encounters periodically throughout nineteenth- and early twentieth-century German letters: a story often and famously cast as one of Germany's affinity with Greece, which is to say with a pre-Roman antiquity that promises to underwrite Europe's true renaissance as a postcapitalist, postimperialist—post-Spanish, -British, or -Napoleonic—modernity. Fichte's version of this story appears simple only as long as we fail to ask after the central matter at hand—the text's definition of Germanness. Etienne Balibar rightly emphasizes that Fichte rejects protoracist possibilities: "even as Fichte places himself in opposition to Kant by granting an ethical importance to language and linguistic unity, he follows him in completely dissociating the notions of stock and people, and opposes the idea that there would be a historical link between linguistic continuity and biological continuity" ("Fichte" 76–77). What makes a *Volk* a *Volk* is not blood descent but linguistic continuity.[25] Nor, in principle, is Fichte interested in the objective characteristics of this or that language. German has nothing special about it grammatically, semantically, or phonetically; all that matters is that it has been continuously spoken (61/55).

As Balibar says, language, for Fichte, is an ethical attitude, "a way of 'living' a language" ("Fichte" 78). And while that claim needs nuancing—Fichte's notorious (indeed, at times inadvertently comical) concern for linguistic purity suggests the difficulty of maintaining a steady distinction between "objective" and "subjective" aspects of language, or between speech acts and linguistic structures[26]—it pays to attend to the Fichtean homology between language and ethical action, for at one point in the *Addresses* this homology stiffens to the point of damaging the linguistic theme. In the seventh Address we encounter the unambiguous claim that "whoever believes in spirituality and in the freedom of this spirituality, and who wills the eternal development of this spirituality by freedom, *wherever he may have been born and whatever language he speaks,* is of our people [*unsers Geschlechts*]; he is one of us, and will come over to our side." Whoever believes the opposite, "*wherever he may have been born and whatever language he speaks,* is non-German [*undeutsch*] and a stranger to us; and it is to be wished that he would separate himself from us completely, and the sooner the better" (122/127, my emphasis).

For though at various points in Fichte's *Addresses* the continuous and living German language seems the precondition of such belief in spirituality and freedom, Fichte's definition of Germanness has so much to do with belief that he is able, at least on occasion, to abandon the linguistic theme as a merely external, disposable *sign* of belief. If one were to try to sum up his definition of Germanness, one would have to venture something like the following: Germanness is an imaginative act that imagines itself as the (national) repetition of itself. The question of *address* is fundamental: as Fichte emphasizes, he speaks to a German nation that in certain crucial respects does not yet exist and must be posited:

> I speak for Germans simply [*schlechtweg*], of Germans simply, not recognizing, but setting aside completely and rejecting, all the dissociating distinctions which for centuries unhappy events have caused in this nation. . . . In the spirit of which these addresses are the expression, I perceive that organic unity [*durcheinander verwachsene Einheit*] in which no member [*Glied*] regards the fate of another as the fate of a stranger, and which must and shall arise, if we are not to perish altogether—I see this unity already achieved, completed, and existing. [14/4]

Fichte further defines his audience under two more headings: first, he assumes (*voraussetzt*) "such German listeners as have not given themselves over in their entire being to a feeling of pain at the loss they have suffered, who take comfort in this pain, luxuriate in their disconsolate grief . . . but rather such as have already risen, or are at least capable of rising, above this justifiable pain to clear thought and meditation" (14/4–5). Second, he assumes "such hearers as are disposed to see things through their own eyes" rather than through "a strange and foreign eyeglass" (15/6). Listeners not meeting these criteria are repeatedly invited to leave. In the seventh address, as we saw, Fichte declares the pessimist "non-German and a stranger to us"; in the twelfth address he proposes as "the certain characteristic [*festen Grundzug*] of the German" the desire to "form an opinion for himself about that which concerns Germans," whereas "a man who does not want to hear or to think about this subject may rightly be regarded, from now on, as not belonging to us" (197/212). The German is he who can posit Germany. If he cannot—being overly mournful, or equipped with a "foreign eyeglass," or pessimistic, or insouciant—he is not *deutsch*, not genuinely of the *Volk*, though he be a Teuton and a native speaker. To be German is to repeat Fichte's own imaginative act in listening to or reading Fichte. To listen—to really hear—Fichte is to imagine Germany, and thereby to begin to enact or realize Germany. The Lutheran note is explicit: "He who has ears, let him hear" (122/127).[27] The language to be heard is that of intuitive experience: "Whoever feels this within him will be convinced; whoever does not feel it cannot be convinced, since my proof rests entirely on that supposition [*Voraussetzung*]: on him my words are lost; but who would not risk [*auf das Spiel setzen*] something so trivial as words?" (146–47/156). Words can be squandered; they are spirit's inessential, if necessary, supplement. What matters is the act of speaking and listening: a communicational circuit that is in itself the imagining of Germany.

The imagined community thus entails an act of positing that at first glance might look like a tautology. If you are truly hearing Fichte you are German by definition; it might seem, therefore, that you didn't need to hear him in the first place—except that it is precisely in the hearing that Germanness constitutes itself as its own future possibility. When Fichte posits as his addressee the German nation ("I see this unity already achieved, completed, and existing") he speaks with the voice of imagination. Imagination (*Einbildungskraft*) is "the power spontaneously to create images [*Bilder*] that are independent of reality and in no way imitations of it [*Nachbilder*], but are rather prefigurations of it [*Vorbilder*]" (31/23). The *Addresses* are proleptic: they address the future; they aim their spirit-charged words at an ear to come. In the aiming or speaking or imagining, the addressee comes into being *as* a future. As is always the case in Fichte, a nontemporal act of positing opens up temporality—here, the time of nation building—thanks to the power of imagination.[28] When Fichte writes that "We must become on the spot [*zur Stelle*] what we should be in any case: Germans" (193/207), he compacts into an instant the temporality of *Bildung:* we who hear Fichte are being educated, albeit in the momentary flame of an inspiration. And the work before us is pedagogical: "most citizens [*Bürger*] must be educated to a sense of fatherland" (145/154). The imagination both enables *Bildung* and constitutes *Bildung*'s object. For in order to imagine the nation, the imagination must be trained:

> The external eye, when accustomed to cleanliness and order, is troubled and distressed, as though actually hurt, by a stain [*einen Flecken*] which indeed causes the body no actual injury, or by the sight of objects lying in chaotic confusion; while the eye accustomed to dirt and disorder is quite comfortable under such circumstances. So too the inner spiritual eye of man can be so accustomed and trained [*gebildet*] that the mere sight of a muddled and disorderly, unworthy and dishonorable existence of its own or a kindred people [*verbrüderten Stammes*] causes it internal pain, apart from anything there may be to fear or to hope from this for its own material welfare. This pain, apart again from any material fear or hope, permits the possessor of such an eye no rest until he has removed, in so far as he can, this condition which displeases him, and has set in its place that which alone can please him. For the possessor of such an eye, because of this stimulating feeling of approval or disapproval, the welfare of his whole environment is bound up inextricably with the welfare of his own self, which is conscious of itself only as part of the whole and can endure itself only when the whole is pleasing. To educate itself to possess such an eye [*Die Sichbildung zu einem solchen Auge*] will therefore be a sure means, and indeed the only means left to a nation which has lost its independence, and with it all influence over public fear and hope, of rising again into life from the destruction it has suffered. [20–21/12]

The subject of this education is being trained to feel pain, and to feel it as an aesthetic experience that is equally an ethical imperative. The unaesthetic nation can be perceived—as pain—in and through the imagining of the nation that one then inevitably works to realize precisely as the national imagining of the nation. For if the nation can be brought to imagine itself, this imagining will itself be the nation's *Sichbildung*. No longer the proleptic vision of an educated, privileged, Fichtean few, the nation will be realized.

The task ahead thus consists "in the fashioning of an entirely new, universal and national self [*in der Bildung zu einem durchaus neuen . . . allgemeines und nationales Selbst*]—one that may have existed before in individuals as an exception, but never as a national self—and in the education of the nation [*Erziehung der Nation*]"(21/13). The heart and soul of Fichte's *Addresses* is his educational plan. Designed to result in the production of a nation, it is a vision of *mass* education. All classes and both sexes are to be educated together; "the subjects of instruction are the same for both sexes" (in this respect, Fichte's solitary concession to the sexism of his time takes the form of the pronouncement that "the general relation of the two sexes to each other, stout-hearted protection on the one side and loving help on the other, must appear in the educational institution and be fostered in the pupils" [169–70/180–81]). Nowhere is Fichte's Jacobin side so visible as in these sections of the *Addresses:* not only is national education to be radically democratic in its generality, but it is to intervene in civil society with the full force of the state. Children, if at all possible, are to be taken from their families and educated in isolation from adult society in state-funded coeducational boarding schools. We may skip over here the details of Fichte's educational theories, many of which derive from Pestalozzi;[29] for present purposes the important point is that Fichte's plan aims at a *total* education, an utter making—or breaking and remaking—of human being: "den Menschen selbst zu bilden" (23/15). Children are to be extracted from the familial unit and educated apart because this new sort of *Bildung* is to reach the very roots (*Wurzeln*) of the subject; it will "completely destroy freedom of will in the soil it undertakes to cultivate" (28/20), so as to produce a new freedom, training the imagination, the foundation of this new *Bildung,* through procedures that stimulate the pupil's own self-determination (32/24). The educated imagination serves a pure moral will: the pupil freely creates, through the proleptic power of imagination, the image of a moral order; he (or, as we have seen, she) then cathects this image and seeks to realize it (39/32). This image is "Germany." The patriotism that results from such *Bildung* transcends the state, for this *Vaterlandsliebe* amounts to nothing less than the love of humanity and the desire for "the blossoming of the eternal and the divine in the world" (131/138). This desire for the eternal "unites first [the patriot's] own nation, and then, through his own nation, the whole human race" (129/136). And despite the small to nonexistent role Fichte gives to the "humanities" (indeed, even to reading and writing) in his educational system, we need to recognize his plan as a program of *aesthetic* education precisely insofar as it sets out to shape the creative faculty it presupposes.[30] For though Fichte's is not a program of acculturation in an Arnoldian sense, it is no less an aesthetic education turned "NATIONAL EDUCATION, the *nisus formativus* of the body politic," as Coleridge would put it twenty years later—"the shaping and informing spirit, which *educing,* i.e., eliciting, the latent *man* in all the natives of the soil, *trains them up* to citizens of the country, free subjects of the realm" (48).[31] The subject is "trained up" to perceive the unperceivable Nation: a nation that is at once Germany and humanity itself. The state is thus in a sense being asked to submit to nationalism, to transcend itself by funding a pedagogical project that exceeds it. ("But that love of fatherland ought above all to inspire the German State, wherever Germans are governed, and take the lead, and be the motive power in all its decisions" [175/187].) Yet it would be more accurate, here and elsewhere in Fichte's text, to speak of an unsteady interplay between nation and state. The state's interests persist: "As to the State's doubt whether it can meet the costs of a national education, would that one could convince it that by this one expenditure it will provide for most of the others in the most economical way...!" Above all, the State would save on military expenses: it would have "an army such as no age has yet seen" in its fit, utterly selfless and self-sacrificing citizen-soldiers (178/190). Fichte's vision of the ethical, pacifist, cosmopolitan nation is always also a vision of total mobilization; and that ambiguity, I suggest, inheres in the very grain of aesthetic nationalism.

Yet for the present, all depends on an exemplary performance—Fichte's. "I was the first one to see it vividly; therefore it fell to me to take the first step. . . . There must always be one who is first; then let him be first who can!" (232/252). His exemplarity resides in his ability to speak with the voice, the living force, of the German language; his exemplarity also hangs, as we have seen, on a structure of address, an ability to image "the German nation" as a receptive ear. And we may return at this point to Benedict Anderson's great insight, and ask after the technical precondition of such an address. For Fichte's task is to communicate his imaginative vision not just to a circle of auditors, but to a nation-to-be that can *only* be imagined:

> You, worthy gathering, are indeed to my bodily eye the first and immediate representatives who make present to me the beloved national traits, and are the visible spark at which the flame of my address kindles itself. But my spirit gathers round it the educated part of the whole German nation, from all the lands over which it is spread; . . . it longs that part of the living force with which these lectures may grip you, may also remain in and breathe from the dumb printed page which alone will come to the eyes of the absent, and may in all places kindle German hearts to decision and deed. [13/3–4]

In his final lecture, Fichte returns to this theme: "I have had in view the whole German nation, and my intention has been to gather around me, in the room in which you are bodily present, everyone in the domain of the German language who is able to understand me." Once again he expresses the hope that he has thrown out sparks that will be gathered, "so that at this central point a single, continuous, and unceasing flame of patriotic disposition may be kindled, which will spread over the whole soil of the fatherland to its uttermost boundaries" (228/248). Fichte's reiterated figures of spark and flame, voice and breath, communicate his understanding of language as spiritual force; yet in an Andersonian spirit we may also remark how irreducible the supplemental role of "the dumb printed page" is in this scene of address. To address the nation is to assemble it "around a speaker by the means of a printed book [*durch den Bücherdruck um sich zu versammeln*]" (195/209).[32] The imagination of the nation presupposes print technology; and as both Anderson and Fichte in their different ways suggest, the imagined nation equally demands the subordination of technics to a trope of "unisonance." A text, in aesthetic-nationalist discourse, must function as technically extended voice. One could say, perhaps a little overimaginatively, that in imagining the aesthetic nation Fichte necessarily imagines the possibility of radio—a haunted radio attuned, like all national transmitters, to the transmissions of the dead and the unborn: "Your fore-fathers unite themselves with these addresses, and make a solemn appeal to you"; "There comes a solemn appeal to you from your descendants not yet born"; "A solemn appeal comes to you even from foreign countries, insofar as they still understand themselves" (242–44/264–66).[33]

To the extent that such an assertion of unisonance depends upon a mis-recognition of its own predicament, it needs to be able to acknowledge and quarantine loss. Aesthetic nationalisms necessarily cultivate sites and occasions of mourning; Fichtean nationalism—understandably, under the circumstances—begins in mourning. The fundamental task of Fichtean aesthetic education, as we saw, is to teach its national subjects how to mourn the figurative wound, the stain or *Fleck,* on the phantasmatic national body. But too much mourning would be crippling. Germans who have become possessed by mourning, who "take comfort in this pain, luxuriate in their disconsolate grief, and think thereby to compromise with the call that summons them to action," are not true Germans, and Fichte posits them out of existence (14/4). The difference between German and not-German might even be said to turn on the question of proper and excessive mourning. Yet in closing his first address Fichte stages a remarkable scene:

> The age [*Die Zeit*] seems to me a shade [*ein Schatten*] that stands over his own corpse [*Leichname*], out of which he has been driven by a host of diseases, and weeps, and cannot tear his gaze from the form so beloved of old, and tries in despair every means to enter again the home of pestilence. Already, indeed, the quickening breezes of that other world, which the departed has entered, have taken her [that is, *die Zeit*] unto themselves and are surrounding her with the warm breath of love; the whispering voices of her sisters greet her with joy and bid her welcome; and already inside her there is stir and growth in all directions toward the more glorious form into which she will develop. But as yet she has no feeling for these breezes or ear for these voices—or if she had them, they have disappeared in the pain of her loss, with which she thinks she has lost herself as well. What is to be done with her? Already the dawn of the new world has broken and gilds the mountain-tops, and figures forth the coming day. I wish, so far as I can, to seize the rays of this dawn and weave them into a mirror, in which our grief-stricken age [*trostlose Zeit*] may see herself, so that she may believe she is still there, perceive her true identity, and see as in prophetic vision her own development and forms. In the contemplation of this, the picture of her former life will doubtless sink and vanish, and the dead body [*der Tote*] may be borne to its resting place without undue lamenting. [26/18]

I have forced the passage a bit by translating the pronouns literally. In the first sentence "the age" (a feminine noun in German: *die Zeit*) is a "shade" (a masculine noun: *Schatten*) who stands and weeps; but after the first sentence Fichte reverts to the feminine pronoun—to, that is, the figure of "die Zeit" herself. The otherworldly "sisters" who greet this mourner lend additional momentum to her personification as feminine, as does the association of long standing between mothers and mourning that we noted earlier in connection with Benedict Anderson's text. Fichte imagines himself weaving the light of the future into a mirror: in this imaginary, specular, and solar moment, the Age will imagine herself back into existence ("believe she is still there"), forget her loss, moderate her grief, and allow her body to be buried. I say "her" body out of respect for the scene's personifying momentum, though the body she mourns is of course grammatically male (*der Leichnam*; *der Tote*).

It is possible, I think, to read this scene as an allegory that speaks to the ambivalence of national mourning. Just as the tomb of the Unknown Soldier remains forever a tomb, marked by the death it abstracts and forecloses, so the Age, in Fichte's scenario, remains bending over her corpse, a Niobe petrified by grief, untouched by the orator's resurrectional rhetoric. She is the modernity that is Germany; but Fichte's living words have not yet reached her, and, like figures on a Grecian urn, they never will. She is the Nation divided from itself, split into soul and body by the mark of difference and death; but the mark is singular and uncertain, the difference between life and death undecidable, and the work of mourning as irreducible as the gap between an allegorical sign and its meaning. The task of nationalism, particularly of what Anderson calls "official nationalism," is to monumentalize such scenes and fence them off. They record, and thus to some extent compensate for, the imagined community's dependence on the unimaginable.

Notes

1. In what follows, the acronym *IC* flags a reference to the second, revised edition of Anderson's *Imagined Communities*; *S* refers to Anderson's *The Spectre of Comparisons*. I thank Jonathan Culler and Pheng Cheah for directing me to this latter text, and more generally for their very helpful comments on an earlier draft of this essay.
2. Wall Street is of course a synecdoche here for the dispersed centers of international capital. It is also perhaps worth underscoring that, as has often been pointed out, global capitalism's homogenizing forces coexist with its systematic exploitation of unevenly developed markets. "Globalization" is thus never simply a description of an actual state of affairs, but is always *also* the ideological narrative of a permanently deferred utopia (or dystopia).
3. "Cosmopolitanism" is a term possessed of much greater range than my commentary here can indicate: see, for example, Cheah and Robbins for a collection of interesting recent attempts to imagine nonuniversalist, local, or finite forms of cosmopolitanism.
4. On the development of aesthetic culture in nineteenth-century Britain see Lloyd and Thomas; see the opening chapter of my *Phantom Formations* for a short history of the emergence of aesthetics as a discourse, and an analysis of the complexities of what, following de Man, I call "aesthetic ideology." For a model of aesthetic politics more up-to-date than those of Schiller or Arnold, see Ankersmit, whose *Aesthetic Politics: Political Philosophy beyond Fact and Value* (1996) is rather surprisingly featured in Stanford's postcolonial-theory "Mestizo Spaces/Espaces Métissés" series. Ankersmit claims to be proposing a non-Schillerian model of the aesthetic state because "aesthetics is invoked here not in order to argue for the *unity* but precisely for the brokenness of the political domain" (18). Predictably, however, "brokenness"

turns out to mean aesthetic play, which permits the reintroduction of unity as aesthetic harmony; for example:

> (Aesthetic) political representation is required since each (civil) society needs an image of itself in order to function properly; without such a mirror image of itself it will stumble around erratically and aimlessly like a blind man. Apart from its better-known and more obvious functions, the state, as the representation of civil society, is such an image of society to itself. And it follows that the clearer and more vigorous the contours of the state are, the better it may be expected to fulfill its function of being a representation or an image of civil society. . . . On the assumptions of an aesthetic political philosophy, the best political world is therefore the one in which a strong state and a strong civil society coexist in a fruitful symbiosis. [191, Ankersmit's parentheses, my ellipsis]

The tropes of mutilation and errancy that pop up here ("stumble around erratically and aimlessly like a blind man") are typical of the aesthetic tradition, and function as signs of the violence with which this tradition is prepared to repress its own instability. For the argument behind that assertion, see my *Phantom Formations* 1–37.

5. These comments target recent work in cultural studies rather than in history or political science, but it is rare for a scholar in any field to put real critical pressure on the figure of "imagination" in Anderson's text. Historians have argued that Anderson's account of the nation's origins in print capitalism fails to explain why the imagined communities enabled by the circulation of newspapers, novels, and so forth would take the specific form of nationalism (see, for example, Breuilly 406–07); and many postcolonialist critics have echoed Partha Chatterjee's question "Whose imagined community?" (Chatterjee 5), but usually without questioning what it means to "imagine" a "community." Within cultural studies, one of the few texts I have encountered that scrutinizes Anderson's arguments is Homi Bhabha's rich essay "DissemiNation" (see esp. 308–11). Bhabha's main object is to complicate Anderson's notion of the "homogenous empty time" of nationalism rather than that of an imagined community per se. But as we shall see, the complication of the one complicates the other, and I take Bhabha's account of the tensions within nationalism and national identity to be compatible with the arguments I shall be elaborating here.

6. From a history-of-ideas perspective the idea of the imagination as a synthetic or articulative faculty capable of transforming sensory impressions into mental images returns to classical roots: for a helpful account see Cocking. For a historical study focused on the eighteenth-century "creation" of "the idea of the imagination as we still understand it today," see Engell (vii).

7. Hegel goes on to link the arbitrariness of the sign with pedagogy, because such signs must be learned. See *Enzyklopädie, III,* par. 457 (unless otherwise indicated, all translations in this essay are mine):

> The sign [*Das Zeichen*] must be declared to be something great. When the intelligence has signified [*bezeichnet*] something, it has finished with the content of the perception and has given the sensuous material a meaning [*Bedeutung*] foreign to it as its soul. Thus a cockade or a *flag* or a *gravestone* means [*bedeutet*] something quite different from that which they immediately indicate [*unmittelbar anzeigen*]. The arbitrariness, here made evident, of the link between the sensuous material and the general representation has as necessary consequence the fact that one must first learn the meaning of signs. This holds notably for linguistic signs. [269, Hegel's emphasis]

8. On the sublimity of the nation, see Ian Balfour, "The Sublime of the Nation," forthcoming as part of a book in progress called *The Language of the Sublime.*

9. "Reading a newspaper is like reading a novel whose author has abandoned any thought of a coherent plot," Anderson comments in a footnote (*IC* 33n54)—which is why the newspaper serves his argument better than the novel does. As soon as questions of emplotment and narrative voice arise, the temporality of narrative becomes irreducible to "a complex gloss upon the word 'meanwhile'" (*IC* 25). An entire subfield in literary criticism, of course, narratology, thrives on explaining how texts construct and manage temporality through

such rhetorical devices as prefiguration, repetition, prolepses and analepses, and so on. Franco Moretti's recent *Atlas of the European Novel* seeks in part to elaborate on Anderson's intuition of a link betwen novels and national consciousness: he argues, for instance, that Jane Austen's heroines, who typically have to travel to different counties to meet compatible partners, are participating in a "national" marriage market and that the novels thereby convey a sense of a middle-sized world, "the typical intermediate space of the nation-state" (Moretti 22). Many of his readings are intriguing and helpful; they are also plagued by factual errors, ranging from Moretti's mixing up the names of the Dickens characters Little Dorrit and Fanny (122: Fanny is the unadmirable older sister of Dickens's eponymous heroine) to his misrepresentation of Goethe's *Wilhelm Meister* as a city-oriented narrative (65)—this last in large part, I think, because Moretti's notion of the genre of the Bildungsroman is heavily distorted by his preference for Balzac and, more generally, for the French and English novelistic traditions over the German.

10. From Derrida's perspective, Anderson may be seen as remaining faithful to a fundamental Marxist insight: "Marx is one of the rare thinkers of the past to have taken seriously, at least in principle, the originary indissociability of technics and language, and thus of tele-technics (for every language is a tele-technics)" [*Specters of Marx* 53].

11. It should also be noted here that although print capitalism is the fundamental precondition of nationalism in Anderson's argument, nationalism actually comes into existence by propping itself up, so to speak, on existing administrative and market units, particularly in the case of the New World "creole nationalisms" that, Anderson emphasizes, animated the first successful nationalist movements. In similar fashion, the absolutist state provides a kind of scaffold or skeleton for national imagining in Europe. Anderson also points to the importance of capitalism's transportation technologies: "The essential nexus of long-distance transportation and print-capitalist communications prepared the grounds on which, by the end of the eighteenth century, the first nationalist movements flowered. It is striking that this flowering took place first in North America and later in the Catholic, Iberian colonies to the south, the economies of which were all pre-industrial" (*S* 62). Anderson thus suggests "the untenability of Ernest Gellner's argument that industrialism was the historical source of nationalism's emergence" (*S* 63n10). (For that argument see Gellner.) The emphasis would rather need to fall on a certain *displacement* effected by developments in transport and communication technologies, rather than on industrialism per se.

12. For a fine reading of *Madame Bovary* that stresses Emma's inability to live in time, see Marder; an extended version of her argument may be found in her *Dead Time: Temporal Disorders in the Wake of Modernity,* Stanford UP 2001.

13. Of Derrida's several classic texts on this subject, see especially "Signature Event Context" and associated texts in *Limited Inc.* My comments here converge with Geoffrey Bennington's assessment that the nation is "always open to its others, or rather, it is constituted only in that opening, which is, in principle, violent" (131); stories of the nation, in contrast, seek "interminably to constitute identity against difference, inside against outside" (132).

14. Leaving aside the broader genealogy of the political as fictional or fashioned that Lacoue-Labarthe sketches, we may note that the link between the nation and the power of will appears everywhere in modern nationalist discourse, playing a central role in traditions as separate in time and spirit as Ernest Renan's nineteenth-century liberal humanism and Alfred Rosenberg's twentieth-century fascist mythologizing. See, for example, Renan: "There is something in man which is superior to language, namely, the will" (16); "A nation is a soul, a spiritual principle. Two things, which in truth are but one, constitute this soul or spiritual principle. One is the possession in common of a rich legacy of memories; the other is present-day consent, the desire to live together, the will to perpetuate the value of the heritage that one has received in an undivided form" (19). I pursue the topic of will and imagination further in my discussion of Fichte.

15. In his chapter "Replica, Aura, and Late National Imaginings" in *The Spectre of Comparisons,* Anderson comments further on the Tomb of the Unknown Soldier and provides some intriguing historical detail:

> The British government, which seems to have pioneered these memorials in the immediate aftermath of World War I, was seriously worried, from the start, about the possibility that the Unknown Soldier might escape or be body-snatched . . . if

his identity could be tracked down. . . . The search for the right remains was thus limited to those who had been killed in the first months of the war, so that, maximally decayed, they would be as much like dust and as little like bodies as possible. Four such remains were picked out by military officials, and one was chosen, by lot . . . " [*S* 55]

16.   I therefore agree with Gopal Balakrishnan's claim that Anderson tends to underplay the importance of "the language and imagery of war" in the constitution of "the pathos of national membership" (Balakrishnan 208).

17.   The association of mourning with maternity has a long and complex filiation in Western culture; for a reading of the mother's role as mourner in ancient Greek culture, see Loraux. In his account of national burial customs and projects during the First World War, Anderson notes as a curious detail the fact that "the [U.S.] Congress felt obliged to finance the round-trip tickets and other expenses of all mothers (not wives) who wished to visit their Europe-interred sons" (*S* 53).

18.   As Friedrich Kittler has shown, the mother becomes closely associated with "language" and language acquisition in German contexts in the early nineteenth century ("The mother as primary instructor is, quite literally, an invention of 1800" [26]). Kittler's is a culturally specific analysis in many respects (see his chapter "The Mother's Mouth" 25–69); but quite apart from the considerable direct influence of Pestalozzi and other German pedagogical theorists of the era on European and American educational theory and practice, it seems safe to say that in a very broad sense Anderson's maternal figure constitutes part of his text's Romantic legacy.

It should be added, however, that Anderson is highly aware of the rhetorical and ideological power of the figure of the family. His fine gloss on Renan's famous comment that "the essence of a nation is that all individuals have many things in common, and also that they have forgotten many things" (11) identifies the trope of the family as the nation's exemplary device for forgetting what it remembers. Violent events become "reassuringly fratricidal" when both parties are retrospectively absorbed into the familiarity of a "France" or a "United States": a war thus becomes a "Civil" War; a bloody anti-Huguenot pogrom becomes "la Saint-Barthélemy" (Anderson 200). Speaking of that second example (which is drawn from Renan), Anderson comments that "we become aware of a systematic historiographical campaign, deployed by the state mainly through the state's school system, to 'remind' every young Frenchwoman and Frenchman of a series of antique slaughters which are now inscribed as 'family history'" (201). The Nation as Motherland can then mourn and celebrate both her sons, thanks to the forgetful power of the memory that preserves the event only by presupposing the nation.

19.   Anderson's ambivalent naturalization of imagination, nation, and language in these passages may be understood as the flip side of his underestimation of nationalism's drive to "naturalize" itself. His much-criticized effort to oppose nationalism to racism ("nationalism thinks in terms of historical destinies, while racism dreams of eternal contaminations" [149]) partly stems, I think, from his effort to resist his own denaturalizing critique. Etienne Balibar is surely right to stress that the "ideal nation" requires something besides language to define itself: language (as Anderson, for that matter, also points out) "assimilates everyone, but holds no one" to the extent that it can be learned or lost; hence the need for the "fiction of a racial identity" as a supplemental principle of closure (Balibar, "The Nation Form" 97, 99). (As Balibar remarks, "One's 'mother' tongue is not necessarily the language of one's 'real' mother.") It must also be said that Anderson's account oversimplifies the relationship between racism and historicism: racism's stereotyping idiom is bound up both with the typographical technologies that made the dissemination of stereotypes effective, and with the typology of aesthetic historicism, whereby the master race prefigures—and, through its dominion, works to achieve—the ever-deferred accomplishment of modernity as the communion of peoples.

20.   On the ideological effectiveness of contemporary nationalist culture's endless stream of banal, quotidian imagery—anthems, flag-motifs, and so on—see Billig.

21.   Double page numbers separated by a backslash refer to the German and English texts of *Addresses to the German Nation,* in that order. The Jones and Turnbull translation has been modified in the interest of accuracy or emphasis.

22. For a history of the reception of Fichte's lectures, see Léon. Etienne Balibar points out that the phrase "war of national liberation" was first coined during Prussia's uprising against Napoleon in 1813, and adds the interesting detail that, a century later, Fichte's text was literally taken into the trenches: in 1915 the German General Staff had hundreds of thousands of copies printed and placed in soldiers' backpacks ("Fichte and the Internal Border" 232n2). Fichte himself, it is only fair to add, hesitated before giving his support to the 1813 war, worrying (rightly) that it was being waged on behalf of reactionary rather than progressively nationalist constituencies.

23. Since at the beginning of this essay I suggested that in a very broad sense one can think of Benedict Anderson as writing within a Romantic tradition, I should pay for that generalization by recalling that if we take Romanticism as what a traditional literary history calls *die romantische Schule*, Fichte does not belong to it, though certainly his relation to Jena Romanticism and its aftermath is hardly simple. "By a remarkable irony," Xavier Léon writes, "the ideas that the Addresses popularized, and that Fichte's genius animated and made enter history, were for the most part German romantic theses: theses that Fichte, in the end, had borrowed only in order to combat the romantics" (133). If Fichte stands opposed to Hegel as the nationalist to the statist, his nationalism intends to have little in common with what he saw as the Catholic and monarchical tendencies of A. W. Schlegel's lectures on literature and art of 1803–04 (from which Fichte borrows liberally, as Léon shows). For some lucid orienting remarks on Fichte's relation to Romanticism, see Behler.

24. Fichte's approach to the classic question of the origin of language is set forth in Surber's *Language and German Idealism,* which includes a translation of Fichte's 1795 monograph "On the Linguistic Capacity and the Origin of Language" ("Von der Sprachfähigkeit und dem Ursprung der Sprache"). Partly in order to protect his revision of Kant against Hamann's critique of critical philosophy (as inattentive to its own dependence on a historically developed language), Fichte seeks, in this short and intriguing early paper, to reformulate the question of language's origin in transcendental terms, so that language could be understood as a product of reason's free purposiveness. In this account, language manifests itself originally as the "hieroglyphic language" of an *Ursprache,* in which signs, while arbitrarily posited by the will, are still mimetically connected to nature. As the *Ursprache* becomes an actual historical *Sprache,* it disappears without a trace:

    > Even with a people that remains free of all external influences, never mingles with another people, never changes its dwelling place, etc., the primitive natural language will gradually perish and be replaced by another which carries in itself not even the slightest trace of the former. Thus, it would be a mistake to believe that the Greeks, Romans, and others never had an *Urspache* because there are no remnants of it in them. Those original sounds [*Urtone*] have gradually disappeared from the *Ursprache* as they were replaced by signs which better corresponded to the civilized spirit of the people. ["On the Linguistic Capacity" 144; *Sämmtliche Werke* 8: 340]

25. Teutons, for Fichte, are inherent leaders, and their genes, as it were, win out; but there is no such thing as a pure Teutonic race anymore, and Fichte has no interest in measuring degrees of purity:

    > [L]ittle importance would be attached to the fact that the Teutonic stock [*die germanische Abstammung*] has intermingled with the former inhabitants of the countries it has conquered; for, after all, the victors and masters of the new people [*Volk*] that arose from this intermingling were none but Teutons. Moreover, in the mother-country [*im Mutterland*] there was an intermingling with Slavs similar to what took place abroad with Gauls, Cantabrians, etc., and perhaps of no less extent; so that it would not be easy at the present day to demonstrate a greater purity of descent [*Abstammung*] than the others. [*60–61/54–55*]

26. For a fine study of Fichte's concern for linguistic purity, see Martyn, who, drawing on modern studies of linguistic borrowing, shows that "the 'domestic' language is diverse—foreign— from the start" (309) by showing that practically no sentence in the *Addresses,* despite Fichte's deliberately "Germanic," Lutheran style, fails to contain hidden borrowings. Even a word

like *Bildung*, as Martyn notes, "owes its formation to a double foreign influence. Coined as a translation of *imaginatio* to mean 'idea' or 'conception,' it later acquired the pedagogical sense that it has in the word *Bildungsroman* under the influence of the English *formation*, for it was first used with that meaning..." (306). A hint of the gravity—or, if one wishes, the absurdity—of Fichte's predicament may be had from the fact that his only word for Teutons is *Germanen*, and that his title and topic hang on the equally Latinate *Nation* (*natio:* the birth of a child, people, nation).

27.   Fichte's writings are consistent in their Protestant emphasis on choice: "What sort of philosophy one chooses depends . . . on what sort of person one is," as the famous line from the First Introduction to the *Wissenschaftslehre* has it. "For a philosophical system is not a dead piece of furniture that we can reject or accept as we wish; it is rather a thing animated by the soul of the person who holds it. A person indolent by nature or dulled and distorted by mental servitude, learned luxury, and vanity will never raise himself to the level of idealism" (Fichte, *Science* 16; *Sämmtliche Werke* 1: 434).

28.   Readers of the *Wissenschaftslehre* will recall the fundamental role of the imagination (*Einbildungskraft*) in generating the possibility of phenomenal experience: see *Science* 188 (*Sämmtliche Werke* 1: 208) and 194 (1: 216–17), where Fichte proposes that the imagination's wavering (*Schweben*) between irreconcilables "extends the condition of the self therein to a moment of *time*." Fichte's reworking of Kant's schematizing imagination ultimately results in the claim that "all reality—for us being understood, as it cannot be otherwise understood in a system of transcendental philosophy—is brought forth solely by the imagination" (202; 1: 227).

29.   A vivid picture (and parody) of this sort of educational scheme may be had in Goethe's descriptions of the Pedagogical Province in *Wilhelm Meisters Wanderjahre* (book 2, chs. 1, 2, 8).

30.   "Reading and writing can be of no use in the purely national education, so long as this education continues. But it can, indeed, be very harmful; because, as it has hitherto so often done, it may easily lead the pupil astray from direct perception to mere signs . . ." (152/162).

31.   Coleridge's editor John Colmer notes that "writers in many fields seized on [the phrase *nisus formativus*], which means 'formative urge, impulse, or force,' with its German equivalent, *Bildungstrieb* . . ." (48n1).

32.   Hence Fichte's determination to publish each address as soon as it was delivered, despite the battles he consequently had to fight with the government censor.

33.   "In this way," as Anderson comments, "we can observe how the national dead and the national unborn, in their uncountable billions, mirror each other, and provide the best sureties of the ineradicable Goodness of the nation" (*S* 364).

Works Cited

Alarcón, Norma, Caren Kaplan, and Minoo Moallem. "Introduction: Between Woman and Nation." Kaplan, Alarcón, and Moallem 1–16.

Anderson, Benedict. *Imagined Communities: Reflections on the Origin and Spread of Nationalism.* 1983. Rev. ed. New York: Verso, 1991.

———. Introduction. Balakrishnan, *Mapping the Nation* 1–16.

———. *The Spectre of Comparisons: Nationalism, Southeast Asia, and the World.* New York: Verso, 1998.

Ankersmit, F. R. *Aesthetic Politics: Political Philosophy beyond Fact and Value.* Stanford: Stanford UP, 1996.

Arnold, Matthew. *Culture and Anarchy. Culture and Anarchy and Other Writings.* Ed. Stefan Collini. Cambridge: Cambridge UP, 1993. 55–187.

Balakrishnan, Gopal, ed. *Mapping the Nation.* London: Verso, 1996.

———. "Mapping the Nation." Balakrishnan, *Mapping the Nation* 198–213.

Balibar, Etienne. "Fichte and the Internal Border: On Addresses to the German Nation." *Masses, Classes, Ideas: Studies on Politics and Philosophy before and after Marx.* Trans. James Swenson. New York: Routledge, 1994. 61–84.

———. "The Nation Form: History and Ideology." Balibar and Wallerstein 86–106.

————, and Immanuel Wallerstein. *Race, Nation, Class: Ambiguous Identities*. Trans. Chris Turner. London: Verso, 1991.

Behler, Ernst. *German Literary Theory*. Cambridge: Cambridge UP, 1996.

Benjamin, Walter. "On Some Motifs in Baudelaire." *Illuminations:Essays and Reflections*. Ed. Hannah Arendt. Trans. Harry Zohn. New York: Schocken Books, 1968. 155–200.

Bennington, Geoffrey. "Postal Politics and the Institution of the Nation." Bhabha, *Nation and Narration* 121–37.

Bhabha, Homi. "DissemiNation: Time Narrative, and the Margins of the Modern Nation." Bhabha, *Nation and Narration* 291–322.

————, ed. *Nation and Narration*. London: Routledge, 1990.

Billig, Michael. *Banal Nationalism*. London: Sage, 1995.

Breuilly, John. *Nationalism and the State*. 2nd ed. Chicago: U of Chicago Press, 1994.

Chatterjee, Partha. *The Nation and Its Fragments: Colonial and Postcolonial Histories*. Princeton: Princeton UP, 1993.

Cheah, Pheng, and Bruce Robbins, eds. *Cosmopolitics: Thinking and Feeling beyond the Nation*. Minneapolis: U of Minnesota Press, 1998.

Cocking, J. M. *Imagination: A Study in the History of Ideas*. Ed. Penelope Murray. London: Routledge, 1991.

Coleridge, Samuel Taylor. *On the Constitution of Church and State*. Ed John Colmer. *The Collected Works of Samuel Taylor Coleridge*. Ed. Kathleen Coburn. Princeton: Princeton UP, 1976. Vol. 10.

De Man, Paul. "Sign and Symbol in Hegel's Aesthetics." *Aesthetic Ideology*. Ed. Andrzej Warminski. Minneapolis: U of Minnesota Press, 1996. 91–104.

Derrida, Jacques. *Limited Inc*. Ed. Gerald Graff. Evanston: Northwestern UP, 1988.

————. *Specters of Marx: The State of the Debt, the Work of Mourning, and the New International*. Trans. Peggy Kamuf. New York: Routledge, 1994.

Engell, James. *The Creative Imagination: Enlightenment to Romanticism*. Cambridge: Harvard UP, 1981.

Fichte, Johann Gottlieb. *Addresses to the German Nation*. Trans. R. F. Jones and G. H. Turnbull. London: Open Court, 1922. Trans. of *Reden an die deutsche Nation*. Hamburg: Felix Meiner, 1955.

————. *Johann Gottlieb Fichtes sämmtliche Werke*. Ed. I. H. Fichte. 8 vols. Berlin: Veit, 1845–46.

————. "On the Linguistic Capacity and the Origin of Language." Surber 117–45.

————. *Science of Knowledge* [Wissenschaftlehre], *with the First and Second Introductions*. Ed. and trans. Peter Heath and John Lachs. Cambridge: Cambridge UP, 1982.

Gellner, Ernest. *Nations and Nationalism*. Ithaca: Cornell UP, 1983.

Hegel, G. W. F. *Enzyklopädie der philosophischen Wissenschaften, III*. Vol. 10 of *Werke*. Ed. Eva Moldenhauer and Karl Markus Michel. Frankfurt am Main: Suhrkamp, 1986.

Kaplan, Caren, Norma Alarcón, and Minoo Moallem, eds. *Between Woman and Nation: Nationalisms, Transnational Feminisms, and the State*. Durham: Duke UP, 1999.

Kittler, Friedrich. *Discourse Networks: 1800/1900*. Trans. Michael Metteer, with Chris Cullens. Stanford: Stanford UP, 1990.

Lacoue-Labarthe, Philippe. *Heidegger, Art, and Politics: The Fiction of the Political*. Trans. Chris Turner. Oxford: Blackwell, 1990.

Léon, Xavier. *Fichte et son temps, II: Fichte à Berlin (1799–1813), deuxième partie: La lutte pour l'affranchissement national (1806–1813)*. Paris: Armand Colin, 1959.

Lloyd, David. "Nationalisms against the State." Lowe and Lloyd 173–97.

————, and Paul Thomas. *Culture and the State*. New York: Routledge, 1997.

Loraux, Nicole. *Les mères en deuil*. Paris: Seuil, 1990.

Lowe, Lisa, and David Lloyd, eds. *The Politics of Culture in the Shadow of Capital*. Durham: Duke UP, 1997.

Marder, Elissa. "Trauma, Addiction, and Temporal Bulimia in Madame Bovary." *diacritics* 27.3 (1997): 49–64.

Martyn, David. "Borrowed Fatherland: Nationalism and Language Purism in Fichte's *Addresses to the German Nation*." *Germanic Review* 72.4 (1997): 303–15.

Moretti, Franco. *Atlas of the European Novel, 1800–1900*. London: Verso, 1998.

Pyle, Forest. *The Ideology of the Imagination: Subject and Society in the Discourse of Romanticism*. Stanford: Stanford UP, 1995.

Redfield, Marc. *Phantom Formations: Aesthetic Ideology and the Bildungsroman.* Ithaca: Cornell UP, 1996.

Renan, Ernest. "What Is a Nation?" Trans. Martin Thom. Bhabha, *Nation and Narration* 8–22.

Schiller, Friedrich. *On the Aesthetic Education of Man, in a Series of Letters.* Bilingual ed. Ed. and trans. Elizabeth M. Wilkinson and L. A. Willoughby. Oxford: Clarendon, 1967.

Scott, Ridley, dir. *Blade Runner.* Ladd, 1982.

Surber, Jere Paul. *Language and German Idealism: Fichte's Linguistic Philosophy.* Atlantic Highlands, NJ: Humanities, 1996.

Weber, Samuel. *Mass Mediauras: Form, Technics, Media.* Stanford: Stanford UP, 1996.

CHAPTER 6

Be–Longing and Bi–Lingual States

DORIS SOMMER

"How sad that people don't keep commitments any more. Even marriages last only about five years."

"Yes, but long-distance marriages can stretch those five years out over weekends and vacations to make relationships last a lifetime."

Benedict Anderson's provocative new book, *The Spectre of Comparisons: Nationalism, Southeast Asia and the World,* raises questions about political relationships over time and over space. Like precarious modern marriages and their corollary "political" kinships (in-laws in Spanish are one's *familia política),* national sentiment today strains with the movements of transnational communities from home to distant enclaves. Over time, ties can unravel as modern subjects choose, or not, to identify with adopted political relatives. Is one's country the bastion of a people reluctant to receive more immigrants? Is it the sender of surplus people who will, in turn, send money home? (Heads of state in El Salvador, Guatemala, and Mexico typically object to United States restrictions on immigration.) Or is it the harbor for many peoples? Does belonging even to a recently invented country anchor an existential need, a *be-longing,* because being a "man"—as Hannah Arendt still called the subject of politics—means striving for recognition among equals? Or, do many citizens today feel like resident aliens (to themselves or to others), belonging rather to ethnic minorities and perhaps—long-distance—to other nations of origin or of choice? Anderson is right to worry about precarious belongings and optional obligations.

In the end though, he finds solace from the threats of egotism and de-spair, and from the social decomposition of too much movement (what Arjun Appadurai calls "modernity at large") in the resilient promise of the "goodness of nations." Confidence in the extrapersonal goals and pride in national belonging appears, almost miraculously, in the last of seventeen chapters. Each of these brilliant and erudite essays will reconfirm our ad-miration for Anderson. My own personal debt includes his extraordinary generosity and the good counsel that encourages me to follow him, some-times with a swerve, as will be evident when my appreciation for be-longing plays bi-lingual games.

The opening pages of *The Spectre of Comparisons* theorize a paradox in the postcolonial condition: the inescapable folly of comparing one's nation to another, or to a mother country. Concepts like nation or culture, after all, take on meaning in their particular contexts and by contrast with others. The core chapters chronicle aborted beginnings and abusive conflations of the nation and the state. But hope has the last word, thanks to three guarantees of national imaginings: the promising and innocent unborn generations; the nation's dead (war heroes); and the living who are ever willing to give the nation another chance, and yet another. Feelings of pride and shame come together in the end, because citizens invest, often against the evidence, in "the goodness of nations" (364). This resilience shows up right after the trouble in chapter sixteen, where shame was the connection between nation and narrator in Mario Vargas Llosa's 1987 novel about Peru. Unfounded but unrelenting, Anderson's hope follows on shame rather abruptly and suggests that shame itself is a sign of our care for our countries.[1] The narrator of *El hablador* had tried to escape from his ill-fated country, his "malhadado país," only to be haunted by it.

My question is whether Anderson's coda to this Peruvian novel is inspired by the same indomitable demon of comparisons that he has been exposing throughout the essays. José Rizal had named the meddling devil to blame it for distracting the Filipino from the lovely garden he saw in Manila, assail-ing him with memories of a European original or model (2). This double vision raises a specter of possible inauthenticity; it undermines meaning as models slip from centers to peripheries. Local concepts lose their partic-ularities in global vocabularies. Anderson calls the movement a "logic of seriality." I prefer to call it *trans-latio*, literally a carrying from one place to another. "Nation" suffers a sea change, as do words like "shame" and "hope" whose meanings and affect get lost on the way. Translation, in fact, is the particular name for loss in Vargas Llosa's guilt-ridden *El hablador*. "Those apostolic linguists of yours are the worst of all," the half-Jewish anthropol-ogist complains just before going native. "They work their way into the tribes to destroy them from within. . . . The others steal their vital space and exploit them or push them farther into the interior. At worst, they kill them physically. Your linguists are more refined. They want to kill them in another way. Translating the Bible into Machiguenga! How about that!" (*S* 95–96; *H* 93–96; see also *S* 162–63; *H* 157). Words work best by *analogy,* that is by the kind of comparison that displays bad fits and remainders alongside the commonality. For example: the Manila garden is to the European garden what Peru is to, say, France; or the Machiguenga tribe is to Peru, let's say, what the Jews were to Poland, a dispensable part. Analogy is the figure that describes genre for Wittgenstein: it is not the particular rules that govern a game, but the similarity of rule-making systems that establishes gaming or identifies an activity. And different rule-bound activities, gaming and drawing, are themselves linked by analogy: "The kinship [of games] is that of two pictures, one of which consists of colour patches with vague contours, and the other of patches similarly shaped and distributed, but with clear contours. The kinship is just as undeniable as the difference" (Wittgenstein, *PI* #76). It is the difference that goes without saying.

For Vargas Llosa's namesake narrator, on my reading, the goodness of nations doesn't translate into Peruvian. The novel is tragic in the classic sense of hopelessly conflicted. Shame is overdetermined and unremitting; it doesn't pause for hope or languish in forgetfulness. Shame comes, and stays, at the impasse between equally hateful and compelling options: one is leaving Peru behind; the other is feeling it thrust in your face. There is no reprieve from or for Peru, no infinitely other chances to make good on the nation. So I take Anderson's sound advice to stay alert for the demon of comparisons and therefore demur at Anderson's own conclusions about this novel (as they already argue with those of my earlier essay "About Face"). Perhaps this specific engagement can suggest general questions (about community and long-distance, about languages and multiple belongings).

The very first sentence of *El hablador* is a stop and start, a double take. Facing the narrator is precisely the thing he had escaped. "I came to Firenze to forget Peru and the Peruvians for a while, and behold, the damned country forced itself upon me this morning in the most unexpected way . . . a window display *stopped me short* [me paró en seco]: bows, arrows, a carved oar, a pot with a geometric design, a mannequin bundled into a wild cotton cushma" (*S*3; *H*7). The promise of recognition grips the narrator, but leads nowhere except in circles around the same sticking point. Peru claims his attention, like a trap, or an obstacle to be wished away. The grip is maddening, because unwanted otherness makes one kind of aggression or another practically inevitable: either denial of oneself to live for (*para*) the other; or elimination of others by translating them into oneself. As a novelist, Vargas Llosa performs both kinds of removal: one narrator removes himself to the jungle and shuns translators; the other wishes the jungle away, along with the whole tangled country. But as a politician, Vargas Llosa has been single-minded about transforming Indians into Creoles: "It is tragic to destroy what is still living, still a driving cultural possibility, but I am afraid we shall have to make a choice.... [W]here there is such an economic and social gap, modernization is possible only with the sacrifice of the Indian cultures" (37).

"We" have to make a choice for (*por*) them. This monological impulse has always been the motor of Spanish American *Creolization.* The word has been analogized in other parts of the world where it evidently realizes more of its ideal meaning as cultural hybrid. In Indonesia, Anderson tells us, Creole really does refer to a modern bureaucratic language invented from Dutch and local languages to administer a heterogeneous colony. Otherwise, what could today's credo "One country. One People. One language" possibly mean in an archipelago of 13,000 islands? The tenuous union may now have to acknowledge stubborn differences of ethnicity, religion, and language, starting with East Timor, where pre-Dutch Portuguese interrupts Indonesian ambitions. "*Unidades,*" reads the tongue-in-cheek graffito on the national monument there to the national credo (see Mydans). French- or Dutch-based Caribbean languages, *créole* and *papiamento,* also strain away from the mother-tongues (see, for example, Bernabé et al.; Dash). But in Spanish and Portuguese America, by definition, ready-made bureaucratic languages were exported wholesale for the Conquest. Antonio de Nebrija's Spanish grammar of 1492 made a selling point of the connection between a stable mother language and an expanding empire. Linguistic purity became a sign of religious and cultural legitimacy, once Moors and Jews no longer deformed the language. "Speak Christian" is still a way to demand clarity in Spain, where it can be heard as an objection to regional languages, and in Spanish America, where Creolization can amount to Hispanization, or cultural "redemption." Even a word like *mestizaje* acknowledges more racial than cultural mixing. Fernando Ortiz invented the term "transculturation" to give an account of the cultural violence in the forging of an admirable Cuban culture by European settlers and their African slaves. But the asymmetrical mix cost Europeans little more than their rhythmic and religious simplicity; Africans lost lives, histories, secular languages.[2] This simple and sober observation may remind us that Creole originally meant "Black born in his master's house"; that is, violently translated from Africa to the Americas. When peninsular Spaniards used the word for whites born in the New World, it was to disdain them (see Lavallé, "Recherches" and "La aparición"). However whites, mulattos, or mestizos resignify the word to describe themselves or others, they all speak the same imported (and imposed) language.

Benedict Anderson objects to the unethical "ventriloquism" of Spanish for Machiguenga in *El hablador* (359). Objection is surely in order, though "translation" may be a better word than "ventriloquism" for violent voice-replacement. The intolerable ventriloquist is Vargas Llosa himself, as Anderson made clear to me, not the fictional Mascarita. The talker lends his voice to others; but the Creole statesman translates others away. (Theirs is a grammatical difference between *para* others and *por* others.) Perhaps Anderson's objections to the analogy between Jew and Indian are overstated; he points out that the Peruvian Jew is in no danger of extinction, since Israel is a vocal and powerful modern country. And Mascarita is only half-Jewish; he is half-*criollo* on his mother's side [358]. The novel, of course, insists on the connection, by making Jewishness the leitmotiv of misfits in Peru. When the narrator speculates that Mascarita's blotchy two-tone face had isolated and allied him to the excluded tribes of the jungle, his friend offers a better theory: "Don Salomón Zuratas, being sharper than I was, had suggested a Jewish interpretation. 'That I'm identifying the Amazonian Indians with the Jewish people, always a minority and always persecuted for their religion and their mores that are different from those of the rest of society.... Okay.... Suddenly being half Jewish and half monster has made me more sensitive to the fate of the jungle tribes than someone as appallingly normal as you [*S*28–29; *H* 30].'" Jews, he suggests, are less normal. Salomón's experience of genocidal World War II, transmitted to his son, makes a lasting and eerie connection with the Indians. The historical connections are analogical, to be sure, but the differences highlight a shared effect. In this "catastrophic age," Cathy Caruth writes, trauma has become an almost banal catch-all description for a range of disorders, both personal and collective. But in its historical and collective meaning (in extermination campaigns, racial persecutions, chattel-slavery), the trauma suffered by different peoples can be the "catch-all" that holds a promise of mutual recognitions [Caruth 10].[3]

I once asked Vargas Llosa about this pairing of Jews and jungle people. Almost an idle question about the obvious, it was meant to go elsewhere, perhaps into the pairing structure of the novel, where chapters of fictional autobiography alternate with native narratives. But the answer I got was about polar extremes. Primitive Indians and prosperous cosmopolitan Jews were at opposite ends of the country's population, he explained. And the novel was an effort to span Peru through its ill-fitting extremities.[4] I was surprised, given the intimacies the novel performs. And, reluctant to pursue the familiar line that cordons off Jews from national constructions, I let the conversation hobble onto other issues. Is it a similar line that leads Anderson to contrast thriving Jews with precarious Peruvians?

The differences between these nomads are not expendable, of course, nor are Anderson's concerns. I share them, in fact, throughout a series of essays called *Proceed with Caution* (1999). They ask why literary interpretation is deaf to tropes of social and historical difference. Our general but limited habits of reader-response flatten the asymmetries between reader and text by inviting us to be intimates, coauthors and conspirators, with books (and with people). Perhaps readers are targets, especially of "minority" writing that "slaps and embraces, slaps and embraces," as Toni Morrison says, to seduce us and to keep us at a distance. A rhetoric of particularism, if we hear it, might caution against overcoming distances and remainders. But circumspection does not always demand silence, as critics of cultural relativism know. And objections to ventriloquism might suggest that speech should be "authentic," perhaps that a particular minority speak only for itself. This is, ironically, the very demand made by the (unfissured) ethnic essentialists whom Anderson wisely worries about. In any case, ventriloquism, along with the "inspired pastiche" that Anderson uncovers in the novel (355) are, after all, the mechanisms of fiction. No wonder some thinkers, from Plato to Austin and Foucault, object to its infelicitous lies. Bakhtin, however, found them most useful, ethically and politically. A good ventriloquist can speak for (*para*) conflicting constituents, with the sacred particularity of each incommensurable voice. Indians haunt Vargas Llosa's fiction; even dead Indians.

But the politician speaks for (*por*) them, intolerant of his divided country. A good part of Peru remains stubbornly native, as it did during the wars of Independence when Indians hardly responded to foreign agitators like San Martín, who dubbed them "Peruvians." But they had supported Tupaq Amaru II's rebellion of 1780 and 1781, which delayed Creoles from seeking independence and arming the natives. On the other side of the division, the country contemplates itself through the specter of *Bovarysme* (Vargas Llosa's Flaubertian version of the ironic inauthenticity or double consciousness that Rizal blamed on *el demonio de las comparaciones*). *El hablador* stages the standoff: Mascarita as *the talker* for "deep Peru," against the modernizing narrator, who is capable of feeling but too practical to be moved. Though Anderson notices the conflict, he concludes—as Bakhtin's contemporaries concluded with Dostoevsky—that it adds up to one authorial stance: "Mascarita is the author's alibi in the court of cultural claims" (359). (Bakhtin, of course, was complaining that the calculation was too simple, that it reduced contradiction to one authorial ideology instead of noticing that conflicts survive in novels.) What good can come of this murderous conflict? It won't admit a multicultural solution, only a Creolization that would finish off conquered peoples.

What is the good? This is the fundamental question of politics that Anderson raises. But he never asks it directly. National unity is apparently better than fragmentation and alienation. The corollary is dismay at ethnic essentialism or identitarian politics, which counts marked heads, meddles long-distance in "home" countries, and unravels civic ties. But the difference between political unity and group identity is another difficulty for translation. Are civic ties the same as cultural ties? Does the imagined political community translate into a cultural or linguistic community? Or do they link up by analogy, showing as much difference as kinship? (Will Kymlicka insists on the remainder in his defense of liberalism as a vehicle for multiculturalism.) Ideally, nationalism should include all subjects of a territory and dissolve racial or cultural exclusiveness, not mask it with modern words like ethnicity or group rights. This is also Vargas Llosa's political ideal. Inclusion, at all cost, whether Indians like it or not. Does this mean that cultural particularists are behind the times when they resist full translation? Are they out of place too, with their demands for political universality? (See Krauss.)

The questions come up both in countries accustomed to cultural conflicts and in traditionally more homogeneous states. Remorseless capital, Anderson points out, is dissolving even those societies into host countries that hardly recognize themselves, as "foreign" populations migrate in global circuits of goods, people, information. Belonging both here and there can be treacherous, even treasonous. Pollard's spying for Israel can be pardoned by some American Jews. Hindu extremists abroad fund anti-Muslim violence in India. Nevertheless, as Anderson adds, some good can also come from doubling and distancing. His example of Filipinos both at home and abroad who conspired to depose Marcos (74) shows that, sometimes, interference can be a good thing. I know it can. A recent *New York Times* article reported on Algerian dissidents who flourish in France; they speak freely and prepare for a comeback [see Riding]. Like them, so many Latin American intellectuals have agitated for their own countries from nearby and far-flung nations. Ethnic identifications are most dangerous when they identify with a state, not when they hobble national coherence. Anderson calls it "menacing nationalism," when it marries the state (26). The slippery difference between the "nation" and the "state" is apparently at work in Anderson's book, available to the trickster demon of comparisons. It is the blind spot from which we might reconsider, and even renew, our love of country, if we could disentangle the terms. Lyotard had also worried about the muddled difference between biological nation (from natality) and artificial *res-publica*. Democracy itself is a contradiction, he fretted, since *demos* is a particular people or "nation," and the political system assumes the neutrality of birth (Lyotard 139; Declaration of 1789).

But Hans Kohn didn't worry, in *American Nationalism* (1956). Without shame, he loved his new country as a state governed by law. Kohn's title is no oxymoronic confusion between birthright and civic rights, because, unlike Europe, America is where "nationalism" is not based on birth—on "pedigree," as he says—but on a mutually binding contract (a secular covenant). Hannah Arendt was another German-Jewish refugee who was at home here and theorized her preference for contract over sentiment as the choice of negotiated democracy over totalitarian passion (see Arendt, *On Revolution*). Differences of birth and creed became irrelevant in America, because civic ties were just that, not ties of blood or soil.

Is it possible that the differences of birth and creed (even of language, taste, cultural practices) are precisely what make contract necessary and therefore what mother its invention? Is the culturally fissured society practically obliged to resort to a neutral public sphere? I like to think so, for several reasons. One reason is that cultural fissures are a reality today; they mark our increasingly complicated countries. Even in the nineteenth century, José Rizal captured the complexity in bilingual games, meant to frustrate the Spanish monolinguals who wouldn't get the Tagalog jokes (Anderson 234, 241). We certainly cannot wish those games away, without risking the sort of stagnant shame and irrepressible violence that haunt Mario Vargas Llosa's novel. Another reason to have patience with the fissures is their promise of pleasure as the language games play in between codes.

***

"*No bueno,*" said the doctor grimly, as he walked in with Barbarita's X-rays. He told Mima, "Ask her if she had TB."

Mima turned to Barbarita. "He says if you have a television?"

"Tell him yes, but in Havana. Not in Miami. But my daughter has a television here."

Mima told the doctor, "She says she had a TV in Cuba, not in Miami. But her daughter has TV here."

"In that case we need to test her daughter for TB too."

Mima translated, "He says he needs to test your daughter's television to make sure it works, otherwise you cannot get your green card."

"Why the television?" asked a puzzled Barbarita with the X-rays.

"How many times did I tell you you needed to buy one? Don't you know, Barbarita? This is America."

—Roberto G. Fernández, "Wrong Channel"

"Ask the defendant if he stole a horse."

"The judge wants to know if you stole a horse."

"*I stole a horse?*"

"The defendant says he stole a horse."

"Ask him if he needed a horse."

"The judge wants to know if you needed a horse."
"*I needed a horse?*"
"The defendant says he needed a horse."
"Ask him why he needed it."
"The judge wants to know why you needed a horse."
"*Me? A horse? Oyf kapures* [to sacrifice, for nothing, I didn't need it at all] *I needed it.*"
"He says he needed the horse for ritual purposes."
  —Jewish-American joke

These jokes work through English, but not entirely in it. They tease and stretch the language toward borders with other codes and cultures in ways that expand the horizons of art—and that could develop those of criticism—beyond the narrowness of a single tradition. What follows is a series of early explorations toward a book in progress on bilingual arts. Neither well coordinated nor developed, I admit, these sections do begin to pose the "bilingual question" to fields that have somehow remained indifferent to it. Politics, aesthetics, psychoanalysis, humor, and the philosophy of language are places to start.

Political philosophy seems more alert than the other discourses. It has already gotten the joke—about official codes that can't hear evidence—and engages in spirited debates about the effects of immigration on liberal, constitutional reasoning. One debate concerns the status of dual nationality. Ten American countries now recognize and even encourage it, along with the generous remittances sent by U.S.-based nationals. But the United States remains suspicious of disloyalty, in case of war, or economic competitions. Is be-longing to two like bigamy?[5] What is the good, and how is it to be achieved? Can rights and obligations refer to more than one, even conflicting contexts? Is politics the sphere for representation or self-interest? Of group rights? National mission? Ethnic pride? Even when all profess respect for human beings as both the ground and the goal of political behavior, political theorists dissent over appropriate techniques, the contours of a (national or international) public sphere, the legitimate (universal or particular) language of political speech acts.

But aesthetics stays almost deaf to the provocations, decidedly deaf, maybe as a reaction to allegedly too much politics and too much critical theory in the past thirty years of literary studies. In 1994, the Association of Literary Scholars and Critics was founded because of "a deep and widespread concern about developments within the humanities that threatened to inhibit the freedom of the literary imagination. What was at stake for the founding members was the breadth and expanse of literature itself, whose power to communicate to the human mind in its multifarious dimensions had been curtailed by a narrowing, often overtly political, within the discipline."[6]

Reacting to this reaction, scholars who defend the political value of literature are loath to favor the kind of aesthetics that amounts to a backlash against their own work. José Limón, for example, frames his *Mexican Ballads, Chicano Poems: History and Influence in Mexican-American Social Poetry* (1992) with respectful debts to Harold Bloom, but objects to his refusal of political responsibility. Bloom responded, deaf to Limón's debts and unwilling to be upstaged. He edited a collection of critical essays, *Hispanic-American Writers* (1998), perhaps only to exclude Limón and to chastise him. In the petulant page and a half that serves as an introduction, Bloom dismisses both the Chicano critic and his favorite subject: "Having acknowledged that I am Limón's devil to Paredes' angel, I shall not venture to defend myself, but instead shall question both. . . . The English-language ballads that Limón quotes are very sincere but, as Oscar Wilde observed, all bad poetry is sincere. I refrain from quoting any excerpts or texts praised by Limón, because they cannot bear quotation. . . . Ideology at best can produce period-pieces, not poems" (2). Not all the engagements are this pitched or personal, I'm glad to note. Increasingly, students of "minority" literatures are exploring its rhetorical features, and "aesthetes" are acknowledging room for rapprochement. Robert Alter, for example, was dismayed "by rumors and suspicions that we represent some sort of right-wing conspiracy" (2); and his successor as ALSC president insists that "literary scholars and critics know perfectly well that no work of art is isolated from its time and place" (Cook 3).

Indifference to aesthetics is a hard principle to defend for literary critics. It is self-dismissive. What is literature, after all, but beautiful writing, or what the Russian formalists described as having the effect of strangeness that renews the world? When historian Paul Veyne pressed himself (after reading Foucault) to distinguish between novels (which cut and paste subjectively selected data, and then speculate on relations of cause and effect) and historical narratives (which do the same), the only—tongue-in-cheek but significant—difference, he concluded, is that novels are interesting, pleasing (18). And part of their pleasure-producing principle is the many-voiced counterpoint that challenges readers to assume different points of view that survive an author's preference for one or another.

Surely political projects will gain ground from aesthetics, if it can be expanded in the direction of those resilient voices. One immediate gain from retooling our talk about the beautiful is the kind of professional agenda that can engage even conservative counterparts, who can be moved to develop their reading lists and their appreciation for art. Another corollary gain is the opportunity, or obligation, to generate names and descriptions for a broad range of rhetorical figures and language games that stretch and push a host language out of its standard, sometimes tired, shape. And the aesthetic reaction to politics would be guilty of bad faith, if it remained deaf to these formal developments, which follow from immigration. They have a venerable tradition.

"Idiota" was what the Venerable Bede called the single-language speaker in ninth-century England. Throughout medieval Europe, macaronic poetry thrived, alongside the diglossia of entire populations who knew enough church Latin to play it off in counterpoint to the vernacular language (see Ziolkowski). But the equivalence between linguistic narrowness and intellectual simplicity was apparently forgotten during Europe's long and often brutal efforts to consolidate modern cultures. The standard Spanish version of that history features Spain as the first truly modern country, to its own eventual sorrow. Spain consolidated reluctant regions into an authoritarian state, its church into an exclusive monopoly on religion, and its centralizing language into a weapon against dissidence (see Dussel). It learned its lesson, during the long period of reflection from the Armada's failure against Elizabeth I to Franco's lamentable success at consolidation. Today, Spain's democratic constitution of 1978 (developed from the Republican model of the 1930s) defends the cultural rights (including language rights) of autonomous regions. It legitimates the kinds of difference that had flourished before 1492. Today, too, other countries experiment with constitutional safeguards for cultural rights (see Prieto). Their reasoning has apparently more to do with demands for recognition than with the possible contributions of cultural difference to democratic life; it has more to do with acknowledging regional or at least local differences that refused to disappear in the rush of modernization than with efforts to accommodate immigrant cultures as participants in host countries.

Can there be stronger arguments for embracing difference, beyond "a politics of recognition" and besides the anxiety about the ways that immigrant cultures might corrupt the norms and procedures of constitutional democracies? Maybe cultural criticism can contribute something here, if it learns a lesson from political philosophy. One of liberalism's challenges, after all, is to turn the cultural dread of difference into a political taste for it.

1. Liberalism Has a Point

The principle of liberalism is quite simple: to defend the rights and freedom of an individual. Unlike corporatist philosophies, which favor group interests over those of their members, liberalism settles competing claims in favor of the personal subject. This bias against group demands discourages some defenders of group rights from pursuing liberal doctrines. The communitarian alternative adjusts the liberal bias in favor of disadvantaged groups (labeled by race, ethnicity, gender, sexuality, religion, language, physical disability).

Group rights to resources and representation, according to Charles Taylor, Michael Walzer, Michael Sandel, and others, cannot prosper in debates that treat the individual as autonomous from group identifications.[7]

But the principle has considerable flex capacity, say defenders of a liberal tradition that can evolve to accommodate multicultural societies. Yes, liberalism favors individual rights, but an individual is neither the product nor the subject of a cultural vacuum, say Will Kymlicka and Jürgen Habermas. And respect for the person implies respect and recognition for his or her culture, race, language, and so on. There is no philosophical reason to distinguish, as Taylor does, between Liberalism 1 (the narrow, personal variety) and Liberalism 2 (the expanded variety that includes "cultural rights" as a good, to be promoted by politics), because one requires the other in logical and organic ways. The individual requires the group as an anchor of identity, a source of taste and values; and the group requires the free and creative participation of the individual, if it is to thrive in a liberal, constitutional state.

Like the ample concept of modernity in Habermas's hands, liberalism can make room for the broadest interpretations. Someone else might have been tempted to deconstruct the the unstable opposition between Liberalism 1 and communitarianism. He might have shown that the terms need one another, that they imply and depend on one another in their very struggle for legitimacy. But Habermas doesn't treat the terms as equally deluded partners; he favors one over the other, because "liberal" includes both the restricted definition of "respect for the individual" and the critiques that will stretch that definition: "individuals identify through collectivities."

Multiculturalism, Habermas writes in response to Taylor, "does not require special justification or an alternative principle. For from a normative point of view, the integrity of the individual legal person cannot be guaranteed without protecting the intersubjectively shared experiences and life contexts in which the person has been socialized and has formed his or her identity. . . . Hence the individual remains the bearer of "rights to cultural membership," in Will Kymlicka's phrase. But as the dialectic of legal and actual equality plays itself out, this gives rise to extensive guarantees of status, rights to self-administration, infrastructural benefits, subsidies, and so on . . ." (129). "A democratic constitutional state that is serious about uncoupling these two levels of integration can require of immigrants only the political socialization. . . . This enables it to preserve the identity of the political community, which nothing, including immigration, can be permitted to encroach upon, since that identity is founded on the constitutional principles anchored in the political culture and not on the basic ethical orientations of the cultural form of life predominant in that country" (139; see also Cornell and Bratton).

What features of national life safeguard the difference between political institutions and a majoritarian culture? What heuristic device will keep them from overlapping and encroaching on one another? An analogy with the distinction between church and state comes to mind. One way to keep them separate is to allow more than one church in a given state. Different religions are incommensurable with one another, which makes unity unlikely and helps to avoid a sloppy equation between religion and politics. The overload, the excess, the presence of plural creeds, demonstrates that religion operates at a level different from politics. It has no one coordinating structure for the country, but rather shows incompatibilities among the options. Religion therefore leaves the work of coordination to the public sphere; it makes that work necessary by cultivating incommensurable differences. To be sure, the public sphere requires a lingua franca, as bilinguals know. Bilingualism is no bastion against learning English (or French, or German, or Spanish; immigrant parents notoriously favor the lingua franca); it obviously describes a convivencia of codes. With a common language as fellow traveler of particular codes, do the public advantages that come from conflicting creeds also come from overloads (even a cacophony) of language, music, sense of humor, and so on, so that cultural difference looks good for democracy?

It is a challenge that we might seize, like an opportunity. Can we afford to ignore it, either ethically—given the practical redundancy of the term "democratic pluralism"—or pragmatically, given the impractical objections to global migrations, transportation, communication? To the extent that politics, including cultural politics, is still a discourse of the nation, national feelings and assumptions color the debates.

2. To Liberalism's Point, Does Aesthetics Make Counterpoint?

Not yet. Calling attention to this opportunity is the ambition of my essay. Biculturalism hasn't yet stretched our general sense of "the beautiful."[8] The whole question can seem irrelevant for agendas in liberal education, as I said, either because aesthetics seems like an unfriendly arena for groups who demand representation, whether or not their cultural expressions seem beautiful to outsiders, or because political considerations seem inimical to an appreciation of the Beautiful. But multiculturalism could be exciting for aesthetics, invited after centuries of monolingual taste into the banquet of bilingual creativity. It's not that diglossia vanished from literature after the Middle Ages; anyone can name occasional experiments, like Pound's, with the more-than-one. And everyone knows that Russian novels, for example, assumed a knowledge of French. Nor are immigration or mass displacements new phenomena. What is new are the great numbers, the visibility, and the postmodern cultural mood that make multilingual experiments a significant feature of literary art. The creativity is *de facto*. Can we expand our critical tools to render the creativity visible, as legitimate contributions to American art? One net gain will be an expanded toolbox that will refine other readings, too. What is the rhetorical name for a code switch that works like an escape route? What do you call purposeful mistranslations, or the sounds-like associations between words of different languages? How would Wittgenstein have continued his investigations if he had described bilingual games? Are there genres of humor that Freud doesn't dare to address? Does Peirce's third part of logic, "abduction," along with induction and deduction, seem like a necessary addition to the critical vocabulary for reading bilingual texts that poach words from a parallel language and feed them to another (see Peirce)?

Another gain will be ethical, because recognizing art has the virtue of acknowledging the agency of an artist. Bilingual wit has the particular virtue of attesting to the kind of intelligence that invents relationships where there had been none. It is often quite clever, sometimes wise. Art performs the autonomy of admirable personhood; it quite literally becomes a per-sona to be heard and acknowledged. The stories people tell of themselves and of others show the miracle "natality," in Hannah Arendt's defense of the novelty and particularity of each person. Art is the trace of miraculous initiative (see Arendt, *Human Condition* 50–52).

The opportunities for aesthetics to play in counterpoint to liberalism need urgent attention, especially in the US, a country of immigrants. Nations like Germany or France may live in denial of the evidence of internal cultural differences (a quarter of the population of a city like Frankfurt, according to Habermas ("Taylor's 'Politics of Recognition'")); the United States cannot. We saw that at least some political philosophers imply the desirability of difference for democracy. But literary criticism can make the claim bold and compelling, if we take a lead, for example, from Mikhail Bakhtin and his recent disciples (see Yúdice et al.). Charles Taylor has used him already for politics, as a way out of the personalist monologism of liberal theory. Taylor avails himself of Bakhtin's term "dialogism" to describe the formative process of human personalities; for Taylor, an intimate and continuous give-and-take of family and community is the character of human life, "what we have in common with people we love; how some goods become accessible to us only through such common enjoyment" (33).

Literary critics will know that this is a hasty alliance with Bakhtin. It is ironically personal for a foe of liberal abuses.[9] Dialogism describes conflict, not community. It is the radical feature of the modern novel that Bakhtin located first in Dostoevsky and then in all novels worthy of the (insubordinate, nonconformist, tirelessly experimental) name of a form too unpredictable to be a genre (see "Discourse in the Novel"). Dialogism refers to unreconciled points of view and to particular uses of language that distinguish one character from an agonistic other as well as from the author, who may occupy one position among several in the book. Bakhtin objected to his contemporaries who noticed Dostoevsky's multivoiced world but "found no other course than to monologize" it into a new artistic will. "Dostoevsky, like Goethe's Prometheus, creates not voiceless slaves (as does Zeus), but rather *free* people who are capable of standing *beside* their creator, of disagreeing with him, and even of rebelling against him. *The plurality of independent and unmerged voices and consciousnesses and the genuine polyphony of full-valued voices are in fact characteristics of Dostoevsky's novels*" (*Problems of Dostoevsky's Poetics* 6, 4, Bakhtin's emphasis). This description surely seems better *taylored* to liberalism's renewed respect for cultural discontinuities than to communitarian idylls of commonality.

One thing is certain, however capriciously one interprets Bakhtin's critique of monologism. He associated it with monolingualism, which he dreaded with a mix of fear and scorn that motivates several important books. Single languages were narrow and dogmatic by definition, because a language—he often repeated—is an entire culture. And it is impossible to get any perspective on that culture from inside it. Only on the linguistic borders, where Rabelais wrote, are true reason, humor, and wisdom available. "The link of these forms with a multilingual world . . . seems to us extremely important. . . . [I]t is impossible to overcome through abstract thought alone, within the system of a unique language, that deep dogmatism hidden in all the forms of this system. The completely new, self-criticizing, absolutely sober, fearless, and gay life of the image can start only on linguistic borders" (*Rabelais and His World* 472).

Tolerating and tarrying at those borders long enough to notice the narrowness on either side, to laugh at it, and to admire the artistic vehicles invented for straddling differences will not be easy. Pausing at an uncomfortable pass, or anywhere else, including love, isn't easy today, says philosopher Stanley Cavell, for whom modernity amounts to a tragic loss of attention span. Modern advice would be to get beyond the difficulty of bi- or multiculturalism, to choose the common linguistic denominator and divide two languages to get one. This advice to get on with one's life not only sounds analogous to the prescription for mourning as the cure for melancholy; it is part of that prescription, and it will haunt the next section of this essay too: leave the burden of lost relationships behind; free yourselves of ghosts who cannot be revived and who threaten your emotional independence. (The Irish, for example, are notoriously—David Lloyd might say aggressively—melancholy in the face of English prescriptions for mental hygiene.)

The face-off, between the good and the beautiful, is hardly a classical posture, of course. For the classics one was a sign of the other, even if Plato finally feared the insubordination of art, philosophy's first love. The philosopher king would control that inclination and choose the good over the beautiful (see Arendt, *Human Condition* 226). Defenders of aesthetics against politics today may find a friendly harbor in Kant's support of art for art's sake; but a long and strong current of politically inflected interpretation, reaching back to Aristotle through Matthew Arnold and forward to Pierre Bourdieu, puts Kant in the company of those who made a salutary distinction between purpose and artistic pleasure, not describing an indifference of one to the other. In his own words, aesthetic ideas facilitate political and moral reflection because they draw out a "concept's implications and its kinship with other concepts" (183).[10] Beauty is autonomous of goodness. If it were not, tastes and values might appear to be so self-evident as to preempt debate and judgment. Autonomy itself is a link between aesthetics and morality, which demands freedom of choice. Just as each individual is endowed with reason, to pursue the good, each can also strive after the beautiful, in works as unique and individual as the liberal subjects who create them. Now autonomy (of beauty, of a poem, of the poet) is a sign of relationship, sometimes of mutuality, not of apathy or of independence. Liberalism depends on autonomous individuals who can engage through politics; engagement is what constructs the public sphere.[11] And, I hope I am arguing here, liberal politics depends on autonomous practices of art, for two related reasons. These respond to the distinction between a narrow definition of liberalism as based on individual rights (Liberalism 1 for Taylor and Walzer) and a more flexible definition that recognizes individuals as members of particular groups (Liberalism 2 for communitarians, who don't trust the flexibility). The reasons are:

(1) Because art is autonomous, of politics, of other works of art, of critics, and so forth, creating art is a performance of the artist's autonomy. To the definition of the liberal subject as one who has rational agency, I'd like to add the dimension of "artistic" agency, as a sign of the autonomous, creative individual who can make legitimate claims to respect in the public sphere.[12]

And (2) because art, however original, depends on the collective elements of a culture, the work of art is evidence of the artist's dependence on that culture. An interesting complication arises here, in the intersection between the politics of expanded liberalism (according to Kymlicka and Habermas) and the autonomy of art. In politics, particular cultural rights may be permitted as long as they don't contradict the "political culture" of the country. Illiberal fanaticism, by definition, cannot fit. The measure of legitimate particularism is the norm of constitutional public culture, not the other way around: particular cultural norms cannot measure the collective public practices of a country. Nevertheless—and here is my point—their very presence alongside a lingua franca interferes with homegrown illiberal tendencies to collapse public culture into one dominant language of religion, art, and etiquette. This collapse can bring multiculturalism down on feminism, for example, as in Susan Moller Okin's objections to group rights because they allegedly oppress women. Her respondents note that she has mistranslated religion as culture and then mistaken culture as closure, so that abuses look like standard practice. They caution that her secularism is an option for liberalism, not a requirement, and that religions often interpret principles and debate practices. She should take note, they say, that debate is not a Western monopoly; her unicultural biases may miss some chances for liberal procedure. In any case, her very intolerance for multiculturalism promotes the abuses that liberals abhor; it creates a hostile environment in which minority groups close ranks and table reforms.

Difference is good for democracy, is a bold way of expressing the healthy side-effects of homegrown diversity and of immigration. Immigration and regional ethnic and gender rights upset the stubborn compact between the (ethnic) nation and the constitutional state, and they stretch liberal practices toward a greater realization of liberalism's own promises. Universalism itself depends on difference, to follow Ernesto Laclau's provocative formulation, shared by some critical legal scholars.[13] The universal has survived classical philosophy's dismissal of particularity as deviation, and it has outlived a European Enlightenment that conflated the universal (subject, class, culture) with particular (French) incarnations. Today's universalism is a paradox for the past, because it is grounded in particularist demands. They unmoor universalism from any fixed cultural content and keep it open to an "always receding horizon" (Laclau 107). The corollary paradox of democracy, Laclau admits without embarrassment, is that it requires unity but depends on diversity. Tension and ambiguity are structural to democracy, which neither Habermas's ideal of communication nor Lyotard's lament over an impasse can acknowledge. The point of politics is to win ground and rights from centers of power, not to dispense with the power that invites struggle (see Butler, Laclau, and Zizek). This is perhaps the closest political philosophy comes to appreciating antagonism as democracy's normal condition.

From France's colonial margins, Fanon had been teaching the metropolis a preliminary lesson in agonistics. Without concluding (as Laclau does) that democracy depends on continual struggle, he did insist that the idea would realize itself through colonial clashes. Struggle against countries that invented democracy but that got stuck in premodern prejudice would demonstrate that the lessons in modern statehood were not hypocritical but simply underappreciated by the authorities.

From those same, and now postcolonial, margins, France is learning the almost perverse pleasures of *Amour bilingue,* to quote a title by Algerian novelist Abdelkebir Khatibi. It is learning that the deterritorialized relationship to language may be neurotic, but not abnormal. One of Khatibi's most ardent readers is Jacques Derrida, who explains, and repeats like an incantation, or like Irish keening, in *The Monolingualism of the Other*, that his only language, the one he thinks, writes, speaks, and dreams in, the one he masters enviably, is not his own. (The ideal is "to speak the other's language without renouncing one's own.") What does the (self-)consciousness of using a foreign language suggest to literary criticism? Is this a question that interrogates the dimensions of multiculturalism? Has it any relevance for a bilingual aesthetics? What differences do these differences between the particular and the universal make for the study of literary art? Curiously, I repeat, these questions haven't yet seemed central to aesthetics.

3. Freud

The Jewish Questions

Asking them would advance, for example, our analysis of humor, along with the various techniques of condensation and displacement that humor shares with dreams and with literary arts. It was Freud who observed those mechanisms, first in dreams and then in humor, he tells us in "Wit and Its Relationship to the Unconscious" (1905). As for the relationship with poetry, it is patent in the very word for condensation, *Verdichtung*, which practically means turning into poetry. This linguistic (aesthetic) turn was, for Lacan, Freud's most important contribution to psychoanalysis. It enabled a practice of reading that could track repressed events and feelings through the creative distortions that had appeared to be nonsense rather than clever disguise. Without the literary training that Freud took for granted (and that Lacan marshals to read metaphors as symptoms, and metonymy as insatiable desire), psychoanalysis is unthinkable (see Lacan, "The Agency of the Letter").

But Freud's joke book has a glaring contradiction at its core, a performative contradiction. The book provides a *universal* science of wit through performances of *particular*, decidedly noninterchangeable, expressions of wit. Practically all the examples are Jewish. Has anyone commented on this before? Sander Gilman remarked on it, but he read the contradiction as thwarted assimilation. I want to add a note of sly vindication for the indelible difference. Freud's contradiction is so dramatic that it seems itself like a joke: his own universalizing project, to study the (ahistorical, culturally nonspecific) unconscious, looks silly, as he tells one Jewish joke after another. What is more, he can tell them *because* he is Jewish; "They are stories which were invented by Jews themselves and which are directed against Jewish peculiarities. The Jewish jokes made up by *non-Jews* are nearly all brutal buffooneries in which wit is spared by the fact that the Jew appears as a comic figure to a stranger. The Jewish jokes which originate with Jews admit this, but they know their real shortcomings as well as their merits, and the interest of the person himself in the thing to be criticized produces the subjective determination of the wit-work which would otherwise be difficult to bring about" (705). Jokes about paupers, about marriage brokers, about primitive habits and incorrigible outsiders. . . . He can't stop, and ends up theorizing their particular and superior qualities. (In fact, Freud already had made "a collection of profound Jewish stories" before he decided what to do with them, as he tells Fleiss in a letter of 1897 [Gilman 262].)

As part of Freud's general design to describe the universal properties and mechanisms of the unconscious, and thereby to depathologize any particular group that notoriously suffered from neuroses, namely the Jews, he attends to wit as a universal feature of human expression (658). Freud was certainly not the first to dignify wit by making it the subject of serious scholarship (references acknowledge leads from Ludovic Dugas, Karl Groos, Alexander Bain, Henri Bergson, Herbert Spencer, and from many others), but Freud gave it an uncommonly central role in his scientific pursuit. Wit works like dreams, he observed from the many jokes that he obviously takes pleasure in telling, so that studying wit is another, and entertaining, route to the unconscious. Like dreams, wit often works through techniques of condensation and displacement to produce apparent nonsense that is, in fact, a disguised wish or a piece of wisdom. The major difference between them, says Freud, is that dreams are personal (they need not be shared nor even understood by the dreamer in order to be dreams); and wit is social, so social that it needs at least three participants to work. What is more, wit seems to work best inside clearly defined, particular societies, a national culture, preferably a minoritarian culture that is misprized and slighted by the majority: Jewish culture, for example.

Paradoxically, particularity is a general feature of other minorities. Difference itself, along with the double consciousness that identifies with both the despised minority and the majority that despises it, can be a commonality. This must be why, as Camille Forbes tells me, a manual for comedians invites minorities to advance quickly, since they already share a sense of the absurd, "Are you Jewish, Black or Italian? Note: If you answered yes to this question, skip directly to chapter two [see Carter]." (It is also why, in Vargas Llosa's novel, half-Jewish Mascarita be-longs to the marginal Machiguenga and presumes to speak for them.) Wit, to return to Freud, is allegedly universal, but Jews happen to be wittier than others. Wit is supposed to work like a dream, but the social dimensions of its highest form, tendency-wit (unlike the harmless message-free variety [693]) directs and determines unconscious transformations. The contradiction is apparent: on the one hand is a claim to general scientific validity for observations of techniques that explode inhibitions with a burst of laughter; and on the other, a particular group that is most adept. "All of us are responsible," in Levinas's ventriloquism of *The Brothers Karamazov;* "but I'm more responsible than the rest."

A contradiction is a crossroads.[14] Lingering there, I notice an uncanny similarity: The mischief that Jewish humor makes with universal wit (engaging it to bring it up short) repeats the kind of mischief that Jewish jokes make with non-Jewish listeners. And it has a distinct resemblance to obscene humor. No, I'm not referring to the tired and offensive association between Jews and dirty jokes, a practically inevitable association in Freud's Vienna, where his "scientific" book on wit wants to cap and to close a small industry of often smutty Jewish joke books. Gilman may be right, partly. I certainly don't doubt his reading of Freud's Jewish self-hatred, nor do I forget the enormous debt I owe to his formulation.

But self-hatred is a funny thing; it keeps the self focused with practically narcissistic attention. Like the allegedly despised and tabu discourse of sex for the Victorians, which locked them in deliciously vicious circles of denials and confessions, Jewish anti-Semitism was both inescapable and desirable. Inescapable because, as Gilman explains, the very effort of escape into good society marks the Jew as an outsider; and charming because (although Gilman doesn't add this) the effort and anxiety that attend to it keep one's attention focused on the self as a fascinating misfit. Self-hatred comes with its own antidote of self-valorization. ("They know their real shortcomings as well as their merits," Freud had written.) The medicine is not enough for a cure, but just enough for a maintenance program, to keep the round of jokes going, at one's own expense and at the expense of outsiders, too.

Minority Humor, Are You in, or Out?

Like erotic humor, Jewish (I'll say minority from now on) wit needs at least three participants: (1) a teller, (2) the object of the joke (a potential conquest; a member of the majority culture); and (3) an intimate to whom the joke is told. It's a stunning resemblance. In both cases, the second player is expendable (693). Neither the "woman" nor the "majoritarian" is meant to laugh; they are hardly necessary at all, and a reference to them will do. Instead, they are props for promoting intimacy "between men," as it were. In both cases, a clash of codes prepares the wit. In one, the clash between the men's desire and the woman's resistance; in the other, the misalignment between minority and majority cultures. Teller and listener share the same assumptions, and their hostage does not. In neither case is the object to "win" (at seduction, or at overwhelming the majority). It is to humiliate the second party and to celebrate one's superiority with a laugh. Freud would hardly have welcomed such a reading. It may be the result of my overinterpreting his preference for Jewish jokes, his delight in telling them beyond the demands of demonstration, into a preference for remaining Jewish. This can only mean distinguishing himself (culturally, emotionally) from non-Jews, and obstructing the universalizing methods of science.

A sense of superiority is probably taken for granted in obscene humor, where men evidently assume advantages over women, although they fear being refused. I'm suggesting that a similar asymmetry works in minority humor, that authority is often on the side of subaltern figures. Whether their superiority is taken for granted, or whether it's constructed by the jokes themselves may depend on circumstances. But the discharge of repressive energy (which Freud repeatedly describes as the mechanism of laughter) in people who have learned humble or angry postures certainly relaxes their bearing. The release is a double pleasure for the listener: both the intellectual satisfaction of getting the joke, and the political pleasure of gloating over the second person who doesn't get it.

What is it that the outside listener doesn't get? That second (structurally unnecessary) person can miss the very fact that wit has been created, along with the tripartite relationship that has just used him as a prop. He or she may laugh too, encouraged by laughter all around, but might mistake wit for a simpler, *comic* form of humor that needs only two participants who *find* a situation funny. The corollary mistake is to imagine that one is the ideal audience, rather than the butt of a joke. Certainly people can pass from one position to another; they can learn multiple cultural codes and become agents of jokes where they had been objects. But without the shared assumptions of fellow players, specifically without the expectation that minority jokesters can be sophisticated and *make* wit, the condescending participant may descend into a baser form of comic *found* humor. Silly laughter from the butt of a joke might well heighten the pleasure in superior wit.

Is gloating a compensation for not getting other things, such as sex, power, money, education, jobs? Respect? Maybe. In any case, those prizes can look as laughable and undignified as the system that holds them like carrots in front of pursuers who are beaten with sticks. The minority joke can play to lose, if loss seems inevitable, which makes it more dignified than winning. Wit can turn the asymmetry of money, power, and public respect on its head, at least for the moment that laughter makes havoc. And the imbalance is especially vulnerable in the clearest case of bicultural wit: the bilingual joke. Freud doesn't tell any Yiddish examples; it may be the only genre of Jewish jokes that he excludes. Playing games that depend on positions of insider and outsider was probably too evidently incompatible with his universalizing project.

He is not deaf to the slide (*Verschiebung*) from one language to another when the ideal listener is himself or another analyst. Lacan mentions an example from the 1927 paper on fetishism, where Freud reported his solution to an enigmatic "shine on the nose" (*Glanz auf der Nase*) that a patient needed to see in order to achieve sexual satisfaction. It turned out to be, not a shine, but a glance, in English, from an early childhood fixation with "a glance at the nose" (the desired phallus) of his mother. (in Lacan, *Ecrits* 170). Lacan doesn't comment on the bilingual structure of the analysis, but I wonder if this is not an apt example of the unstable bar between signifier and signified that he privileges as the core intuition of Freud's science, even before Saussure formulated it as S/s.[15] Veering from one signifier to another, in ways that affect the signified, is a technique of disguise, or escape, or privileged association that is probably typical in language games for multilinguals.

Whether or not Freud might have pursued this line of escape in (private) dream-work, he chose to stay in plain view when he tells (social) jokes. If they depend on a language other than German, it is either French (which he assumes any educated reader will know); or Italian, which he translates in parentheses (the story about Napoleon's complaint that Italians dance so badly: "Non tutti," answered his hostess, "ma, buona parte"). But he avoids the very popular jokes, meant mostly for Jews, that mistranslate from laughable, recalcitrantly particularist, almost-German (Yiddish) to the official version. Gilman mentions that Freud's own letters to Fleiss are laced with funny Yiddishisms, but Freud objected to the barbarous mistakes of his "half-Asian" brother-in-law from Bucharest.[16]

I Need an Unconscious?

Bilingual wit must have threatened the importance of Freud's discovery of an unconscious. Without the unconscious, he has no science; and bilingual humor can do without it. Without it he has no position to stand outside the limited world attributed to Jews, to distance himself through a new discourse that replaces ethnic languages with a universal science. In Freud's version, wit needs to dip into the unconscious in order to free a conscious thought toward a repressed association. Without the dip, the flash of inspiration that amounts to a loss of control, there is no wit.[17] But a good bilingual joke doesn't depend on repressed associations; it dips into a perfectly visible and shared pool of alternate words and associations. It is clever and yet widely available, sophisticated but democratic. What would Freud have done with this riotous border-crossing that managed to sidestep a murky unconscious, while it also practiced an art of cultural border making? For him, the competent reader is the universal reader. Nevertheless, he had to admit, different personal circumstances do affect what we find funny (700).

The bilingual jokes that I told at the beginning of this essay use monolingual listeners as the butt of humor. And they know it, usually after the fact and with some resentment. But at another level, the object of the humor is the same bilingual subject (or someone of his nation, as Freud would say) who can tell the joke and get it right away. This is a reflexive genre; it has a boomerang effect that—directed at the monolingual who won't find it funny—ultimately targets the teller for a gentle variety of scorn. Reflexive can also mean split, between an agent and its object, as it does in Freud's 1927 paper on "Humor," which is like wit, he says, but more wise. Humor targets the self, through a split between the teller—a mature superego that can laugh at defeat and therefore shore up narcissism against external judgments—and the object of humor, a laughably childish ego to be cajoled into disengaging from useless affect by the parental voice. Translator James Strachey notes that in "Humor," "for the first time we find the super-ego presented in an amiable mood (160). Are the bilingual jokes witty, and by definition tendentious, with a target external to the self? Or, are they humorous, in a self-contained circuit that others can enjoy vicariously and unscathed, where the emotionally painful expenditure to repress suffering finds release in saving the energy by dismissing the childish problem? Or, again, can bilingual jokes do double duty, have their listeners coming and going, breaking and entering the distinctions between outside and inside that Freud's mature paper presumes to defend?

To be sure, Freud's intuition about the split between ego and superego helps to locate the language divide in bilingual humor between competence and fragility.[18] It can locate cracks in the brittle egos of newly minted Americans, whose precarious English, as we heard, keeps them waiting for doctors to approve visas and keeps them worrying about lawyers who misrepresent them at court. The costs of this "wisdom" can be high to egos that don't just imagine insecurity but live it, too, unless the jokes merely acknowledge the high costs of bad fits and (in Freud's economistic reasoning) save grateful listeners the trouble. Costs can run very high, if wisdom itself is sacrificed to a tendency; that is, if the allegedly "childlike" ego remains recalcitrant and too proud to laugh away some injustice. Then the ego makes common cause with a superego that stands too erect to be reflexive. Instead, it jokes at the doctors, lawyers, and lawmen who are limited to one language. Freud's intuition says nothing about this language divide, the one between monolingual simplicity and the complexity of more-than-one. Isn't this where the doctor in Roberto Fernández's "Wrong Channel?" seems foolish for missing the ambiguity between TB and TV while he presumes to say two words in bad Spanish? Isn't it here that the judge in the horse joke might have mistaken the defendant's *Oyf kapures* for the almost nonsensical *oy vey,* instead of his figurative dismissal of guilt? Isn't this also where another story about a stolen horse misses what a simple "no" means in a courteous and detailed report? In the sheriff-shooting scene that ends badly for the hero of

The Ballad of Gregorio Cortez (1983), his virtuosity in Spanish outruns the competence of both Anglo authorities and Anglo audiences.[19]

Melancholia

The jokes play to lose; they denigrate the jokers, and yet they take pleasure in it. I've begun to suggest why this is so. Perhaps there is enough satisfaction in watching the monolingual outsiders stay outside of the game. Or, maybe the light touch on heavy subjects makes the burden seem silly, inessential, bearable. Is there a comfort in losing, even a pride in refusing to play by someone else's rules? An either/or response seems out of line here. Why choose one effect over another, as if playing a single game in a tidy field when what we are considering is precisely overloads, unorthodox juxtapositions? These games are double-barreled jokes that shoot off in more than one direction. Some observations have led back to Freud's early speculations about wit as the most social form of humor, and others will lead forward to a new field of "bilingual aesthetics" that we should name and call into being. It will acknowledge the specific sophistication of language games that operate in more than one code. And in between the step back to Freud's work on wit and the one forward, past Wittgenstein's monolingual games, we should pause at the uncanny paradox (so familiar and yet so strangely unacknowledged) that I've already noted about bilingual sophistication: it plays monolinguals for inferiors; and it is also self-denigrating, sometimes bitter, others philosophical. Even worse, it can also covet the laughable simplicity of the culture one scorns.

"[A]dmiras su eficacia, sus comodidades, su higiene, su poder; y más te duele saber que por más que lo intentes, no puedes ser como ellos. . . . Porque después de todo, di: ¿tu visión de las cosas, en tus peores o en tus mejores moments, ha sido tan simplista como la de ellos? Nunca" (Fuentes 32–33).

Along with the complaint is a reluctance to take the cure. Because, for Cruz, taking the cure of efficiency and hygiene would be to kill off the complicated Mexican patient. He stays inside, looking out with a mixture of envy and disdain.[20] Freud must have known that some jokes were melancholic, the profound ones that named a human failing and refused to remedy it. Why? What for? Are humans perfect? This is the lesson in wisdom that he appends as the deeper level of the joke about the disgruntled young man who whispers to the marriage broker a list of faults about the perspective bride: "You can speak up," says the *schadchen*. "She's deaf, too." "But here, as it often happens, the jest betrays the seriousness of it. We shall not err if we assume that all stories with logical facades really mean what they assert even if these assertions are deliberately falsely motivated. . . . The suitor really makes himself ridiculous when he collects together so sedulously the individual charms of the bride which are transient after all, and when he forgets at the same time that he must be prepared to take as his wife a human being with inevitable faults . . ." ("Wit" 701–02). Almost luxuriating in the incurability of the human condition, Freud makes self-deprecation a stable feature of his Jewish jokes.[21]

Melancholia was not a likely word for Freud to use, as he tried to legitimate wit-work as the necessary partner to dream-work. It dams up the circuits of pleasure with unconscious repressions; while wit releases them. One haunts, the other sets free. One acknowledges unspeakable loss, the other dares to speak it with the tremble of laughter. But by the 1927 essay on "Humor," he had come to the conclusion that the two are paradoxical partners: "The alternation between melancholia and mania, between a cruel suppressing of the ego by the super-ego and the liberation of the ego after this oppression, suggests some such shifting of cathexis; and this conception would, moreover, explain a number of phenomena in normal mental life. If, hitherto, we have but seldom had recourse to this explanation, it has been on account of our customary caution" ("Humor" 219). A symptom of this alternation is, I think, Freud's own reluctance to be entirely "cured" of Jewishness.

The word *melancholia* is out of vogue in the social sciences, where *mourning* now describes both normal and neurotic expressions of grief.[22] The single word is no doubt meant to suggest an unstable boundary between the two. That boundary has a particular name in Ricardo C. Ainslie's essay about the (melancholic) incomplete mourning among Mexican immigrants in Austin, Texas; it is *La Pulga*, the Flea Market, which he cleverly calls a "transitional space" between the safe inside of Mexican culture and the threatening outside of an Anglo American world. *La Pulga* extends the immigrants' ordeal of loss, he says, "because they retain the hope of return, and cannot fully mourn the fact that they have had to leave in the first place" (295). But Peggy Leavitt asks Ainslie why he seems eager to move beyond that space. Is it simply a matter of health and maturation, as if one psychological trajectory fit all life stories, universally? Does this space not have a value in itself; is it merely a crutch, a scaffolding, a transition (301–02)? In fact, Chicano cultural critics call it "a third space," and they call it home (see Brady; Barcelo; Soja; Estill; Langston). Perhaps living there, in the cultural overload (*en el desborde*, to use Norma Alarcón's inspiration), is a therapeutic response to immigration, because it preserves treasures from being exiled to the trash heap. This is David Lloyd's option too, when he defends an Irish sadness that refuses the English cure in favor of cultural autonomy and its almost perverse sense of agency. The recalcitrant art of keening for the dead is an affront to English good advice to leave the past behind. The Irish understand it as a demand to give up the ghost.[23]

Ainslie, among many others, would cure perversity and purge the ghost. He might prefer a slight deformation (quite normal to my Puerto Ricanized ear) of that Flea Market from *la pulga* to *la purga*. The very play on words enjoys Spanish as its lively and current medium. Spanish is not a vestige of lands in transition toward forgetfulness, but a source of treasures for creativity. *La pulga* is a gadfly to assimilation.[24]

4. Wittgenstein

For some reason, the kinds of doubly satisfying bilingual games that jokes represent have not gotten much serious attention. Neither traditional aesthetics (including rhetoric), nor the philosophy of language has thought beyond single codes. Bilingualism is a political and a pedagogical problem in many industrialized countries, almost a pathology. Somehow it is not a cultural field, although cultivation there might follow Wittgenstein's advice for language pathologies: don't cure them, just describe normal uses. What's normal, in bilanguage games, says *barrio*-based linguist Ana Celia Zentella, is creative virtuosity. She compares them to expert basketball and to dancing salsa. They are shared art forms, vehicles for solidarity as well as a space for personal creativity (3).

Wittgenstein never described bilingual uses. Deaf to his own advice, he cured them. One of the things that can "happen" when you try to express an idea or a feeling while writing a letter, Wittgenstein says, is that you think of something in a foreign language and then strain to translate it into your mother tongue. He goes from one thing to the other, as if from cause to inevitable effect. He has rushed ahead, darted from an English stimulus to a desired German response, practically collapsing the two into one event. How strangely impatient he seems with the interference; how unexpectedly prescriptive this goal of monolingual performance appears, in the *Philosophical Investigations*, where tolerance is the remedy for philosophical problems. "Look and see," was his repeated exhortation to thinkers who had lost touch with the world. Rather than theorize about what can and cannot be done with language, Wittgenstein is busy doing things with it, like writing a letter.

Yet he seems stuck in at least one abstract parameter of language philosophy: that is, its reduction of everyday functions to the operations in one linguistic code. The fact that Wittgenstein himself thought and communicated in more than one language (I suspect that many philosophers of language do), stays underremarked and undeveloped. With the gate around monolingual therapies still closed, an English expression comes to Wittgenstein, and he acts indifferent to the ways it works. He hardly looks, doesn't quite see, and certainly doesn't skip a beat before dismissing it "to hit on the corresponding German one" (*PI*#335). How would the *Investigations* develop, if the gate around monolingual therapies were to open? They would surely consider the ways in which language often, and perhaps increasingly, works in association with another. A second language may be as limited as the first, but in different, occasionally liberating ways. Among other things that a code switch can do, it evidently can free his thought into finding words, English words. He might have noticed that, before he forced the words away, because "Once we register the damage wreaked by propositional reductions," Wittgenstein sighed, "We feel as if we had to repair a torn spider's web with our fingers" (*PI* #106).

Immigrants who hold onto a web of home languages after coming to the United States are not necessarily ungrateful; they are complicated.[25] Offended neighbors may bristle at feeling excluded when they don't understand home languages spoken on the street (in bars, hospitals, businesses).[26] But displaced people will defend their freedom of speech and continue to live in normally double (or multiple) codes, sometimes for generations. If pressed to embrace the host culture after moving across the border—or being crossed by it politically or economically in transnational circuits—creative migrants are likely to double their response. They defer and demur, in counterpoint. Their language games can thrive under pressure, as the charm of traditional cultures survives in posthumous displays of originality. They notice the charms of purposeful mistranslation, a postponed punchline, and relief from the law of one language by reprieve from another:

> sonriéndose se empina el vato la botella
> and wagging chapulín legs in-and-out
> le dice algo a su camarada
> y los dos avientan una buena carcajada
> y luego siguen platicando
> mientras la amiga, unaffected
> masca y truena su chicle
> viéndose por un espejo
> componiéndose el hairdo [*Vigil-Piñón*]

These are some of the games that prosper in the tight spots where one language rubs against another. They may not be quite modern when they hold something back from the universal embrace.[27] Maybe these slightly intractable games are postmodern, because they know how to play with difficulty in language and don't dismiss it as noise. Bilinguals understand the arbitrariness of language even more intensely than do theorists who, after Paul de Man, call language allegorical because words are of a different order from their elusive referents.[28] Beyond elusive, everyday language can be downright opaque when it confronts another one, sometimes intentionally opaque, as a reminder of surviving cultural differences. "We have a right to our opacity," begins Édouard Glissant's manifesto for Caribbean cultural self-determination.[29]

I will want to consider some of the vanguard practices that relieve the conspicuous normalization of culture. They are the bi- (or multi-)lingual games that take advantage of dissonant residues of assimilation (or that bear the erroneous but often pleasing consequences), after particular languages are forced into universal codes.[30] Interruptions, delays, code switching, syncopated communication are rhetorical features of bicultural language games; they are also symptoms of democratic engagement that should not presume mutual understanding among citizens.[31] However much we may grieve over the real losses of cultural difference in the wake of modernity, it would be even sadder, and counterproductive, to let lamentation drown out the sounds of cultural counterpoint and creative survival.

Of course it is possible that lots of people are producing goods for the international export market. And the pattern of migrations that—host countries complain—overwhelms national cultures, might prompt a skeptic to ask if there are enough educated consumers left in the home market to read more "authentic" stuff (see Owen). The grounds for complaint are more than possible.

"Possible, but not interesting"

This is how Borges's independent detective responded to the reasonable police inspector. With that dismissal, detective Eric Lönnrot of "Death and the Compass" (1945) overrides the inspector's truth claim and his instant solution of the homicide case in favor of a more interesting, literally erroneous, sidetrack. (Lönnrot turns out to bear more than one resemblance to the proverbial rabbi who responds to an obviously correct biblical exegesis with a disdainful "That's only one answer to the question," because right answers overlook the inexhaustible mystery of sacred texts.) Plausible solutions to a murder mystery, or justified complaints against globalization, are not the most creative responses to the challenges at hand. If detective Lönnrot were at today's scene of violence against cultures, he would probably delay any conclusions about guilt or damage in order to develop more interesting questions: does everyone suffer losses? When victims incur damage, is it a net loss, or are there mitigating factors? Lönnrot might have observed, mischievously, that inside Argentina, and other Latin American countries where European and North American books have long been staples of reading, strong national traditions continue to thrive. Educated Argentines, who sometimes learn their first lessons in English, or French, or German, may be amused at an almost provincial anxiety over eroding linguistic specificity. Perhaps they feel the satisfaction of watching the whole literate world finally advance toward Argentina, southward, where Argentines have always found their frontier. There, and in Mexico, or Cuba, or anywhere in Latin America (especially in Brazil), patriots have long known that economics and education oblige them to cross national lines and languages. And the most "authentic" literature can be hilariously hybrid. Think of Cabrera Infante's novel written in "Cuban," *Tres tristes tigres,* where Sam Clemens follows San Anselmo in the list of Enlightened Philosophers (269). The book opens with a very funny, imperfectly bilingual, nightclub routine that could certainly have added a few ironic lines about a First World worried that creativity is lost in translation.

> *Showtime!* Señoras y señores. *Ladies and gentlemen. Muy* buenas noches, damas y caballeros, tengan todos ustedes. . . . *In the marvelous production of our Rodney the Great. . . .* En la gran, maravillosa producción de nuestro GRANDE, ¡Roderico Neyra! . . . *"Going to Brazil"* . . . Intitulada, *"Me voy pal Brasil"* . . . Taratará tarará, taratará tarará taratareo . . . *Brazuil terra dye nostra felichidade. . . . That was Brezill for you, ladies and gentlemen. That is, my very very particular version of it!* . . . en el idioma de *Chakespeare,* en *English.* [15]

Borges's detective Lönnrot obviously preferred playing games over winning them. Even after he finally loses, the player's last words manage to adjust the rules of the game for a rematch in another life. He could have closed the first homicide case with unimaginative answers; instead he opened it up with arcane questions that send us on a delightfully brainteasing chase. Had the case been merely solved, it could not have been Borges's vehicle for one of his favorite themes, the theme of codependence between law and crime, detectives and delinquents, signs and things. Detective Lönnrot was notorious in the underworld for his clever skirmishes with crime; this time, he is lured to engage through a hermeneutical sidetrack that the murderer apparently left as a personal trap. Lönnrot, in fact, (mis)construes a piece of circumstance into an inviting sign. He takes up the invitation, confident that he is at least equal to his prey. Their deadly game begins by spelling out God's unspeakably holy Hebrew name.

The story works along the faultlines of the common language, in the loose connections where restricted codes can play. Law (in Spanish, or in English translation) is a system that includes everyone; it is clear, uniformly available, and therefore indifferent to foreign distractions. But some speakers, bored by the uniformity, prefer the distractions. Why repeat the tedious game of being right, when the game of being clever is more fun? So Lönnrot takes up the sacred language and communes with his counterpart. Their game may have little to do with the original texts that make it possible. Maybe the Hebrew language itself is vehicle enough for the special connection between the players. Not that the special vehicle leads to a conflict with the public language. Nothing here happens outside the law, nor despite it, and certainly not against it. Lönnrot, after all, has defended the law so effectively that criminals target him personally as enemy number one. But the inclusive code is thin in places; it is tedious or otherwise unimpressive, when compared to the option of a particular language that the law finds irrelevant. Thanks to the very indifference or dismissal of foreign signs ("The inspector regarded them with dread, almost with repulsion"), players can sometimes revel unpoliced while staying inside a generally powerful system. Their games are collective, but restricted, hermeneutic adventures. And though their virtuosity seems pointless to the policeman and to the newspaper editor, to the protagonists it is the medium of creative communication.

How strange that the shared language should be the mechanism of exclusion, and that minor characters are distinguished by their ignorance of a minor language. Yet the paradox can surprise only monolinguals. Those who hear nothing but the universal language in Borges's story (and in many others) actually miss the available fun. Specifically, his language game depends on the option to spar in a difficult, privileged language. More generally, it depends on the simultaneous availability of universal and particularist languages. To stay inside only one is already to forfeit the possible games, or to be their target.[32]

I might have noticed the literary charms of code switching as long ago as my first reading of "Death and the Compass," or far earlier, in the multilingual games we immigrant children would play at the expense of competent English-only speakers, including our teachers. But theory can lag embarrassingly behind practice; and catching up now that the practice is so general, varied, and culturally significant is hardly an intellectual risk. It's more like a pedagogical obligation. We live inside dominant languages that often sparkle with the survivals of resistant speech, yet teachers either decline to notice or they feel beleaguered by the range of references that somehow, they feel, should be mastered. Otherwise, what could they add to a reading? Sometimes educators conclude, prematurely, that multicultural games are meant to enrich the dominant experience, so they complain if the material is hard to digest.[33] In fact, the appetite for enlarged and improved master codes misses the point of some particularist games. They are played at the center's expense. Self-authorized readers are sometimes the targets of a minority text, not its coconspirators. Lönnrot confronted the difference at the end of his story, when the Jewish crook who had scoffed at the *goyim* who dabble in Cabala took aim and shot the detective.

The point is that foreign disturbances can be flagrant, on purpose. They can be signatures of particular languages through a universal medium. In the asymmetry of reception that they impose, in the deferred stress or delayed apprehension of meaning, in the skipped beat of a conversation that achieves the rhythm of a joke, spaces open up aesthetics in two different

but codependent moves, as a corollary mixed blessing of double consciousness: one direction is toward the aesthetic effects that the formalists called
"making the familiar strange"; and the opposite direction is noticing that
the "strange" or foreign is intimately familiar.

These are the apparently contradictory spaces between nation and state
that liberal theory explores today. It is nudged along by the multilingual
players who get in the way of mistranslating culture into society. The wel-
come interference performs the difference between particular cultures and
a common sense of procedural civility.

Notes

1. I am grateful to Pheng Cheah for his advice on this and other points.
2. See Ortiz; Sommer, "A Vindication of Double Consciousness."
3. This brings to mind, also, Paul Gilroy's deliberate connections between one diaspora and
    another, and the specific mention of Du Bois in Europe during the Dreyfus case, passing for
    a Jew (211–12).
4. I am grateful to Mario Vargas Llosa for his personal generosity and attention during that
    conversation of October 23, 1993, during his teaching semester as John F. Kennedy Professor
    of Latin American Studies at Harvard University.
5. "The bigamy analogy comes up a lot among critics of dual nationality" (Jones-Correa 19),
    which suggests the nineteenth-century "Foundational Fictions" motif of sliding from Eros
    to Polis that I considered in that 1991 book.
6. "Austin Quigley, ALSC President for 1998/99, put it this way: 'The goal of the association
    is to restore an intellectual terrain in which readers can exercise their capacity to think for
    themselves, rather than rely upon various kinds of theoretical/political machinery to do their
    thinking for them' (from flier for membership drive). . . . 'I agree with Christopher Ricks,'
    said fellow member David Bromwich, 'the problem is not the presence of politics at the
    M.L.A., but the absence of nonpolitics'" (see Grimes 15).
7. See also Laponce, who develops the linguistic argument. I thank Silvana Seabra for this
    reading.
8. Dispensing with the sometimes perverse charm of baroque excess, and collapsing the dis-
    turbing category of the sublime back into a preromantic category of the beautiful, Elaine
    Scarry purges the term of cultural overloads (see Scarry). Multiculturalism becomes a series
    of translatable equivalences, not a field of resistant differends.
9. Homi K. Bhabha, for example, comments on Taylor's reluctance to budge from the position
    of Ideal Observer in a reading that parallels my own (see Bhabha).
10. See also Pierre Bourdieu, "It is within history that the principle of freedom from history
    resides" (248); and Guillory.
11. See Paul Guyer for development of the moral implications in Kant's aesthetics.
12. See Arendt's extended definition of Athenian politics as performance: Pericles, and no less
    Homer, defended the *vita activa* as enacting memory of greatness, good and evil deeds; unlike
    moral judgment, greatness in the performance itself. For Aristotle, "work" was to live well,
    apart from any means-ends logic; it was Politics as Performance; a formulation of politics as
    above work and labor; it is appearance (*Human Condition* 205–08).
13. Citing Robert Paul Wolff, in "Beyond Tolerance" (*Critique of Pure Tolerance* 4, 17), Neil
    Gotanda defends racial-cultural diversity as a positive good in the polity, rather than some-
    thing to be merely tolerated and benignly overlooked. (Gotanda 53). Gotanda also quotes
    Justice Brennan, whose decision in *Metro Broadcasting v. FCC* draws from *Regents of Uni-
    versity of California v. Bakke:* "Just as a 'diverse student body' contributing to a 'robust
    exchange of ideas' is a 'constitutionally permissible goal' on which a race-conscious univer-
    sity admissions program may be predicated, the diversity of views and information on the
    airwaves serves important First Amendment values. The benefits of such diversity are not

limited to the members of minority groups . . .; rather, the benefits redound to all members of the viewing and listening audience" (57). Thanks to Susan Keller for directing me to this article.

14. This one could simply have disabused me of the pretension to scientific truth that deluded Freud, that is, if I valued him only as a scientist. Of course, the disciples who revered his science were practically indifferent to the joke book. Or, they felt embarrassed by its apparent levity. They didn't engage it long enough to notice, or to worry about its untenable defense of universality. Freudian psychoanalysis remains, though, a set of practices, or an art. Science doesn't generally revere him anymore; but many practitioners of literary criticism do. This is not a demotion, if you ask a literary critic, but a side-move which Lacan helped to negotiate. It was Lacan who dusted off the joke book, and reframed it at the center of Freud's contributions. Because in it, Freud showed how the spirit works through words. The unconscious is hard to map, by definition; the spirit is hard to articulate, too. Yet Freud's techniques for reading the games that words play as signposts of human mysteries gave Lacan and legions of other fans material traces to work with.

   Another response to the contradiction might have been to go on a deconstructive mission against allegedly universal unconscious structures and mechanisms (by way of wit and then including revelations in dreams). Alternatively, it could have made me ponder the intricate relationships between science and circumstance, between predictable pattern and messy actualization. I confess to following a route less ambitious than any of these. Mine doesn't go very far at all. Instead, it lingers in the sidetracks of theory, where universal claims go astray into particular dead ends. There is where mischief is made with abstractions. In other words, I'm content to stay inside the contradiction, and to wonder at Freud's fascination with Jewish humor. Why does he let it continually take the lead, even when it interferes with his scientific goals?

15. The innovation, Lacan points out, is not about the "arbitrariness of the sign, as it has been elaborated since the earliest reflections of the ancients"; it is about "the illusion that the signifier answers to the function of representing the signified" (Lacan, *Écrits* 149). To the disappointment of logical positivists, the signifier has a way of slipping into the signified. "We are forced, then, to accept the notion of an incessant sliding of the signified under the signifier—which Ferdinand de Saussure illustrates with an image resembling the wavy lines of the upper and lower waters . . . a double flux marked by fine streaks of rain" (Lacan, *Écrits* 154). Isn't this what happens when "glance" slides into "Glanz"?

16. While the 1905 book acknowledges the Yiddish shift in stress as funny (one Jew asks another, "Did you take a bath?" "Why?" asks the other, "Is one missing?"), the jokes are generally embedded in "good" German, as Gilman notes (263), even though standardizing the language undercuts the humor. "In his study Freud dismisses the use of *jargon,* that is, Yiddish, as a source of humor . . . he observes that jargon weakens the effect of the joke, since the tale relies on the effect of the language rather than the content of what the language expresses (8: 108, 114). For it is not merely the self-deprecating content of the jokes that makes them Jewish, as Freud claims, but also the very use of language, which Freud then rejects as superficial. The Jews in Freud's jokes speak an easily identifiable language" (Gilman 265).

17. One clear difference between wit and the comic is that comedy can stay at conscious levels. Comedy draws associations between consciousness and "foreconsciousness," something forgotten but familiar, rather than repressed, like childish behavior in an adult.

18. I thank Jane de Almeida for focusing me on this split.

19. See chapter three of my *Proceed with Caution,* "Cortez in the Courts." The movie is in English and Spanish with no subtitles, and sets a trap for Anglo viewers. Meaning escapes monolinguals for as long as Cortez manages to escape his pursuers, after shooting the sheriff of a Texas border town. The movie, in other words, makes us worry about more than what we watch; it corners us into considering who watches and from what position on the language divide. Most Anglos don't question the competence of the translator who accompanies the sheriff on an investigation of a theft. But bilinguals know enough to laugh with Cortez, master of Spanish (which should have been an official Texan language, he may be reminding his listeners, according to the Treaty of Guadalupe-Hidalgo). He denies having traded *un caballo, ahora.* It was a mare, and he traded her two days ago. They know enough to wince over linguistic incompetence. From his first mispronounced greeting to the last and

fatal mistranslation, the translator is both funny and infuriating. He twists each informative answer into practically dumb noncompliance. And, after telling a joke at the translator's expense, Cortez goes on the run, until he is caught and locked up for the next dozen and debilitating years in one jail or another.

20. Freud evidently appreciates that threshold as the stage for performing a minority identity, when he considers the inside-trading of witticisms between a teller and someone of his "nation." Surely bilingual jokes reconfirm this collective identity more surely than do the monolingual culture clashes that he stages in his collection of jokes, simply because outsiders don't easily cross the language divide. When they eavesdrop they can even be the measure of insider sophistication. If monolinguals think they get the point, what they get can be something laughable, but basely and barely laughable comedy, an absurdity, some nonsense that is found, rather than a witticism that is created. Does the doctor laugh at Mima's confusion in "Wrong Channel," like the judge who may be laughing at the gesticulating defendant who never stole a horse, or like the sheriff's translator, who may find Cortez's predicament funny, for a short moment? If they do, it is on the simple, two-dimensional plane of comedy, which is a funny place to see them stuck.

21. At least this goes for the ones that he most enjoyed, like the one that introduces and recurs throughout the book: Heine's description of the Baron Rothschild, who treated the pauper at his table just like family, forgotten family, very "famillionare." It will later inspire Lacan's extended riffs: 1."Le famillionnaire," 2."Le fat-millionnaire," 3. "Le Miglionnaire" (see "Les structures freudiennes de l'ésprit").

22. I take this lesson from Marcelo Suarez-Orozco.

23. The Irish preference for the burden of memory of the dead, of imperial outrages, memories of hunger, of massacre, of slavery (Robert Southey was sent to Brazil at the beginning of the nineteenth century to study its exemplary system of forced labor, in order to recommend improvements in managing Irish workers) refuses the relief of absolution. Relief for whom?

    Over a century ago, Ernest Renan understood a profound paradox of patriotism. Countries, he said, consolidate their identities, not through collective memories, but through collective forgetfulness. Logically, peoples who are forgotten by that process in official histories (those who have lost wars, commerce, language, religion) respond differently. They refuse the therapies that, they sense, serve the oppressor better than the oppressed. Why forget the trouble that turned them into the oppressed, when forgetting would mean losing the means to account for the present? Without memories of historical cause, other causes might be invented, such as alleged deficiencies, a lack of talent, or industry. There is, I want to suggest, a charm in melancholia. It may be a vaccine against worse ailments, a dose of understandable sadness that defends undervalued people from more serious depression. The joke, of course, is that the malady is also a defense against those who would cure it.

24. *Melancholia* may have faded from a scientific vocabulary, but it remains perversely radiant in literary criticism, a "black sun," in the metaphor Julia Kristeva borrows from Gerard de Nerval. It is a goad to creativity, as compensation and catharsis, therapies that alleviate sadness but don't cure it. Melancholia has also been the guide to philosophy. It "is not a philosopher's disease but his very nature, his *ethos*. . . . With Aristotle, melancholia, counterbalanced by genius, is coextensive with man's anxiety in being. It could be seen as the forerunner of Heidegger's anguish as the *Stimmung* of thought. Schelling found in it, in similar fashion, the 'essence of human freedom,' an indication of man's affinity with nature.' The philosopher would thus be 'melancholy on account of a surfeit of humanity'" (Kristeva 7). Is there an analogous surfeit of cultures, identities, be-longings in bicultural subjects? Is the reluctance to streamline the surfeit into one clear cultural option a refusal of mourning as therapy?

25. Suzanne Oboler calls them strategically ambivalent, that is, ironic, subtle (see her *Ethnic Labels: Latino Lives* for examples: 11–12; 93–98; 145–50; 161–62).

26. Consider the complicated California case of telemarketing employees, hired for their Mexican-American bilinguialism and repeatedly censured for gossiping about Anglo coworkers in Spanish. Management's exasperated response was to forbid casual conversation in Spanish. The workers brought suit, and the boss relocated (NPR report of 19 Feb. 1998: 637efe6e-b91f-lldl-aldc-8a) This is certainly a more interesting illustration than the judge who fined a mother for speaking to her daughter in Spanish, alleging that she was dooming the child to the life of a maid.

27. Nevertheless, what Wallace Lambert coined "subtractive bilingualism," in his study of French-Canadian immigrant children, prevails for recent immigrant children generally. They are apparently losing their native languages more quickly than did earlier groups. "The only difference is that the process appears to be taking place much more rapidly today. Few among us realize what is really happening. Quite the contrary. Over the past several years, there has been an increasing concern among educators, policymakers, and members of the public that the new immigrants are not assimilating fast enough" (qtd. in Fillmore 324).

28. "One particular advantage that bilingual children have is in the area of metalinguistic awareness—the ability to analyze the form as well as the content of language, knowledge of how to talk about language, and control over nonliteral uses of language, like puns, irony, and figures of speech. Certain kinds of metalinguistic skills—such as recognizing that words have no intrinsic connection to the objects they refer to—typically emerge several years earlier in bilingual than in monolingual children. Nor is it surprising that the process of learning a second language or of switching back and forth between two languages would heighten one's likelihood of becoming aware of the formal aspects of the linguistic system and one's understanding of the arbitrariness of the linguistic code" (Snow 65).

29. "Nous réclamons le droit à l'opacité" (Glissant 11). And Henry Giroux argues that the "politics of clarity . . . becomes a code word for an approach to writing that is profoundly Eurocentric in both context and content" (166). Della Pollock glosses his argument against flattening the relationship between language and audience, dismissing subaltern claims on language use: "Claims for such writing assume a correspondence theory of language that effaces questions of voice, style and difference" (77).

30. Néstor García Canclini develops similar observations about everyday artisanal productions among working-class and rural populations in Mexico [see *Hybrid Cultures*]. On the creativity of error, see Lipsitz.

31. This is a commonplace of political philosophy: "liberalism as a political doctrine supposes that there are many conflicting and incommensurable conceptions of the good, each compatible with the full rationality of human persons" (Rawls 248); "There has to be at least a conflict based on an actual lack of homogeneity for what is distinctive about justice to become relevant" (Fisk 1); see also Dahl.

32. When asked in an interview whether the future of Latin America is to constitute only one country, Borges said: "I would rather say that the future of the world is in only one country. Afterwards, we could join with the other America, to speak two languages: Castilian and English. Russian is very difficult. Chinese, spoken by millions and millions of people, is so difficult that the Chinese from different regions can only understand each other in writing. I think that if in the primary school both languages would be taught, we would have a bilingual humanity."

33. Enrichment is what Bill Buford hastily celebrated when he praised contemporary Indian authors for refreshing the English language. They responded, however, that English enrichment was neither the goal nor the most significant effect of their writing (see Buford, "Declarations of Independence," *New Yorker* June 23 and 30, 1997, and responses in the same issue by Salman Rushdie, G. V. Desani, Abraham Verghese, Amit Chaudhuri). I Thank Greta Slobin for this reference.

Works Cited

Ainslie, Ricardo C. "Cultural Mourning, Immigration, and Engagement: Vignettes from the Mexican Experience." *Crossings: Mexican Immigration in Interdisciplinary Perspectives.* Ed. Marcelo M. Suárez-Orozco. Cambridge: DRCLAS, 1998. 283–300.

Alter, Robert. *ALSC Newsletter* 3/3 (Spring/Summer 1997): 2.

Anderson, Benedict. *The Spectre of Comparisons: Nationalism, Southeast Asia and the World.* London: Verso, 1999.

Appadurai, Arjun. *Modernity at Large: Cultural Dimensions of Globalization.* Minneapolis: U of Minnesota Press, 1996.

Arendt, Hannah. *The Human Condition.* 1958. Intro. Margaret Canovan. Chicago: U of Chicago Press, 1998.

———. *On Revolution.* New York: Viking, 1963.

Bakhtin, M. M. *The Dialogical Imagination.* Trans. Caryl Emerson and Michael Holquist. Austin: U of Texas Press, 1981.

———. *Problems of Dostoevsky's Poetics.* 1929. Trans. R. W. Rotsel. Ann Arbor, MI: Ardis, 1973.

———. *Rabelais and His World.* Trans. Helene Iswolsky. Cambridge: MIT Press, 1968.

Barcelo, Margarita Theresa. "Geographies of Sturggle: Ideological Representations of Social Space in Four Chicana Writers." Diss. U of California, San Diego, 1995. DA9526968.

Benítez-Rojo, Antonio. *The Repeating Island: The Caribbean and the Postmodern Perspective.* Trans. James Maraniss. Durham: Duke UP, 1992.

Bernabé, Jean, Patrick Chamoiseau, and Raphael Confiant. *Éloge de la créolité.* Paris: Gallimard/ Presses universitaires créoles, 1989.

Bhabha, Homi K. "Culture's in Between." *Multicultural States: Rethinking Difference and Identity.* Ed. David Bennett. New York: Routledge, 1998.

Bloom, Harold. *Hispanic-American Writers.* Philadelphia: Chelsea House, 1998.

Borges, Jorge. "Death and the Compass." Trans. Donald A. Yates. *Everything and Nothing.* New York: New Directions, 1999.

———. Interview with Ramón Chao and Ignacio Ramonet. *Espectador* 7 Aug. 1994. First published in *Triunfo y le monde.*

Bourdieu, Pierre. *The Rules of Art: Genesis and Structure of the Literary Field.* Trans. Susan Emanuel. Stanford: Stanford UP, 1992.

Brady, Mary Patricia. "Extinct Lands, Scarred Bodies: Chicana Literature and the Reinvention of Space." Diss. U of California, Los Angeles, 1996. DA9705531.

Buford, Bill. "Declarations of Independence: Why Are There Suddenly So Many Indian Novelists?" *New Yorker* 23–30 June 1997: 6–11.

Butler, Judith, Ernesto Laclau, and Slavoj Zizek. *Hegemony, Universality, Contingency.* London: Verso, 2000.

Cabrera Infante, Guillermo. *Tres tristes tigres.* Barcelona: Seix Barral, 1967.

Carter, Judy. *StandUp Comedy: The Book.* New York: Dell, 1989.

Caruth, Cathy. Introduction [to a special issue]. *American Imago* 49.2 (1992): 9.

Cavell, Stanley. "The Avoidance of Love: Must We Mean What We Say?" Cambridge: Cambridge UP, 1976.

Cook, Eleanor. "Skills in Reading." *ALSC Newsletter* 4/4 (Fall 1998): 1–4.

Cornell, Drucilla, and William W. Bratton. "Deadweight Costs and Intrinsic Wrongs of Nativism: Economics, Freedom and Legal Suppression of Spanish." *Cornell Law Review* 84/3 (March 1999): 595–695.

Dahl, Robert. *Dilemmas of Pluralist Democracy: Autonomy Versus Control.* New Haven: Yale UP, 1982.

Dash, Michael. *The Other America: Caribbean Literature in a New World Context.* Charlottesville: U of Virginia Press, 1998.

Dussel, Enrique. "Beyond Eurocentrism: The World-System and the Limits of Modernity." *The Cultures of Globalization.* Ed. Fredric Jameson and Masao Miyoshi. Durham: Duke UP, 1998.

Estill, Adrianne. "Lyric Cartographies: Space, Body, and Subject in Contemporary Mexican and Chicano Poetry." Diss. Cornell UP, 1997. DA9727873.

Fernández, Roberto G. "Wrong Channel." *An Anthology of Really Short Stories.* Ed. Jerome Stern. New York: Norton, 1996.

Fillmore, Lily Wong. "When Learning a Second Language Means Losing the First." *Early Childhood Research Quarterly* 6 (1991): 324.

Fisk, Milton. "Introduction: The Problem of Justice." *Key Concepts in Critical Theory: Justice.* Atlantic Highlands, NJ: Humanities, 1993. 1–8.

Freud, Sigmund. "Humor." 1927. *The Standard Edition of the Complete Psychological Works of Sigmund Freud.* Trans. James Strachey. 24 vols. New York: Hogarth, 1957. 21: 160–66.

———. "Wit and Its Relation to the Unconscious." 1905. *The Basic Writings of Sigmund Freud.* Trans., ed., and intro. A. A. Brill. New York: Modern Library, 1938.

Fuentes, Carlos. *La muerte de Artemio Cruz.* Mexico City: Fondo de Cultura Economica, 1962.

García Canclini, Néstor. *Hybrid Cultures: Strategies for Entering and Leaving Modernity.* Trans. Christopher L. Chippari and Silvia L. Lopez. Minneapolis: U of Minnesota Press, 1995.

Gilman, Sander L. *Jewish Self-Hatred: Anti-Semitism and the Hidden Language of the Jews.* Baltimore: Johns Hopkins UP, 1986.

Gilroy, Paul. *The Black Atlantic: Modernity and Double Consciousness.* Cambridge: Harvard UP, 1993.

Giroux, Henry. "Language, Power and Clarity or 'Does Plain Prose Cheat?'" *Living Dangerously: Multiculturaism and the Politics of Difference.* New York: Peter Lang, 1993.

Glissant, Édouard. *Le discours antillais.* Paris: Seuil, 1981.

Gotanda, Neil. "A Critique of 'Our Constitution is Color-Blind.'" *Stanford Law Review* 44.1 (Nov. 1991): 1–68.

Grimes, William. "Does the Tab Seem Higher? Probably, It Is." *New York Times* 9 December 1994: C15.

Guillory, John. *Cultural Capital: The Problem of Literary Canon Formation.* Chicago: U of Chicago Press, 1993.

Guyer, Paul. *Kant and the Experience of Freedom: Aesthetics and Morality.* Cambridge: Cambridge UP, 1993.

Habermas, Jürgen. "Struggles for Recognition in the Democratic Constitutional State." *Multiculturalism: Examining the Politics of Recognition.* Ed. Amy Gutmann. Princeton: Princeton UP, 1994.

———. "Taylor's 'Politics of Recognition.'" *The Inclusion of the Other.* Ed. Ciaran Cronin and Pablo de Greiff. Cambridge: MIT Press, 1999.

Jones-Correa, Michael. "Under Two Flags: Dual Nationality in Latin American and Its Consequences for the United States." David Rockefeller Center for Latin American Studies. Working Papers on Latin America. Paper No. 99/00-3.

Kant, Immanuel. *Critique of Judgment.* Trans. Werner S. Pluhar. Indianapolis, IN: Hackett, 1987.

Khatibi, Abdelkebir. *Amour bilingue.* Montpellier: Fata Morgana, 1983.

Kohn, Hans. *American Nationalism.* New York: Macmillan, 1957.

Krauss, Clifford. "A Revolution Peru's Rebels Didn't Intend." *New York Times* 29 Aug. 1999: A1.

Kristeva, Julia. *Black Sun: Depression and Melancholia.* New York: Columbia UP, 1989.

Lacan, Jacques. "The Agency of the Letter in the Unconscious or Reason since Freud." 1957. *Écrits, a Selection.* Trans. Alan Sheridan. New York: Norton, 1977.

———. *Écrits, a Selection.* Trans. Alan Sheridan. New York: Norton, 1977.

———. "Les structures freudiennes de l'esprit." *Le séminaire de Jacques Lacan.* Ed. Jacques-Alain Miller. Paris: Seuil, 1998. 9–64.

Laclau, Ernesto. "Universalism, Particularism and the Question of Identity." *The Identity in Question.* Ed. John Rajchman. New York: Routledge, 1995.

Langston, David J. "Time and Space as the Lenses of Reading." *Journal of Aesthetics and Art Criticism* 40.4 (1982): 401–414.

Laponce, J. A. *Languages and Their Territories.* Toronto: U of Toronto P, 1987.

Lavallé, Bernard. "La aparición de la palabra criollo y su contexto en el Perú del siglo XVI." *Kuntur: Perú en la cultura* 1 (July–Aug. 1986): 20–24.

———. "Recherches sur l'aparition de la conscience créole dans la vice-royauté du Pérou (l'antagonisme hispano-créole dans les ordres religieux XVI–XVII siècles). Lille, 1982.

Leavitt, Peggy B. "Response to Ricardo C. Ainslie." *Crossings: Mexican Immigration in Interdisciplinary Perspectives.* Ed. Marcelo M. Suárez-Orozco. Cambridge: DRCLAS, 1998. 301–05.

Limón, José. *Mexican Ballads, Chicano Poems: History and Influence in Mexican-American Social Poetry.* Berkeley: U of California Press, 1992.

Lipsitz, George. "'It's All Wrong, but It's All Right': Creative Misunderstandings in Intercultural Communication." *Mapping Multiculturalism.* Ed. Avery F. Gordon and Christopher Newfield. Minneapolis: U of Minnesota Press, 1996. 403–12.

Lloyd, David. Lecture. Binghamton U. Binghamton, NY. April 1999.

Lyotard, Jean-François. "The Other's Rights." *On Human Rights: The Oxford Amnesty Lectures 1993.* Ed. Stephen Shute and Susan Hurley. New York: Harper Collins, 1993.

Mydans, Seth. "The World: Indonesia's Many Faces Reflect One Nation, Divisible." *New York Times* 5 Sept. 1999: Week in Review.

Oboler, Suzanne. *Ethnic Labels: Latino Lives.* Minneapolis: U of Minnesota Press, 1994.

Okin, Susan Moller, and respondents [Azizah Y. Al-Hibri, Abdullahi An-Na'im, Homi K. Bhabha, Sander L. Gilman, Janet E. Halley, Bonnie Honig, Will Kymlicka, Martha C. Nussbaum,

Bhikhu Parekh, Katha Pollitt, Robert Post, Joseph Raz, Saskia Sassen, Cass R. Sunstein, Yael Tamir]. *Is Multiculturalism Bad for Women?* Ed. Joshua Cohen, Matthew Howard, and Martha C. Nussbaum. Princeton: Princeton UP, 1999.

Ortiz, Fernando. *Cuban Counterpoint of Tobacco and Sugar.* 1940. Intro. B. Malinowski (1947). New intro. Fernando Coronil. Durham: Duke UP, 1995. 98–102.

Owen, B. Stephen. "National Literatures in a Global World?—Sometimes—Maybe." *Fieldwork.* Ed. Marjorie Garber, Rebecca L. Walkowitz, and Paul B. Franklin. New York: Routledge, 1996. 120–29.

Peirce, Charles S. *The Essential Peirce: Selected Philosophical Writings.* Ed. Nathan Houser and Christian Kloesel. 2 vols. Bloomington: Indiana UP, 1998.

"Peru's Unanticipated Revolution." *New York Times* 29 Aug. 1999: A1.

Pollock, Della. "Performing Writing." *The Ends of Performance.* Ed. Peggy Phelan and Jill Lane. New York: NYU Press, 1998. 73–103.

Prieto de Pedro, Jesus D. "Democracy and Cultural Difference in the Spanish Constitution of 1978." *Democracy and Ethnography.* Ed. Carol Greenhouse. Albany: State U of New York Press, 1998.

Rawls, John. "Justice as Fairness: Political Not Metaphysical." *Philosophy and Public Affairs* 14 (1985): 223–51.

Riding, Alan. "Replanted in France, Algerian Arts Bloom." *New York Times* 17 July 1999: A13+.

Scarry, Elaine. *On Beauty and Being Just.* Princeton: Princeton UP, 1999.

Snow, Catherine. "Rationales for Native Language Instruction: Evidence from Research." *Bilingual Education: Issues and Strategies.* Ed. Amado M. Padilla, Halford H. Fairchild, Concepción M. Valadez. 60–74.

Soja, Edward W. "The SocioSpatial Dialectic." *Annals of the Assn. of American Geographers* 70.2 (1980): 207225.

Sommer, Doris. "About Face: The Talker Turns toward Peru." *Proceed with Caution* 234–70.

———. "Cortez in the Courts." *Proceed with Caution* 92–112.

———. *Foundational Fictions: The National Romances of Latin America.* Berkeley: U of California Press, 1991.

———. *Proceed with Caution, When Engaged by Minority Writing in the Americas.* Cambridge: Harvard UP, 1999.

———. "A Vindication of Double Consciousness." *A Companion to Postcolonial Studies.* Ed. Henry Schwarz and Sangeeta Ray. Cambridge, MA: Blackwell, 2000.

Taylor, Charles. "The Politics of Recognition." *Multiculturalism: Examining the Politics of Recognition.* Ed. Amy Gutmann. Princeton: Princeton UP, 1994.

Vargas Llosa, Mario. *The Storyteller.* Trans. Helen Lane. London: Faber and Faber, 1989. [S] Trans. of *El hablador.* Barcelona: Seix Barral, 1987. [H]

———. *A Writer's Reality.* Boston: Houghton Mifflin, 1991.

Veyne, Paul. *Writing History.* Trans. Mina Moore-Rinvolucri. Middletown: Wesleyan UP, 1984.

Vigil-Piñón, Evangelina. "Por la Calle Zarzamora." *Thirty an' Seen a Lot.* Houston: Arte Publico, 1982.

Wittgenstein, Ludwig. *Philosophical Investigations.* Trans. G. E. M. Anscombe. Oxford: Blackwell, 1997.

Wolff, Robert Paul. *A Critique of Pure Tolerance.* Ed. Robert Paul Wolff, Barrington Moore, Jr., and Herbert Marcuse. 1965.

Yúdice, George, et al. *On Edge: The Crisis of Contemporary Latin American Culture.* Minneapolis: U of Minnesota Press, 1992.

Zentella, Ana Celia. *Growing Up Bilingual.* Oxford: Blackwell, 1997.

Ziolkowski, Jan. "Cultural Diglossia and the Nature of Medieval Latin Literature." *The Ballad and Oral Literature.* Cambridge: Harvard UP, 1991.

CHAPTER 7

Authority, Solidarity, and the Political Economy of Identity

The Case of the United States

DAVID A. HOLLINGER

Theorists of nationalism tend to circle around the United States like boy scouts who have spotted a clump of poison oak. The nationalism of the United States has figured small in the robust and wide-ranging discourse about nationalism that has involved sociologists, historians, political scientists, philosophers, and literary scholars during the past two decades. Although there are significant exceptions to this pattern of avoidance—David Miller and Liah Greenfeld are convenient examples—several prominent cases illustrate the pattern. The United States is mentioned in only a single footnote in Ernest Gellner's *Nations and Nationalism*. The United States is given short shrift in three of the most important collections of the 1990s: Homi Bhabha's *Nation and Narration,* John Hutchinson and Anthony D. Smith's *Nationalism,* and Geoff Eley and Ronald G. Suny's *Becoming National.* Montserrat Guibernau mentions the United States only twice, and in passing, in her *Nationalisms: The Nation-State and Nationalism in the Twentieth Century.* The United States gets less attention than Canada and the Ukraine in John A. Hall's rich, state-of-the-art collection of 1998, *The State of the Nation.* Ronald Beiner's *Theorizing Nationalism* has much more to tell us about Quebec than about the United States, which is alluded to even in passing by only half the contributors to this valuable anthology of

1999. That "nationalism is unknown" in the United States is claimed by Elie Kedouri, even in the fourth edition of his classic text *Nationalism* (143). But the most interesting case of all is that of nationalism's most creative and influential theorist, Benedict Anderson.

Anderson provides only episodic treatment of the United States while discussing "creole nationalism" in his influential book *Imagined Communities*. To be sure, Anderson's demonstration of the similarities between a large number of similarly situated, comparably developing national projects among creole populations in the New World is no cause for complaint. It is a signal contribution, and still insufficiently absorbed by a persistently Europe-centered discourse about nationalism. Anderson's recent book, *The Spectre of Comparisons*, also deals episodically with the United States, which Anderson now tells us explicitly has proved "too sui generis for ready-to-hand" (336) comparisons with other national projects in the Western Hemisphere. Most of *Spectre of Comparisons* is about Southeast Asia, just as the preponderance of *Imagined Communities* is about Latin America. Fair enough.

My point is not to find fault with Anderson for being an Area Studies specialist in so many areas of the world outside the United States. Nor do I have any significant quarrel with what little Anderson does say about the United States. What is worth remarking upon is simply that even the least Eurocentric of our era's leading *theorists of nationalism in general* has emerged not from the study of the United States, but from the study of Southeast Asia and Latin America. This is less a comment about Anderson than about the class of theorists of which he is a member. The scholars whose careers focus on the United States are "area studies specialists" of a kind, but few of them have intervened tellingly in the cross-disciplinary discussion of nationalism. One who did was the historian David Potter, whose still-powerful article "Historian's Use of Nationalism and Vice Versa" was published nearly forty years ago but is rarely cited today.

The poison oak effect among theorists of nationalism would not be worthy of notice were it not for one fact that might be expected to attract rather than repel these theorists: the United States is the most successful nationalist project in all of modern history. What makes it "successful" is its longevity, its absorption of a variety of peoples, and its sheer power. Two-and-one-quarter centuries after its founding and 135 years after its Civil War, it is by far the most powerful nation-state in the world. No other major nation in the twenty-first century still operates with a constitution written in the eighteenth. It manages to get done a lot of what nations are expected to do. It has managed to incorporate a great variety of ethnoracial groups through immigration, conquest, and enslavement-and-emancipation. This process of incorporation has often been marked by the systematic mistreatment of people on the basis of color, language, and religion, but the national project of the United States remains, from the viewpoint of a comparative history, a story of relative stability.

One can lament the success of the United States, or at least the evils by which it has been achieved. One can instead rejoice in it, or be morally indifferent to it. And one can explain it in a number of different ways. But no matter how one may judge the national project of the United States morally, and no matter how one may explain its raw success, the downplaying of that project by theorists of nationalism remains a bit odd. It makes as much sense as a literature on rock and roll that treats Chuck Berry as just another performer with a guitar and a southern accent. To be sure, the study of small cases like Quebec or Ghana may turn out to prompt the most profound insights into the generic phenomenon of nationalism. Anderson's work is a commanding example of how much one can contribute while paying relatively little attention to the big case. But when we look at an entire literature of a generic, world-historical phenomenon, magnitude surely counts for something. Unless one eliminates the United States by way of a frankly "American exceptionalist" position eschewed by most theorists of nationalism, the United States is the Chuck Berry of nationalism.[1]

Moreover, the case of the United States might prompt a slight but productive change in the theorizing of nationalism, and one that would entail neither American exceptionalism nor the assimilation of the case of the United States into universal theories of nationalism. Rather than putting so fine a point on what is and is not a *nation*, and running endless variations on Renan, we might instead strive for an analysis of *political solidarity*, with the understanding that the diversity of what we call "nations" is part of a larger diversity of a yet larger class of communities. Political solidarities obviously include subnational and transnational formations, some of which are more "nationlike" or "protonational" than others. Political solidarities are to nations what genus is to species, and what species is to varieties: the lines between the levels of classification are fuzzy at the edges, as Darwin taught us long ago. What enables the United States to stimulate this shift from nation to political solidarity is the capacity of the Old Republic to challenge the categories without ceasing to be a "nation."

The wisdom of stepping back from nations and nationalisms in order to address something more inclusive is indicated by Anderson's own recent engagement with the notion of "seriality." In an analysis distinguished by the heightened abstractness of its basic terms, Anderson offers a distinction between unbound and bound seriality. He argues that each style of seriality generates its own kind of "politicization and political practice." And it is in talking about the bound seriality exemplified in the institution of the census that Anderson, interestingly, undertakes one of his more sustained discussions of the United States. It is the census carried out by the United States government since 1790 that provides Anderson with his key example of "bound" seriality, which "has its origins in governmentality," and which classifies each individual monolithically. For a vivid example of "unbound" seriality, Anderson takes the rough-and-tumble, non-bureaucratic, identity-transforming world experienced by a character from a fictional tale of the revolutionary movement that developed in Java at the end of the period of Japanese occupation. This young woman, in the tale by Pramoedya Ananta Toer quoted by Anderson, "found a circle of acquaintances far wider than the circle of her brothers, sisters, and parents." She occupied a "defined position" as "a woman, a typist in a government office, as a free individual." But the "plasticity and universality" of each series that now defines this woman socially "can never appear in a census," notes Anderson, "not merely because they cannot be enumerated and totaled," but because the meaning of each series for her is integrated into her sense of herself as a revolutionary (Anderson, *Spectre* 29, 36–37, 41–42). Hence Anderson comes close to saying—but does not quite say—that his distinction between unbounded and bounded seriality tracks the classical distinction between voluntary and ascribed identities.

Yet Anderson's choice of examples is ironic in view of the fact that the United States, home of the census and of oodles of ascribed and monolithic administrative identities, is also a site for an enormous history of multiple identities, identity transformations, contingent identities, and celebrations if not practices of voluntary identity. Many of the world's other societies are marked by greater continuity of the "collective subjectivities" that are Anderson's chief concern. If one is looking for a site in which unbounded as well as bounded seriality flourish, bump up against one another contentiously, and present striking challenges to theorists of political solidarity, collective subjectivity, and nationalism, the United States has a lot to offer.

The poison oak effect is difficult to throw off, however, especially when we approach the possibility of even a haltingly favorable judgment about nationalism. Anderson closes *Spectre of Comparisons* with a pensive meditation on "The Goodness of Nations" in which he remarks upon the sometimes wholesome result that respect for a nation's dead can have in maintaining the aspiration that a national community will eventually live up to its highest self-conception. Yet in a juxtaposition the irony of which is hard to miss, Anderson treats all nations as on virtually a moral par, while judging negatively a New Haven cemetery's even-handed honor of that city's dead soldiers, who had died in a series of wars of which some were more honorable than others. Of the monument to the dead soldiers of New Haven,

Anderson writes the following decidedly moralistic description:

> The four faces on its pedestal are inscribed with the names of men and boys who died in four very different old wars: the heroic war of Independence against George III's England; the unheroic skirmishes against the same foe in 1812; the louche imperialist adventure against Mexico in 1848; and the traumatic Civil War of 1861–65. It is remarkable that the monument treats all these dead as absolutely equivalent: it makes not the slightest difference whether they met their lives on a glorious or shameful battlefield. The sacrifice of their lives is thus radically separated from historical Right or Wrong. [*Spectre* 363]

Yet about nations Anderson concludes by stringing together the patriotism of Max Weber about the future of Germany (mocked by what happened to Weber's beloved nation in the following generation) with the patriotism of contemporary Americans about the United States (Anderson's concluding image of which is the reticent disinclination of Clinton-hating Americans to speak of Clinton in the same language of rape American soldiers applied to Saddam Hussein in the Gulf War). "No matter what crimes a nation's government commits and its passing citizenry endorses," Anderson observes, the nation's dead prompt the sentiment "My Country is ultimately Good" (*Spectre* 368).

Is the goodness of all nations equal? Are all varieties of national solidarity equally promising? Is the uncritical affirmation of a national tradition—against the cavalier dismissal of which Anderson cautions wisely—a generic phenomenon that the student of nationalism is simply to observe? When does an ostensibly neutral language mask an invidious judgment? Poison oak still?

I will not repeat here what I have said elsewhere about the national project of the United States and its salience to the discourse on nationalism (see Hollinger, all works listed). Instead, I want to call attention to several recent contentions within and about the national project of the United States that sharpen some of the general theoretical issues about identity, descent, and nationality. Although what follows is a decidedly Americocentric discussion grounded in American-style liberal theory, the issues on which I focus here appear to be of increasing importance in Europe and elsewhere as migrations, diasporas, and conflicts over human rights complicate relations between tribe, ethnos, nation, state, and species. The point is not to uphold the United States as a model for the world, but to urge closer scrutiny of the case of the United States in discussions of identity, descent, and nationality.

***

In the United States today, *identity,* whatever else it may be, is a zone of disputation within which various claims concerning an individual's social character and obligations press against each other. At issue, ultimately, is the distribution of solidarity. Identity is understood to be performative and social: one's identity carries implications for the distribution of one's affections, resources, and energies and for the claims one can make on the affections, resources, and energies of others. Whether identity is understood as monolithic or multiple, enduring or contingent, it has a "political economy" in the sense that identity is distributed in one way or another on the basis of authority.

This is not the way identity used to be understood in the United States. Identity once had to do primarily with psychological integration, not with group affiliation. In the heyday of Erik Erikson, identity was something a sound personality achieved, usually after a youthful crisis. The concept of identity applied to societies as a whole only when they were construed as analogues of an individual's personality, or "character" [see Erikson]. Some writers of the 1950s did analyze the national community of the United States in these terms. But this holistic style of analysis, often associated with "consensus history," was widely discredited in later decades. Throughout the 1980s and 1990s, however, a somewhat similar style of holistic analysis, under the sign of identity, came back into vogue when talking about ethnoracial communities. By then, "American identity" was understood to be a shallow concept, masking diversity and implying a conformist mentality. The concept was to be thrown out along with old copies of Boorstin and Hartz. But "Chicano identity," "Asian-American identity," and "black identity" were presented as deep concepts, expressing a vital unity in each case. Holism can thus wax and wane in relation to sentiments about just what wholes and parts are to be affirmed or denied. One party's whole can be another party's part, and vice versa.

Identity became a way of establishing circles of "we" and "they": who is in and who is out of the particular group that matters when identity is asserted or ascribed? This usage extends beyond ethnoracially defined collectivities; the movement for "Catholic identity" is a means by which some colleges and universities of Catholic affiliation have sought to counteract the influence on campus culture of Protestants, Jews, and freethinkers. Even Notre Dame, which has a strong Catholic identity movement of its own, led by its current President, finds itself accused by voices from other campuses of having failed to achieve and maintain a truly Catholic identity. It is no coincidence that the most far-out of the American religious-right affiliations has taken for its name "Christian Identity." And this effect is not limited to the United States: in the fall of 1999, Dominican Republic citizens trying to oust Haitians, to push them back across the border that divides the island they share, carried signs reading, "Dominican Identity."

One specific location in which we can see identity in its capacity as a commodity to be distributed by authority is the controversy over the federal census. The advocates of a mixed-race classification might be seen as practitioners of the politics of recognition. They want a census category that registers their mixtures, and treats these mixtures as authentic identities in their own right. The opponents of this classification, concerned with the distribution of government benefits, might be seen as practitioners of the politics of distribution. These opponents of the mixed-race category worry that without accurate accounts by traditional color categories, it will be more difficult to administer remedies for discrimination that has traditionally ignored mixture, as with the application of the one-drop rule. It is easy to understand the feeling of these opponents that the mixed-race advocates should look to arenas other than the census to gain recognition for their mixtures. Yet neither of the two sides to this debate, nor the Census Bureau, nor the Congress of the United States, which supervises the census, has been willing to separate color from culture and hence the politics of distribution from the politics of recognition. As a result, the two sides hold each other's virtues hostage. And mixed-race advocates are openly accused of breaking down the solidarity of descent communities that need antidiscrimination remedies. Some of the people with mixed descent, in turn, answer that by identifying themselves primarily as black or as Asian-American they are denying the solidarity they feel with the parts of their family that are not black or Asian-American.

The Census might, after all, ask two questions, one about color giving free play to the politics of distribution and one about culture giving free play to the politics of recognition. "Do you have the physical characteristics that render you at risk of discrimination at the hands of white people, and if so, do those characteristics make you black, red, yellow, or brown?" This question speaks exactly to the justified concern of opponents of the mixed-race category. Many mixed-descent individuals, moreover, could easily answer yes without violating their cultural identity. The latter could be elicited by another question, "Do you consider yourself to be a member of any of the following ethnoracially defined cultural groups?" This second question might be asked in relation to a list of ethnoracial categories that would include various specific mixtures, and should include the opportunity to write in something not included in the list. Tiger Woods can describe himself as he wishes in response to this second question, but a census official would have good reason to resist if, in answer to the earlier question about physical characteristics, Woods denied that he should be classified as "black."

But we will not have the two questions so long as all the parties cling to the doctrines that identity is singular, that color and culture go together, and that one can't really choose one's culture because, after all, one's culture is indissolubly bound up with one's color. Hence the politics of recognition and the politics of distribution remain linked even when there is a chance to separate them, and to allow each to do its own good work without obstructing the other. One might argue that identity is, or should be, one thing, while solidarity is, or should be, another. But that is not the way life in the United States is understood.

In the context of the awareness that identity now has a political economy, several closely related questions present themselves.

What is the authority by which claims about an individual's identity are warranted? To what extent does this authority reside in the will of the individual? If individual will is not a sufficiently authoritative basis for identity, who has the authority to ascribe identity to an individual, and what is the theoretical foundation for that authority? And on the basis of what considerations do these "ascribers" select, even to their own satisfaction, one identity rather than another to assign to a given individual?

A striking feature of identity discourse in the United States is how rarely these questions are asked. What makes this noticeable is the fact that the country is filled with people who are quite willing to tell other folks what their identity is, and isn't. Identity ascription flourishes best when no one asks hard questions about it. It is easier for the ascribers if no one challenges their authority or questions their principles of classification.

The dynamics of identity ascription might become clearer if we consider a certain class of contests over identity: those in which an individual declares an identity at variance with prevailing expectations. An "African-American" or an "Asian-American" might self-identify as "white," or simply as "an American," or perhaps as "a Christian." Or a person we think of as "white" suddenly announces that he or she is Osage or Cherokee. We, as a society, generally resist such declarations, or trivialize them as subsidiary, on the authority of (1) the physical evidence of skin color and morphological traits, and (2) the historical evidence that these physical features determine so much of any individual's social destiny that these physical features must therefore be central to identity. So heavily do we rely upon this combination of authorities that when we encounter persistent self-identification at odds with them—a self-identification that conflicts with the marks of physical descent—we often dismiss this self-identification as somehow false (one can't pretend to have a differently shaped and hued body than one has, can one?) and somehow wrong (isn't it immoral, or at least unattractively self-centered, to diminish solidarity with those with whom one shares a social destiny however much that destiny may be the product of prejudicial treatment at the hands of empowered racists?).

We resist especially the substitution of civic-national ("I'm an American") and religious ("I'm a Christian") identities for descent-community identities, apparently because such substitutions seem to be evasions of primal truths about "the way things are," and thus serve to invite the further victimization of peoples whose "true" interests are served by solidarity with their community of descent. We seem the most willing to accept multiple identities when there is a clear hierarchy placing identity by descent-community first (ahead of identities by religion, civic nationality, sexual orientation, professional calling, and so forth). And we seem the most willing to accept individual choice when it validates social expectations created by the physical marks of descent. In all of these decisions, we seem to regard identity as an essentially cultural phenomenon that exists within space largely determined by physical phenomena. Even when identity is conceived as a consciousness, or subjectivity (as in "the Chicano subject" or "the white subject"), the ordinance of perceived shared physical descent over proclaimed individual consent is strong.

This authority of the physical marks of descent in the political economy of identity invites scrutiny in the context of liberal theory's commitment to the expansion of the perimeter of the freedom of individuals. We might suppose that liberal theory would favor identity choice over identity ascription, even though liberals sometimes do find that other considerations override individual choice. Consider four public policy issues that pit individual choice against an ostensibly justified constraint. All four of these issues are widely discussed by American liberals in our time. One issue is the "right to work" rather than to be subjected to collective bargaining. Liberals usually say that the social benefits of collective bargaining easily trump the individual's "choice" of terms of employment. It's the conservatives who rejoice in the decline of unions. A second is flagged by the mantra "taxation is theft." Individuals ought to be able to choose how to spend what they earn, rather than have a certain percentage of their earnings taken by the state and then spent for them as the state sees fit. People on the left generally respond that an individual's earnings are facilitated by governmental policies created by the national community as a whole, and insist that the interests of the society trump the individual's choice of how the entirety of his or her earnings should be expended. It's the far right that finds taxes problematic on principle. A third is what is increasingly called "school choice." Self-styled progressives usually defend the existing system of public schools as superior to a voucher system on the basis of the larger interest of the society. Equality in this view is more likely to be achieved by perfecting a system of public education universal to the society than by parceling out education into a series of tax-supported but de facto private schools. It's the conservatives, again, who most push for vouchers. Yet a fourth issue is reproductive choice.

A woman should have access to contraceptives and abortion, rather than to be subject to restrictions on reproductive choice. Now in this fourth case, unlike in the first three, liberal theorists almost always deny that sweeping restrictions on the reproductive choices of adult women are justified by some larger social interest. It is the political right wing that finds "pro-choice" a sham, overruled by the social benefits of restraining individual choice. Liberals who resist certain other claims to "choice" offered in the name of an individual's freedom, then, often defend reproductive choice vigorously, and with well-theorized confidence.

Identity choice might well be compared with reproductive choice. Yet the widespread willingness to tolerate and even to encourage identity ascription implies the contrary. Those who acquiesce in, or encourage, identity ascription implicitly count this restriction on choice as more comparable to collective bargaining and taxation and public schools than to restrictions on reproductive choice. Voluntary identities are surely to be preferred to ascribed identities on classically liberal grounds. Encouraging individuals to make their own decisions about cultural identity, about who to affiliate with, about how to distribute their own capabilities for solidarity would seem to be a classically liberal program.

But it turns out that for many people of many different political orientations, including the left, identities, affiliations, and communities are attractive because they are understood to be *not* chosen. To recognize the human need for nonchosen imperatives is often considered the mark of a profound mind. From that point of view, the principle of "affiliation by revocable consent" is superficial.[2] This principle urges that we, as a society, allow individuals to make up their own minds about just how much energy they put into their communities of descent. Where the conditions for choice do not exist, as they so often do not, the principle urges that educational and public policy try to create conditions more conducive to choice. The principle of affiliation by revocable consent does not cut against strong affiliations, but it does cut against ascription. The principle of revocable consent "supports the renewal and critical revision of those communities of descent whose progeny choose to devote their energies to these communities even after experiencing opportunities for affiliating with other kinds of people" (Hollinger, *Postethnic America* 118). This principle takes for granted that some people will have good reasons for choosing to identify with and contributing to their communities of descent even when prejudice does not eliminate the possibility of exit.

But I encounter, again and again, the feeling that a true community, a true identity, must entail a significant element of coercion. True belonging, it is said, is not something to which you can consent. An affiliation consented to, in this view, is somehow less worthy, and less real, than an affiliation over which you have no control. To encounter this outlook is rather like talking with someone who does not believe in divorce: a marriage is a meaningful commitment only if there is no escape from it. These are classically conservative sentiments. This way of looking at the relation of individuals to groups has a long history, some of which is honorable, some not.

Holocaust survivor Konrad Latte, whose story was told recently in the *New York Times Magazine,* shocked Israeli journalists when he told them that he did not consider himself to be a Jew. His only felt connection to Jewishness was having been persecuted as a Jew. He did not want to grant Hitler the authority to determine his identity, to tell him with whom to associate even in the wake of the Shoah.[3] How should one respond when African-Americans or Japanese-Americans reject the authority of white racists to tell them who they are? When the Louisiana-born writer Anatole Broyard tried to enact such a rejection, he could get away with it, as Henry Louis Gates, Jr., has pointed out, only because Broyard was sufficiently light-skinned to pass as white throughout his career in New York City. Broyard did this at the cost of cutting off nearly all contact with his early life and his family of birth, and being obliged to live his life under the principle of whiteness, which appears to have stunted his creativity as much as liberated it (see Gates). In the United States today, Jewish identity is often treated as a matter of revocable consent. As a prominent historian of American Jewry recently put the point, affiliated Jews in recent American history "would continue being Jews because they wanted to, not because they were being forced to" (Shapiro 36). But not so with African-American affiliation. Not yet, if ever, affiliation by revocable consent.

And this brings us back to the census, and to the contractions that bedevil the debate over the mixed-race category. Perhaps someone will yet design sensible questions that serve the needs of both cultural affirmation and antidiscrimination, and thus respond both to the imperatives of identity choice and to some of the concerns behind identity ascription. Perhaps someone will even be able to build a political constituency strong enough to enact such a reform of the census. But in the meantime there is another reason for keeping the old census categories intact, even though many people now think the long-term goal of equality would be best served if the census would stop counting people by any and all ethnoracial categories. Marriage and reproduction across so-called "racial" lines are increasing at a high rate. It is surely important that the census keep us accurately informed about this remarkable development. Here, again, it is the physical rather than the cultural characteristics that matter. The census should continue to measure the so-called "races" and their mixing, if only to give us a record of one vital aspect of the struggle of Americans to overcome the power of "race" to control their individual lives, including their identities.[4]

The census of 1990 is already a decade out of date, but it shows the demographic base of the national project of the United States to be different from that of most other nations with a racist tradition as strong as that of the United States. The rate of marriage and reproduction across ethnoracial lines has been increasing rapidly even during a period when assimilation has been severely criticized in the interests of preserving descent communities. Census data show that 81 percent of married Polish-Americans between the ages of twenty-five and thirty-four had married outside their ethnic group, and that 73 percent of Italian-Americans had done so. But the figures concerning non-European groups demand the greatest emphasis, given the long-term history of Eurocentric attitudes in the United States. After all, we are talking about a nation that did not even allow Asians to become naturalized citizens until 1952. Of married persons between the ages of twenty-five and thirty-four in 1990 who had been born in the United States, about one-half of those with Asian ancestry had "outmarried." Among Hispanics, about 35 percent had acquired a spouse of non-Latino descent. About 60 percent of Indians reported being married to non-Indians. Black-white marriages continued to be rare, but they were considerably more frequent than only a few decades previously. In 1990, 3.75 percent of married black women in the twenty-five-to-thirty-four age cohort were married to white men, and 8.5 percent of the married black men were married to white women (see Farley).

These last figures concerning black-white unions provide little support for the predictions of Stanley Crouch and other social commentators that ethnoracial distinctions will disappear in the twenty-first century. Blacks still marry outside their descent community at a much lower rate than do other nonwhites. But these statistics do indicate an extent of publicly proclaimed and officially recognized black-white mixing significant for a society that in 1990 stood only twenty-three years from *Loving v. Virginia,* when the Supreme Court of the United States ruled unconstitutional all state laws forbidding interracial marriage. Until that ruling of 1967, black-white marriages were illegal in most of the states in which a large percentage of the population was black. An intriguing feature of the increase in black-white marriages is their location in very different parts of the class structure: among those most likely to marry across the black-white color line are enlisted personnel in the military and doctoral graduates of elite universities.

When all of these results of the 1990 census are considered in relation to the rest of the world, the old "melting pot" notion of the United States regains some of its credibility, although devoid, of course, of the sense of natural progression so long innocently associated with quotations from Crevecour and Zangwill. A political and legal struggle that continues today has been required to diminish the ethnocentric social attitudes and public policies put in place and long enforced by dominant Anglo-Protestants. But the United States now displays a degree of structural assimilation not to be found even in such other diverse societies as India, Switzerland, and Belgium, to say nothing of more homogeneous societies like Germany, Japan, the Netherlands, Austria, and Poland.

This relatively high degree of structural assimilation helps to mark off the contemporary nationalist impulse in the United States from many of the nationalist movements of today that sustain understandable suspicion of nationalism. I refer to the nationalist movements recently launched or renewed by Basques, Croats, Flemings, Kurds, Macedonians, Serbs, Sikhs, Slovakians, Tamils, and Ukrainians. The United States case is different even from the somewhat less ethnocentric nationalist movements of the Catalonians, Quebecois, and Scots. Nationalism is not of a piece, and the variety represented by the United States has much less blood-and-soil exclusivity than do several of the ones just named, and even less linguistic particularism.

By the same token, the nationalist impulse of the present American moment differs from that found in this country during the Progressive Era and the 1920s. Anyone who thinks we are about to replay the nativist politics of the 1920s might imagine the conservative Republican candidate of 1924, Calvin Coolidge, acting like his conservative Republican counterpart of 2000, which would mean trying to win votes by speaking Yiddish or Italian. In 2000 even Bob Jones University has given up its ban on black-white dating, while in 1924 it was still within the bounds of respectable public discussion among white conservatives to advocate the exporting of the entire black population to New Guinea and the Belgian Congo. The right-wing politicians and white-supremacist militias who today replay and extend the Anglo-Protestant chauvinism of Madison Grant are not to be ignored, but they are at the margins of American politics, as their predecessors decidedly were not. Exaggerating the power of cryptofascist racism in the United States today trivializes the suffering of those who were abused by even worse versions tolerated by established authority in past generations.

What is right up front in the American case today, considered in relation to such other ethnoracially plural societies as Belgium, Brazil, India, Indonesia, New Zealand, and Switzerland, is the frequency with which the descent communities that are considered "standard" change from generation to generation. The historical process by which a number of European-based immigrant groups became "white" has been widely discussed by historians. The "whiting" of economically successful Asian-Americans is a staple of everyday conversation in California, where Japanese-Americans were taken off to concentration camps actually quite recently, within my own lifetime. Yet the most striking case is that of American Jews. As recently as 1940 Jews were a stigmatized group often called a "race," only about three percent of whom outmarried. They were systematically excluded, by legal authority, from many spheres of employment, housing, and public accommodations. Yet by the 1980s between one-third and one-half of all marriages involving Jews entailed the acquiring of a non-Jewish spouse, and Jews had become so thoroughly assimilated into the "European" community of descent that they had ceased to be counted as a distinctive group when issues of ethnoracial representation and under-representation were discussed.

This American sort of "diversity," in which the very categories of diversity change, is different from the sort of diversity displayed by nations featuring several historically continuous descent communities that remain sharply separate from one another. One need not fall into the trap of a mystical "American exceptionalism" to recognize empirically warranted differences between the United States and certain other, specific nations and to appreciate, in the current world-historical context, the value of any political order that diminishes the constraints that often follow from ascribed status according to descent. The United States may not be unique, but it is a formidable engine of ethnoracial change. In this particular, modest respect, the United States since 1945, for all its manifestly counter-revolutionary actions in Vietnam and Guatemala, in Chile and the Congo, has proved to be a truly revolutionary power.

As such, it is a distinctive episode in the history of national solidarities. If the critical, necessarily guarded scrutiny of the United States can help the species find a future in which the varieties of humankind are less afraid of intimacy with one another, and can draw its various circles of the "we" more deliberately and less prejudicially, that will be all to the good.

Yet the very idea of the United States serving as a valuable example of a certain kind of civic nation mediating between the species and multiple communities of descent needs to be carefully formulated. I refer to an "example," not a "model." The historical particularity of each nation's situation militates against so arrogant a notion as a model to be copied, especially when the candidate for model status is the world's preeminent military and economic power. I intend "example" in what might be called its softest sense: it is simply a case that can be scrutinized critically by people who have reason to be interested in it. And now, when so many countries, especially in Europe, contemplate a future with larger immigrant populations, there is global interest in political communities that cross ethnoracial barriers without pretending to be universal. The case of the United States is important because racism is so deeply structured into its national history. This case, depending on the specific path it follows, may yet serve humbly to remind a heavily racialized world that even a society with a deeply racist past can incorporate individuals from a great variety of communities of descent on terms of considerable intimacy within a civic solidarity.

Notes

For helpful conversations about the issues I address in this paper I want to thank three colleagues, none of whom are likely to be fully comfortable with my formulations: Samuel Scheffler, Pheng Cheah, and Peter Zinoman. I want also to acknowledge the critical advice of Richard Bernstein, Nancy Fraser, and Joan Heifetz Hollinger.

1. Or, if this image is too benign for such problematic entities as nationalism and the United States, a different figure of speech can serve just as well: we would look askance at a theory of earthquakes that paid only passing attention to evidence from California; the United States could then be described as "the San Andreas Fault of nationalism."
2. The defense of this principle is a chief concern of my *Postethnic America*.
3. "I can't let the Nazis have the last word. I can't let them tell me, 'You're a Jew, you belong in this corner, this drawer'" (qtd. in Schneider 54).
4. For an excellent analysis of the difficulties created for social scientists, humanists, and political actors by the unresolved tensions that now reside within the concept of "identity," see Brubaker and Cooper, which appeared too late to be of use in the preparation of this essay.

Works Cited

Anderson, Benedict. *Imagined Communities: Reflections on the Origin and Spread of Nationalism.* 2d ed. London: Verso, 1991.

———. *The Spectre of Comparisons: Nationalism, Southeast Asia, and the World.* New York: Verso, 1998.

Beiner, Ronald. *Theorizing Nationalism.* Albany: SUNY Press, 1999.

Bhabha, Homi, ed. *Nation and Narration.* New York: Routledge, 1990.

Brubaker, Rogers, and Frederick Cooper. "Beyond 'Identity.'" *Theory and Society* 29 (2000): 1–47.

Eley, Geoff, and Ronald G. Suny. *Becoming National.* New York: Oxford UP, 1996.

Erikson, Erik. *Childhood and Society.* New York: Norton, 1950.

Farley, Reyonds. "Racial Issues: Recent Trends in Residential Patterns and Intermarriage." *Diversity and Its Discontents: Cultural Conflict and Common Ground in Contemporary American Society.* Ed. Neil Smelser and Jeffrey Alexander. Princeton: Princeton UP, 1998. 85–128.

Gates, Henry Louis, Jr. "White Like Me." *New Yorker* 17 June 1996.

Gellner, Ernest. *Nations and Nationalism.* Oxford: Blackwell, 1983.

Greenfeld, Liah. *Nationalism: Five Roads to Modernity.* Cambridge, MA: Harvard UP, 1992.

Guibernau, Montserrat. *Nationalisms: The Nation-State and Nationalism in the Twentieth Century.* Cambridge: Polity, 1996.

Hall, John A. *The State of the Nation: Ernest Gellner and the the Theory of Nationalism.* New York: Cambridge UP, 1998.

Hollinger, David A. "National Culture and Communities of Descent." *Diversity and Its Discontents.* Ed. Neil Smelser and Jeffrey Alexander. Princeton: Princeton UP, 1998. 247–62.

———. "Nationalism, Cosmopolitanism, and the United States." *Immigration and Citizenship in the Twenty-First Century.* Ed. Noah Pickus. Lantham, MD: Rowman and Littlefield, 1998. 85–99.

———. "National Solidarity at the End of the Twentieth Century: Reflections on the United States and Liberal Nationalism." *Journal of American History* 84 (1997): 559–69.

———. *Postethnic America: Beyond Multiculturalism.* New York: Basic Books, 1995.

Hutchinson, John, and Anthony D. Smith, eds. *Nationalism.* Oxford: Oxford UP, 1994.

Kedouri, Elie. *Nationalism.* Oxford: Blackwell, 1993.

Miller, David. *On Nationality.* Oxford: Clarendon, 1995.

Potter, David. "The Historian's Use of Nationalism and Vice Versa." *American Historical Review* 67 (1962): 924–50.

Schneider, Peter. "Saving Konrad Latte." *New York Times Magazine* 13 Feb. 2000: 54.

Shapiro, Edward S. *A Time for Healing: American Jewry since World War II.* Baltimore: Johns Hopkins UP, 1992.

CHAPTER **8**

Anderson's Utopia

PARTHA CHATTERJEE

Imagined Communities was, without doubt, one of the most influential books of the late twentieth century. In the years since it was published, as nationalism unexpectedly came to be regarded as an increasingly unresolvable and often dangerous "problem" in world affairs, Benedict Anderson has continued to analyze and reflect on the subject, adding two brilliant chapters to his highly acclaimed book and writing several new essays and lectures. Some of these have been brought together, along with a series of essays on the history and politics of Southeast Asia, in *The Spectre of Comparisons*. The publication of this volume provides an opportunity for other scholars in the field to reassess the work of, and pay tribute to, a major intellectual of our time.

1

Theoretically, the most significant addition that Anderson has made to his analysis in *Imagined Communities* is his attempt to distinguish between nationalism and the politics of ethnicity. He does this by identifying two kinds of seriality that are produced by the modern imaginings of community. One is the unbound seriality of the everyday universals of modern social thought: nations, citizens, revolutionaries, bureaucrats, workers, intellectuals, and so on. The other is the bound seriality of governmentality: the finite totals of enumerable classes of population produced by the modern census and the modern electoral systems. Unbound serialities are typically imagined and narrated by means of the classic instruments of print capitalism, namely, the newspaper and the novel. They afford the opportunity for individuals to imagine themselves as members of larger than face-to-face solidarities, of choosing to act on behalf of those solidarities, of transcending by an act of political imagination the limits imposed by traditional practices. Unbound serialities are potentially liberating. As Anderson quotes from Pramodeya Ananta Toer's tale *Dia Jang Menjerah,* which describes such a moment of emancipation experienced by one of its characters:

> By now, Is knew the society she was entering. She had found a circle of acquain-
> tances far wider than the circle of her brothers, sisters and parents. She now
> occupied a defined position in that society: as a woman, as a typist in a govern-
> ment office, as a free individual. She had become a new human being, with new
> understanding, new tales to tell, new perspectives, new attitudes, new interests—
> newnesses that she managed to pluck and assemble from her acquaintances.
> [quoted in *Spectre* 41]

Bound serialities, by contrast, can operate only with integers. This implies that for each category of classification, an individual can count only as one or zero, never as a fraction, which in turn means that all partial or mixed affiliations to a category are ruled out. One can only be black or not black, Muslim or not Muslim, tribal or not tribal, never only partially or contextually so. Bound serialities, Anderson suggests, are constricting and perhaps inherently conflictual. They produce the tools of ethnic politics.

I am not sure that the distinction between bound and unbound seriality, despite its appearance of mathematical precision, is the appropriate way to describe the differences in political modalities that Anderson wants to demarcate. It is not clear why the "unbound" serialities of the nationalist imagination cannot, under specific conditions, produce finite and countable classes. Explaining unbound seriality, Anderson says it is that which "makes the United Nations a normal, wholly unparadoxical institution" (29). But surely, at any given time, the United Nations can have only a finite number of members. And that is because, with its explicitly laid-down procedures and criteria of membership, the imagining of nationhood has been reduced to the institutional grid of governmentality. Again, if by revolutionaries we mean those who are members of revolutionary political parties, then the number of revolutionaries in a country, or even in the whole world, will also be finite and countable, in the same way that the census claims to provide a figure for, let us say, the number of Hindus in India. It is also not clear in what sense the serialities of governmentality are "bound." The series for Christians or English speakers in the world is, in principle, without end, since to every total that we count today one more could be added tomorrow. But, of course, the series is denumerable, exactly like, say, the series of positive integers, even though at any given point in time such a set will contain a finite number of members.

Some years ago, Ben Anderson asked me what I thought of Hegel's idea of the "wrong infinity." I must say that I was stumped by the suggestion that a somewhat quaint remark by the long-dead German philosopher might call for some sort of moral response from me. After carefully reading Anderson's "logic of seriality," I can now see what he was asking me. The denumerable but infinite series, such as the sequence of positive integers, which is the basic form of counting used by governmental systems like the census, is, for Anderson, of the same dubious philosophical status as it was for Hegel. To describe change or "becoming" by means of a sequence of finite quantities, which is what the statistical logic of governmentality would prescribe, is not to transcend the finite at all, but merely to set one finite against its other. One finite merely reappears in another finite. "The progression of infinity never gets further than a statement of the contradiction involved in the finite, viz. that it is somewhat as well as somewhat else. It sets up with endless iteration the alternation between these two terms, each of which calls up the other" (Hegel, *Encyclopaedia* 137). This is the "wrong or negative infinity." Hegel makes a withering comment on those who try to grasp the infinite character of, say, space or time by following in this way the endless progression of finite quantities:

> In the attempt to contemplate such an infinite, our thought, we are commonly informed, must sink exhausted. It is true indeed that we must abandon the unending contemplation, not however because the occupation is too sublime, but because it is too tedious. It is tedious to expatiate in the contemplation of this infinite progression, because the same thing is constantly recurring. We lay down a limit: then we pass it: next we have a limit once more, and so on for ever. All this is but superficial alternation, which never leaves the region of the finite behind. [*Encyclopaedia* 138][1]

The "genuine infinity," by contrast, does not simply negate one finite by its other, but also negates that other. By doing so, it "returns to itself," becomes self-related. The true infinity does not set up an abyss between a finite this-world and an infinite other-world. Rather, it expresses the truth of the finite, which, for Hegel, is its ideality. It encapsulates in its ideality the infinite variability of the finite.

I have not brought up this abstruse Hegelian point merely to obscure the distinction between unbound and bound serialities on which Anderson hangs his argument about the residual goodness of nationalism and the unrelieved nastiness of ethnic politics. On the contrary, I think Hegel's idea of the true infinity is an example of the kind of universalist critical thought characteristic of the Enlightenment that Anderson is keen to preserve. It is the mark of what is genuinely ethical and indeed—I use this word in sincere admiration—noble in his work.

Hegel's true infinity, as I said, is only an example. One will find similar examples in Kant or (at least in the standard readings) in Marx. Faced with the indubitable facts of historical conflict and change, the aspiration here is to affirm an ethical universal that does not deny the variability of human wants and values or cast them aside as unworthy or ephemeral but rather encompasses and integrates them as the real historical ground on which that ethical universal must be established. Much philosophical blood was spilt in the nineteenth century over the question of whether there was an idealist and a materialist version of this aspiration and, if so, which was the more truthful. Few take those debates seriously anymore. But as the sciences and technologies of governmentality have spread their tentacles throughout the populated world in the twentieth century, the critical philosophical mind has been torn by the question of ethical universalism and cultural relativism. The growing strength of anticolonial nationalist politics in the middle decades of this century contributed greatly to the recognition of this problem, even though the very successes of nationalism may also have led to the chimerical hope that the cultural conflicts were merely the superficial signs of the production of a richer, more universal, modernity. Decolonization, however, was soon followed by the crisis of the third-world state, and the culture wars became identified with chauvinism, ethnic hatred, and cynically manipulative and corrupt regimes. To all intents and purposes, nationalism became incurably contaminated by ethnic politics.

Ben Anderson has refused to accept this diagnosis. He continues to believe that the politics of nationalism and that of ethnicity arise on different sites, grow on different nutriments, travel through different networks, mobilize on different sentiments, and fight for different causes. But unlike many in the Western academy, he has refused to soothe the liberal bad conscience with the balm of multiculturalism. He has also remained an outspoken critic of the hard-headed developmentalist of the "realist" school whose recipes for third-world countries flow out of a cynical double standard that says "ethics for us, economics for them." Anderson closes *The Spectre of Comparisons* with an evocative listing of some of the ideals and affective moments of nationalism and remarks: "There is something of value in all of this—strange as it may seem. . . . Each in a different but related way shows why, no matter what crimes a nation's government commits and its passing citizenry endorses, My Country is ultimately Good. In these straitened millennial times, can such Goodness be profitably discarded?" (368). Idealist? I think the question is quite meaningless, especially since we know that Anderson, more than anyone else in recent years, has inspired the study of the material instruments of literary and cultural production that made possible the imagining of modern political communities in virtually every region of the world. Romantic? Perhaps, but then much that is good and noble in modern social thinking has been propelled by romantic impulses. Utopian? Yes. And there lies, I think, a major theoretical and political problem, which is also the chief source of my disagreement with Anderson.

2

The dominant strand of modern historical thinking imagines the social space of modernity as distributed in empty homogeneous time. A Marxist could call this the time of capital. Anderson explicitly adopts the formulation from Walter Benjamin and uses it to brilliant effect in *Imagined Communities* to show the material possibilities of large anonymous socialities being formed by the simultaneous experience of reading the daily newspaper or following the private lives of popular fictional characters. It is the same simultaneity experienced in empty homogeneous time that allows us to speak of the reality of such categories of political economy as prices, wages, markets, and so on. Empty homogeneous time is the time of capital. Within its domain, capital allows for no resistances to its free movement. When it encounters an impediment, it thinks it has encountered another time— something out of precapital, something that belongs to the premodern. Such resistances to capital (or to modernity) are always thought of as coming out of humanity's past, something people should have left behind but somehow haven't. But by imagining capital (or modernity) as an attribute of time itself, this view succeeds not only in branding the resistances to it as archaic and backward, but also in securing for capital and modernity their ultimate triumph, regardless of what some people believe or hope, because after all, as everyone knows, time does not stand still.

It would be tiresome to pile on examples of this sort of progressive historicist thinking because they are strewn all over the historical and sociological literature of at least the last century and a half. Let me cite here one example from a Marxist historian who was justifiably celebrated for his antireductionist view of historical agency and who once led a bitter attack against the Althusserian project of writing "history without a subject." In a famous essay on time and work-discipline in the era of industrial capitalism, E. P. Thompson spoke of the inevitability of workers everywhere having to shed their precapitalist work habits: "Without time-discipline we could not have the insistent energies of the industrial man; and whether this discipline comes in the form of Methodism, or of Stalinism, or of nationalism, it will come to the developing world" (399).

I believe Ben Anderson has a similar view of modern politics as something that belongs to the very character of the time in which we now live. It is futile to participate in, or sympathize with, or even to give credence to efforts to resist its sway. In *Imagined Communities,* he wrote of the modular forms of nationalism developed in the Americas, in Europe, and in Russia which then became available for copy by the anticolonial nationalisms of Asia and Africa. In *Spectre,* he speaks often of "the remarkable planetary spread, not merely of nationalism, but of a profoundly standardized conception of politics, in part by reflecting on the everyday practices, rooted in industrial material civilization, that have displaced the cosmos to make way for the world" (29). Such a conception of politics requires an understanding of the world as *one,* so that a common activity called politics can be seen to be going on *everywhere.* Politics, in this sense, inhabits the empty homogeneous time of modernity.

I disagree. I believe this view of modernity, or indeed of capital, is mistaken because it is one-sided. It looks at only one dimension of the time-space of modern life. People can only imagine themselves in empty homogeneous time; they do not live in it. Empty homogeneous time is the utopian time of capital. It linearly connects past, present, and future, creating the possibility for all of those historicist imaginings of identity, nationhood, progress, and so on that Anderson, along with others, have made familiar to us. But empty homogeneous time is not located anywhere in real space—it is utopian. The real space of modern life is a heterotopia (my debt to Michel Foucault should be obvious). Time here is heterogeneous, unevenly dense. Here, even industrial workers do not all internalize the work-discipline of capitalism, and more curiously, even when they do, they do not do so in the same way. Politics here does not mean the same thing to all people. To ignore this is, I believe, to discard the real for the utopian.

Obviously, I can make my case more persuasively by picking examples from the postcolonial world. For it is there more than anywhere else in the modern world that one could show, with almost the immediacy of the palpable, the presence of a dense and heterogeneous time. In those places, one could show industrial capitalists waiting to close a business deal because they hadn't yet had word from their respective astrologers, or industrial workers who would not touch a new machine until it had been consecrated with appropriate religious rites, or voters who could set fire to themselves to mourn the defeat of their favorite leader, or ministers who openly boast of having secured more jobs for people from their own clan and having kept the others out. To call this the copresence of several times—the time of the modern and the times of the premodern—is only to endorse the utopianism of Western modernity. I prefer to call it the heterogeneous time of modernity. And to push my polemical point a little further, I will add that the postcolonial world outside Western Europe and North America actually constitutes *most* of the populated modern world.

Having said this, let me return to Anderson's distinction between nationalism and the politics of ethnicity. He agrees that the "bound serialities" of governmentality can create a sense of community, which is precisely what the politics of ethnic identity feeds on. But this sense of community is illusory. In these real and imagined censuses, "thanks to capitalism, state machineries, and mathematics, integral bodies become identical, and thus serially aggregable as phantom communities." (*Spectre* 44). By contrast, the "unbound serialities" of nationalism do not, one presumes, need to turn the free individual members of the national community into integers. It can imagine the nation as having existed in identical form from the dawn of historical time to the present without requiring a censuslike verification of its identity. It can also experience the simultaneity of the imagined collective life of the nation without imposing rigid and arbitrary criteria of membership. Can such "unbound serialities" exist anywhere except in utopian space?

To endorse these "unbound serialities" while rejecting the "bound" ones is, in fact, to imagine nationalism without modern governmentality. What modern politics can we have that has no truck with capitalism, state machineries, or mathematics? The historical moment Anderson seems keen to preserve is the moment of classical nationalism. Referring to today's politics of ethnicity in the United States and other old nation-states, he calls it (perhaps overlooking the deep moral ambivalence of Dostoyevsky's characterizations) "a bastard Smerdyakov to classical nationalism's Dmitri Karamazov" (*Spectre* 71). When he chastises the "long-distance nationalism" of Irish-Americans for being so out of touch with the "real" Ireland, he ignores the fact that "Ireland" here truly exists only in utopian space, since the real space of this politics is the heterotopia of contemporary American social life.

Anderson's posing of the opposition between nationalism and ethnicity can be traced, therefore, to the distinction between popular sovereignty, enshrined in classical nationalism's equation of the people with the nation, and governmentality, which really came into its own in the second half of the twentieth century. But how are we to understand this opposition? As an opposition between the good and the bad? Between something that should be preserved and something else to be abjured? Or should we say, following the course of capitalist modernity in the twentieth century, that the opposition between popular sovereignty and governmentality expresses a new set of contradictions in a capitalist order that now has to maintain class rule under the general conditions of mass democracy?

I believe it is no longer productive to reassert the utopian politics of classical nationalism. Or rather, I do not believe it is an option that is available for a theorist from the postcolonial world. Let me end by commenting briefly on Anderson's perspective on comparisons.

Anderson begins *The Spectre of Comparisons* with a report on an experience in 1963 when he acted as an impromptu interpreter of a speech
by Sukarno in which the Indonesian president praised Hitler for being so
"clever" in arousing the patriotic feelings of Germans by depicting the ideals
of nationalism. Anderson

> felt a kind of vertigo. For the first time in my young life I had been invited to see
> my Europe as through an inverted telescope. Sukarno ... was perfectly aware of
> the horrors of Hitler's rule. But he seemed to regard these horrors ... with the
> brisk distance from which my schoolteachers had spoken of Genghiz Khan, the
> Inquisition, Nero, or Pizarro. It was going to be difficult from now on to think
> of "my" Hitler in the old way. [2]

This "doubled vision," looking "as through an inverted telescope," is what
Anderson, borrowing from José Rizal, so felicitously calls "the spectre of
comparisons." It forced him to look at "his" Europe and "his" Hitler as
through the eyes and mind of Sukarno, just as Sukarno himself had learnt to
look at Europe as through the eyes and minds of his Dutch teachers. This is
the critical anthropologist's vision, which does not shy away from having to
come to terms with a fundamental relativism of worldviews. Ben Anderson's
work, including all of the essays contained in this book, is a wonderful
example of the struggle to grapple with this doubled vision, carried out in
his case with acute analytical skill and outstanding intellectual and political
integrity.

What Anderson does not seem to recognize is that as comparativists
looking upon the world in the twentieth century, the perspective of the
Indonesian can never be symmetrical to that of the Irishman. One's comparative vision is not the mirror image of the other's. To put it plainly, the
universalism that is available to Anderson to be refined and enriched through
his anthropological practice could never have been available to Sukarno, regardless of the political power the latter may have wielded as leader of a
major postcolonial nation. The universalist ideal that belongs to Anderson
as part of the same inheritance that allows him to say "my Europe" can
continue *to encompass* its others as it moves from older national rigidities
to newer cosmopolitan lifestyles. For those who cannot say "my Europe,"
the choice seems to be to allow oneself *to be encompassed* within global cosmopolitan hybridities or to relapse into hateful ethnic particularities. For
Anderson, and others like him, upholding the universalism of classical nationalism is still an ethically legitimate privilege. For those who now live
in the postcolonial nations founded by the Bandung generation, charting a
course that steers away from both global cosmopolitanism and ethnic chauvinism means necessarily to dirty one's hands in the complicated business of

the politics of governmentality. The asymmetries produced and legitimized by the universalisms of classical nationalism have not left room for any ethically neat choice. Even the patriotic absurdities of diasporic communities, which Anderson so dislikes, will seem, by this reckoning, less the examples of perverse nationalism and more those of a failed cosmopolitanism.

At a recent meeting in an Indian research institute, after a distinguished panel of academics and policymakers had bemoaned the decline of universalist ideals and moral values in national life, a Dalit activist from the audience asked why it was the case that liberal and leftist intellectuals were so pessimistic about where history was moving at the end of the twentieth century. As far as he could see, the latter half of the twentieth century had been the brightest period in the entire history of the Dalits, since they had gotten rid of the worst social forms of untouchability, mobilized themselves politically as a community, and were now making strategic alliances with other oppressed groups in order to get a share of governmental power. All this could happen because the conditions of mass democracy had thrown open the bastions of caste privilege to attack from the representatives of oppressed groups organized into electoral majorities. The panelists were silenced by this impassioned intervention, although one or two could be heard muttering something about the inevitable recurrence of the Tocquevillian problem. I came away persuaded once more that it is morally illegitimate to uphold the universalist ideals of nationalism without simultaneously demanding that the politics spawned by governmentality be recognized as an equally legitimate part of the real time-space of the modern political life of the nation. Without it, governmental technologies will continue to proliferate and serve as manipulable instruments of class rule in a global capitalist order. By seeking to find real ethical spaces for their operation, the incipient resistances to that order may be allowed to invent new terms of political justice. As the counterpoint to what I believe is a one-sided view of capitalist modernity held by Anderson, I continue to adhere to Marx's methodological premise:

> capital drives beyond national barriers and prejudices as much as beyond nature worship, as well as all traditional, confined, complacent, encrusted satisfactions of present needs, and reproductions of old ways of life....
>
> But from the fact that capital posits every such limit as a barrier and hence gets *ideally* beyond it, it does not by any means follow that it has *really* overcome it, and, since every such barrier contradicts its character, its production moves in contradictions which are constantly overcome but just as constantly posited. Furthermore. The universality towards which it irresistibly strives encounters barriers in its own nature, which will, at a certain stage of its development, allow it to be recognized as being itself the greatest barrier to this tendency, and hence will drive towards its own suspension. [Marx, *Grundrisse* 410][2]

Notes

1. Hegel makes specific use of his distinction between the true and the false infinity to criticize Fichte's arguments about the legal and moral validity of a contract (see Hegel, *Philosophy of Right* 61).
2. I am indebted to a recent reading of Dipesh Chakrabarty's "Two Histories of Capital" which reminded me of this apt citation from Marx as well as of the article by E. P. Thompson cited earlier.

Works Cited

Anderson, Benedict. *Imagined Communities: Reflections on the Origin and Spread of Nationalism.* London: Verso, 1983.

———. *The Spectre of Comparisons: Nationalism, Southeast Asia and the World.* London: Verso, 1998.

Chakrabarty, Dipesh. "Two Histories of Capital." *Provincializing Europe: Postcolonial Thought and Historical Difference.* Princeton: Princeton UP, 2000.

Hegel, G. W. F. *Encyclopaedia of the Philosophical Sciences.* Part 1. Trans. William Wallace. Oxford: Clarendon, 1975.

———. *Philosophy of Right.* Trans. T. M. Knox. London: Oxford UP, 1967.

Marx, Karl. *Grundrisse.* Trans. Martin Nicolaus. Harmondsworth: Penguin, 1973.

Thompson, E. P. "Time, Work-Discipline and Industrial Capitalism." *Customs in Common.* London: Penguin, 1991. 352–403.

CHAPTER 9

Ghostly Comparisons

Anderson's Telescope

H. D. HAROOTUNIAN

While the formation of area studies in the universities and colleges of the United States was initially inaugurated as a response to the Cold War "necessity" to win the hearts and minds of the unaligned, many of whom were new refugees of decolonization, one of its unintended consequences was to foster the development of comparative perspectives of study across disciplines and different cultural regions. But this secondary goal was often diverted by the principal purpose of area studies programs to supply authoritative information on regions outside of Euro-America (the second and third worlds) considered crucial to the national security and to private businesses thrown increasingly into an expanding global market seeking new regions capable of providing buyers, workers, and materials. In time, the vocation of comparison became part of the unconscious of area studies, as the unit of the nation-state took precedence over all other considerations. Instead of envisaging genuinely interdisciplinary agendas that were able to integrate different disciplines, area studies have too often settled for simple multi-disciplinarism, substituting coverage for comparison, language acquisition for method, the nation-state for the totality of the cultural region. Benedict Anderson's recent *Spectre of Comparisons* reminds us of the role played by area studies programs in the American academic profession during the nervous days of the Cold War and the wartime exigencies that led to their postwar organization and installation in a number of universities. But it also recalls for us the comparative promise associated with area studies and how it was either redirected to a multidisciplinary approach poorly disguised as interdisciplinarism or simply incorporated into large developmental narratives like modernization theory. It is instructive to see how Anderson's own work, rather than Southeast Asian area studies, has been able to achieve the remote goal of integration and comparison in a number of stunning examples that have eluded the collective efforts of many institutional programs. This singular success magisterially discloses how he was trained to envisage the region as a "unified" area studies program, even though little more than a geographical term named this unity, and what he needed to do to actually realize the dim prospect of achieving some sort of larger, integrated understanding, which was eventually inscribed in his seminal book, *Imagined Communities*. At the most basic level, Anderson was able to secure this effect first by roaming around the area (turning his banishment from Indonesia in 1972 to good use by shifting his attention to Thailand and then the Philippines). Yet, as his essays show, there were other, more intellectually and epistemologically compelling reasons which, if amplified, might provide such diversity with a sense of commonality that only geography and the putatively integrative approach of an area studies program seemed willing to promise even as they failed to deliver.

Anderson situates his own intellectual trajectory within the institutional circumstances of the region as an area studies which he and his contemporary fellow students "helped give a certain reality" (*Spectre* 19). In fact, "Southeast Asia" has always been the common frame that structured the particular relationship between Europe of the colonizers and its Asian colonized and thus became the location that best exemplified for him the peculiar nature of the "haunting," as he puts it, as both the place of comparison and the necessity of comparability. In other words, Southeast Asia was the locus that best afforded a sighting of the spectacle of specters that recalled authorizing sister images in Europe and provided a perspective that was necessarily comparative. In Anderson's reckoning, comparison first referred to the circulation of images between metropole and colony and secondly between the various colonial sites that constituted Southeast Asia. As a result, Southeast Asia, and by extension all colonies, became the overdetermined place of haunting.

Beyond the agency of the war, of course, was the experience of colonialism and those first modern interpreters of Asia who, as administrators, spent long years in the field serving imperial bureaucracies and who were in the incomparable position of examining such sites comparatively. This was especially true of the Southeast Asian colonies that recruited a diversely national cohort of administrators who became scholars of their particular precincts. Anderson recognizes that even though these scholars contributed to transforming this geographical location into an object of study, it was still marked by the experience of a "strange history of mottled imperialism." (*Spectre* 4). As a unit in area studies, Southeast Asian Studies was therefore organized later than the study of other regions, such as East Asia, the Middle East, and Latin America, owing to its staggered schedule of decolonization. Yet its prior history of colonial subjugation prefigured this delayed recognition of the region as a unit of study. Only Belgium and Italy were missing from Euro-America's participation in this mottled imperialism, which itself dates back to the sixteenth century, when the first Portuguese and Spanish appeared in search of booty and converts. Unlike the colonization of Africa, which mainly took place in the late nineteenth century; of South Asia, the fruits of Great Britain's victory over the French in the eighteenth century; or even of East Asia, which became the object of intense imperial competition in the nineteenth and early twentieth centuries, Southeast Asia's long encounter with "mottled imperialism" seemed to condense the whole, diverse history of Euro-American expansion and colonization, and served as the "central factor" that differentiated the region from others. Moreover, imperial powers, fearing rivalry with contiguously close neighbors, often sought to close off their newly acquired territories from nearby colonies. In this way, Anderson proposes, the inhabitants of Batavia were more familiar with Amsterdam than with other peoples in the vicinity, despite sharing with them ethnic, cultural and historical ties, "while their cousins in Manila knew more about Madrid and New York than about the Vietnamese littoral a short step across the South China Sea" (*Spectre* 5). This combination of imperial segregation and geographical remoteness, according to Anderson, worked to prevent envisaging the region as a unity and even inhibited giving it a name that might stand in for the absence of coherence.

It was World War II and its aftermath that supplied the region with a name that conferred a unitary identity and promoted the process of transforming this heterogeneous congeries of diverse imperial possessions into an "imagined reality" at the moment of decolonization. Anderson, I think, overlooks or perhaps understates the irony that a region whose history, peoples, and cultures constantly imbricated each other for over a thousand years has been locked in a state of segregation since the colonial powers were forced to surrender their control and leave. To be sure, Cold War policy and the establishment of interregional organizations like SEATO (1954), ASA (1961), and ASEAN (1967), implemented in response to what Anderson calls "an alarming profile" consisting of Communist insurgencies throughout the region in the wake of decolonization, sought to reinforce regional solidarity but usually under American sponsorship. The United States has often appeared as the true successor of the mottled imperialism of European nations and has, with disastrous consequences, tried to reconstitute precisely what decolonization promised to eliminate. In place of nationally diverse colonial possessions, we now have diverse nation-states serving as clients to a unitary neocolonial power. Anderson doesn't say this but provides ample testimony to its reality. Absent in Anderson's account is a consideration of the Bandung Conference—the first meeting of newly formed unaligned countries in Sukarno's Indonesia—which sought to find a different mode of integration by allying many of the states of Southeast Asia with Nasser's Egypt, Nehru's India, and Tito's Yugoslavia. All of these former colonial regimes claimed some sort of affiliation with non-Soviet socialism, including the Royal Buddhists of Cambodia. Instead, Anderson assesses the career of Communism in Southeast Asia in the apparent aftermath of Bandung and the failure of Communism in the subsequent reconstitution of political radicalism. Yet the trajectory of Communism in Southeast Asia and its ultimate failure by no means represent the only possible legacy of the Bandung Conference, which easily—and wrongly, I believe—was assimilated to Cold War narratives by American policy makers already obsessed by the fear that the region was becoming the staging ground for the enactment of the notorious "domino theory." I should say, though, that I am not accusing Anderson of contributing to this historiographical fiction.

Added to the goals of American policy to create an anti-Communist bulwark in the area and to diminish the establishment of an alternative, non-Soviet socialist bloc of nation-states was, of course, the formation of area studies programs like Anderson's at Cornell University, devoted to the teaching and training of regional specialists. These programs were initially funded by major foundations like Ford and Rockefeller and later supported by the federal government in the wake of national panic caused by the Soviet Union's success in putting Sputnik into space. Like the more established area studies programs on East Asia, the Middle East, and Russia and Eastern Europe, these new Southeast Asian programs invariably were linked to the state through federal funding aimed at augmenting language study and training experts who could gather useful information about areas crucial to American security (and, later, business) interests. While Anderson correctly recognizes that these new programs concentrated on fields of study different from the more generalized scholar-colonial bureaucrats of the prewar days, the first generation of trainees, like those in East Asian studies, were, for a variety of reasons, closely bonded to the security state and, despite the heroic figure of George McT. Kahin of Cornell and a few, older "China hands" like John Service and Owen Lattimore, most American Asia specialists had been produced by the war and retained strong sympathies with United States policy in Asia. While Anderson has a more generous view of the role played by area studies programs than I hold (undoubtedly attesting to a better experience at Cornell), I should say, in any case, people like Kahin and him were exceptions to the more familiar products of such programs and therefore do not really count in any effort to justify the continued existence of such research enclaves, much less their past, and the role they were supposed to have played in familiarizing Americans with the world outside Euro-America. Most area studies programs have contributed far more to keeping their cultural regions on the outside and as objects of US strategic and economic interests. What so many area studies programs have managed to accomplish has been, in fact, the reproduction of the political vocation of its inaugural generation. In this regard, there is less difference between those intrepid colonial bureaucrat-scholars who first studied the region in their spare moments and their post–World War II successors who, in their own way, were as devoted to serving the state. Helen Hardacre's recently edited and overpriced volume on Japanese Studies in the United States recalls for us nothing more than those Hollywood B movies titled *The Land Time Forgot* or *The Land Where Time Stood Still*, correctly conveying the sense of a neolithic scene.

It is, in any case, this locus, a geographical region, and its development into a unified subject of scholarly inquiry, that has been Anderson's site for seeing through his own ambitious program of comparative study. His program has been double-tiered: the primary focus of comparison has been between "my Europe," as he puts it, and its Southeast Asian inflections; and secondarily, the comparative possibilities among the several societies that constitute the region. But it is important that his grasp of the first level of comparison determines how he envisages the second. Long before Anderson imagined his program, Walter Benjamin—prompted by Marx's recognition of the mystical, and thus ghostly, dimension of the commodity form—proposed a view that sought to see history as spectral, inasmuch as events that seek to restore what had been lost, forgotten, or repressed come as specters, apparitions that seek to trouble the settled boundaries of the present and that are always on the point of arriving (see Benjamin 159–235). In his *Spectre of Comparisons*, Anderson immediately alerts us to one of the excluded possibilities lived by societies outside of Euro-America but still implicated in its imperial expansion and colonial expropriations whose modern forms were introduced through the export of capital and its deterritorializing machinery. Through a reading of José Rizal's late nineteenth-century novel *Noli me tangere*, Anderson is able to perceive how Rizal looked upon the gardens of Manila as being "shadowed . . . by images of their sister gardens in Europe" (2). The images can no longer be seen in their immediacy but only from a double perspective simultaneously close-up and far away. The author, according to Anderson, names this simultaneous doubling the "spectre of comparisons" (*el demonio de las comparaciones*—perhaps, too, bedeviling comparisons, carrying with it the association of a bad or difficult comparison, the dilemma of not knowing which way to look). Moreover, Anderson, with Rizal's help, designates "Southeast Asia" as the site of this "haunting" or devilish vision, housing this specter, the primary place where this ambiguous optic and the difficulty of comparison has materialized. But Anderson could just have easily seen in the novelistic form itself the sign of this devilish doubling, which would prefigure the dilemma of subsequent sister images. For Anderson, concerned with resituating Southeast Asia, which like most of the colonial and Asian worlds remained as Europe's outside, in contemporary analysis, the doubling effect (noted years earlier by the Japanese philosopher Watsuji Tetsuro, who could not have read Rizal yet curiously echoing W. E. B. DuBois's "double consciousness" of black folk) necessitated thinking simultaneously about Europe and its colonial outside and thus mandated a comparative perspective in which comparison was always identified with a haunting. Yet Anderson employs the metaphor of the inverted telescope, which provides us with an up-to-date example of the camera obscura and still another vision of comparisons. By looking through the large lens and opposite end of the telescope, he sights another image, which must be smaller, miniaturized, distant. Since he is the subject who is gazing through the telescope he has, I believe, magnified his own position at the expense of miniaturizing and diminishing the sighting of Southeast Asia. In fact, the distancing implied by this gaze resembles the kind of distance necessary for the formation of the exotic project of an earlier generation of Westerners like Victor Segelan who always insisted on keeping the object at arm's length. Under this arrangement, there cannot be an equal doubling but rather a hierarchicizing of a large original and a small copy. The diminution and distancing of the image means only that it has won its putative difference from an original by sacrificing the equality of scale and size.

Although Anderson warns us that he is not trading in "imitations," "copies," and "derivative discourses," his appeal to the trope of the telescope more than offsets his logic of bound and unbound seriality and its goal to dispel unwanted "bogeys" (*Spectre* 29). Hence, it is the purpose of this logic to grasp the "remarkable planetary spread, not merely of nationalism, but of a profoundly standardized conception of politics, in part reflecting on the everyday practices, rooted in industrial material civilization" (29). To be sure, he reminds us in his earlier, influential *Imagined Communities* that the idea of the "nation" could claim no patent since it was continually "pirated" by different peoples with often "unexpected" results. Here and elsewhere Anderson has identified "print capitalism" as the agent of this process of spreading and transformation, undoubtedly emanating from the metropolitan centers of industry in Euro-America and diffusing its deterritorializing power to undermine all cultures of reference. The idea of the nation often resembled the process of mechanical reproduction and the eventual loss of the original in the copies. Perhaps a better way of dealing with this problem of original and copy is to suggest that with ceaseless repetition there is always the mandatory necessity of difference, as Borges reminded us years ago in his story "Pierre Menard, the Man Who Wrote *the Quixote*." Yet we must recognize that this agency is more about print than the political economy of capitalism, more about communicating commonalities than the destructive leveling of capitalist productive relations and forces. So powerful has this force of deterritorializing and reterritorializing been in shaping the world outside of Euro-America that it has prompted Anderson, among others, to fix the source of the spread in its nationalistic form in the great industrial centers of the West, without reducing all subsequent manifestations of nationalism and modernity in the formerly colonial world to a relationship between a ventriloquist and a dummy. In fact, it might be instructive to contrast Anderson's idea of seriality and replication with the conception of alternative modernity that has recently gained a certain currency in contemporary discussions and that constitutes perhaps an extreme polar opposite. If Anderson wishes to propose an approach that must take into consideration the role of some form of replication by Asian societies embarked upon the course of capitalist modernization and national liberation, the proposition of an alternative modernity based upon resuscitating a romantic and antimodern communitarianism free from the corrosions of colonial (and thus Western) mediation in figuring a national identity must be seen as simply a recuperation—however unintentional—of the second term of the established binary (West/East, civilized/primitive, developed/undeveloped) it is attempting to bypass.

Anderson's interpretative strategy has invited criticism from proponents of postcolonial discourse—the subaltern wing—who charge that it is simply another Western narrative that has played no role in fostering a genuine anticolonial nationalism in imperially occupied countries. Specifically, the complaint has sought to put into question the relationship between the original and copy that Anderson's comparisons seem to have recuperated despite his own disclaimers. Partha Chatterjee, perhaps the most energetically vocal among Anderson's postcolonial critics, asks: "If nationalisms in the rest of the world have to choose their imagined community from certain 'modular' forms already made available to them by Europe and the Americas, what do they have left to imagine?" (5). Continuing in this mode of special pleading, Chatterjee wonders whether the formerly colonized are destined to be nothing more than permanent consumers of modernity. But the modernity he is fearful of consuming is a strategic and ideological misrecognition of capitalism, which in this instance refers to the reproduction of capital accumulation, not a specific or even modular form of modernity, as such. It is important for him, and others, to displace the movement of capitalism by the conception of an indeterminate modernity which we are persuaded to identify as a unitary West. Behind this complaint is, I believe, the inadvertent desire to recuperate the status of the late developer in the interest of promoting the modular example of an alternative modernity. In fact, the conceptualization of an alternative modernity is based on the necessary transmutation of a quantitative temporal lag into a qualitative difference (thus reinforcing the myth of the time lag so dear to developmentalist theory in American social science years ago). Moreover, it demands the placement of an impossible unity called the "West" and thus a unified experience empowered to override all local differences. This is, of course, the kind of "spirit" Edmund Husserl constructed when he identified Europe with Greek philosophy and thus encouraged Japanese like Nishida Kitaro and Kuki Shuzo to imagine a complementary unity, equally impossible, called the "East" which reflected affect or no-thing rather than Being. This act of promoting an alternative modernity also requires positing the prior existence of a hegemonic model of modernity, whatever that might be, in order to imagine the possibility of an alternative that will easily qualify as its other.

Despite the strangely displaced romantic quest for originality that owes as much to nineteenth-century Europe as it does to any indigenous South Asian aesthetic and the nostalgia for the loss of something that probably never existed, the whole operation reinforces and reifies the very binary that current postcolonial discourse seeks to overcome and misreads Anderson's view of the role played by capitalism in the serial spread of nationalism and modernity. Nothing could be further from the ceaseless deterritorializing force of capitalism than the prospect of alternative modernities based upon the refiguration of the national community according to the reservoir of native resources that have remained both hidden and exempt from the narrative of capitalism but are always ready to supply guidance in any national present.

While an alternative modernity is simply an alibi for once more promoting a desire for identity in difference, an exceptionalism, it never really gets around to answering the question of what it is an alternative to, other than assuming that it is more than a "shallow homogenisation" and "struggles for other . . . richer definitions of the 'nation' and the future political community" (Gyanendra Pandey, qtd. in Chatterjee n.p. [opening epigraph]). What seems to be at stake in this complaint is the repression of an indigenous imagination capable of generating a nationalism and presumably a modernity from native resources that have managed somehow to remain immune to the contamination of colonialism and capitalism. Yet what can be said of an indigenous imagination that must depend for its form upon precisely those narratives it wishes to overcome and whose leading concepts derive from thinkers like Antonio Gramsci? In this regard, the subaltern desire to envisage a national identity unique to an indigenous India experience unaffected by colonialism comes very close to the Japanese who, in the notorious conference on modernity of 1942, tried to find a way to "overcome the modern." At the heart of this desire for an alternative modernity, based on a naive and totally indefensible vision of the agency of cultural purity, is the recuperation of a binary that separates an external, outer world of colonialism and capitalism (the world of materiality) from an inner realm of native sensibility (the domain of spirit) that apparently has remained intact since the Stone Age (see Lazarus 131–33). But such an appeal can only rest on the presumption of an existing ground of authenticity whose persistence guarantees the retention of an essential difference, as Japanese in the interwar period believed when confronted by accelerated capitalist modernization. In fact, capitalist modernization was seen by thoughtful Japanese and Chinese between the wars as a totalizing process that was altering every part of society (see Harootunian). This historical experience is crucial to an understanding of precisely the colonial episode postcolonial critics currently wish to theorize as knowledge and which Anderson has addressed, despite Chatterjee's refusal to acknowledge it. To have recognized this history will have shown the impossibility of imagining what some have insisted on identifying as an "anticolonial nationalism" and its figuration from an uncontaminated autonomous native culture at the heart of colonialism. What this reveals, apart from a leap of faith, is the conviction that the disempowered seemed to have involuntarily recuperated the space of nonreification Lukács once reserved for the proletariat and their struggle to break free from the constraints of bourgeois ideology because they were involved in manual labor, not mental labor, which would have colonized consciousness more completely. In making this move, adherents of postcolonial discourse misrecognize an identity between capitalism and its putative claims of universalism and thus couple homogeneity, albeit a "shallow" one, with capitalism even more readily than the most enthusiastic capitalist would. As a result, they fail to see, according to Pierre Vilar, that capitalism has universalized history to the extent that it has established systematic relations of social interdependence on a global scale that have eventually encompassed noncapitalist societies. In this regard, it has managed to fix a standard of measurement—world time—produced by a "single global space of co-existence," within which forms of action and the occurrence of events are subject to a single, quantifiable chronology. But because different social practices, especially at the level of everyday life, exist are outside this abstract measure, capitalism has not "unified" history (Vilar 41). The most unobservant visitor to Calcutta, London, Tokyo, or Shanghai will be immediately struck by the fact that at the level of everyday experience, people are living vast differences even though all of these metropolitan centers constitute centers of capital. By his own acknowledgment, it has been Anderson's intention to grasp a "standardized politics" by "reflecting on everyday practices." But the world envisaged by postcolonial discourse, inhabiting a moment that is chronologically after colonialism, seems committed to preserving a prior time by trying to rescue "imagination" and the claims of an inner, spiritual life that were exempted from the corrosive effects of (colonially inspired) nationalism and modern capitalism. This strategy, as a result, seems bent on escaping the performative present for an authentic and indeterminate past, virtually an eternalized everydayness as once envisaged by the Japanese native ethnologist Yanagita Kunio in the 1920s, which he believed existed before capitalist modernization. Through the alchemy of authenticity, thinkers and writers believed they were able to change the baser metal of their present into the pure gold of an eternal experience unaffected by history. Yet we know that Anderson has refused to risk carrying out this alchemical operation which is just as likely to produce a fool's gold in the form of a culturalist argument because "the rise of nationalism meant a change of consciousness so thoroughgoing that a prenationalist consciousness had become inaccessible and thus had to be substituted for by History and Tradition" (*Spectre* 21).

The response to what Frantz Fanon called the "sacking of cultural patterns," where the "social panorama is destructured" and "values are flaunted, crushed, emptied," was expressed in the form of a fear of loss of identity that was associated with a conception of exceptional culture that embodied enduring and unchanging value and meaning. It was precisely because the Japanese and the Chinese believed their imagination had been colonized by the commodity form that they turned to finding a sanctuary of enduring and unchanging value that had existed in an indeterminate history prior to the coming of capitalism and that was still available for ("pirating"?) recall in their present. In fact, this conception of cultural value was simply the other side of the commodity form where the search for stable meaning replaced the market-driven price and the endless circulation of goods, constantly changing but remaining the same. In this regard, it is best to recall Fanon's own, dim estimate of all those attempts to rescue difference by rooting it in a "folklore." The appeal to such autonomous resources, immune to capitalism in its colonial form, is a fiction not worth "delving into. A national culture is not a folklore, nor an abstract populism that believes it can discover the people's true nature. It is made up of the inert dregs of gratuitous actions, that is to say, actions which are less and less attached to the ever-present reality of the people" (233).

It is important to recall that Anderson is on record for acknowledging the differences experienced by the new states of Southeast Asia after World War II and his own, explicit rejection of the iron necessity of the Euro-American model for all latecomers. Yet the logic of his ghostly comparisons and the optic of his inverted telescope goes a long way toward reinforcing an image of relentless linear seriality that transforms everything in its path and a frame that structures a relationship between copy and copy or, as he puts it, replicas without originals. While he is undoubtedly correct in seeing the transformation of these societies according to capital logic, this does not necessarily preclude the possibility of realizing differences. The problem of difference is always present in these transformations; what is lacking is an essentialized difference that would guarantee the achievement of an alternative modernity. Anderson's appeal to the instrumentality of the inverted telescope, as I've already suggested, produces only a difference of scale, since the image of the transformed states and societies of Southeast Asia will appear miniaturized, distant, small. In his essay on "Elections in Southeast Asia," he argues that the pattern of electoralism in Southeast Asia "followed closely the one that can be observed in the historical evolution of the electoral mechanism in the areas from which it was imported . . . Western Europe and the United States: in other words, the development of national-level legislatures and the expansion of the suffrage followed a certain democratization of political life rather than brought it into being" (265). The actual experiences of the "democratization of political life" in Siam, the Philippines, and Indonesia have only approximated Western-style bourgeois democracy. With Siam, Anderson observes that the outcome has, in actuality, been "superficial"; in the Philippines, owing to a historically weak state in the twentieth century, electoralism came earlier; and in Indonesia "electoralism preceded the creation of a genuinely powerful and national civil apparatus, and part of the price has been the effective nullification of any serious form of popular representation for the past quarter of a century" (284). Here, Anderson recognizes a difference from those political practices associated with electoral processes found throughout bourgeois democracies and proposes that in their Southeast Asian inflection they have no positive policy outcome, as he puts it, and are meaningful only as forms of expressing dissatisfaction with the leadership. (But what does this imply about the performance of the electoral process in contemporary Euro-America, which, far from providing the forum for changes in policy, has become mired in endless, simple reproduction?)

It is hard not to conclude from this that political modernization in these newer states is being measured against another experience which if it is not necessarily modular is, nonetheless, larger in its scale of effectiveness. But it may well be that these replicas represent precisely the only kind of differences that native resources are capable of imagining under specific historical circumstances, a way in which a specific social reality cannot but appear at a particular moment. And this sense of appearing, as Etienne Balibar has proposed, "constitutes a mediation or necessary function without which, in given historical conditions, the life of society would be quite simply impossible" (61). Anderson's analysis shows how the specific histories mediate these "democratizing" achievements. We are reminded of examples like Japan's one-party democracy, which, at least in the official view of United States policy and many professional Japanologists, was always regarded as no less democratic. Too often, in the effort to speak of paradigmatic and hegemonic models, an ideal type is necessarily projected that is made to appear as embracing all of the necessary requirements, which immediately are misrecognized as a historical example. Too often, moreover, these comparisons are concerned with large structures, institutions, and processes rather than the lived experiences of everyday life that invariably write their own, very different comparative histories. In other words, if the inverted telescope miniaturizes and distantiates the image, looking through it the "correct" way will magnify the scene. Although the inverted telescope taught Anderson that it was no longer possible to take Europe for granted, perhaps it is equally important to remember at the same time that one ought not take the outside—Asia, Africa, and Latin America—for granted since, in their own way, they constitute the specters Euro-America will have to confront as they return to "haunt" and retaliate against a world that kept them beyond the horizon of consciousness and continues to forget them in innumerable ways. In Anderson's gaze, Europe still appears dangerously magnified.

While I would agree with Anderson that the power to refigure life at the everyday level is an insurmountable force and must remain the minimal unit of any proper comparison, it is an analysis of the movement and behavior of the specters that best offers a defense of the kind of difference he has been seeking to represent and that might still the denunciations of romantic authenticists and cultural exceptionalists. But by sensitizing us to the specter of comparison and opposing it to what must constitute its real body, "My Europe," in order to better understand the scene of Southeast Asia, Anderson has inadvertently, I believe, committed himself to a different kind of alchemical maneuver than the operations devised by postcolonial discourse. He seeks to explain the "alchemical transmutation that converts one into the other," and thus provide a narrative of transubstantiation that works to change the body and flesh into its apparition to define for comparative study its true vocation. By implementing this strategy he has situated himself "ambiguously" between an ontology, which since the Enlightenment has made comparison possible through the instrumentality of a transcendental subjectivity, and what Derrida has called a "hauntology," which, according to Pierre Macherey, forces the recognition of the "horror" "but also the derision, of a reality of specters, and which is perhaps only the specter of itself and its own 'reality'" (22). It is important to acknowledge that this sense of comparability—the power and necessity of instrumental rationality to grasp knowledge and experience—was, at the same time, made available to precisely all those Asians like Watsuji, Soetomo, and even Chatterjee who took its possibility for granted in constructing their own critical strategies. Anderson proceeds from the presumption that the flesh, the body—Europe—was actually and initially the ghostly, owing to the relationship between the culture Europe exported and the commodity form. In his scheme, then, there is no effort to distinguish between the apparition and its reality. Ironically, this perspective resembles that of an alternative modernity, which, in seeking the domain of pure culture to ground its difference, must opt for the primacy of spirit or the ghostly that promises to transmute it into a different (alternative) reality. Anderson slides the ontology under the hauntology, thus assimilating the apparition to the real, and fails to draw a demarcation between the two. Yet it is important to establish boundaries, because it is in the nature of ghosts to cross such lines and transgress them in order to do the work of unsettling the stable boundaries of time and space, as I will suggest later on.

Since the place of Anderson's haunting, Southeast Asia, is also the site that demands comparison, the hauntology or spectrality and comparison become one and the same thing. The realm of comparison is identical to the space of spectrality—comparability involves examining the specters of the real, of Europe, its shadow and silhouette but not its body. This is not the ghost usually associated with a forgotten history and past which memory has somehow repressed; it is the ghost of another reality, the long shadow Euro-America has managed to cast around the globe. As a result, this place seems less haunted than merely a haunt, albeit miniaturized and distant because of the inverted telescope, the space of a shrunken shadow and an ambiguous silhouette. Shadows are not the same as ghosts or specters that haunt and terrify the living, even though they can, on occasion, scare the hell out of us. Anderson never really maps out the domain of spectrality apart from insisting upon the simultaneity of a double vision that sees the image from close up and afar. Missing in this ghostly perspective is, of course, the past of Southeast Asia, which its specular present has simply superscripted, erased, and consigned to another existence to prevent its "surplus" from unexpectedly surfacing to create trouble as a haunting. But this is closer to the task of correcting a difficulty that had been produced by cultural diplopia. The problem of comparison, as Anderson sees it, seems to be less the activity of specters than the action of aporias, the difficulties encountered in making a comparison between faraway and nearby images, in assigning the status of reality or its appearance to phenomena. By identifying the project of comparison with the locus of Southeast Asia, making one into the other, a haunted house, so to speak, and by not keeping the lines between them demarcated, Anderson risks robbing the specter of its powers to actually haunt and return as an unwanted excess that was supposed to have been repressed and that unexpectedly takes its revenge upon the present that has "forgotten" it (see Ivy 84 ff.). He also risks restoring the aporetic question of trying to determine the status of an original and its copy as the purpose of comparison without accounting for the possibility of seeing this relationship as one involving repetition and difference. But repetition in this connection would resemble the Heideggerian *Wiederholung,* whereby the heritage of possibilities is repeated in a "moment of vision" necessitated by the "concrete futurity of vision," which succeeds in installing a temporal difference in the present instead of merely restoring the legacy of a past and thus an identity with it (see Osborne 168–69).

In Anderson's sensitive reading of *Memories,* by Soetomo, who lived in a colonial environment between older Java and the yet-to-be nation-state of Indonesia, there is still the momentary possibility to remember the past and try to resituate it in the present so that different modes of being and temporality will be able to coexist in the future. The example of Soetomo shows a form of colonial consciousness rarely encountered in our scholarly and intellectual interventions, which invariably focus on those like the Japanese folklorist Yanagita Kunio, who sought to exhume the past in his present and preserve it as a living museum of custom in a capitalist society that had already achieved nation-statehood, resituating the timeless in the midst of an historical society, or those who, like current postcolonialists, look back longingly for signs of what Adorno once called "frozen emanations" that might serve to supply their decolonized present with the aura of anticolonial authenticity. While Yanagita and his followers searched tirelessly for the survival of older customs and practices throughout rural Japan in the 1920s and 1930s, they were confident that their retention would signify an enduring and unchanging order of things that was coterminous with the remote past. And the philosopher Watsuji Tetsuro, as I've already suggested, envisaged a stratigraphic history that he called "double life" (*niju seikatsu*) in which the everydayness from Japan's remote past remained as a living layer beneath later impositions that would constitute modern strata. To this end, Watsuji identified the Japanese house (*ie*) and the way it organized social relationships and moral conduct as the fundamental layer of everyday which still survived in his day (1930s) despite the immense material transformations the nation had already experienced. The older and putatively original stratum of life would inevitably filter through the overlays and operate very much like a palimpsest. In this regard, these responses differed from their later postcolonial successors who searched not their present but history itself for these "living" residues that had remained uncontaminated by the colonial presence and which were copresent with a long but indefinite past. Whatever the case, like Hegel's owl, both (Japanese and Indian) efforts came too late and faced the inescapable reality of encountering specters and ghosts of a past that refused to remain passed. It could be argued that both, in their own way, have produced their texts in the effort to placate the unwanted excesses of a past that refuses to go away. But these examples from Japan and South Asia at different historical moments, representing different lived histories which can be multiplied with illustrations from other areas, are still somewhat different from the experience of Soetomo and the desire of his generation to forge an Indonesian nation.

By the same measure, I am convinced that Soetomo's own concern with the interrelationship between a premodern, indigenous past and a mixed present, like the Japanese and Indians who were concerned with a similar problem, envisaged a comparative approach that differed from Anderson's telescopic method even though it was made possible by the same instrumental rationality that had produced it. If Anderson's conception of comparison is identical with his notion of specter, more nearly the shadow of Europe stretching across Southeast Asia, it is, as I've suggested, one that has no power to actually "return," since it is already inscribed in the present. The shadow, or in this case Anderson's specter, has only a singular temporality. In this script, temporality is always measured from one, base timeline since, it was believed, true time was kept by the modern West. The actuality of the Southeast Asian present is merely the shadow of the body—Europe—whose lengthening across the region darkens the received reality and clouds the possibilities it has to offer. There can be no chance for the "autonomization" of the "ghostly effect," because the ideas or thoughts have not been severed from a living body to which they can return; they are only pale, distantly miniaturized reflections of another's body (Derrida 126). But a perspective that must account for a disappearing past on its way to becoming mere excess provides the opportunity for something—the ghosts of an unremembered history—to return to a body from which it has been separated by history; it is a vastly different present, one that has forgotten the past because it has become the place of mixed temporalities coexisting with each other, what both Marx and Benjamin called the present conjuring up the past. We need not explore here the vast consequences of this form of conjuration but only note that it has been the principal sign of what it means to become modern. What is made possible by this conjuration and the approach it authorizes is the recognition that the cultural unevenness everywhere capitalism has implanted its regime is a necessary condition of modernity and not a marking of either late development, incompletion, or simple imitation. Cultural unevenness has primarily privileged the spatial realm and thus coexistence and cohabitation of different modes of being, as it were, and temporalities within a modern capitalist society. Similarly, this cultural unevenness is often isomorphic and coexistent with uneven and unequal development in the political economy, even though it is not necessarily reducible to it. Although uneven political and economic development testifies to the laws of capitalism, which demand sacrificing one region for the growth of another, the locus is once again more spatial and fixed than temporal and fluid despite the claims of achieving an eventual even ground.

This involuntary surfacing of the forgotten past—the specter—constitutes a haunting because it comes from a place outside of time. Moreover, a society that has been transformed by the encounter with capitalist Euro-America but is seen merely as its easily forgotten shadow, which means putting it and its History on the outside, can now return as the unanticipated ghost seeking reunion with the body from which it been torn, the past of Euro-America, and threatening to retaliate against those who had forgotten their own role in the violent history that reshaped Asia and Africa. With the establishment of any modern nation-state, often accomplished on the condition of forgetting the past, the potentiality represented by Soetomo and his generation—the actual possibilities promised by their past—has thus vanished. The stage is set for the return of real specters and ghosts from outside of time to wreak their revenge on the present, which can have no control over the unscheduled arrival of the revenant and the horror of discovering a reality that is, at the same time, filled with the ghosts of another time and history, the undead among the living, groaning in the shadows of a discarded and now-forgotten history, demanding to be heard and remembered. This is precisely the fate Soetomo's text is trying to avoid in a future he can only dimly perceive but which promises the eventual realization of a decolonized nationhood. Once the state is put into place, as Anderson recognizes, all such appeals to the past become nothing more than culturalist reductions, romantic fantasies, fetishized seductions—the Chatterjee effect—employing History and Tradition as stand-ins for the history of cultural memory that even Soetomo must, in part, already represent. But there is still time not simply to rescue the past from the grips of the colonial state or an independent state to come, even if such plural histories could be offered by the supermarket of culture, but to resituate its exemplars in the present as a living presence, as Soetomo hoped to embody for his times. Soetomo's *Memories* show that the past he was trying to install was less spectral than the one still living in and through him and others of his generation, a past that had not yet been beaten down to the ground by capitalism and colonialism but living a fugitive existence as a cultural repressed.

With Soetomo, the specters never move the way they should. Educated in a colonial environment, which meant both Dutch and Indonesian idioms, Anderson is right to reject the more familiar (and meaningless) reading of

Memories as another instance of struggle between tradition and modernity. Soetomo is already "enlightened" and understands the protocols of a theory of knowledge that permits him to conjure up in his present a distant Javanese past that structured his childhood. This comparison between past and present is made within a form that seems to oscillate between older and newer literary and linguistic practices. But what seems to be important, according to Anderson's account, is this comparative thrust—surely more in keeping with Soetomo's modern, enlightened, rational education than with his Javanese cultural inheritance, which probably would have inhibited this kind of reach and the making of temporally bound juxtapositions. It is evident that this absence of concern for comparability marked other cultural orders in East Asia, where the project of comparison came with capitalism, colonialism, and a capacious conception of instrumental reason that presumed the imperative to grasp the world as an object of knowledge and to understand everything according to the rules of science and laws of nature. Again, it is interesting to see how the Japanese ethnologist Yanagita Kunio and his associates, at the turn of the century, committed their intellectual energies to what they called "Ghost Studies" (*Yokai kenkyu*) in order to satisfy an earlier nativist perception that the world is filled with unexplainable wonder not even the "logic" (*rikkutsu*) of the "Chinese mind" (*karagokoro*) could possibly elucidate. Even in a modernizing Japan it was still possible to believe that Western enlightened and instrumental reason was equally insufficient to account for the mysteries and wonders of what was called "ghostly knowledge." It was precisely this episode that drove Yanagita further to found a "science" devoted to custom and community and that explains why his first collection of folk tales (*Tono monogatari*) concentrated on a spectral knowledge lived and experienced by Japan's 'ordinary folk' before the coming of capitalism. At the time he collected these tales in the early twentieth century, people were still living their lives according to this ghostly knowledge in the remote reaches of rural Japan, still believing that the visible world of the living was coterminous with the hidden world of the spirits and constantly subject to it.

As for the Javanese cultural endowment that constituted so much of Soetomo's intellectual make-up, his fear grew that this past was on its way to being remaindered, forgotten. In order to avert this tragic karma, he pledged himself to try to restore it in his present by demonstrating how his own life had fulfilled the ancestral desire to imitate the forefathers by not imitating them. Soetomo desired to make himself, perhaps, as an exemplar of how the two temporalities must coexist. If the present fails in some way to remember the ancient model and implement its discipline, it risks inviting the specters of precisely that past which, because it has been forgotten, is now excess that will return and demand recognition, like Yanagita's ancestors

exacting remembrance and respect from their living successors, or if unsat-
isfied, threatening to wreak revenge on settled boundaries like subject and
object, real and unreal, history and timelessness. What is to be avoided, as
Watsuji Tetsuro tried to realize with his layering of different everydays so
that the most basic and enduring (representing *the* "authentic" ground) is
never lost to sight, is a past that becomes surplus and is always in a position to riotously spill over from constraints that were supposed to have
kept it hidden and repressed, to triumphantly return as the uncanny. The
irony of Soetomo's *Memories,* serving as the vehicle of a spectral past, is
that a colonial education made comparison a necessity in the first place, as
it did with Rizal, and thus allowed the capacity to forge a vision that sees
the possible coexistence of two, vastly different temporalities as a condition
for realizing modern nationhood. During Soetomo's time, Indonesia was
not yet an achieved reality, and it was momentarily possible to envisage an
arrangement where these two temporalities and their modes of existence
might coexist without antagonism and conflict. But, as Anderson shows,
Soetomo was already engaged in that destructively modern reflex of conjuring up the past in his present to remind his contemporaries of what had
thus far been sacrificed in the interest of becoming modern. Like Yanagita,
Soetomo lived in a moment when it was still possible to experience a kind of
hybrid reality—the condition of colonial encounter everywhere—the folklorist called "mixed civilization" (*ainoko bunmei*), which he discerned in
all ports of East Asia in the 1930s. Yet this state of balance could not last
forever, despite the obvious observation that cultural coexistence was better
than the total destruction of local cultures of reference. It is because the
kind of world Soetomo envisaged cannot last and must be made an unwilling sacrifice to modern nation-statehood that Asia's modernity, the locus of
Anderson's intervention, is always the place of the haunting and, for Asians
like Soetomo, the scene where the past comes onstage as ghosts demanding
to be placated. Yet the specular indeterminacy of a factual present and absent
past that is constantly being summoned constitutes not so much a resistance
to the modern as its principal condition of possibility and what it means
to become modern; contemporaneity and the appeal to the timelessness of
memory invariably disclose a structure of desire and deferral that repetition
seeks to resolve though it stimulates even greater anxiety.

We must acknowledge our debt to Anderson for having early and forcefully made us aware that precisely the excluded possibilities lived by societies
outside Europe were, at the same time, deeply implicated in its imperial expansion, whose modern forms were thus introduced through the export
of capital and colonial deterritorialization. The forms that evolved from
this violent encounter and involuntary transformation were not modular
imitations or even superficial mutations that stifled the native imagination

and emptied it of all power to mediate and appropriate creatively what plainly came uninvited from elsewhere. For Anderson, the untimely intrusion necessitated thinking about Europe and its outside simultaneously, which required the installation of comparative perspectives in which comparison was always a "haunting." Like all such ghostly arrivals, the appearance of the apparition in the form of comparison works to unsettle the inside—Euro-American civilization—which had enabled the comparison in the first place. In other words, Euro-American modernity is already inscribed in its "shadow," in the apparition, which is always in a position to outdo the "original," even though the "original" can never, in revenge, turn on its shadow to undo it. Beyond Anderson's identification of the ghostly is, I believe, the larger spectrality of societies deeply involved in fashioning a modernity coeval with Euro-America yet whose difference is dramatized by the revenant, the past and the premodern culture of reference, which appear as ghosts that have not yet died but have become repressed excess left behind, ready to return from this place outside of time to haunt and disturb the historical present. These remains roam about like the dead, or better yet, the undead among the living—what Benjamin once called "involuntary memory"—who wait for their hour to upset the living present, like avenging specters who desire to be remembered. But we must recognize here a double haunting. If the ghosts of the past return to haunt the present that has forgotten them, the inflected modernity becomes the specter to the Euro-America that inspired the models that forcefully powered the vast transformations in Asia and Africa into modern orders only to exclude them by characterizing them as either colonialism, some form of imitation and the status of a copy, or as "consumers of modernity" for whom there is nothing left to imagine. In this way, the inflections of Euro-America's modernity turn back to become a critique of it. In other words, while the return of the ghosts of a not-yet-completed past disturb the present of the modernity lived throughout Asia, the revenant from outside returns to unsettle Euro-America's own modernity, a reminder of having been excluded, an unremembered past, now demanding release from its indeterminate state of impossibility—existing as the undead among the world of the living.

Works Cited

Anderson, Benedict. *The Specter of Comparisons: Nationalism, Southeast Asia and the World.* London: Verso, 1998.
Balibar, Etienne. *The Philosophy of Marx.* Trans. Chris Tucker. London: Verso, 1995.
Benjamin, Walter. *The Origins of German Tragic Drama.* Trans. John Osborne. London: NLB, 1977.
Chatterjee, Partha. *The Nation and Its Fragments.* Princeton, NJ: Princeton UP, 1993.
Derrida, Jacques. *Specters of Marx.* London: Routledge, 1994.
Fanon, Frantz. *The Wretched of the Earth.* New York: Grove, 1968.

Hardacre, Helen, ed. *The Postward Developments of Japanese Studies in the United States*. Leiden: Brill, 1998.

Harootunian, H. D. *Overcome by Modernity: History, Culture and Community in Interwar Japan*. Princeton, NJ: Princeton UP, 2000.

Ivy, Marilyn. *Discourse of the Vanishing: Modernity, Phantasm, Japan*. Chicago: U of Chicago Press, 1995.

Lazarus, Neil. *Nationalism and Cultural Practice in the Postcolonial World*. Cambridge: Cambridge UP, 1999.

Macherey, Pierre. "Marx Dematerialized, or the Spirit of Derrida." *Ghostly Demarcations*. Ed. Michael Sprinker. London: Verso, 1999.

Osborne, Peter. *The Politics of Time*. London: Verso, 1995.

Vilar, Pierre. "Marxist History, a History in the Making, towards a Dialogue with Althusser." *Althusser, a Critical Reader*. Ed. Gregory Elliott. Oxford: Blackwell, 1994.

CHAPTER 10

Desire and Sovereign Thinking

LYDIA H. LIU

It may sound like a truism that the modern nation cannot imagine itself except in sovereign terms. But what is this truism saying or, rather, withholding from us? When Benedict Anderson wrote his influential study of nationalism in 1983, he circumscribed the imagining of the nation as "both inherently limited and sovereign" and relied on this basic understanding to explain the global transformation of dynastic empires into nation-states (*Imagined Communities* 6). That insight, however, has not drawn to itself as much attention or scrutiny as some of his other concepts, like "print capitalism" or "creole nationalisms." If one were to name a few of the blind spots in the contemporary discussions of nationalism, cosmopolitanism, and diaspora, one of them would be the place and placing of sovereignty and sovereign right. To those of us whose initial purpose has been to historicize the nation and nationalism, this blind spot cannot but raise some serious methodological and interpretive questions. Insofar as sovereignty articulates a major mode of exchange between nation and empire in recent history and moreover figures prominently in the realm of what Anderson calls "quotidian universals" (*Spectre of Comparisons* 33), the truism of its truth needs to be unpacked carefully.

Hence, I would like to raise some tentative questions about desire and sovereignty, not in terms of legal studies, but in light of what we have learned about colonial exchange and its production of difference, fetishism, identity, and the logic of reciprocity. I am going to show that these intellectual and material developments have had significant bearings on the making of international law such that our inquiry into the latter can no longer be confined to the self-explanatory evolution of legal discourse. For sovereign thinking is one of those areas that must be reexamined, to borrow Edward Said's words, "according to a detailed logic governed not simply by empirical reality but by a battery of desires, repressions, investments, and projections" (18).

In this essay, I begin with a critical analysis of Benedict Anderson's work, focusing on the interplay of the historical and the universal in his study of the nation. I am particularly interested in examining what Anderson chose to do, or not to do, with sovereignty in his theory of nationalism, and I raise some questions about his idea of the "modular," whereby the universal takes on the role of a migrant figure making histories here and there. Section two introduces the subject of fetishism and desire into the discussion by linking the display of the thrones of Chinese emperors in British museums to significant moments of sovereign thinking in the reign of Queen Victoria and the Empress Dowager of China at the turn of the century. In section three, I attempt a detailed discussion of the sovereignty complex of Ku Hung-ming, a diasporic subject who grew up in colonial Malaysia, was educated in Europe, and ended up serving China as his adopted sovereign country. My analysis centers on Ku's well-known defense of the Empress Dowager during the popular nationalist uprising of 1900 and his work as a translator and publicist in Anglo-Chinese military confrontations. Finally, I turn to the theories of international law itself and ask how nineteenth-century jurists revised the notion of sovereignty to arrive at a new constitutive theory of recognition in the heyday of imperialist expansion. I argue that any attempt to explain the rise of the modern nation-state must take full account of this significant revision in the early nineteenth century, because the revision signaled a paradigmatic shift from natural law to positivist jurisprudence to the effect that a constitutive understanding of sovereign right would eventually overcome and displace the natural law notion of universal sovereignty.

Sovereign Thinking in Migrant Nationalisms

In *Imagined Communities,* Anderson pointed to sovereignty as a necessary condition in thinking about the nation when, for example, he suggested that "nations dream of being free, and, if under God, directly so. The gauge and emblem of this freedom is the sovereign state" (7). The point seems well taken and indisputable on historical grounds. Anderson did not, however, go on to elaborate beyond the obvious truism of sovereign right what he meant by "freedom," leaving the readers to guess how we are supposed to comprehend the "universal" condition of any nation's dream for freedom when that dream must first be figured as a desire for the sovereign state. Indeed, what is the thing that renders the truth of *sovereign right as freedom* self-evident, powerful, inevitable, and universal?

The answer, in a way, lies in what Anderson calls the "modular" status of certain historical formations and knowledges (primarily from the West) that are capable of being imitated, replicated, and pirated just as the technology of print capitalism can produce instantaneous copies of itself in the diverse languages and dialects of the world. The plurality of independent states arises out of this process of multiple modeling and comes back to confirm "the validity and generalizability of the blueprint" (*Imagined Communities* 81). The argument strongly implies a circular movement between plurality and generality. Before we submit too quickly to this tempting scenario of the universal, let us reconsider briefly the case of "official nationalism," an idea Anderson had borrowed from Hugh Seton-Watson to help account for the situation of a secondary, reactionary modeling of nationalism in Europe. Anderson characterizes this secondary modeling as "a willed merger of nation and dynastic empire" that took place *after* and *in reaction to* the popular nationalist movements proliferating since the 1820s. He states that "these 'official nationalisms' can best be understood as a means for combining naturalization with retention of dynastic power, in particular over the huge polyglot domains accumulated since the Middle Ages, or, to put it another way, for stretching the short, tight skin of the nation over the gigantic body of the empire" (*Imagined Communities* 86). The examples he calls up in the book, such as Czarist Russia and the British empire, demonstrate that the Machiavellian "official nationalism" has enabled dynastic states and the ruling classes to exploit elements of the existing models ("creole-republican" and "ethnolinguistic") of popular nationalism for their own survival. Commenting on the historical function of this brand of nationalism, Anderson goes on to say:

> Such official nationalisms were conservative, not to say reactionary, *policies,* adapted from the model of the largely spontaneous popular nationalisms that preceded them. Nor were they ultimately confined to Europe and the Levant. In the name of imperialism, very similar policies were pursued by the same sorts of groups in the vast Asian and African territories subjected in the course of the nineteenth century. Finally, refracted into non-European cultures and histories, they were picked up and imitated by indigenous groups in those few zones (among them Japan and Siam) which escaped direct subjection. [*Imagined Communities* 110]

Anderson rightly points out the migrant tendencies of "official nationalism" and its oppressive politics but is less convincing on the issue of how the non-European societies modeled themselves on European innovations. What becomes of sovereign right in this picturing of "official nationalism"? Is the desire for sovereignty a result of universal modeling or something else? Would Anderson, for example, entertain the possibility that the triumph of the constitutive notion of sovereign right over the natural law idea of universal sovereignty could have made a decisive impact on how "official nationalism" behaved in empires and nations or compelled other nations and empires to behave likewise in the nineteenth century?

In his 1991 edition of *Imagined Communities,* Anderson sought to revise his "modular" idea of the universal, especially in view of what he had said about non-European cultures and histories. Reflecting on his earlier position in a spirit of self-criticism, he wrote:

> My short-sighted assumption then was that official nationalism in the colonized worlds of Asia and Africa was modelled directly on that of the dynastic states of nineteenth-century Europe. Subsequent reflection has persuaded me that this view was hasty and superficial, and that the immediate genealogy should be traced to the imaginings of the colonial state. At first sight, this conclusion may seem surprising, since colonial states were typically anti-nationalist, and often violently so. But if one looks beneath colonial ideologies and policies to the grammar in which, from the mid-nineteenth century, they were deployed, the lineage becomes decidedly more clear. [*Imagined Communities* 163]

The above remarks are contained in one of the concluding chapters Anderson added to the 1991 edition of his book, in which he took up the issue of how colonial knowledge making managed to create three modern institutions of power: the census, the map, and the museum. The belated postcolonial, Foucaultian bent in the proposed genealogical study significantly tempers his earlier "modular" approach in the sense that instead of universal modeling, one sees a shared and negotiated moment of knowledge making throughout colonial history that has helped fashion modern Europe no less than it created Europe's colonial other. Does this suggest new directions in Anderson's work? It struck me, however, that the figure of "grammar" in the above quotation continues to trouble Anderson's analysis of non-European societies, because it insists on modular thinking at yet another level of discourse, which seems to go against his stated purpose of historicizing international relations. If colonial ideologies and policies are expressions of a grammar more fundamental than themselves, what accounts for the grammar? The figure of "grammar" suggests a subtle methodological move between historicity and ahistoricity, because the argument now is one of generality producing an infinite number of pluralities, which is not so drastically different from his earlier mode of analysis, which emphasized the uncertain circularity between plurality and generality.

In *The Spectre of Comparisons,* Anderson further identifies this "grammar" as the logic of seriality and refines his modular idea of the universal by proposing two contrasting types of serialities, bound and unbound. He states:

> Unbound seriality, which has its origins in the print market, especially in newspapers, and in the representations of popular performance, is exemplified by such open-to-the-world plurals as nationalists, anarchists, bureaucrats, and workers. It is, for example, the seriality that makes the United Nations a normal, wholly unparadoxical institution. Bound seriality, which has its origins in governmentality, especially in such institutions as the census and elections, is exemplified by finite series like Asian-Americans, *beurs,* and Tutsis. It is the seriality that makes a United Ethnicities or a United Identities unthinkable. (29)

Serialization appears to be a more enabling process than imitation, because it generates new series, not just copies. What the new theoretical language does here is to allow Anderson to make further revisions to his theory of the modular. If earlier he had relied on the interplay of the model and its copies to explain the development of the calendrical simultaneity of apparently random occurrences in newspapers and periodicals, unbound and bound seriality cuts into the troublesome question of how universals are made or unmade in the modern world from a new angle. "It is from within this logic of the series," says Anderson, "that a new grammar of representation came into being, which was also a precondition for imagining the nation" (*Spectre* 34). To the author, the proposed bound series and unbound series serve the purpose of drawing a useful analytical distinction between nationalism and ethnicity and, in a related, indirect fashion, that between universality and "cosmopolitan" hybridity. Although I cannot dwell here on the epistemic feasibility of Anderson's analytical divide between bound and unbound series, I would like to examine briefly his critique of collective subjectivities and cosmopolitanism, since the critique touches on identitarian politics in nationalism and, indirectly, sovereign thinking in international law.

Anderson sees the contemporary practice of cosmopolitanism and long-distance nationalism as an extension of imagined, census-style, bounded series. The identitarian conception of ethnicity in these practices is conservative in his view precisely because integral bodies become identical (the Hispanics, Asian-Americans, African-Americans, and so on), and serially aggregable as phantom communities when they participate in the operations of capitalism, state machineries, and mathematics. He writes:

> Ethnic politics are played out on the basis of people's prior *national* entitlement as voters, and are justified on the basis of proportionality within the framing

of the existing census. When, or better if, a *soi-disant* ethnic group reimagines itself as a nation (as, for example, has been happening with the Québecois), and seeks to acquire an independent state, then it discards this census in the name of a new one of its own figuring. It is exactly at the moment of independence, however, that the logic of proportionality reemerges, within a new "n." [*Spectre* 43–44]

Anderson's observation makes perfect sense when it is directed toward those who maintain a naïve faith in the liberating potential of census-style identity politics whereby to reinscribe the logic of proportionality within the familiar domain of the independent state, if not official nationalism. I myself share some of his reservations about the limits of identity politics but feel that Anderson's polemical treatment of such politics obscures an important link, namely, the role of sovereign thinking in the conjuring of phantom communities. After all, the desire for independence requires a preliminary, if not single-minded, investment in the projected plenitude of sovereign rights. This is readily documented in official nationalism, past and present, but no less so in popular nationalism, which is entirely capable of imagining itself within the purview of sovereign thinking. In both instances, the meaning of "freedom" appears rather narrow but precise, which is borne out by the result of decolonization as well as of the other struggles for national independence.

That sovereignty has always been keenly contested in international law and nationalist movements goes to show that the emergence of national identity must be analyzed in view of what the international is doing within the national imaginary, not just beyond its borders. This may be one of those simple lessons that dialectical reasoning can teach us, but it is not so simple when it comes to making personal choices at particular times. The choice of personal identity or bio-political belonging, of which citizenship is but part of the game, is very much constrained by the types of questions we can or cannot ask of sovereign rights in the modern world. Indeed, what is personal, what is sovereign, and what is national and international? The state of schizophrenia—the euphemism of which is cosmopolitanism— which Frantz Fanon probed so poignantly in *Black Skin and White Masks,* may require a different sort of explanation once we begin to approach the problem of "inferiority complex" in colonial and postcolonial subjects in the direction I would like to suggest here.

One way of recasting that problem is to theorize the classic Fanon concern as a *desire for the sovereign* (which is invariably gendered) in the broadest sense. One may think of that desire in terms of a psychic love affair: a longing perpetuated by a sense of loss and distance impossible to cross. The roots of that desire are deeply historical and, in some cases, traumatic because the loss of sovereignty (understood in the legal, historical sense) and yearning for its recovery are capable of producing its own repertoire of fixations. What it means for colonial and postcolonial subjects is that one cannot possibly live in a mythical state of ambiguity or hybridity except, perhaps, by denying or otherwise coping with that desire. The cosmopolitan sublimation of the desire for the sovereign is anything but freedom from the nation.

Moreover, the sovereignty complex of the colonized tends to figure itself negatively by recognizing or indexing what seems to be the necessary condition of imperial desire that identifies itself with the metropolitan center. This (imperial) desire and that (sovereignty) complex appear to be mutually constitutive, for neither is the modular nor the copy of the other. They must be explicated on a basis of mutual determination because the imperial desire and the sovereignty complex of the colonized inhabit the same structure of what Ashis Nandy appropriately terms the "cultural pathology" of colonialism (35), which has crippled both the oppressor and the oppressed. Does the cultural pathology belong to Anderson's bound series or unbound series? Perhaps neither; yet it has everything to do with the question of collective subjectivities that Anderson brings up in *The Spectre of Comparisons*. The circulation of cultural pathology between the colonizer and colonized makes it impossible for us to romanticize popular nationalism, as Anderson tends to do in his book, when we critique official nationalism.

A familiar symptom of that pathology among the colonizers is what one might call the fetishizing of the dynastic throne, as is commonly encountered in the museums of the West. The display of the looted regalia of non-Western sovereigns never fails to fascinate visitors, but museums tend to be reticent about how and why those objects got there in the first place. The imperial throne, in the form of a spectral seat, is ostensibly unoccupied but seems, in another sense, crowded with old dreams, new fantasies, and much, much more.

My emphasis, however, is not on the museum as an imperial institution, which has been treated extensively by other scholars and by Anderson himself.[1] Rather, I am primarily interested in the economy of sovereign thinking that has produced specific targets of neurotic fixation in the colonizer as well as in the colonized during the global circulation of people, objects, goods, and fantasies. In the section that follows, I offer a few personal reflections on the question of imperial nostalgia. My argument is that the familiar display of the thrones of Chinese emperors in British museums must be linked to significant moments of sovereign thinking in recent history, especially during the reign of Queen Victoria and that of the Empress Dowager of China. One of the catastrophic events marking the end of the overlapping years of the Qing era and the Victorian era was the 1900 uprising of the Battalion for Universal Righteousness and Harmony (hereafter, the 1900 uprising) in northern China.[2] It was the defeat of this popular nationalist movement by the British and their allies that led to the second round of massive looting of Chinese artifacts by Western powers and their subsequent possession of some of the imperial furniture that ended up in Western museums. (The first looting episode took place in 1860 at the conclusion of the second Opium War [see Hevia, "Looting China 1860, 1900"].)

Fascination, Nostalgia, and Imperial Regalia

More than a decade ago, I watched Bernardo Bertolucci's *Last Emperor* for the first time and found myself baffled by the oppressive pull of nostalgia that the film sought to produce and force into the subjectivity of the viewer. That strange narrative of obsession was blatantly seductive, if not immobilizing, as it attempted to regale the audience with a hypnotic rhetoric of imperial regalia. Bertolucci's camera seizes on the royal throne, in particular, with a fetishistic intensity and piety that requires the repeated appearance of that object throughout the film. The throne is there to haunt the viewer. I, for one, tend to lose track of the total number of shots devoted to that singular object, but the last shot of the imperial site is truly unforgettable. That scene includes several sentimental close-up shots of Pu Yi, who is making what appears to be his last visit to the Forbidden City, where he encounters a young boy playing innocently around the seat of the vacant throne. The boy's age is roughly the same age as Pu Yi's when he had first been initiated into the Forbidden City to become the boy emperor of China. No doubt the film is trying to stage an allegorical encounter between Pu Yi and his former self across the monumental divide of the Republic revolution, World War II, and the Communist revolution. For a period of time, I struggled unsuccessfully to figure out why this particular brand of nostalgia had been able to cast such a spell on its audience and why the experience of watching Bertolucci's film both repelled and fascinated me.

Looking back on it now, I realize that I must have been fascinated by the West's own fascination with the Chinese throne but had been unable to put my finger on either source of the fascination until I visited Britain in the mid-nineties. During that trip, I chanced upon what looked like a Chinese throne-chair on display in the Asian Art Museum in Edinburgh. The caption indicated that this handsome object had been donated to the museum by a Scottish brigadier and his wife yet did not disclose how the couple had come to own it. For the second time, I was brought face-to-face with a reified imperial throne, but this time I was also astonished to discover that I had somehow failed to pay attention to any of the imperial throne-chairs on display in the Forbidden City itself, where I had made numerous visits before journeying to the West. It was through someone else's eyes—a Bertolucci camera and a museum exhibition—that I began to take notice of an object that could have existed in another time and place as far as I was concerned.[3] In any case, what must have baffled me about the film *Last Emperor* has been clarified since my visit to the Asian Art museum in Edinburgh. It is not that I rediscovered the colonial and postcolonial life story of the imperial regalia through someone else's eyes but rather this: *I was fascinated with someone else's fascination.*

The art historian Craig Clunas, who has published a number of articles about the looting of the imperial thrones of China, gives us a poignant account of his own adolescent experience at the Victoria and Albert Museum, where he had his first encounter with the imperial throne. Clunas writes:

> When I was fourteen I came to London with my father. We were on the way to Cambridge, where I was to investigate the possibility of studying Chinese. I visited the Victoria and Albert Museum for the first time, and there in a large room titled "Far Eastern Art" I was enthralled to see a great carved lacquer seat, labeled "Throne of the Emperor Ch'ien-lung." While the uniformed warder looked or pretended to look away, I knelt down and put my forehead to the black linoleum in homage. [*"Oriental Antiques"* 318]

Commenting on his "scandalous" performance, Clunas perceives, retrospectively, elements of "embarrassing personal engagements and secret fetishisms, which threaten to reopen the space between the viewer and the artifact" (318). Indeed, such mimicking of the imperial ritual before a vacant Chinese throne *and* in the setting of a British museum immediately brings to mind the story of what James Hevia calls "the scandal of inequality" generally associated with Lord Macartney's mission to the court of Emperor Qianlong in 1793. Clunas's transgression of the code of viewing at the V & A may be construed as an unintended assault on the image of the upright, freestanding Western man that had fueled the Macartney controversy for over a century. For it was on the ground of bodily posture that Lord Macartney had found the rituals of kneeling and *koutouing* to Emperor Qianlong particularly offensive and humiliating.[4] As Hevia points out, "It was precisely at the site of interstate ceremonial that the new notions of diplomacy and commerce converged with emerging pronouncements about acceptable bodily posture for the bourgeois gentleman" ("Scandal" 100). Embodied through diplomatic rituals, sovereign rights came to be negotiated on a basis of *equality qua reciprocity,* of which free trade served as both a secular model and as its raison d'être.

The Macartney audience was one of those century-long fixations that had preoccupied the imperial subjects who fought to defend the British interests in the Opium War, the Arrow War, and the subsequent suppression of the 1900 popular nationalist uprising. The overwhelming sentiment and rhetoric for waging war against China invariably evoked the perceived need to redeem the honor and cultural superiority of the British, which had been compromised in the earlier encounter between Lord Macartney and Emperor Qianlong. The voluminous official dispatches and unofficial exchanges between the British and Chinese governments preserved in the imperial archive of the Public Record Office in London attest to the startling level of neurotic fixations that drove the British ruling class to one military campaign after another in China.[5] One must, however, be vigilant about reading such emotional behavior as a mere ideological sham to cover up the commercial interests of the British in the nineteenth century. Without meaning to downplay the economic factor, I would like to suggest that the will to retaliate against the Chinese because of their humiliation of the British on the diplomatic front was very real, no less so than the economic interest. And this psychic investment often exceeded the calculated political and economic objectives of the British, leading to the most costly and fanatic destruction of human lives and property in a series of military campaigns. By taking possession of the "throne-chair" of Emperor Qianlong and having it displayed in the V & A, the British state was, in fact, settling an old score with an emperor who had been long dead (since 1795) but whose memory survived in the form of phantasmagoric retaliations. Such retroactive acts of moral vindication point up the neurotic fixations of the conqueror despite its triumphant display of the throne-chair of the Emperor.

In a study of several cases of looting in India, the last of which involves the British pillage of Delhi after the suppression of the Indian uprising in 1857 (three years preceding the first looting episode in China), Richard Davis provides an illuminating perspective from which we may reinterpret the meaning of looting and the loot in the nineteenth century:

> When we trace the histories of these objects, often we find that they have been dislodged from their initial settings during moments of official pillage, where the practice of looting has been public, more or less orderly, lawful (within the moral parameters of the looting party), and motivated as much by symbolic and representational as by economic intentions. This kind of looting most often forms part of imperial projects, by which conquering polities have sought to establish and represent asymmetrical political relations and cultural hegemonies. [293]

Indeed, military looting should not be taken for granted as a natural expression of human greed any more than the assumption that the throne of Emperor Qianlong was a war trophy claimed by the victorious British army during their military campaigns. As Clunas's study has shown, this late eighteenth-century chair embarked on a somewhat obscure trip abroad after having left its original home at the imperial hunting park in the Nan haizi to the south of Beijing. The chair had been looted from the Nan haizi during the allies' occupation of Beijing but did not turn up on London's art market until twenty years later. The owner of the chair at the time was Michael Girs, a White Russian émigré and former Tsarist ambassador who sold the piece for 2250 pounds. The donor of those funds, George Swift, earned the personal thanks of the queen.[6] At the time of its acquisition by the V & A in 1922, the director, Cecil Harcourt Smith, wrote to Swift: "I have had an opportunity of bringing the gift to the personal notice of the Queen who had already seen the Throne and expressed a hope that, by some means, it might find a place in our collections; and I am commended to inform you that Her Majesty desired me to convey to you her warm appreciation of your generosity and spirit."[7] Indeed, from the time of its acquisition to the removal of the collection at the coming of World War II, the throne was the main focus in a galley (room 42) devoted to Chinese and Japanese lacquer and woodwork. It was singled out as the most significant item in the room by the author of *The Victoria and Albert Museum: Brief Guide* (London, 1924) and of *The Victoria and Albert Museum: A Short Illustrated Guide* (London, 1937).

The queen's interest in "The Throne of the Emperor Qianlong" may well be read as a direct assertion of the sovereign rights of the British crown vis-à-vis those of the Chinese state. This understanding of sovereignty seems to suggest a mode of reciprocity familiar to us all. Clunas suggests, for example, that by acquiring the throne in 1922 "the British state was obtaining more than a splendid piece of craftsmanship, it was staking a claim which supported at a symbolic level the political and commercial rights that it had extorted from the government of the Chinese empire, and would uphold against the claims of the Chinese Republic" ("Whose Throne" 50). While I agree with much of what Clunas says in his fine study, the notion of the "symbolic" does not seem to capture the performativity of sovereign rights as a belated act (more than a century had elapsed between the Emperor's death in 1795 and Britain's possession of the throne-chair in 1922). I would argue that this significant time lag was none other than the long nineteenth century, during which the natural law notion of universal sovereignty came to be replaced by the positive construct of sovereign rights as something to be "recognized" by the family of nations. Hence the idea of a nation's "entrance" into the family of nations. In other words, by possessing the throne-chair, the British state was not only staking a symbolic claim to the political and commercial rights it had extorted from the Qing regime but asserting a certain view of sovereignty and of the universal that bore the imprint of the nineteenth century, as distinguished from, say, Europe's own earlier theories of international law. Before taking up the centuries-long evolution of the legal discourse of sovereign rights, let me dwell a little longer on the nineteenth century, especially the interesting triangulation of sovereign thinking among the British empire, Southeast Asia, and China.

Ku Hung-ming: Colonial Negativity and the Sovereignty Complex

> A boy in a Board school was lately asked to define Roman citizenship, when he gave this answer: "Roman citizenship was a ship on which the Romans went out 'fishing free of charge.'"
> —Ku Hung-ming, *Papers from a Viceroy's Yamen*

The central figure in this narrative is a diplomat and translator named Ku Hung-ming (1857–1928), whose steadfast loyalty to the Empress Dowager of China provides us with a fascinating angle from which to reexamine the meaning of sovereign thinking during the hostile exchanges between the British empire and the Qing empire at the turn of the century. During the allies' military campaign and looting of Beijing in 1901, Ku was in the diplomatic service of the Manchu government and published numerous articles deploring these imperialist acts. What he did before and after arriving in China came very close to exemplifying what Anderson calls "long-distance nationalism," yet Ku's enthusiasm for China was never a simple case of patriotism or displaced ethnic loyalty. Being a former colonial subject of the British crown and having adopted China as a sovereign nation in his mid-twenties, Ku seems to exemplify the sovereignty complex of the *migrant modern intellectual* better than he represents Chinese nationalism. The latter, if understood in ethnic terms, would have obliged Ku to adopt the exact opposite course of action and rebel against the Manchu regime and the Empress Dowager rather than serve them. A good example was Sun Yat-sen and the other long-distance nationalists whose patriotism was driven by a revolutionary agenda and the unambiguous racial call to restore the place of the Han Chinese against minority groups, especially the ruling Manchus. In contrast, Ku's sovereignty complex tells us a very different story about long-distance nationalism and Chinese nationalism. For reasons that I will go into shortly, his is the story of colonial negativity masquerading as patriotism.

Ku was born in the British colony of the Straits Settlements, Penang, in 1857. He spent the early years of his youth living in and migrating between Southeast Asia and Europe before renouncing his colonial identity. He arrived in mainland China in the mid-1880s and rose to become the top aide and translator for the powerful imperial official Viceroy Zhang Zhidong. During the 1900 popular nationalist uprising, Ku emerged as the most outspoken critic of British imperialism and defender of the Empress Dowager of China. Curiously, however, Ku harbored ambivalent sentiments toward Queen Victoria and seemed on occasion to want to shield the British Crown from the imperialist crimes committed by the British troops. His unresolved ambivalence toward Queen Victoria and adopted loyalty to the Empress Dowager should help us glimpse a vital moment of sovereign thinking in this early moment of long-distance nationalism, one that was specifically triangulated among Europe, Southeast Asia, and China. I emphasize further that a sovereignty complex such as Ku's must be understood with reference to the dynamic interplay of nation and empire, rather than through purely psychological or cultural gymnastics. The formidable legacy he left behind concerns intellectual migration and conversion and, of course, a host of unresolved questions concerning comparative work on nations, sovereign rights, and universals.[8] That legacy suggests an instructive connection between the complex geopolitical formations of Southeast Asia that Benedict Anderson has analyzed with fresh insight in *The Spectre of Comparisons* and the set of issues I intend to bring up and explore in this section.

Unlike the other prominent critics of Western imperialism in China, Ku wrote the majority of his works in English and published them mostly in the news media of the West and its colonies. His writing and idiosyncratic translations of the Confucian classics were eagerly read and discussed by liberal intellectuals in Europe; the British novelist Somerset Maugham even traveled to China to pay homage to him. In an essay called "The Philosopher," Maugham recalls: "here lived a philosopher of repute the desire to see whom had been to me one of the incentives of a somewhat arduous journey. He was the greatest authority in China on the Confucian learning. He was said to speak English and German with facility. He had been for many years secretary to one of the Empress Dowager's greatest viceroys, but he lived now in retirement" (147–48).

Ku received Maugham in his Beijing home in 1921. When the two met, Maugham quickly saw that Ku was an eccentric character who had the knack of turning an ordinary conversation into a disaster. Maugham writes: "I hastened to express my sense of the honour he did me in allowing me to visit him. He waved me to a chair and poured out the tea. 'I am flattered that you wished to see me,' he returned, 'Your countrymen deal only with coolies and with compradores; they think every Chinese must be one or the other.' I ventured to protest. But I had not caught his point. He leaned back in his chair and looked at me with an expression of mockery" (149–50).[9] It is interesting that Ku emerges from the pages of Maugham's book as a ranting old man who seemed bitter, lost, and deeply insecure on behalf of his adopted country. It is almost as if Maugham's physical presence weighed on him so much that he had to fight it off in self-defense. In one of the poignant moments Maugham has recorded from that memorable occasion, Ku reportedly says:

> "Do you know that we tried an experiment which is unique in the history of the world? We sought to rule this great country not by force, but by wisdom. And for centuries we succeeded. Then why does the white man despise the yellow? Shall I tell you? Because he has invented the machine gun. That is your superiority. We are a defenceless horde and you can blow us into eternity. You have shattered

the dream of our philosophers that the world could be governed by the power of law and order. And now you are teaching our young men your secret. You have thrust your hideous inventions upon us. Do you not know that we have a genius for mechanics? Do you not know that there are in this country four hundred millions of the most practical and industrious people in the world? Do you think it will take us long to learn? And what will become of your superiority when the yellow man can make as good guns as the white and fire them as straight? You have appealed to the machine gun and by the machine gun shall you be judged." [153–54]

Maugham did not enjoy Ku's impassioned oratory, and in the commentary that follows he takes objection to Ku's mannerism and tone of speech. But was this the voice of a schizophrenic or an uncanny prophet?[10] (If we substitute the nuclear warheads for the machine gun, Ku's words would probably ring true as the new millennium witnesses yet another round of military buildup and the nuclear arms race in the Asian Pacific region.) Confident in his power of judgment, Maugham states: "I could not help thinking him a somewhat pathetic figure. He felt in himself the capacity to administer the state, but there was no king to entrust him with office; he had vast stores of learning which he was eager to impart to the great band of students that his soul hankered after, and there came to listen but a few, wretched, half-starved, and obtuse provincials." (154–55). Maugham's disappointment seems genuine enough, but I am not sure that he comprehended the full pathos of Ku's seemingly neurotic behavior or the intense irony of the situation he so describes, using such interesting tropes as "office" and "administering the state." For all we know, the man he encountered could have been speaking to the ghosts of his own memory or the ghost of a former self that had lingered behind in Penang, Singapore, Berlin, Edinburgh, or a host of other places where he had lived and studied.

Ku was born to a family of *nanyang* ethnic Chinese (*nanyang* meaning "southsea," the old Chinese term to be later replaced by "Southeast Asia") and received his early schooling at the Prince of Wales' Island Central School. At the age of thirteen, he was brought to Edinburgh by his Scottish godfather Forbes Brown and stayed with the Brown family to further his education in Europe. For the next decade or so, Ku immersed himself thoroughly in the European humanistic curricula and mastered an impressive array of languages, including Greek, Latin, French, German, and other modern European languages. As one of the handful of Eurasians or ethnic Chinese who majored in the humanities in nineteenth-century Europe, Ku became conversant with the classics as well as with the modern literature and philosophy of the West.[11] After finishing an MA degree at the University of Edinburgh, he went on to study civil engineering in Germany for a period of time. In 1880 he returned to Southeast Asia and started a career in the colonial administration of Singapore (see Huang).

By Ku's own account, a chance encounter with the Chinese scholar and senior diplomat Ma Jianzhong, who visited Singapore and Penang in 1881, brought about a miraculous transformation in his outlook on life and cultural identity.[12] Almost immediately after the two met and had their historic conversation, Ku made what would become for him a lifetime decision: he quit the job with the Colonial Secretary in Singapore and renounced his identity of "an imitation Western man." According to one of his biographers, Ku told the episode of his transformation forty years later: "I was too impatient to wait for my boss's reply to the note of resignation. I simply jumped on board a departing steamer and returned to my old home Penang. The moment I arrived, I announced to the head of our clan, who was my cousin then, that I was going to grow a queue and adopt the Chinese long gown."[13] Undaunted by the fact that he had to pick up Mandarin and classical Chinese in his mid twenties in order to become Chinese, Ku plunged into an intensive course of study, and, within a period of three years, he had learned to read and write classical Chinese and had a tolerable command of the Confucian classics. In 1885, Ku sailed for China and was appointed the top secretary-interpreter in the office of Viceroy Zhang Zhidong, who was one of the most powerful Qing officials in late nineteenth-century China. Ku himself would soon become a senior diplomat in Zhang's office of foreign affairs and play an important role in the management of the 1900 crisis.

Ku's conversion was both thorough and tragically at odds with his own time. Not only did he declare himself an orthodox Confucian when classical Chinese learning was in the process of disintegrating and giving way to models of Western education in which he himself was brought up, but he began to insist on the importance of the queue as a sign of his Manchu-Chinese identity and loyalty to the Qing dynasty which was itself on the verge of a catastrophic collapse. Indeed, with the demise of the Qing in 1911, the much-hated queue, long regarded as an oppressive foreign code imposed upon Chinese males by the Manchu regime since 1644, was the first to go, and often had to go by violent means. Ku's steadfast refusal to cut his queue many years after the overthrow of the Qing turned him into a national laughing stock in the young Republic and caused him no small measure of pain and isolation at Beijing University, where he taught English literature on the faculty of the Department of Foreign Languages until retirement. During his meeting with Maugham, Ku is said to have drawn attention to his queue: "'You see that I wear a queue,' he said, taking it in his hands. 'It is a symbol. I am the last representative of the old China'" (Maugham 154). (Ku was better known as a Confucian philosopher in the West than he was in China, especially after his English works had been translated into French, German, and Japanese. In Europe, where Ku was called a *vieux-chinois,* his free interpretation of Confucianism won the admiration of many educated readers like Maugham, Tolstoy, and Georg Brandes.)[14]

Ku's lifelong devotion to the sovereign in the body of the Empress Dowager and the Qing regime has struck many as oddly conservative. One can hardly overlook the irony that, after renouncing his earlier colonial identity, Ku should declare allegiance to a Manchu sovereign whose alien authority had been contested and fought by the Chinese for over two hundred years. Is it not obviously contradictory to let the queue stand or fall as a symbol of the old China? as his critics would say. In addition to the need to address the matter of authenticity or lack thereof, one sometimes also encounters a serious argument directed at Ku's monarchism and political conservatism. Now, my question is, Can we settle on one or the other of these predrawn conclusions regarding Ku's monarchism and claim to authenticity?

Let us briefly consider the circumstances of Ku's writing to see what new light it might shed on our understanding of his sovereignty complex. My point of departure is that Ku's desire for the sovereign is historical, but decidedly *not* accessible to the evolutionist discourse of modern politics, any more than schizophrenia is inherently conservative or progressive. One must therefore avoid reading Ku's writings from the hindsight of the 1911 revolution and declaring him a conservative monarchist, but proceed from those years when he had thought it necessary to publish his famous defense of the Empress Dowager. Ku's writing was concerned not with the revolution but with Kolonial Politik, sovereignty, justice, peace, imperialism, and international order. Two interesting details stand out in this scenario. First, Ku's central piece in defense of the Chinese sovereign was published in response to the allies' retaliation against the popular anti-imperialist movement in 1900.[15] Secondly, Ku wrote and published those views exclusively in English with specific groups of English-speaking audiences and specific diplomatic imperatives in mind.

The majority of Ku's articles during the 1900 crisis appeared first in an English-language newspaper called the *Japan Mail* issued from Yokohama and *North China Daily News,* the largest circulating English newspaper printed in Shanghai. As one of the influential advisors on foreign affairs for Viceroy Zhang Zhidong and a senior diplomat privy to Zhang's decision making on the treaty negotiations, Ku's vocal criticism of the Western press coverage of the antimissionary sentiment and popular resistance movements in China did not go unheeded. He wrote: "Whenever modern scientific men of Europe meet with any extraordinary manifestation of human soul which they cannot explain, they call it fanaticism. But what is fanaticism? It is this.

The only impulse which can drive men to extraordinary acts of courage and heroism, and make them sacrifice themselves, is the impulse inspired by a desire to defend something which they in their hearts admire, love and reverence" (*Papers from a Viceroy's Yamen* 20–21). The "something" Ku endorses turns out to be the sovereign ideal as embodied in the person of the Empress Dowager. As will be discussed shortly, the stakes of the sovereign were extremely high at this time because the allies were demanding the heads of the princes and "Boxer" rebels. Ku published those views in the *Japan Mail* in order to counter the overwhelmingly damaging portrayal of the 1900 movement in the Western press and to stop further bloodshed.

The British commander Lord Salisbury found Ku's frequent criticism of "bastard" British imperialism a nuisance and lodged a formal complaint to H. E. Viceroy Zhang to shut him up. Ku stubbornly went on to expose Lord Salisbury's blackmail by publishing a short notice preceding his article "For the Cause of Good Government in China" in the *Japan Mail:* "I understand the British authorities have taken umbrage at my writing, and have formally complained to H. E. the Viceroy. I, of course, hold myself amenable to His Excellency's displeasure. I do not know whether the action of the British authorities is sanctioned by the British government. But in view of it, I think it useful here to bring publicly to the notice of Lord Salisbury, a cipher telegram which I sent to his Lordship last summer" (*Papers* 82).[16]

Ku wrote his chief piece defending the Chinese sovereign on July 27, 1900, when the allied forces had advanced to Beijing and were seeking revenge against the Manchu princes and the Empress Dowager. In response to the impending disaster, Viceroy Zhang had entrusted him with the task of translating a joint official telegram on behalf of the southern viceroys urging the British authorities and the allies to respect the personal safety of the Empress Dowager.[17] In the course of translating the telegram, Ku took the initiative of elaborating on the official statements and turning the text into a lengthy article, which he subsequently published in the *Japan Mail* with the title "Moriamur pro Rege, Regina! A Statement of the True Feelings of the Chinese People towards the Person and Authority of H. I. M. the Empress Dowager."[18] In a letter to the editor of the newspaper, Ku explained the circumstances under which he wrote the article:

> I had at first obtained authority from H. E. the Viceroy to prepare a translation of the substance of his telegram for publication. But afterwards on learning that I had made a long article of his telegram, His Excellency, under advice and other extraneous influence, which I could not control, withdrew his authorization. I did not submit to His Excellency my whole article beforehand, because, for one reason, in order to make him see the force of it, it would have taken me a long time to put the article into proper Chinese literary form, and, in the agony of the situation, every minute was precious. *For I had intended with this article to*

save Peking as well as the Legations there. I believed then, —and I almost believe it now,—that if I could have succeeded in arresting and allaying somewhat the storm of indignation, natural at the moment, on the part of foreigners against H. I. M. the Empress Dowager and her Government, the panic and mutual agony on both sides would calm down a little to enable those responsible persons in authority to take a clearer view of the situation and to solve it without any unnecessary bloodshed. [*Papers* 25–26, my emphasis]

In an admirable but doomed attempt to stop the war and influence the policy of Britain and the allies, Ku took steps to send his article to the attention of Lord Salisbury, who was incensed by Ku's open criticisms and sought to undermine his credibility with Viceroy Zhang. Although the allies spared the life of the Empress Dowager in the aftermath of the suppression, they punished the princes and rounded up victim after victim for execution.[19] Ku wrote: "the cool, callous, persistent demand for heads was, I must say, an act of moral helplessness and cynicism on the part of responsible statesmen more disgraceful to the state of civilization at the present day than even the savagery of the foreign troops in North China. I really pity the men who were responsible for the suicide of the Chinese Princes and State Ministers" (*Papers* iii).

As suggested earlier, the essay "Moriamur pro Rege, Regina!" was motivated by the need to defend the Empress Dowager as the supreme sovereign of the Chinese people. In the process of making that argument, Ku stepped outside the limits of his official duty as a translator by presenting his case in a way that ran contrary to Viceroy Zhang's political objective; namely, to extricate the Empress Dowager from the actions of the insurgents. Ku defended the insurgents as well as the Empress Dowager on the ground that these men were trying to protect "the mother of the nation," whom he calls *guomu,* and did so by throwing down their young lives before the muzzles of modern European guns. His argument ran:

It is plain therefore that the real "causa belli," the real passionate impulse which has led the people of China to assume a warlike attitude actually in the North and virtually in the South, is the conviction that insult was offered or intended to be offered to the person and liberty of H. I. M. the Empress Dowager. It is, I may say, a war of the people, not of the Government; in fact, it is rather in spite of the Government. That is the unfortunate reason why what are called the strict rules of civilized warfare have not been scrupulously observed.

Now, I do not know whether the more or less democratic people of Europe and America, who are at the present day very enthusiastic about "patriotism," are able or willing to remember from their past history that there is still a more genuine word than modern patriotism, a word the meaning of which I have tried to convey by using the Latin phrase at the head of this article, namely "Loyalty," the loyalty of the servant to his master, the loyal devotion of a child to his parents, of a wife to her husband, and lastly, summing up all these, the loyalty of a people to their sovereign! If the people of Europe and America will

remember the meaning of that word, they will understand why the Chinese
people—and not the Government—are now in a state of war, at bay against the
whole world. For the cry from one end of China to the other is "Moriamur pro
Rege, Regina!" [22–23]

Ku's comment on the loyalty shown by ordinary people to the sovereign is
worth pondering. Whether or not the author correctly diagnoses the origins
of the 1900 movement is beside the point, because we are not reading a historical essay for the author's objective assessment of the situation any more
than we can trust the objective archival value of the contemporary eyewit-
ness accounts given by missionaries like Arthur Smith or Arthur Brown.[20] It
is the mode of argumentation, in the form of what Benedict Anderson calls
the "quotidian universals" (*Spectre* 41) of newspaper writing, that mattered
at the moment and shaped the moment. Ku's manner of securing the universals of the "people" and their "sovereign" among a set of exchangeable
registers—history, loyalty, patriotism—appears very much like a free translation between Chinese and English. The argument of the *guomu* makes
sense only insofar as the Empress Dowager is understood as an equivalent of
the British crown (mother of nation and empire?) and China as an equivalent
of other sovereign nations. The exchangeability and reciprocity of sovereign
rights articulate the legal ground on which Queen Victoria and the Empress
Dowager should act and be seen to act. Indeed, in the naïve hope that the
Anglo-Chinese problem could be resolved through direct communication
between the female heads of the state, Ku proposes toward the conclusion of
"Moriamur Pro Rege, Regina!": "That H. B. M. the Queen, as the Doyenne
of the Lady Sovereigns of the world, be graciously pleased to send, as soon
as possible, a direct open telegram to H. I. M. the Empress Dowager—not
in official language, but in simple language of the heart,—expressing sympathy for the trials and hardships which H. I. M. the Empress Dowager,
her son and her suffering people have gone through in the present trouble"
(*Papers* 27). Ku confesses that his proposal appears sentimental in the context of the war but justifies it by the hard, commonsense, practical reason
of "politique du cœur." It bears asking, though, what kinds of hypothetical
equivalence obtain between the British crown and the Empress Dowager.[21]
Does his choice of equivalents (like *guomu*) presuppose reciprocity between
the languages, philosophies, and political discourses of two vastly different
intellectual traditions?

If Ku's language in the above quotation is marked by the rhetoric of
patriarchal Confucian moralism, the circumstance of his writing requires
that we take a careful look at the theoretical underpinnings of his notion of
sovereignty in the larger context of international law and ask how sovereignty
figured in the relations of reciprocity as understood to exist among the family
of nations in his time. Ku addressed these issues directly in a treatise called

"For the Cause of Good Government in China," where the language of Confucianism was conspicuously absent. He wrote:

> The broad and vital issue of the Chinese Problem is this. The foreign Powers must distinctly and absolutely decide either to take over the responsibility of Government in China or to leave that responsibility to the Imperial Government. If the Powers decide to take over the responsibility: well and good. But if the Powers, on the other hand, decide to demand responsibility of good government from the Imperial Government, then the Powers' plain duty is to absolutely recognize and respect all the rights of the Imperial Government as an independent State—with the exception, at present, of jurisdiction over foreign subjects. [*Papers* 71]

Notice that the author begins to speak the language of international law here, not Confucianism, and, moreover, he appeals to a nineteenth-century positivist understanding of international law that requires reciprocal recognition of sovereign states. When recognition is employed as a discretionary instrument of making or unmaking sovereign entities, it suggests that we are in the realm of a positivist logic of reciprocity that began to prevail in the nineteenth century. Since sovereign right is the foundation of positivist jurisprudence, nineteenth-century positivist jurists essentially sought to reconstruct the entire system of international law on the basis of that understanding.[22]

It is worth recalling that Henry Wheaton was one of the first legal theorists to conceive a constitutive notion of recognition, in the third edition (1846) of his *Elements of International Law* (the first book of international law to be translated into Chinese). In that edition, Wheaton states that while the independence of a state is sufficient to establish its internal sovereignty, its external sovereignty "may require recognition of other States in order to render it perfect and complete." He emphasizes this crucial distinction with regards to the rights of the new state, arguing that as long as a state confines its action to its own citizens, and to the limits of its own territory, it may well dispense with the recognition by others.

> But if it desires to enter into that great society of nations, all the members of which recognize rights to which they are mutually entitled, and duties which they may be called upon reciprocally to fulfil, such recognition becomes essentially necessary to the complete participation of the new State in all the advantages of this society. Every other State is at liberty to grant, or refuse, this recognition, subject to the consequences of its own conduct in this respect; and until such recognition becomes universal on the part of other States, the new State becomes entitled to the exercise of its external sovereignty as to those States only by whom that sovereignty has been recognized. [28–29]

By the late nineteenth century, the English jurist W. E. Hall would go so far as to assert: "States outside European civilization must formally enter into the circle of law-governed countries. They must do something with the acquiescence of the latter, or of some of them, which amounts to an acceptance of law in its entirety beyond all possible misconstruction" (40). This concept of sovereignty would have sounded novel to the naturalist jurists of the previous centuries such as Grotius, who had assumed the sovereignty *de facto* of those state entities who had conducted businesses and signed treaties with one another on a basis of the universal law of nations. What happened at the turn of the eighteenth and nineteenth centuries? And why was the change deemed necessary? In this regard, I find C. H. Alexandrowicz's earlier study of the history of international law in the context of the East Indies illuminating: he suggests that "The replacement of the universal law of nations by positive European International Law meant the reduction of non-European State entities which had enjoyed full legal status within the pre-nineteenth-century family of nations to the position of candidates for admission to its membership or for recognition by the founder members of the European community of States" (*Introduction* 10).

One of the remarkable developments that had preceded and conditioned Ku Hung-ming's treatises on sovereignty was the translation and publishing of the third edition of Wheaton's *Elements of International Law* in classical Chinese in 1864 by the American missionary W. A. P. Martin in collaboration with four Chinese scholars assigned by Prince Gong to help him with the task (see Liu, "Legislating the Universal"). This translation had been mandatory reading for all top Chinese/Manchu officials and provincial governors twenty years before Ku joined Viceroy Zhang's foreign service. Known as *Wanguo gongfa*, the Chinese text introduced what seemed to be the first hypothetical equivalence between "sovereignty" and its Chinese equivalent in the neologism *zhuquan*. Ku, therefore, did not freely designate the meaning of "sovereignty" in the confrontations between the British and Chinese when he assembled the quotidian universals in his treatises; those universals had already been attempted by missionaries and translators and more or less fixed through official publications. As significant as the Chinese equivalent of "sovereignty" was the adoption in *Wanguo gongfa* of the compound *quanli* to serve as the Chinese equivalent of "right." The existence of these and other hypothetical equivalents in *Wanguo gongfa* assumes the double function of both securing the mutual intelligibility of philosophical and political discourses of two vastly different intellectual traditions and raising for us some fundamental issues concerning the logic of reciprocity in international law and its physical circulation. So I turn next to the articulation of reciprocity and cultural difference by international law before and during the nineteenth century and ask how the notion of sovereignty has changed over the centuries to provide nations with a new set of conditions for the imagining of collective subjectivities and global universals.

Sovereignty and the Logic of Reciprocity

The extraordinary manner in which the British annulled the 1793 diplomatic exchange between King George III and Emperor Qianlong makes a powerful statement about reciprocity in the nineteenth century. James Hevia reveals in a recent article that during the 1860 looting and destruction of the Gardens of Perfect Brightness (Yuanming yuan) the British not only looted the Chinese objects but repossessed some of the gifts that King George III had given to the Chinese emperor. In October 1860, British soldiers found some cannons of European manufacture and identified them as gifts from King George III to Emperor Qianlong that had been brought to China by Lord Macartney. Thereupon "the commander of all British forces in China, General Hope Grant, ordered that the cannons, which bore a name plate recording their place of manufacture, be repatriated to the Royal arsenal at Woolwich" (Hevia, "Loot's Fate" 319). This behavior was very different from what Margaret J. Wiener has discovered in her research on the Dutch looting of the royal regalia of Klungkung in Bali in 1908. After the Dutch military sacked the royal palace of Klungkung's king, they found a silver tea service, a gift from the governor general, as well as a number of other European objects. "Significantly, there is no record of what became of the European artifacts discovered in the palace—the saddle, the tea service, the portraits of the Queen, and ammunition. Such things may have caught the eyes of journalists, but they could have no ethnological value since they failed to encode the necessary distance between European selves and Balinese others" (Wiener 353).

The repatriation of the royal gift to Woolwich allegorizes a different mode of reciprocity. The rivalry between the British empire and the Qing empire is one of the main factors that caused the scenario to emerge; furthermore, their rivalry was caught up in the paradigmatic shift I mentioned earlier with respect to the international politics of recognition. The repatriation of the royal gift suggests nonrecognition and denial of universal sovereignty. Such acts of nonrecognition introduce a typical moment of colonial abjection and the desire for sovereignty. When Ku Hung-ming, for example, felt the need to migrate between the sovereigns, it was almost as if positive existence—the overcoming of colonial abjection—required sovereign imagining. Seizing on Chinese nationalism, Ku took its promise of sovereignty to be the only path toward dignified existence outside the colonial regimes of power. If the decolonization of his hometown in Southeast Asia seemed somewhat remote at the time, when it did arrive, the decolonization movement had no choice but to strive in a similar manner toward a satisfactory resolution of sovereign rights. It is in these processes (colonization and decolonization as nation building), I argue, that sovereignty successfully evolved into the ultimate, universal test of independence, freedom, equality, reciprocity, and dignity, as well as the principle of exchange among nations, that which has since become intimate knowledge. Our intimate knowledge further betrays the fact that we are living with the consequences of an earlier paradigmatic shift and, moreover, in the shadows of the long nineteenth century.

Insofar as the logic of reciprocity introduces difference and universal equivalence (value) into international law, it cannot but structure the basic mode of exchange among nations. What I have in mind is more than a state of affairs or a theoretical argument, as one might expect in any discussion of colonial and cultural encounter. By the logic of reciprocity, I am alluding, first of all, to a set of formal registers in theoretical and intuitive knowledge that make difference thinkable as a problem of equivalence and cannot do so without tautology. Secondly, the same conceptual registers govern the terms of exchange and comparison whereby the common sense of difference and its equivalence with respect to other differences can then be secured (see Liu, "The Question of Meaning-Value"). The tautology of difference as value within a structure of unequal exchange victimizes that difference by translating it as lesser value or nonuniversal value on an assumed ground of equivalence.

The ground of equivalence in unequal exchange is one of those areas that has received very little philosophical attention in recent empire studies, postcolonial theory, and comparative scholarship. When it does appear, it is usually studied as an issue of universalism within the metaphysical tradition of the West, in which case we are deprived of the opportunity to examine a more interesting problem: the need to account for the scenario of "competing universalisms" on a global scale. The notion of sovereignty, for example, is a product of centuries-long treaty making and reciprocal dealings that involved many parts of the world, including the European states. It was only after the nineteenth century that this dynamic process was reduced to the common sense that international law has evolved solely within the paradigm of universalist aspirations of European legal discourse.

To question this common sense, we must ask how sovereignty arose as a problem in the first place through centuries of reciprocal trading of differences and universalisms. That seems to be the path to take especially if we wish to avoid the myopia of European exceptionalism. But a formal issue must be settled first: how does the logic of reciprocity work *as form?* Let us consider the primary category of deixis in language for initial comprehension. In an ordinary speech context or epistolary instance of writing, two or more interlocutors engage in a reciprocal exchange of the pronominal "I" as each addresses the other as "you." The ground of equivalence in this instance lies in the production of difference through the deictic exchange of person and the simultaneous leveling of that difference with respect to the same reciprocal address. Emile Benveniste, who has theorized deixis extensively, speaks of the phenomenon of "pronominal forms" in these terms:

The importance of their function will be measured by the nature of the problem they serve to solve, which is none other than that of intersubjective communication. Language has solved this problem by creating an ensemble of "empty" signs that are nonreferential with respect to "reality." These signs are always available and become "full" as soon as a speaker introduces them into each instance of his discourse. Since they lack material references, they cannot be misused; since they do not assert anything, they are not subject to the condition of truth and escape all denial. Their role is to provide the instrument of a conversion that one could call the conversion of language into discourse. It is by identifying himself as a unique person pronouncing I that each speaker sets himself up in turn as the "subject." [219–20]

In the immediate context of his writing, Benveniste is primarily concerned with the linguistic construction of subjectivity and its philosophical implications. After the work of Derrida and other deconstructionists, however, this aspect of his work appears not as redeemable as some of his other insights, like the above point about the absolute reciprocity of deictic address.[23] Colonial encounters abound in situations where the absolute reciprocity of deictic address figures powerfully in the emergence of relations of domination, as implied in the mutually exclusive determination of deictic address: "I am I because I am not you" in almost all articulations of universals and cultural difference.

The tautology of difference and equivalence that is served so well by deictic address need not rely on discursive utterance or pronominals at all times. Daniel Defoe's novel *Robinson Crusoe* may be taken as an archetypal figuring of deixis as physical "pointing" in a broad sense that requires little verbal assistance. The fact that Friday speaks no English in their "first encounter" does not prevent Robinson Crusoe from carrying out his project of educating the "savage" and letting Friday know his place in relation to the European master. The ingenuity of Crusoe lies in his intuitive grasp of how nonverbal deixis can produce the desired semiotic effect under the circumstances:

so to let Friday understand a little what I would do, I call'd him to me again, pointed at the Fowl which was indeed a Parrot, tho' I thought it had been a Hawk, I say pointing to the Parrot and to my Gun, and to the Ground under the Parrot, to let him see I would make it fall, I made him understand that I would shoot and kill that Bird; according I fir'd and bad him look, and immediately he saw the Parrot fall, he stood like one frighted again, notwithstanding all I had said to him; and I found he was the more amaz'd because he did not see me put any Thing into the Gun; but thought that there must be some wonderful Fund of Death and Destruction in that Thing, able to kill Man, Beast, Bird, or any Thing near, or far off, and the Astonishment this created in him was such, as could not wear off for a long Time; and I believe, if I would have let him, he would have worshipp'ed me and my Gun: As for the Gun itself, he would not so much as touch it for several Days after; but would speak to it, and talk to it, as if it had answer'd him, when he was by himself; which, as I afterwards learn'd of him, was to desire it not to kill him. [153]

In this rehearsal of the "first encounter" with Friday, Crusoe need only *point to kill* in an intransitive sense to communicate the precise meaning of violence, fear, and death. Crusoe points literally with his finger and then with his gun, yet the gun should not be taken merely as a killing machine: the object figures, first and foremost, as a deixis of power in the initiation ritual of colonial domination and fetishism. Hence the novel's fascination with Friday's worship of Crusoe and his civilization. The unchallenged power of Crusoe's superior technology establishes him as the master, the lord, and the sovereign of the Caribbean island. By the same token, the gun glosses the meaning of the "uncivilized" by way of circular reasoning: the American Indians are uncivilized because they are unable to defend themselves against military attack.

What is the place of international law in this deictic figuring of sovereignty and colonial power and its articulation of reciprocity in the European conquest of America? The question brings us to what might be called the early beginnings of international law in the work of the sixteenth-century Spanish theologian and jurist Francisco de Vitoria (for background see Scott). Commonly designated as the founding texts of the discipline, Vitoria's seminal lectures "De indis noviter inventis" and "De jure bellis hispanorum in barbaros" place the rise of international law squarely in the early moment of colonial encounter. Vitoria developed his doctrine of sovereignty, in particular, for the purpose of justifying Spanish title over the West Indies while trying to engage with the thorny issue of difference between the colonizer and the colonized in matters of religion and culture. As Anthony Anghie has observed in a recent article, Vitoria's approach to the law of nations is by no means an application of existing juridical doctrines developed in Europe that he then borrowed to determine the legal status of the Indians. Rather, Vitoria's work raises a prior set of questions. "Who is sovereign? What are the powers of a sovereign? Are the Indians sovereign? What are the rights and duties of the Indians and Spaniards? How are the respective rights and duties of the Spanish and the Indians to be decided?" (Anghie, "Francisco de Vitoria").

Vitoria writes that the Indians are "barbarians" and are guilty of mortal sins and forms of heresy, but he contends that the moral and religious inferiority of the Indians "constitutes no legal ground for civilized Europeans to deny them their legal rights or deprive these people of their land" (Vitoria 156; qtd. in Gong 36). His judgment is based on an argument of basic "natural rights" that presumably can be applied to both the "believers" and "non-believers"; however, as Gerrit W. Gong has argued, "for Vitoria, the issue is less one of faith and more one of protecting certain natural rights. The Indians maintained their legal rights and protection so long as they guaranteed the 'safety and peace' of Spaniards journeying, trading, or preaching the Gospel. With this emphasis on freedom of trade, travel, and proselytizing, the requirements Vitoria seeks to uphold presage their later explicit definition as part of the standard of 'civilization'" (37). The reciprocity of "natural rights" stipulates further that, if the Spanish right to trade with the Indians and to sojourn in their lands were violated, then the Spanish had "against the Indians all the rights of war, and might take possession of their lands. If after recourse to all other measures," Vitoria states, "the Spanish are unable to obtain safety as regards the nature of the Indians, save by seizing their cities and reducing them to subjection, they may lawfully proceed to these extremities" (Vitoria 155; qtd. in Gong 37).

In Vitoria's resolution of the problem of jurisdiction governing Spanish-Indian relations, the universal system of divine law administered by the Pope is displaced by the universal natural law system of *jus gentium,* whose rules may be ascertained by the use of reason. Anthony Anghie's interpretation of this important shift from divine law to secular natural law suggests the emergence of a new doctrine of sovereignty at this time whereby "natural law administered by sovereigns rather than divine law articulated by the Pope becomes the source of international law governing Spanish-India relations" ("Francisco de Vitoria" 325). Vitoria's concept of sovereignty is developed primarily in the matter of the sovereign's right to wage war. He grants the Indians their natural rights but denies them sovereignty on the basis of cultural difference by determining that, like the Saracens, the Indians are incapable of waging a just war and that the sovereign by definition cannot be an Indian. Thus, "the most characteristic and unique powers of the sovereign, the powers to wage war and acquire title over territory and over alien peoples are defined in their fullest form by their application on the non-sovereign Indian" ("Francisco de Vitoria" 325).

The fact that Vitoria's primitive concepts of rights, sovereignty, the law of war, and *jus gentium* derived from the circumstances of colonial encounter with non-European peoples in the West Indies suggests the norm rather than an exception in the development of the law of nations. The work of Hugo Grotius, for example, who has long been regarded as the principal forerunner of European international law, had been conceived and probably commissioned to make a direct intervention in the Dutch-Portuguese dispute over the East Indies.[24] In his extraordinarily detailed analysis of the Grotius-Freitas controversy and the history of treaty making and diplomatic relations between Europeans and Asian sovereigns, C. H. Alexandrowicz presents us with a strong case to correct the received parochial view of international law as something that first arose in Europe and only later granted its membership to non-European nations. "For to consider the European nucleus of States as the founder group of the family of nations to the exclusion of Asian Sovereigns in the East Indies was to view the origin and development of that family in the light of positivist conceptions which were only born at the turn of the eighteenth and nineteenth centuries" (*Introduction* 11).

Europeans who entered the East Indian scene found themselves unexpectedly in the middle of a network of organized states. In terms of the law of nations of the sixteenth century, there was no room for the application of titles of discovery or occupation of *terra nullius* in the East Indies. Nor was this possible from the point of view of local interstate custom, which counted treaty making, cession of territory, and conquest among its established legal institutions. Toward the end of the sixteenth century and the beginning of the seventeenth century, the Dutch began to challenge Portuguese monopoly of trade and navigation in the East Indies. Grotius, in his *Mare Liberum* (1608), attacked it from the legal point of view and defended at the same time the rights of the East Indian communities against Portuguese claims. Freitas offered his reply many years later, in 1625, and adopted his own approach to East Indian problems, greatly influenced by canon law. Both writers covered a wide range of legal arguments, concentrating on questions of classification of sovereignty and territorial rights and concerning themselves with the problem of freedom of navigation and trade in the East Indies.

Alexandrowicz calls our attention to the central fact that Grotius carried out his study of the regimes of the Indian Ocean in the archives of the Dutch East Indian Company, formulating the doctrine of the freedom of the sea on the basis of what he knew of Asian maritime custom. At a time when the doctrine of mare clausum was more prevalent in European state practice than the freedom of the high seas, the Asian maritime custom served as a legal precedent for his purposes (*Introduction* 65).[25] Grotius wrote his seminal text *Mare liberum* when his opinion was solicited on the case of the *Santa Catherina*, in which a Dutch naval commander (Heemskerck) captured a Portuguese galleon loaded with a valuable cargo in the Strait of Malacca in 1602. The ship, the *Santa Catherina*, was brought to Amsterdam and sold as a prize, and the proceeds of sale were to be distributed as part of the profit of the Dutch Company. It has been suggested that Grotius probably acted in the case as a counsel for the Dutch East Indian Company, and it is beyond doubt that he had access to its documents, which revealed to him the importance of the East Indies to European trade and led him to an examination of the position of Asian rulers in the law of nations.

Grotius eliminates the possibility of conceiving the East Indies as a legal vacuum as far as the law of nations is concerned, for he argues: "These islands [Java, Ceylon, and the Moluccas] of which we speak, now have and always have had their own Kings, their own government, their own laws and their own legal systems" (*Introduction* 45). European powers coming to this part of the world could not acquire territorial or other rights by discovery, occupation of *terra nullius*, papal donation, or any other unilateral act carried out in disregard of the sovereign authorities governing the countries of the East Indies. They could consider themselves sovereigns only over territories acquired by cession or conquest in accordance with the rules of the law of nations. The Portuguese could not, therefore, by virtue of any fictitious right of sovereignty, prevent the Dutch from access to the East Indies or from dealing with Asian sovereigns. In defense of Dutch interests against the Portuguese, Grotius concedes to East Indian sovereigns a defined legal status in the law of nations.

The long history of treaty making between Europeans and Asian sovereigns bears this out by way of testing how the concept of sovereignty actually worked in diplomatic relations. Not until the nineteenth century did positivist jurists begin to imagine East Asian countries as existing outside the family of nations and in need of being (re)admitted into the order of international communities. Alexandrowicz writes that "Positivism discarded some of the fundamental qualities of the classic law of nations, irrespective of creed, race, colour and continent (non-discrimination). International law shrank into an Euro-centric system which imposed on extra-European countries its own ideas including the admissibility of war and non-military pressure as a prerogative of sovereignty. It also discriminated against non-European civilizations and thus ran on parallel lines with colonialism as a political trend" (*European-African Confrontation* 6). The commonsensical narrative of East Asia's belated entrance into the family of nations that we routinely find in twentieth-century scholarship is largely indebted to the situation of this positivist turn in international law.

I began this essay with a critical analysis of Benedict Anderson's work and questioned the universal condition of any nation's dream for freedom when that dream needs to be figured as a desire for the sovereign state. I have argued that the truth of *sovereign right as freedom* must be unpacked for it to yield new insights into the making of modern nation-states. Consider the sovereignty complex that drove Ku Hung-ming from Southeast Asia to Europe and China, or the imperial desire that caused the fetishistic displacement of the imperial throne chair from Beijing to London. These stories are powerful, interlocking narratives about the desire for the sovereign, colonial memory, and imperial nostalgia. Such desires and memories continue to shape or trouble people's consciousness or national identities through interpellations by a film like *The Last Emperor* or a London museum like the Victoria & Albert. In reopening the question of reciprocity in the articulation of international relations, I have tried to come up with a new way of interpreting the paradigmatic shift from natural law to positivist jurisprudence that would account for the legal ramifications of the symbiosis of imperial desire and the sovereignty complex. The historical impulse of this study has led me in general to consider the changing notion of sovereignty central to the rethinking of the nation and nationalism. If the positivist turn of sovereign right, along with the familiar worldview it has helped inculcate, is among the most entrenched legacies that the long nineteenth century has left to us, it also issues the most difficult challenge to the future: can we dream a different dream of freedom?

Notes

I am grateful to Pheng Cheah, Jonathan Culler, Peter Zinoman, and Rudolf Wagner for their valuable criticisms and comments, which greatly strengthened the present essay, and to Cui Zhiyuan for calling my attention to some of the recent postcolonial legal scholarship on sovereignty. The Center for Chinese Studies at the University of California, Berkeley, and Göttingen University in Germany each provided me with an opportunity to present this research and test my ideas and conclusions.

1. For recent studies on the Western museum as a social institution, see Bennett; Karp and Lavine.

2. The Battalion for Universal Righteousness and Harmony, or *Yihe tuan,* was negatively dubbed the "Boxers" by Western missionaries and journalists in China, hence the name Boxer Rebellion. It is yet to be determined whether the Chinese pejorative term *quanfei* was a contemporary source for the English term or a Chinese translation of "Boxers." Interestingly, Chinese scholars have consistently used the name *Yihe tuan,* which the Battalion for Universal Righteousness and Harmony themselves had used, whereas to this day respectable Western scholarship uniformly refers to the Battalion as "boxers," or *quanfei.* See note 21 for an alternative English translation by a contemporary who contested the Western media caricature of *Yihe tuan.*

3. The emperor's throne chair on display in the Hall of Supreme Harmony in the Forbidden City had been banished to an obscure corner of a warehouse by General Yuan Shikai in 1915, four years after the Republican revolution. Decades later, this chair was rediscovered in 1959 by the scholar Zhu Jiajin, who was instrumental in its subsequent restoration to the Hall of Supreme Harmony for display. The process of the rediscovery is a fascinating story, because it was entirely due to the fact that Zhu had chanced upon a 1900 photograph of the old throne-chair taken by a Japanese photographer during the allies' occupation of China. Zhu became curious and searched through the warehouses of the Forbidden City to find the throne-chair. This finding has a special meaning for the present study because the pre-Bertolucci photograph was taken apparently during the same military campaign that led to the disappearance of the other chair from Nan haizi, of which Craig Clunas has written extensively (see Zhu Jiajin).

4. For a new study of Lord Macartney's mission to Emperor Qianlong's court, see Hevia, *Cherishing Men from Afar.*

5. For a radical new departure in the interpretation of the Opium War and the Arrow War, based on a comprehensive examination of these archives, see Wong.

6. For a detailed study of the life story of this chair, see Clunas, "Whose Throne Is It Anyway?," and his "Oriental Antiques/Far Eastern Art" 318–55.

7. *Nominal File: J. P. Swift,* Victoria and Albert Registry; qtd. in Clunas, "Whose Throne is It Anyway?" (48–49). Among the looted objects earlier presented to Queen Victoria, there had been a famous Pekingese dog that the queen adored and had appropriately named Looty (see Hevia, "Looting China, 1860, 1900").

8. Ku Hung-ming is the romanized spelling of this author's name, under which he wrote and published all his writings in English. The romanization Ku used for matriculation at the University of Edinburgh was Hong Beng Kaw. However, the commonly adopted spelling of his family name in Penang is Koh. According to the Pinyin romanization that is the standard system used today in the PRC and elsewhere, Ku's name should be spelled Gu Hongming. To avoid confusion, I use his published name, Ku Hung-ming, in this essay.

9. Ku had ignored Maugham's previous, informal request to see him until the latter wrote a polite letter asking for his permission to visit (Maugham 148).

10. G. Lowes Dickinson (1862–1932), a Cambridge professor, adopted Ku's persona without actually naming him and made similar remarks in his best-selling book *Letters from John Chinaman,* published in 1901. In this book, Dickinson invented the character of John Chinaman to criticize European imperialism in the manner of Ku, who had previously signed himself as "a Chinaman" in the articles he published before 1901. Thus John Chinaman and Ku merge into one as we read the following quotation from *Letters from John Chinaman:*

> "They [the Chinese] believe in right," says Sir Robert Hart—let me quote it once more—"they believe in right so firmly that they scorn to think it requires to be supported or enforced by might." Yes, it is we who do not accept it that practise the Gospel of peace; it is you who accept it that trample it underfoot. And—irony of ironies!—it is the nation of Christendom who have come to us to teach us by sword and fire that Right in this world is powerless unless it by [sic] supported by Might! Oh do not doubt that we shall learn the lesson! And woe to Europe when we have acquired it! You are arming a nation of four hundred millions! a nation which, until you came, had no better wish than to live at peace with themselves and all the world. In the name of Christ you have sounded the call to arms! In the name of Confucius, we respond!" [40]

A similar view was expressed in Ku's essay "For the Cause of Good Government in China," published in January 1901. In it, Ku alludes to the prophetic words of Sir Robert Hart, who warned about a future of "Boxdom" in China and argues that the literati can learn the art of war just as quickly as they had unlearned the same in the past, but "the question of whether the Chinese nation will have to fight or not, is a very grave question for the cause of civilization in the world" (Ku, *Papers from a Viceroy's Yamen* 79). There is no need for me to bring out every technical detail that blurs the textual boundaries between Ku and Dickinson. Suffice it to suggest that Maugham's portrait of Ku in "The Philosopher" may be a fascinating collage of all three images of the invented persona of a Chinese critic: Ku the author of *Papers from a Viceroy's Yamen,* Dickinson's John Chinaman, and Maugham's own reaction to Ku's reaction to his visit.

11. Ku's ethnicity is by no means settled. While the majority of my sources indicate that he was an ethnic Chinese, a few suggest, on the basis of first-hand physiognomic evidence, that he was probably a Creole with Caucasian blood from his mother's line.

12. Ma Jianzhong (1844–1900), who had studied in France, is better known as the author of the first grammar book of the classical Chinese language (1898) and single-handedly initiated comparative grammatical studies in Chinese scholarship. Ma was sent on a diplomatic mission to India in the summer of 1881 to discuss with the British authorities the possibility of reducing and eventually terminating the export of opium to China. On his way, he visited the Straits Settlements, where he called on the British officials (Cecil Clementi Smith and Sir Frederick Aloysius Weld) and had talks with the local merchants who ran the opium refineries there. The Straits Settlements (Singapore Island, Penang, and Melaka) was a British crown colony at the end of the Malay peninsula, just above the equator. Singapore served as a transit center for the manufacture, sale, and distribution of prepared opium in the British colonial economy. Chinese scholarship on Ma Jianzhong is extensive. The only monograph I was able to find in English is Tang Yen-lu's PhD dissertation, "The Crumbling of Tradition: Ma Chien-chung and China's Entrance into the Family of Nations."

13. See Huang 18–19. Huang suggests that Ku had had a queue as a child but cut it off sometime after he arrived in Scotland. Ku was apparently without a queue and wore a Western suit when he met with Ma Jianzhong in Singapore.

14. For other contemporary accounts of Ku, see Paquet viii.

15. Interestingly, Ku did not use the same argument of sovereignty in an earlier article called "Defensio populi ad populos," published anonymously (signed "a Chinaman") in the *North China Daily News* in 1891.

16. Attempts to discredit Ku also include casting doubt on his authorship because of his race. When Ku's article "Defensio populi ad populos" first appeared anonymously in English (signed "a Chinaman") in the *North China Daily News* in 1891, the London *Times* is said to have responded by carrying a lead article suggesting that the essay was probably not written by a Chinese author, because the language would not have "had that repose which stamped

the caste of Vere de Vere." Anticipating further attempts to discredit his writing because of his race, Ku posted an introductory letter to the editor of the *Japan Mail* to be printed along with his treatise "Moriamur pro Rege, Regina!" in 1900. The letter goes:

> Now, as an unknown Chinaman appearing to speak publicly for the first time in his own name and on his own responsibility, I think the civilized world has a right to ask my qualifications to speak on this great and important question. I think it therefore necessary to say that the present writer is a Chinaman who has spent ten years of his life in Europe in studying the language, literature, history and institutions of Europe, and twenty years in studying those of his own country. As for his character, I will only say this much: although the present writer cannot boast to be *chevalier sans peur et sans reproche,* yet, I think those foreigners in China who have known me personally and come in contact with me in any relation will bear me out when I say, that the present writer has never, by any unworthy act, sought the favour or deserved the disfavour of the foreigners in China. [*Papers 32*]

17. The southern viceroys Zhang Zhidong and Liu Kunyi had issued a declaration of independence of the provinces south of the Yangzi river in order to distance themselves from the 1900 movement and contain the encroachment of the Western fleets from the North. This was known as Jiangnan huzhu (Mutual assistance movement in the southern provinces). For a recent discussion of Ku's role in this incident, see Huang 108–33.
18. In a poignant way, Ma Jianzhong's death in 1900 was linked to his diplomatic service as a translator. As I mentioned in an earlier footnote, Ma had been instrumental to Ku's conversion in Singapore. He retired from government diplomatic service toward the last years of the nineteenth century and devoted himself to the writing of his grammar book as well as working for business firms. When the 1900 crisis broke out, Ma was once again called upon by Governor General Li Hongzhang to help with his negotiations with the Western powers. In August 1900, Russia sent a 7000-word telegram to the effect that if China did not accept its terms, Russia would blockade the area of Wusong. Ma's brother recalled: "Jianzhong spent the night translating the telegram. When he finished the translation, he was utterly exhausted and fell ill with a high fever. He died of sheer exhaustion on the morning of August 14." See Ma Xiangbo 404, as quoted in Yen-lu Tang 137.
19. It has been suggested that Ku's articles in the *Japan Mail* and *North China Daily News* did have some influence on public opinion and helped soften the allies' attitude toward the Empress Dowager, if not toward the princes, in the aftermath of the 1900 movement (see Shen 172–84). Two highly embellished versions of Ku's role in the 1900 crisis also exist. One of them, written by his student Zhao Wenjun, gives a dramatized account of Ku's story told in Ku's own voice and the other is found in the late Qing novel *Niehai hua* (*The Flowers in the Sea of Evil*). Chapters thirty-one and thirty-two of that novel recount Ku's adventures at the pleasure quarters of Beijing and his relationship with Sai Jinhua, the famous courtesan, who is said to have had an affair with the German army commander. Ku's name in the novel is written as Ku Ming-hung instead of Ku Hung-ming.
20. To this very day, the majority of Western scholarship draws on missionary accounts and Western journalism as reliable sources of information and fails to mention or consider Ku's writing in English on the subject, even though we know that Ku's published writing exerted an indirect impact on the allies' decisions about the aftermath of the 1900 movement and their plans for the punishment of the Manchu princes. James Hevia is the first historian to draw attention to the imperial value of the writings of Smith and Brown on the 1900 movement and the allies' attacks on Beijing. See his "Leaving a Brand in China: Missionary Discourse in the Wake of the 1900 Movement."
21. Being a professional translator, Ku was fully aware of the political stakes of translation in diplomatic intercourse and the print media. For instance, he objected to the negative rendering of the Chinese *Yihe tuan* as "the Boxers" in the Western press and proposed that "The name of the original legitimate first so-called 1900 society 'Yi-ho-t'uan' may be translated as 'friendly society of good men and true' or 'society of honest men for mutual defence'" (*Papers from a Viceroy's Yamen* 17).
22. For a new study of the relationship between positivism and colonialism, see Anthony Anghie, "Finding the Peripheries."

23.   See Jacques Derrida's critique of Saussure and the logocentrism of structural linguistics in *Of Grammatology,* esp. 27–73.
24.   For a discussion of primitive legal concepts, see David Kennedy, "Primitive Legal Scholarship."
25.   Grotius was confronted with the fact that navigation east of the Red Sea to the confines of the Pacific had been free and that local state practice never treated the Indian Ocean as "mare clausum." But the Islamic-Portuguese conflagration in the East changed the whole situation in the Indian Ocean, and the arrival of the Dutch made it still more precarious.

Works Cited

Alexandrowicz, C. H. *The European-African Confrontation: A Study in Treaty Making.* Leiden: Sijthoff, 1973.
———. *An Introduction to the History of the Law of Nations.* Oxford: Clarendon, 1967.
Anderson, Benedict. *Imagined Communities: Reflections on the Origin and Spread of Nationalism.* 2d ed. London: Verso, 1991.
———. *The Spectre of Comparisons: Nationalism, Southeast Asia and the World.* London: Verso, 1998.
Anghie, Anthony. "Finding the Peripheries: Sovereignty and Colonialism in Nineteenth-Century International Law." *Harvard International Law Journal* 40 (Winter 1999): 1–80.
———. "Francisco de Vitoria and the Colonial Origins of International Law." *Social and Legal Studies* 5.3 (Sept. 1996): 321–36.
Bennett, Tony. *The Birth of the Museum: History, Theory, Politics.* London: Routledge, 1995.
Benveniste, Emile. *Problems in General Linguistics.* Trans. Mary Elizabeth Meek. Coral Gables, FL: U of Miami Press, 1971.
Bertolucci, Bernardo, dir. *The Last Emperor.* Hemdale, 1987.
Clunas, Craig. "Oriental Antiques/Far Eastern Art." *positions: east asia cultures critique* 2.2 (Fall 1994): 318–55.
———. "Whose Throne Is It Anyway? The Qianlong Throne in the T. T. Tsui Gallery." *Orientations* 22.7 (July 1991): 44–50.
Davis, Richard H. "Three Styles of Looting in India." *History and Anthropology* 6.4 (1994): 293–317.
Defoe, Daniel. *Robinson Crusoe.* Ed. Michael Shinagel. 2nd critical ed. New York: Norton, 1994.
Derrida, Jacques. *Of Grammatology.* Trans. Gayatri Chakravorty Spivak. Baltimore: Johns Hopkins UP, 1974.
Dickinson, G. Lowes. *Letters from John Chinaman.* London: Allen & Unwin, 1901.
Fanon, Frantz. *Black Skin and White Masks.* Trans. Charles Lam Markmann. London: MacGibbon and Kee, 1968.
Gong, Gerrit W. *The Standard of "Civilization" in International Society.* Oxford: Clarendon, 1984.
Hall, W. E. *A Treatise of International Law.* 2nd ed. Oxford: Clarendon, 1884.
Hevia, James. *Cherishing Men from Afar.* Durham: Duke UP, 1995.
———. "Leaving a Brand in China: Missionary Discourse in the Wake of the 1900 Movement." *Modern China.* 18.3 (July 1992): 304–32.
———. "Looting China, 1860, 1900." *Tokens of Exchange: The Problem of Translation in Global Circulations.* Ed. Lydia H. Liu. Durham: Duke UP, 1999. 192–213.
———. "Loot's Fate: The Economy of Plunder and the Moral Life of Objects 'From the Summer Palace of the Emperor of China.'" *History and Anthropology* 6.4 (1994): 319–45.
———. "The Scandal of Inequality: *Koutou* as Signifier." *positions: east asia cultures critique* 3.1 (Spring 1995): 97–118.
Huang Xingtao. *Wenhua guaijie Gu Hongming* [*Ku Hung-ming, the Cultural Eccentric*]. Beijing: Zhonghua shuju, 1995.
Karp, Ivan, and Steven D. Lavine, eds. *Exhibiting Cultures: The Poetics and Politics of Museum Display.* Washington, DC: Smithsonian Institute Press, 1991.
Kennedy, David. "Primitive Legal Scholarship." *Harvard International Law Journal* 27.1 (Winter 1986): 1–98.
Ku Hung-ming. *Papers from a Viceroy's Yamen: Chinese Plea for the Cause of Good Government and True Civilization of China.* Shanghai: Shanghai Mercury, 1901.

Liu, Lydia H. "Legislating the Universal: The Circulation of International Law in the Nineteenth Century." Liu, *Tokens of Exchange* 127–64.

———. "The Question of Meaning-Value in the Political Economy of the Sign." Liu, *Tokens of Exchange* 13–44.

———, ed. *Tokens of Exchange: The Problem of Translation in Global Circulations.* Durham: Duke UP, 1999.

Maugham, Somerset. *On a Chinese Screen.* London: Heinemann, 1922.

Ma Xiangbo. *Ma Xiangbo wenji* [*Collected Essays of Ma Xiangbo*]. Peiping: 1947.

Nandy, Ashis. *The Intimate Enemy: Loss and Recovery of Self under Colonialism.* Oxford: Oxford UP, 1983.

Paquet, Alfons. Foreword. *Chinasverteidigung gegen Europäische Ideen.* By Ku Hung-ming. Jena: Eugen Diederichs Verla, 1921.

Said, Edward. *Orientalism.* New York: Vintage, 1978.

Scott, James Brown. *The Spanish Origin of International Law: Francisco de Vitoria and His Law of Nations.* Carnegie Endowment for International Peace. Oxford: Clarendon, 1934.

Shen Laiqiu. "Luetan Ku Hung-ming [Some Thoughts on Ku Hung-ming]." *Wentan guaijie Ku Hung-ming* (*Ku Hung-ming, the Strange Literary Genius*). Ed. Wu Guoqing. Changsha: Yuelu shushe, 1988. 172–84.

Tang Yen-lu. "The Crumbling of Tradition: Ma Chien-chung and China's Entrance into the Family of Nations." Diss. New York U, 1987.

Vitoria, Francisco de. *De indis et de iure belli: Reflectiones.* Ed. Ernest Nys. Carnegie Institute of Washington. Washington, DC: Gibson Brothers, 1917.

Wheaton, Henry. *Elements of International Law.* Oxford: Clarendon, 1936.

Wiener, Margaret J. "Object Lessons: Dutch Colonialism and the Looting of Bali." *History and Anthropology* 6.4 (1994): 347–70.

Wong, J. Y. *Deadly Dreams.* Cambridge: Cambridge UP, 1997.

Zeng Pu. *Niehai hua* [*The Flowers in the Sea of Evil*]. Shanghai: Guji chubanshe, 1979.

Zhu Jiajin. *Gugong tuishi lu.* 2 vols. Beijing: Bejing chubanshe, 1999.

CHAPTER **11**

Responses

BENEDICT ANDERSON

I have read through the chapters of this book several times, always with a sense of embarrassment, shot through with a pleasure often guilty. From time to time, therefore, I thought that the shortest and most honest response would be: "How right you are! How stupid I have been! A thousand thanks!" (If this did not end up sounding like something out of Gogol).

To this pleasurably masochistic embarrassment must be added some anxieties. Most of the contributors are skilled specialists in literature and literary criticism, fields with which I have only had the most amateur acquaintance. (My own discipline seems light years away, now that Partha Chatterjee has moved to anthropology.) When the fool realizes he has rushed in where angels fear to tread, how is he to explain himself? And: twenty years have passed since the original publication of *Imagined Communities,* and the era of its appearance seems today far more remote than that. How should I look back on it? With the sadness of old age for a lost youthful vigor and ambition, or with the ironic nostalgia of an adult flipping through his or her baby pictures?

In any case, it seems impossible to offer "a" response to so varied a set of essays. So what I will try to do below is to "converse" with each contributor, especially on matters where they have opened my eyes. But before doing that I would like to thank from my heart all the contributors, and especially Jonathan Culler and Pheng Cheah, for all the care and trouble they have taken in putting the book together. If I do not discuss Pheng's penetrating introduction below it is because I have learned so much from him since the time he was my student that I often can not separate my present thinking clearly from his.

Ernesto Laclau

The careful reservations expressed in Ernesto's lapidary contribution point gently to weaknesses in *Imagined Communities* of which every year I become more aware. When he suggests that the images or symbols of the nation (indeed of any modern type of imagined community) have to be "tendentially empty, for they have to signify not only the given but also the infinitude of what is not given," I can only agree. I should have perceived this twenty years ago when writing about the peculiar spectrality of cenotaphs and tombs of the Unknown Soldier. For aside from the national dead of the particular war for which they were created, they open themselves to the future national dead along an infinitely receding horizon. I imagine that today very few English people think of the London Cenotaph as exclusively attached to 1914–18. In the ironical chapter on "The Goodness of Nations" in *The Spectre of Comparisons,* I tried to show how and why the monochrome (empty) future of the nation is a key element in the establishment of its ethical value.

Ernesto further remarks that I exaggerated the universality and the world-dominance of the national form, pointing to the enormous importance of socialism/communism for much of the twentieth century, the complex ambiguities of the European Community, and the idiosyncratic aspects of the Middle East where "the last twenty years have seen the decline of Arab nationalism and the rise of Islamism." On the European Community, there is no doubt that I was evasive. On socialism/communism, I can only repeat that the immediate political occasion for writing *Imagined Communities* was the triangular warfare between the *soi-disant* revolutionary states of China, Vietnam, and Cambodia at the end of the 1970s. These wars struck me as clear evidence that transnational socialism was being trumped by nationalism and that this was an ominous portent for the future. The developments of the last twenty years have more than confirmed this premonition. In the case of the Middle East, I believe Ernesto is right to see "Arab" nationalism as in secular decline, in a manner that reminds one of the decline of Bolívar's pan-Spanish American nationalism, and of the pan-Turkish nationalism of the Young Turks. But this does not necessarily mean any decline in Lebanese, Egyptian, Algerian, or Palestinian nationalism, indeed may suggest the reverse: that these mirror the "smaller" nationalisms that created Venezuela, Paraguay, Chile, and Argentina. Nor does it mean that a looser fellow-feeling does not link the nation-states of the Arab world, parallel to what exists in the Spanish-speaking world in the western hemisphere. The strong Arab (and larger Muslim) sympathy with the cause of the Palestinians rests primarily on nationalist, and only secondarily on religious grounds. I also believe that the rise of "Islamism" has everything to do with the interminable foreign-backed despotisms that pervade the region like no other in the world. The entrenchment of these despotisms has everything to do with the Cold War, oil, Israel, and the United States.

Ernesto's final point about the inextricability of particularism and universalism echoes Etienne Balibar's long-standing arguments. It is true that in *Imagined Communities* I tried hard to separate nationalism from xenophobia and racism. (But I still think that racism is more characteristic of domestic than of interstate politics). At the same time, xenophobia is also changing its physiognomy. The change arguably stems from a conjuncture probably peculiar to our time, which I date back to about 1945. On the one hand, the near-universality of the nation-state form, and the ever-deepening sacredness attached to national territory, means that the age-old tradition of territorial conquest has, at least for the time being, come to an end. Hitler and Stalin were the last legatees of that tradition. Since 1945, with a few very minor quasi-exceptions like the Indian occupation and absorption of Goa (but it was still a Portuguese colony, not a nation when it was taken over), no state except Israel has significantly enlarged its territory. The obstacles in the way of Israel annexing other territories that it has occupied for decades, suggests the power of the international taboo. Where national boundaries have changed, the cause has been internal fission (Old Pakistan, Old Ethiopia, Old Yugoslavia) rather than external incorporation. On the other hand, the unification (however uneven) of the world economy and the rapidly steepening abyss between the rich countries and the poor has been creating unprecedented migratory flows, mostly from south to north. This is true even for so notoriously "homogenized" a country as Japan. It is under these combined circumstances that xenophobia more and more faces inward toward in-migrating "foreigners," rather than outward, toward predatory neighboring nation-states. In this conjuncture, an earlier pretty clear line between xenophobia and racism is becoming menacingly blurred.

Jonathan Culler

Jonathan Culler's essay is a characteristic mixture of brilliance, lucidity, and gentlemanly courtesy. He is absolutely right to underscore the repeated shifty slides in my discussions of the relations between the nation and the novel. My embarrassment is all the greater since in chapter two of *Imagined Communities* I quite self-consciously started my analysis of the relationship with a firmly abstract "graph" of the structure of an imaginary novel with no locatable social or national context. Not Ahab, Queequeg, Ishmael, and

Pip, but A, B, C, and D. He is also quite right in pointing out that the form of the novel creates a social space of interaction analogous to, but not isomorphic with, the geographic space of nation. I should have seen this clearly and failed to do so. All I can say in my defense is that I was then obsessed with what I believed to be a discovery, i.e., that the form of the novel's multiple narratives was based on Benjamin's "homogenous, empty time," which took simultaneity for granted. Hence, the novel's social space was necessarily subtended by this kind of time—which was also the time of nations. Behind Jane Austen's English social space was the ticking of thousands of inaudible, coordinated clocks.

Jonathan makes a further powerful point in reminding me that in mid-nineteenth century France there were no "national" newspapers. Regions and cities (including Paris) had their own presses, so that in principle it is not easy to see how newspaper-reading in itself could conjure up the nation before subscribers' mental eyes. He writes: "None of this matters if the argument depends upon the fact that the community of readers of a novel or newspaper is the *model* for the imagined community of a nation, but it does matter if the national community is supposed to be that imagined by those simultaneously reading a newspaper." Probably the easiest reply to this criticism is to start by stressing Jonathan's penultimate little "a." I am not sure if it is necessary for everyone to read "the" same newspaper. One can sit in a London tube and observe people reading half a dozen different newspapers printed in the capital. When I was young, Londoners could even be seen reading the *Manchester Guardian* when it was still in Manchester. I suspect that still more important will turn out to be the internal structure of provincial, municipal, and national newspapers, in other words, how the news is classified. A friend of mine who has studied the earliest Argentine newspapers tells me that from the start there was a clear spatial division between "foreign news" and "national news," and that inside national news there was a subsection for "local news." It would be nice some day to compare different newspapers in the France of the 1840s to see if this kind of internal classification existed and was more or less standard. If so, I think some of Jonathan's objections could be met.

But for me the most eye-opening part of Jonathan's essay is that devoted to the question of the readers addressed by novels. He takes beautifully apart my analysis of the opening of José Rizal's *Noli Me Tangere* to show that Rizal's very language clearly addresses a readership far wider (and vaguer) than Manileños or Philippine patriots or even Spaniards. Tellingly and, for me, most embarrassingly, he underlines my failure to translate the key word *allá* in the phrase *[si tu] quieres ver cómo son las reuniones allá en la Perla del Oriente* (if you wish the see how parties are given "yonder" in the Pearl of the Orient). *Allá* is necessary only for people living far away from the

Philippines, who know little about it, and hence might have some curiosity about its social life.

This critique has also, however, led me to reflect further on Andrew Parker's just criticism of my interpretation of Rizal's *demonio de las comparaciones* and my ambiguous borrowing of "double-consciousness" from W.E. DuBois.[1] This is what then occurred to me: one has to imagine a half-starved, near-penniless Rizal, writing the novel in the bitter winter of 1886–87 in Berlin. From Berlin, Manila is indeed "*allá.*" But he then describes his alter-ego hero, Crisostomo Ibarra, as looking at the dilapidated botanical garden in Manila, and being "pestered" by visions of botanical gardens *allá* in Europe, doubtless including Berlin. *Allá* thus has no stable location, since the writer in Berlin imagines a character *allá* in Manila who is thinking about gardens *allá* in the German capital. Needless to say, this cannot be anything like DuBois's "double consciousness."

Furthermore, Ibarra's *allá* is not tied to any colonial (or even postcolonial) binary, since what comes to Ibarra's mind's eye is *los jardines botánicos de Europa* (not *España*). This in turn suggests that among Rizal's intended readers were non-Spanish Europeans. The most obvious example is the distinguished Austrian ethnologist, Dr. Ferdinand Blumentritt, a close friend with whom he had a lengthy correspondence, mainly in German and Spanish, over the years. Through Blumentritt, he got to know many German-speaking Orientalists (*Perla del Oriente!*), and some of their opposite numbers in France and England. It is unlikely that all the anthropological detail noted by Jonathan in the opening chapter of *Noli Me Tangere* was meant for Spaniards, but rather for his potential political allies in Northern Europe. This idea is perhaps confirmed by the sentences that in translation run: "The dinner was being held at a house on Anloague Street. Since we do not recall the street number, we shall describe it in such a way that it may still be recognized—that is, if earthquakes have not destroyed it." If one asks recognized by who? The answer must again be North European sympathizers, including Blumentritt, who knew the colony well from books but had never been there, and whom Rizal hoped one day would be able to make a visit.

Jonathan's critique of my interpretation of *El Hablador* makes a parallel point—quite correctly—about Mario Vargas Llosa's targeted readership, which, he believes, in line with the theses in Pascale Casanova's *La République Mondiale des Lettres,* is not primarily Peruvian, but rather international and cosmopolitan. I am sure that subconsciously I knew this, but half-suppressed it in my eagerness to establish *El Hablador* as a nationalist novel. But it is possible that his argument is pressed a little too far. He quotes the uneasy opening of the novel as follows: "I came to Firenze to escape Peru and Peruvians for a while, and suddenly my unfortunate country forced itself on me this morning in an unexpected way, I had visited Dante's restored house, the little Church of San Martino del Véscovo, and the lane where, so legend has it, he first saw Beatrice, when in the little Via Santa Margherita a window display stopped me short: bows, arrows, a carved oar, a pot with a geometric design, a mannequin bundled into a wild cotton cushma." He continues: "What sort of narrative audience is addressed here? It is first of all one that does not need explanation of the easy references to Firenze and to Dante's glimpse of Beatrice. Proper names, taken for granted, delineate the European scene, but when the narrator turns to the materials from the jungle in the window display and then to the photographs that 'suddenly brought back to me the flavor of the Peruvian jungle,' he does not use proper names or technical terms, such as the objects might be known by in Peru, but 'bows, arrows, a carved oar.'" But I think that behind this judgment lurks an absent *allá*. Jonathan re-mentions bows, arrows, and a carved oar but not the cushma, which is left completely unexplained. While one can be sure that most educated Peruvians have at least heard of Firenze, Dante and Beatrice, we can be far from sure that European readers recognize what a cushma is, while Peruvians will recognize it at once. There is also the telling phrase about escaping Peru and Peruvians "for a while," which I think can only be addressed to Vargas Llosa's fellow-Peruvians.

Similarly, if we think about the kind of faux-Machiguenga Spanish that Vargas Llosa creates for the *hablador* in this novel, it is very unlikely that most Spanish readers, except perhaps those in Ecuador, Peru, and Bolivia, will recognize the peculiar traits of this language. But all educated Peruvians, who have been brought up on José Maria Arguedas's *Los Rios Profondos* (a book about which Vargas Llosa has written affectionately, admiringly, and critically), will immediately recognize the hanging gerunds with which Arguedas tried to recreate the flavor of *altiplano* Quechua and Quechua-inflected mestizo Spanish. This borrowing from Arguedas, which has angered many . . . Peruvians!—who think it shows Llosa's carelessness about the speech of the Amazonian Machiguenga—serves, perhaps, two functions. First, it makes unmistakably clear that the language of the *hablador* is intentionally pastiche, that is, consciously "not correct." Second, it no less unmistakably interpellates Peruvian readers: exactly their irritation—and no one else's—will show their acknowledgment of this haunting taunt.

Andrew Parker

Andrew's essay recalls for me one of my own private "primal scenes." When I was quite young I had on one occasion to play the piano for a small audience. I was so nervous that I forgot most of the time about the pedal and, as if to make up for this, at various moments held the pedal down long enough to create an atonal blur. My mother rushed to the rescue, insisting to her friends that my mistakes were the genial inventions of a prodigy. All I could do was grin sheepishly and keep my mouth firmly shut.

Most of his "motherly" essay makes me feel sheepish in just this fashion, perhaps especially when he finds passages in my writing that echo the deeper ruminations of Jacques Derrida, a great man with whom political science has barely a nodding acquaintance.

In response, I will confine myself to two small points, since the primal scene tells me clearly when to keep mum.

First and foremost, I accept completely his criticism, which parallels that of my brilliant former student Pheng Cheah, that I am a late Romantic with a decadent tendency to believe in the Fall. Both rightly argue that the lines I have often tried to draw between a "true" uncontaminated popular nationalism and the kind of Machiavellian nationalism emanating from the state and from threatened aristocracies and monarchies, is theoretically implausible and leads me back to contrasts between the true and the false, the primal and the derivative, that many other texts I have written are intended to destroy. I think this muddle is especially true of *Imagined Communities*, maybe less so of my work these last years.

Part of the explanation for the error is simply a matter of history. One side of my father's ancestry (through his mother) was a line of Irish nationalists going back to the last years of the eighteenth century. Two young members of that generation joined the ill-starred Young Ireland rebellion in 1798 and were jailed for their pains. Much later they were close aides of Daniel O'Connell in the movement for Catholic Emancipation. In the next generation, one youngster was involved in planning the Fenian rebellion of 1848, and had to flee Ireland for good, via Istanbul to New York. In the third generation, two became members of Parnell's Home Rule bloc of MPs in Westminster. On the other hand, at age 26 I left for an Indonesia then still ruled by the country's nationalist Founding Father Soekarno, while nationalist leaders like Nkrumah in Ghana, Sekou Touré in Guinée, Nehru in India, Ho Chi Minh in Vietnam, and Tito in Yugoslavia were still widely admired in the Bandung Conference spirit. When I returned to the United States in 1964, the Vietnam War was looming on the horizon, and the long 1960s were well under way. In the Cold War context, Third World nationalism looked very attractive, and most of my age-mates in academia were very sympathetic. It was thus easy enough later on, watching the decay of the Nkrumah, Soekarno, Nehru, Tito, and Touré regimes, to view it in terms of a Fall, given these men's impressive records in fighting for independence.

It has also to be remembered that *Imagined Communities* was written in a polemical spirit, against (especially British) colonialism and imperialism. I remember my pleasure when a women wrote in to complain that while I referred to the rulers of other Europeans countries in the standard manner—Louis XIV, Carlos III, and so on—I had unfairly always referred to British rulers as if they were ordinary people—Victoria von Saxe-Coburg-Gotha, and so on. But it is true that the rhetoric of polemical writing often means sentimentality and impossibly crude distinctions.

At the same time, what struck me quite early on about nationalism was what in a facetious moment I called its attachment to the Future Perfect. Monarchical dynasties might last for centuries, but they were always marked for Decline and Fall. Nationalism might linger *cariñosamente* on ancient glories, but it was oriented to a permanent future, the first political form to be so—in a strictly intramundane framework. As I have said elsewhere, here is the reason why the term genocide had to be coined. For a long time, it was difficult for me to associate this secular messianism with the *techne* of the state, and only too easy to locate it in the spontaneous (hence "authentic") sphere of the People.

Andrew is also gently critical of the metaphor of the inverted telescope, which I have often used, while this criticism is expressed more sharply—and I think mistakenly—in the essays of Partha Chatterjee and Harry Harootunian. That three such keen intelligences should have misunderstood me indicates that at the very least I expressed myself badly. So it may be appropriate to have another try. The effect of looking through a reversed telescope is to make the large and close-at-hand suddenly seem small and remote. Thus when in 1963 I heard President Soekarno calmly associating Adolf Hitler with other nationalist leaders, and was obliged to translate what he said for a distressed fellow-European, the sensation was like seeing Hitler in miniature—very distant, and even unfamiliar. My vision was not at all that of Soekarno, who surely was looking through his telescope the right way round, bringing the remote up close for himself and his audience. "This is Hitler, about whom you probably know very little." Nor was it that of any other "Third World" person. Hitler had been for my family a close presence; a V-2 bomb had dropped very close to my grandfather's home in London, smashing every window in the house, and the old gentleman found it prudent to move to a rented house well away from the metropolis. My aunt had worked in a hush-hush sonar factory during the War, as part of the fight against Hitler's submarine fleet, and she often used to talk to us children about her life then and the regular Nazi bombing in her neighborhood. But in 1963 I did not have a name for my new experience, and only found one much later when I stumbled on Rizal's memorable *demonio de las comparaciones*. It was not that I had the exactly same angle of vision as the First Filipino, but that I sensed that in Europe the wide, familiar Philippines had for him become remote, small, and, of course, "comparable." Rizal in Berlin, I myself in Djakarta, were struck by the same dislocation: a new, inescapable oscillation between small and big Philippines, big and small Führer. Looking back, I suspect that it was around 1963 that I dimly started to look for a comparative frame which could encompass not merely this oscillation but many others, depending on where I stood with my reversed telescope and what I watched through it. Certainly no stable ground, more a useful *Entfremdung*.

Marc Redfield

To Marc Redfield's brilliant chapter, I have no adequate answer beyond a *mea culpa* and a little Irish fretfulness at being described as "British-commonsensical." He has a perfect eye for those mushy, non-commonsensical or rather perhaps simply nonsensical paragraphs in *Imagined Communities* which my wiser brother urged me vainly to delete from the manuscript. I suppose I should also say that over twenty years my view of nationalism has become drier. The chapters on "Replica, Aura, and Late Nationalist Imaginings" and "The Goodness of Nations" in *The Spectre of Comparisons* are thus written in a sardonic style mostly foreign to *Imagined Communities*. "Late nationalism" itself, as a universal, rhymes with Late Antiquity.

But none of the above is "dried" enough to meet Marc's powerfully argued criticism that I borrowed from Benjamin but bowdlerized him and that my typical valorization of spontaneous popular nationalism over "official" and state-sponsored nationalism foolishly occludes the *techne* that they must all share. This is a central problem that I think Pheng Cheah was the first to analyze in these terms. Marc's great series of riffs on "anonymity" have been a real eye-opener for me. In a certain way, through these passages, I can dimly hear the ghost of Ernest Gellner, who always insisted that nationalism was a pedagogical project of modernity designed to create an absolute "interchangeability" of human beings within the division of labor under the control of each industrial or industrializing state.

Rather than trying to defend what is indefensible, let me rather offer brief ruminations on two sub-themes in Marc's discussion.

In the remarkable, poetic three-volume memoir, *Dari Pendjara ke Pendjara* (From Prison to Prison), by the veteran Indonesian Communist Tan Malaka—who briefly led Indonesia's Communist Party in the early 1920s, served for a while as the Comintern representative for Southeast Asia, and was finally demonized by his comrades as a "Trotskyist"—there is an extraordinary, rhapsodic apostrophe to the locomotive. Railways had come to the Netherlands East Indies in the early 1880s (about fifteen years after they became significant in Holland itself), not initially to transport human beings, but rather sugar, tobacco, tea, oil, and so on: a central agent of colonial exploitation and primary accumulation. But Tan Malaka addresses the locomotive as a comrade in a headlong, exhilarating rush towards the future perfect. Less eloquently expressed, one can find many comparable raptures over the telephone, the airplane, the radio, the motorcar, the bicycle, and the steamship. Tan Malaka's generation (the generation of the first Indonesian nationalists as well as communists) greeted these astounding novelties with enormous excitement. Finally the world, their World, was on the move. This exhilaration is almost contemporaneous with Benjamin's fraught discussion of the shock of modernity—indeed Tan Malaka, murdered in 1949, outlived Benjamin by almost 9 years. How was the lack of fit managed?

One possible answer is that these innovations arrived "cargo-like" out of the blue, from the other side of the world. They were not made in the colonies, which had then no experience of decades of deepening industrialism. Sugar-mills there were, of course, but they were not of the satanic metallurgical kind that had made a gloomy inferno of so much of England's—and Germany's—green and pleasant land. The working class was still tiny and, so to speak, first generation. It would thus be difficult to argue that in the colony the rhythms of American and European films effectively corresponded with the lived experience of most colonial subjects. Of course, Benjamin never went outside Europe, and Asia hardly appears in his philosophical writings.

Marc wryly notes that the cenotaphs and tombs of the Unknown Soldier about which I wrote were and are characteristically products of the state and of official nationalism, and he endorses Gopal Balakrishnan's remark that I seriously underestimate the importance of war in the creation of nationalism's pathos. I accept the first criticism fully, but the second only in part. Only a small minority of ex-colonial national states have ever fought wars against external enemies, though they have experienced plenty of domestic civil wars, often the result of big power interventions. Malaysia? Venezuela? Jamaica? Fiji? Ghana? Lithuania? Bulgaria? The argument of Balakrishnan is strongest for big-power Europe. Even there, it is possible to exaggerate if one is not careful. The force of so accomplished a work as Linda Colley's *Britons: Forging the Nation, 1707–1837* on the centrality of wars with Catholic, Revolutionary, and Napoleonic France in creating British nationalism is, to my mind, undercut by her casual exclusion of Ireland, which till the early 1920s was very much part of the United Kingdom. The Irishman General Sir John Moore died on the battlefield of Coruña (1809)—and was later celebrated by Irish poet Charles Wolfe—only a decade after the rebels of Young Ireland had looked eagerly for practical and ideological support from revolutionary France. Perhaps the mourning of nationalism comes from other sources. Modernity cuts short personal genealogies. We rarely know much about our grandparents, let alone earlier ancestors. Our children leave us to live lives of their own. In this modern solitude, and facing our own mortality, the immortality of the nation acquires its own importance. But this immortality must also be marked by the endless haemorrhage of everyday deaths. Including one day our own. Mourning, the site where death and immortality encounter one another, is crucial to what Michael Billig shrewdly describes as "banal nationalism."

Doris Sommer

Doris's essay simply reinforces the powerful effect that her wonderful book *Proceed with Caution* had on me a few years back. Rather than arguing with some passages where I have cautious doubts, it strikes me as more useful to start by asking myself how far it can be applied to states that are not "bilingual" in the American sense that she intends. (One could deny that the United States is really bilingual; the national state is effectively monolingual, while sections of the citizenry speak a wide variety of languages and patois in their everyday lives; but of course, Spanish-speakers do form the only potential challengers to the dominance of American English). In fact, in much of the ex-colonial world outside the Americas, monolingualism is quite a rarity. In some cases, the language of the former colonial ruler lives on as the language of state (sometimes even of the nation), of print, and of the elite, partly because it has come to seem "neutral" between the claims of rival local languages, partly because it provides easy communicative access to the dominant West. In other cases, such as Burma, or Algeria, a determined effort has been made to displace the colonial language by that of the majority of the population. In both policies—for we are speaking of the policies of post-colonial states—one can see efforts to find a linguistic analogue to the "unity" of the newly-liberated nation, in the face of a turmoil of local and not-too local languages (e.g. Arabic in some parts of Africa and different kinds of "Chinese" in parts of Southeast Asia). This hubbub marks Asia and Africa off from the Americas in which for the most part European settlers exterminated or decisively marginalized the indigenous populations.

My reservations about the generalizability of Doris's themes are, however, far less important than the stimulus her ideas have been to the most recent work on which I have been engaged. In *Imagined Communities*, I stressed the uniqueness of the linguistic practices of nineteenth and twentieth century Dutch colonialism, which built on two earlier centuries in which the great United East India Company ruled substantial parts of today's Indonesia. The core of these practices was the extensive use made by the Dutch of an old lingua franca, which we can call Malay, in traditional inter-island commerce. The Dutch language only began to be taught in the early twentieth century, and then on a small-scale and rather halfheartedly. Many Dutch refused to be addressed by a native in Dutch. Hence the peculiar fact that when in the 1880s a commercial press began to appear the dominant language was precisely this lingua franca (though newspapers in Dutch, Arabic, Javanese, and other local languages also emerged). The lingua franca was, in the market place, a truly "free language." People writing in it genially or sarcastically inserted vocabulary, idioms, spellings, and grammatical forms from their mother tongues, and, in order to reach their intended multifarious readerships, comparable pieces of these people's home-languages. This Rabelaisian "pandemonium" began to disturb the authorities from the end of the nineteenth century, and a distinguished linguist was assigned the task of going to British Malaya, where, it was thought, "true" traditional Malay was born and still used, and of finding the means there to establish a correct grammar, spelling, and vocabulary for future official administrative and paedagogical use. A little more than a decade later, this standardized official Malay entered school textbooks, along with "correct" dictionaries and grammars; a well-financed state agency was also established to publish "literature" in the "correct" language and disseminate it through a colony-wide system of libraries. But the state was never able to control the market and in March 1942 was itself overthrown by Hirohito's armies.

Of all the thousands of people who wrote for the market in the first half of the twentieth century, none is more remarkable than Kwee Thiam Tjing (1900–74), a prominent left-liberal journalist in the 1920s and 1930s, who wrote, underground, his masterpiece *Indonesia Dalem Api dan Bara* [Indonesia in Fire and Embers] in 1947 in his hometown of Malang, revolutionary East Java, then just reoccupied by Dutch military forces. Kwee's ancestors had been in Indonesia for seven generations, and had long lost any knowledge of written Chinese if they had ever had it. From early childhood he spoke the Hokkien of the local "Chinese" community (which then could only be written in romanized form) as well as the Javanese of the majority of the native population. His father managed to get him into one of the few Dutch-language primary and secondary schools around (where he had the rare privilege of engaging, sometimes successfully, in fistfights with Dutch boys without being punished), so that his Dutch became perfect. Reading newspapers and his own entry into journalism brought him an equal command of lingua franca Malay. Four languages by the time he was twenty. The prose style that he brought to perfection involved the witty intercalation of Dutch, Javanese, and Hokkien with market-Malay. He was from the outset a brave fighter for Indonesia's independence (a rarity then among people of Chinese descent in the colony) and served several terms in prison for his outspokenness.

One nice example of his inimitable style consists of a sort-of sentence composed of four words in three languages. Describing the sleazy behavior of the local Chinese elite in Malang, who, in response to Japanese demands that Chinese youths be trained to help fight against a possible Allied invasion, excused their own children and sent off those of the poor, Kwee maliciously described their stance as: *of romusha of tjaptoen*. *Of* is the Dutch for "either . . . or," *romusha* was a Japanese euphemism for wartime forced labor under inhuman conditions, while *tjaptoen* is colloquial Hokkien for the equivalent of "ten bucks," i.e. a bribe. In effect an ultimatum to needy parents: either pay us a bribe or your son risks his health and life. Kwee knew that his readers would understand what *of . . . of* meant, that they were all terrified of the Japanese and of the *romusha* programs, and that they could easily guess the meaning of *tjaptoen* even if they had never come across it before. He also knew that only in this colony out of all the colonies in the world would this three-language phrase, embedded in a market-Malay larger sentence, be calmly understood. Had he turned the phrase into Malay, all its malice would be drained away. For only his target, the Chinese elite, was accustomed to speak in a mix of Dutch and Hokkien.

Now the strange thing. After independence, his great book disappeared from the marketplace, and was almost immediately forgotten. When I found a single secondhand copy in 1963, no one I asked had read it or even heard of it. And no one seemed to have any idea of the identity lying behind the *nom de plume* of the author, *Tjamboek Berdoeri* (Thorned Whip). It was not until late March 2002 that I found documentary proof that Thorned Whip was actually Kwee Thiam Tjing. He had died a quarter of a century earlier in near-complete obscurity.

There were surely many political reasons why the book vanished. These reasons need not detain us here. The really crucial thing was what happened to the lingua franca. As early as 1928, young nationalist activists had renamed it as *bahasa Indonesia* (the Indonesian language or the language of Indonesia), and vowed to make it the national language. Not then with much effect. But with the coming of independence, it was formally established as the national language and language of the state; the official colonial spelling was altered, but the late colonial policy of standardization, normalization, purification, and prettification was effectively continued. The nation-state managed quickly to do what the colonial state had never managed: to take such control of the lingua franca, with such political authority, that the independent power of the market was completely curbed. Sentences like *of romusha of tjaptoen* had now become intolerable, and Kwee's brilliant, sardonic, often hilarious prose-style was under sentence of death.

An experiment is now under way. Kwee's book is about to be republished in its original form, along with a glossary and footnotes which have become necessary for young readers; and I have written for it a long introduction with an account of Kwee's life and work and of its Renanesque obliteration from national memory. This account is written in a contemporary pastiche of the great man's style, a form of Indonesian which returns it to its lingua franca origins, irregular spelling, borrowings from other languages, and the like.

Needless to say, the idea is to follow in Doris's creolizing steps. We shall soon see whether this experiment is a huge flop, or gets something useful going.

David Hollinger

David is perfectly right in underscoring the relative absence of the United States in the work of the best-known "theorists of nationalism." I myself have long been somewhat puzzled by this. But this oddity is embedded in others. For example, if one draws an arbitrary time line at the onset of World War One, thus ignoring Renan's brief but illuminating essay *Qu'est-ce qu'une nation?* and Otto Bauer's enormous chef d'oeuvre *Die Nationalitätenfrage und die Sozialdemokratie,* one is struck by a curious fact. Most of the key figures are European Jews (Kohn, Hobsbawm, Gellner, Kedourie, and Smith, for example), and most lived and worked in the United Kingdom, but with strong familial ties to the Austro-Hungarian Empire and the cities of Prague and Vienna. (Carleton Hayes is the notable exception, but alas he is not often remembered, even by fellow-American David Hollinger.)

It is difficult to escape the idea that Vienna and London were the capitals of two of the last three important European states from whose names no nationality can be derived. From this, one is led to ask a question which I cannot answer easily. Why should European Jews, attached to supranational imperial states, not have readily embraced the United States where Jews have done at least as well as in those states? A further question to which I find no easy answer is: why has the vast army of American scholars and intellectuals not itself produced what Europe has failed to do? Any foreigner who lives for a while in the United States will feel the hurricane force of American nationalism. Yet some years back when I asked a distinguished Americanist colleague what were the best books on American nationalism, she reacted with surprise and hesitation, finally settling on a rather old book about Manifest Destiny. I had the feeling from this suggestion that American nationalism was seen as something long gone, along with Mahan and Theodore Roosevelt. It is always possible, of course, that grand theory is not an American habit.

In my own case, it has to be confessed that I wrote *Imagined Communities* for a specific audience and with specific and self-conscious prejudices. It was aimed polemically at the United Kingdom, not the United States, and was meant to be a sort of response to Tom Nairn's terrific *The Break-up of Britain.* I was also eager to resist, as far as possible, the temptation to write mainly about the "important states," and so gave unusual space and attention to the small and/or the marginal. Ranajit Guha's initial reaction to the book included irritation that India was mentioned almost in passing; Chinese friends have sometimes felt the same way about the slight attention given to China. Russia, and Brazil too, probably, if I had many friends in those giants. The United States' status in the book is in fact larger than that of any of the above-mentioned big states. My favorite footnote is devoted to a phantasmically Americanized Queequeg.

What makes me a little uneasy about David's intervention is not really the above, but its scope. He concludes the essay by remarking justly that the United States should be taken as an example, not a model, for modern national solidarity. If it is "an" example, then it belongs along with other examples for comparative study. But he does not offer any comparable examples or suggest clearly in what framework these examples should be analyzed; furthermore the texts he cites are all in English, and mostly published quite recently in the United States. In fact, there is at least one example that should be perfect for his needs, and this example is brilliantly illuminated in François Noiriel's seminal book *Le Creuset Français*, now available in English as *The French Meltingpot*. Noiriel's work demonstrates that proportional to population France took in more immigrants than the United States from the 1870s to the 1930s and Frenchified them at least as successfully as America Americanized its own newcomers. In both countries the immigrants formed the tortured backbone of the industrial workforce. The decisive difference is that until very recently French formal jurisprudence largely—and purposefully—ignored ethnicity and religion and French censuses followed suit. This had its own effects on French historians and sociologists who were largely taken by surprise by his findings on the huge numbers of Eastern and Southern Europeans who initially poured into the country followed later by people from the Middle East, Africa, and Asia. But a success it undoubtedly was. And now? The success is visibly threatened by a large influx from the Muslim world, and the French state is under pressure to "notice," i.e., census-count, "minorities," for the first time.

It remains to be seen how well America does with its own growing numbers of Muslims. At this moment of writing, the outlook does not seem terribly encouraging.

Partha Chatterjee

Partha is, of course, one of my oldest and most acute critics, so I feel very touched by the kindness and generosity of his essay. With much of its argument I find myself today in agreement. But there are two important claims about which I have some reservations.

The first of these concerns "homogeneous empty time," which he argues is the utopian time of capital, an inhuman abstraction that does not correspond to the temporal heterogeneity experienced by uncountable millions of people in postcolonial societies. If one wished to see the most utopian instantiation of "homogenous empty time," one could not do better than glance at China. In the era of the Old Republic, dominated by native and foreign capitalists, feudal landlords, and thuggish militarists, China had several time zones, following GMT rules, as well as the local habits of the sun. However, when the CCP came to power in 1949 and began the dismantling of capitalism and feudalism, it also broke temporally with the immediate past. From that time, through the radical experiments of the 1960s, until today, all of China has been governed by one man-made time: that of Peking. When dawn appears over the Forbidden City, it is still the dead of night in Urumchi, but it is 6 am in both places. In practice, of course, Peking bureaucrats have learned not to telephone offices in Urumchi before their own lunch time and officials in Urumchi do not bother to call Peking after 2 pm. There is thus a weird, organized dys-simultaneity below the unified surface. Nonetheless, it hard to see how the time of the Great Leap Forward can be easily termed the time of capital.

I am also not so sure that the insulation of the postcolonial masses from the time of capital is as firm as Partha claims. I cannot speak of Partha's India, but in Indonesia and the Philippines the telephone is in constant use even among the very poor. The needy father in Java who telephones his daughter in Sumatra is not at all surprised to be able to talk to her instantaneously; and he knows enough not to call her between 8 am and 5 pm local time because she will be at work, nor after midnight because she will be asleep. The rhythm of these calls is absolutely determined by the synchronized local clocks in his village in Java and her town in Sumatra. He takes this coordination completely for granted. Indonesian engineers, some of them, of course, consult astrologers, but so did President Reagan and his lady. The really heterogeneous time is the supramundane time of religion, but this time is not accessed only in postcolonial societies, I suspect.

Partha's objection to the sharp line I have often drawn between nationalism and ethnicity (why do we not have in common use an "ethnicism"?) is quite fair, and I have ruefully discussed above this failing and the reasons for it. He is probably right in saying that what he terms my defense of classical nationalism is utopian, but I disagree that this nationalism is irrelevant. I think that it is precisely this utopianism, the utopia of an endlessly receding horizon "over the rainbow," that makes it relevant. There is no escaping what Partha calls the dirty business of governmentality and everyday politics, and this is as true of the United States as it is of India. This is not too different from describing our everyday personal lives as messy and often dirty: lies, evasions, cruelty, treachery, laziness, greed, frivolity, and the rest of anyone's long list. But, if only in others, we recognize these sins as what they are, and criticize them in the name of ethical principles, which can derive from religion, humanism, socialism, and also nationalism. The nation in effect offers a receding ethical horizon. There are many young Indonesians today who speak of giving up on Indonesia, i.e. of no longer giving it another chance. It seems to them an incurable site of governmentality, ethnic and religious brutality, greed, corruption, and utter cynicism. But they do so with great sadness, as if about to lose something irreplaceable. What they think they are being robbed of is an honorable Future. But their language also says something else. When they ask themselves: Why have we Indonesians become so degenerate? What is Indonesia good for these days? We can see there is no replacement for "Indonesians" after "We," and nothing better to fill the space between "What is" and "good for" than "Indonesia."

Harry Harootunian

To my own surprise, I find I do not have much to say in response to Harry's essay. I am generally in agreement with his caustic account of the rise of Area Studies in the United States. I can only add the obvious irony that Southeast Asian area studies "flourished" most—in an institutional and financial sense—during the Vietnam War. (With George Kahin already a distinguished expert on Southeast Asia in Cornell's Government Department, the possibility of a second appointment with same area focus in the same department—my own in 1967—is inconceivable outside the context of that war.) A substantial part of his text is devoted to a duel with Partha to which I find myself tangential.

Harry does make three points, which I think depend on misreadings of some elements in my work. The most of obvious of these is his understanding of the metaphor of the telescope—surely the result of my clumsy formulation of it—which I have discussed above. Beyond that it is plainly not the case that I find the origin of nationalism (if for the moment the word "origin" can be tolerated) in Europe. A major polemical point of *Imagined Communities* was to start with the Americas before turning to the "second wave" in Europe. This, in turn leads to another issue. If I had really believed that industrial capitalism explained the condition of possibility of nationalism, as Gellner indeed claimed, it would have been odd to start my historical account in the Americas, which in the late eighteenth and early nineteenth centuries were almost completely innocent of industrialism. For my analysis—and this is why the work of Fèbvre and Martin was so illuminating for me—it was merchant (not industrial) capitalism, and its peculiar sub-genre print capitalism that was decisive.

As for the complex final section of Harry's exegesis, after reading it over many times, I had the unwelcome feeling that Marc was perhaps right after all about my British-commonsensical outlook. Harry's discussion of revenants, hauntings, and spectres felt too removed from any empirical grounding that I could easily recognize. When I read Marilyn Ivy's brilliant *Discourse of the Vanishing* some years ago, I regularly asked myself whether such a book could be written about the nation-states that I knew best—Indonesia for example, whose muddled Latin-Greek name was casually invented by a German pedant in the second half of the nineteenth century, and whose contemporary extent was not formalized till the first decade of the twentieth century. It is a country with hundreds of "ethnic groups" and languages, Muslims of many persuasions, Catholics, a clangorous riot of Protestants, "Hindus," Buddhists, Taoists, Jews too, as well as a myriad of animisms and mysticisms. Revenants at the "national level," so to speak, seem to me improbable. Locally? In these last years, "head-hunting" reappeared in west and central Borneo, leading to horrifying massacres of poor Madurese immigrants. But these systematic killings were carried out in name of a Dayak people and a Dayak grand tradition popularized only in the last two decades by frustrated and ambitious Dayak intellectuals and politicians. They were aided and manipulated by military people of non-Dayak provenance who were eager to seize control of the regions' rich mines and forests in the aftermath of dictator Suharto's downfall. Nor were these massacres really new. During the Japanese occupation of 1942–45, behind-the-lines British officers encouraged a revival of headhunting to terrify the occupiers; and in 1967, the anticommunist dictatorship of Suharto arranged a similar controlled revival against residual Communist pockets among the local Chinese. I have no idea, alas, whether this is the sort of revenancy that Harry has in mind.

Lydia Liu

Lydia's essay, full of engaging detail and acute theoretical rumination, makes riveting reading. Her argument that in *Imagined Communities* I exploited the concept of sovereignty without thinking too much about it, except in a superficial way, is certainly right.

What I would like to do here, by way of a response, is simply to raise some of the reflections that her text has stimulated. Needless to say, *el demonio de las comparaciones* is there sitting on my shoulder as I write.

Let me begin with the strange figure of Ku Hung-ming, who may not be that strange in the end. Lydia notes that he was born in Penang in 1857, nine years before Sun Yat-sen. (They were of the same generation, but Sun was born to a peasant family in Kwangtung, a place where illusions about the Ch'ing dynasty were not easily sustained.) Penang was the first point of British penetration into the strategic zone of the Malacca Straits, which form the fastest and safest channel between the Indian Ocean and the South China Sea. Settled scantily in 1791, it was formally ceded to the East India Company by the Malay Sultan of Kedah in 1800. Its importance did not last long. The company took control of Singapore Island—much better positioned for control of maritime trade—in 1819, and Penang became a relative backwater soon after. It seems unlikely that Ku's forebears' presence on the island predated the British settlement, so that the family's location there probably did not go back more than two generations. But had they come from China, or from older diasporic Chinese settlements along the west coast of the Malay Peninsula? Did his parents speak any Chinese language? If they did, it perhaps accounts for the speed with which he later mastered classical Chinese. But this is guessing.

The year of his birth was also the year of the Great Indian (Sepoy) Mutiny which, though barbarously suppressed, finished off the East India Company and, the following year, turned India as well as Penang and Singapore into true colonies. When he was 17, the British Crown started its military and diplomatic interventions on the mainland, leading by stages to full colonization of the Peninsula. But by then Ku had already been four years in England. He did not return to Penang till 1880 (having studied in Scotland and Germany) and stayed there barely a year before leaving for China for good. It strikes me therefore as less than likely that his departure was a reaction to coloniality. Reading Lydia's vivid account, I could not help but notice analogies between the obsessions of Ku and those of Prince Wachirawut of Siam, who in 1910 ascended the throne in Bangkok as Rama VI. Wachirawut was born in 1881, a full generation after Ku, but he too was sent to England in early adolescence (1894) and spent almost a decade there. In Thailand today he is often regarded (with some anxiety given his open homosexuality and spendthrift ways) as the founder of Thai nationalism, and this view is not entirely incorrect. But he always equated the (threatened) sovereignty of Siam with his own person as a wannabe absolutist sovereign. This is why, for his coronation in 1910, just a decade after Ku's dramatic defense of the Empress Dowager and the "Boxers," he spent an enormous amount of money and invited all the world's "leading" royal families to attend in recognition of this doubled sovereignty. Perhaps surprisingly, he managed to get most of them (including the Japanese, but not the Chinese) to send over princes or princesses for the grand occasion.

This situation is not as odd as it may now seem. Europe was still a congeries of monarchies, with the notable exception of France (which had, however, only dispensed with its last monarch in 1870). Thus most people in Europe were still not citizens of nations, but the subjects of monarchical sovereigns whose status, here and there *gemildert* by constitutionalism, especially after

1848, still reflected the legacy of Absolutism. Furthermore, many of these sovereigns were "foreigners" in person or in origin. Germans, for example, ruled in Greece and Rumania, and even Victoria herself, famously related to every ruling family in Europe, was of not too distant German origin. But catastrophes were already on the horizon. The following year the Ch'ing dynasty was overthrown. Within less than ten years almost all of the grandest sovereigns, in Berlin and Istanbul, Vienna, and St. Petersburg, vanished— deposed, exiled, or killed. By 1920 the League of Nations had appeared, of which Wachirawut made strenuous efforts to become a member.

The point of all this is that I do not think one can understand Ku without taking into account the fact that most of his political career was carried on in an age when sovereignty in the person of a sovereign monarch was still internationally "normal." He was already 54 years old when the Ch'ing dynasty was finally destroyed. Lydia reads as a bit pathetic and neurotic Ku's eagerness to have Victoria communicate directly with the Empress Dowager, but my guess is that this reading may be anachronistic. For most of the nineteenth century, private communication between European sovereigns on key matters of state was well-established practice. And Ku's confusion of the personal Sovereign with the sovereignty of the state mirrors not only the attitude of Wachirawut but also the outlook of legitimists all over Europe.

While I find very impressive Lydia's lucid discussion of the way in which natural law conceptions of sovereignty were supplanted by positive law as the tide of European imperialism mounted, I think it would have been even better if she had taken into consideration the gradual transformation in the features of the sovereign sketched out above. We can observe the beginnings of the transformation quite well in Jefferson's 1776 Declaration of Independence, which after its famously eloquent opening fades off into a long string of whining complaints, not about the English/British, but about "him," George III, the sitting sovereign—till the Virginian put pen to paper—of the thirteen colonies. We can also note that "We, the People," is a polemical gloss on "We, Georgius Rex." Sovereignty was escaping from the physical person to the abstract national community. This change had vast consequences. Monarchs could talk to each other, marry each other, and, if need be, visit with each other within an interstate status system which marked them as special human beings, residually God-anointed. But nations could not chat with each other, marry each other, or visit with each other. As the nation won the long war with Legitimacy, mutual recognition and equivalency necessarily had to be calibrated along new and abstract axes. One of these axes was surely positive law, as man-made as the nation itself.

A final note on looting. It would be easy to get the impression from Lydia's essay that there was something horribly unique about the double looting of imperial Peking. In fact, however, looting was an age-old practice not merely of European armies but also of their Asian counterparts. Chinese armies sacked and looted the grand Burmese capital of Pagan, Burmese armies sacked and looted the grand Thai capital of Ayutthaya, Thai armies sacked the grand Khmer capital of Angkor. Napoleon sacked Moscow, the British looted Venice, and the Nazis looted everything in Europe they could get their hands on. In this matter there is a historic equivalence that should not be forgotten.

Bangkok, February 2003

Note

1. I now agree that my translation of *demonio* as "spectre" was a real mistake. When visiting the Philippines a few weeks ago, I noticed for the first time that *demonio*, which has long made an easy, unnoticed entry into Tagalog, is used all the time in one quite specific social context, and no other. Harried mothers, driven to distraction by ceaselessly energetic, naughty, and noisy small children, yell at them: *Demonio ka!* Which obviously cannot be translated as "You Spectre!" But also not as "You Demon," "You Bogeyman," or even I think "You Devil." The connotation is "You Pest!" Comparisons are like that, they buzz, and buzz, and refuse to go away or to be quiet. Irritating and distracting, but not spectral.

Contributors

Benedict Anderson, author of the important works discussed in this volume, is the Aaron L. Binenkorb Professor of International Studies, Emeritus, at Cornell University.

Partha Chatterjee is Director, Centre for Studies in Social Sciences, Calcutta, and Visiting Professor of Anthropology, Columbia University. He is the author of *Nationalist Thought and the Colonial World* (1986) and *The Nation and Its Fragments* (1993).

Pheng Cheah teaches in the Rhetoric Department of the University of California, Berkeley. He is coeditor of *Cosmopolitics: Thinking and Feeling beyond the Nation* (1998). His new book, *Spectral Nationality: Passages of Freedom from Kant to Postcolonial Literatures of Liberation,* is forthcoming from Columbia University Press.

Jonathan Culler is Class of 1916 Professor of English and Comparative Literature at Cornell. His most recent book is *Literary Theory: A Very Short Introduction.*

H. D. Harootunian is currently Director of the East Asian Studies Program and Professor of History at New York University. His most recent publications are *History's Disquiet: Modernity, Cultural Practice and the Question of Everyday Life* (2000) and *Overcome by Modernity: History, Culture and Community in Interwar Japan* (2000).

David A. Hollinger's most recent book is *Science, Jews, and Secular Culture: Studies in Mid-Twentieth-Century American Intellectual History.* He is Chancellor's Professor of History at the University of California, Berkeley.

Ernesto Laclau is Professor of Politics at Essex University and Professor of Comparative Literature at SUNY Buffalo. He is the author of *New Reflections on the Revolutions of our Time, Emancipation(s), Hegemony and Socialist Strategy* (with Chantal Mouffe), and *Contingency, Hegemony, Universality* (with Judith Butler and Slavoj Zizek).

Lydia H. Liu is the Helmut F. Stern Professor in Chinese Studies and Professor of Comparative Literature and Asian Languages and Cultures at the University of Michigan. She is the author of *Translingual Practice* (1995), editor of *Tokens of Exchange* (1999) and co-editor of *Writing and Materiality in China* (2003). Her new book *Desire and Sovereign Thinking* is forthcoming from Harvard University Press.

Andrew Parker is Professor of English at Amherst College. His edition of *The Philosopher and His Poor* by Jacques Rancière is forthcoming.

Marc Redfield is Professor of English at Claremont Graduate University and holds the John D. and Lillian Maguire Chair in the Humanities. He is the author of *Phantom Formations: Aesthetic Ideology and the Bildungsroman* (1996) and *The Politics of Aesthetics: Nationalism, Gender, Romanticism* (2003).

Doris Sommer is Professor of Romance Languages and Literatures at Harvard University. She is the author of *Foundational Fictions* (1991) and *Proceed with Caution, When Engaged by Minority Writing in the Americas* (1999).

Index

Adorno, Theodor, 184
Ainslie, Ricardo, 131–32
Alarcón, Norma, 131
Alexandrowicz, C. H., 211, 216–17, 218
Alter, Robert, 116
Anderson, biography, 230–31, 232;
    reputation, 2–3, 53, 77, 161
Anghie, Anthony, 215, 216, 221n22
Ankersmit, F. R., 98n4
Arendt, Hannah, 114, 120, 123, 137n12
Argentina, 134–35
Arguedas, José Maria, 62, 230
Aristotle, 137n12, 139n24
Arnold, Matthew, 76, 84
Auerbach, Erich, 22, 58
Austen, Jane, 35
Austin, J. L., 60

Bakhtin, Mikhail, 112, 120–21
Balakrishnan, Gopal, 49, 101n16, 234
Balfour, Ian, 99n8
Balibar, Etienne, 91, 101n19, 102n22, 182,
    227
Balzac, Honoré de, 41, 47
Basadre, Jorge, 60
Bauer, Otto, 238
Bede, Venerable, 117
Beiner, Robert, 145
Benjamin, Walter, 19n5, 44, 64, 71n8, 79,
    81, 82, 88, 165, 175, 233, 234

Bennington, Geoffrey, 100n12
Benveniste, Emile, 213–14
Berry, Chuck, 147
Bertolucci, Bernardo, 198
Bhabha, Homi, 50n1, 99n5, 137n9, 145
Billig, Michael, 235
Bloom, Harold, 116
Borges, Jorge Luis, 134–36, 140n32, 177
Bossuet, J-B 19n3
Bourdieu, Pierre, 137n10
Brennan, Timothy, 34, 44–5, 50n3, 53
Brown, Forbes, 204
Broyard, Anatole, 155
Buford, Bill, 140n33

Cabrera Infante, 135
Canclini, Nestor García, 140n30
Caruth, Cathy, 111
Cavell, Stanley, 121
Chakrabarty, Dipesh, 170
Chatterjee, Partha, 14, 17, 55–57, 70n2,
    99n5, 177–79, 183, 186, 225, 239–41
Cheah, Pheng, 51, 57, 231, 233
China, 18, 197–212, 240
Clunas, Craig, 199–201, 219n6
Colley, Linda, 46–49, 234
comparative method, vii–viii, 1–2, 9, 12–16,
    18, 168–69, 172, 183–84, 189
Crouch, Stanley, 156
Culler, Jonathan, 8, 54, 58, 227–30

De Man, Paul, 8, 79, 133
Defoe, Daniel, 214
derivative discourse, 55–58, 67, 70, 176
Derrida, Jacques, 51n9, 55–56, 59, 63, 67,
    70n5, 81, 83, 86, 100n10&12, 124,
    182, 185, 214, 231
Dickinson, G. Lowes, 220n10
Dostoevsky, Fyodor, 121
double-consciousness, 10–12, 15, 176
DuBois, W. E. B., 10, 19–20n7, 137n3, 176

Erikson, Erik, 150
European Community, 226

Fanon, Frantz, 10, 123, 180, 196
Fichte, Johann Gotrtleib, 78, 89–98
Forbes, Camille, 125
Foucault, Michel, 166
France, 30–31, 36, 37, 41, 47, 49, 101n18,
    239
Franco, Jean, 71n10
Freud, Sigmund, 81–2, 124–31, 138n14,
    138n16, 139n20
Fukuyama, Francis, 16

Gates, Henry Louis, 155
Gellner, Ernst, 19n2, 59–60, 100n11, 145,
    233, 241
Germany, 23, 78, 89–98
Gilman, Sander, 124, 126
Gilroy, Paul, 10, 137n3
Giroux, Henry, 140n29
Girs, Michael, 201
Glissant, Edouard, 134
Gong, Gerard, 215–16
Gotanda, Neil, 137n13
Gramsci, Antonio, 26, 179
Grant, Hope, 212
Great Britain, 35, 48–49, 231–32, 234, 238
Grotius, Hugo, 211, 216–18, 222n25
Guerrero, Leon Maria, 69
Guha, Ranajit, 239
Guibernau, Montserrat, 145
Guyer, Paul, 137n11

Habermas, Jürgen, 118
Hall, John A., 145
Hall, W. E., 210–11
Harcourt-Smith, Cecil, 156
Harootunian, Harry, 15, 232, 241–42
haunting, 60, 69–70, 97, 172, 175–76,
    182–89, 242

Hegel, G. F. W., 2, 55, 58, 79, 99n7, 102n23,
    163–64
Heidegger, Martin, 184
Heine, Heinrich, 139n21
Hevia, James, 199, 212, 221n20
Hitler, Adolph, 13, 68, 155, 168, 232
Hollinger, David, 17, 18, 238–39
homogeneous empty time, 4–5, 7, 19n4, 22,
    33, 80–83, 99n6, 165–66, 228, 240
Husserl, Edmund, 178

Imagined Communities, 2–3, 9, 14, 22–28,
    29–34, 36–41, 48–50, 53–59, 79–83,
    86–87, 146, 161–8, 226–29, 231–33,
    241
imagined community, 5–8, 21–28, 53–55,
    93–94, 96, 99n5, 154–55, 167, 226–27
India, 169, 200
Indochina, 78
Indonesia, 11–12, 13, 19n10, 33, 59, 104–8,
    110, 181, 184–88, 217, 233, 235–38,
    241, 242–44
Ireland, 34, 167, 231, 234
Islamic nationalism, 27, 226–27
Israel, 227
Ivy, Marilyn, 60, 242

Jameson, Fredric, 50n4
Japan, 179, 184–85, 187
Jefferson, Thomas, 244
Jiajin, Zhu, 219n3

Kahin, George, 174, 241
Kant, Immanuel, 122
Kedouri, Elie, 146
Kennedy, David, 222n24
Kerr, Lucille, 51n13
Khatibi, Abdelkebir, 123–24
Kittler, Friedrich, 101n18
Kohn, Hans, 114
Kristeva, Julia, 139n24
Krystal, Efrain, 51n11, 51n13, 51n14
Ku Hung-ming, 18, 192, 202–12, 218,
    219n8–16, 221n19–21, 242–44
Kunio, Yanagita, 184, 187
Kwee Thiam Tjing, 236–38
Kymlicka, Will, 113, 118

Lacan, Jacques, 124, 127–28, 138n14&15,
    139n21
Laclau, Ernesto, 7–8, 51n9, 123, 226–27
Lacoue-Labarthe, Philippe, 77, 100n14

Lambert, Wallace, 140n27
Latte, Konrad, 155
Leavitt, Peggy, 131
Levinas, Emmanuel, 126
Limón, José, 116
Liu, Lydia, 17, 18, 242–45
Lloyd, David, 33–34, 75–76, 131
long-distance nationalism, 17, 18, 113, 167, 202
Lukács, Gyorgy, 19n5, 179
Lyotard, Jean-François, 19n5, 113

Ma Jianzhong, 220n12, 221n18
Macartney, Lord, 199–200, 212, 219n4
Macherey, Pierre, 182
Malaka, Tan, 233–34
Marder, Elissa, 100n12
Martyn, David, 102n26
Marx, Karl, 5, 6, 19n2, 169, 175
Maugham, W. Somerset, 203–5
Mayer, Enrique, 70n4
Melas, Natalie, 51n12
minorities, 34, 41–47, 61–62, 112, 125, 150–58
modular nationalism, 22–23, 55–57, 70n2, 166, 177–78, 188, 192–95
Moretti, Franco, 35–36, 48, 50n3, 51n15, 79, 100n9
Morrison, Toni, 112
Moss, Daniel and Jennifer Wilder, 71n7
Musil, Robert, 58

Nairn, Tom, 238
Nandy, Ashis, 197
Nebrija, Antonio de, 110
Nettement, Alfred, 51n6
newspapers, 9, 31, 36–37, 80, 83, 99n9, 228
Noiriel, François, 239
novel and the nation, 7, 8, 19n4–5, 31–50, 54, 80, 228–30

O'Bryan-Knight, Jean, 51n13
Oboler, Suzanne, 139n25
Okin, Susan Moller, 123
Ortiz, Fernando, 110

Pandey, Gyanendra, 178
Parker, Andrew, 8, 229, 230–33
Peru, 13, 16, 17, 42–47, 60–67, 108–14
Petronius, 58
Philippines, 10, 12–14, 16, 38–41, 50, 68, 113, 181

Pierce, Charles Sanders, 120
Plato, 77
Potter, David, 146
print capitalism, 6, 17, 31–32, 36, 80, 83, 96, 100n11, 176–77
Pu Yi, 198

Qianlong, Emperor, 197, 200
Quigley, Austin, 137n6

Rabelais, 121
Rama, Angel, 62, 67
Rawls, John, 140n31
Reagan, Ronald, 240
Redfield, Marc, 8, 233, 242
Reid, Roddey, 36
Renan, Ernest, 30–31, 50n1, 100n14, 101n18, 139n23, 238
Rizal, José, 10, 13, 32, 38–41, 49–50, 58, 68, 108, 114, 175–76, 228–29, 232
Rousseau, Jean-Jacques, 1, 63
Rowe, William, 70n4

Said, Edward, 192
Saussure, Ferdinand de, 128
Scarry, Elaine, 137n8
Schelling, F. W. J., 139n24
Schiller, Friedrich, 76,
Schmitt, Cannon, 70n3
Schmitt, Carl, 51n9
Sengalen, Victor, 176
seriality, 9–10, 15, 17, 18, 57, 108, 147–48, 161–64, 167, 176, 183, 195–97
Seton-Watson, Hugh, 193,
Shikai, General Yuan, 219n3
Siam, 12, 181
Singapore, 205
Snow, Catharine, 140n28
Soekarno, see Sukarno
Soetomo, Dr., 184–88
Sommer, Doris, 17, 34–35, 45–46, 51n5, 51n14, 70n4, 112, 235–38
Southeast Asia, vii, 2, 3, 4, 13, 16, 172–76, 180–89
Southey, Robert, 139n23
Spain, 117
Spectre of Comparisons, The, vii, 3–4, 9, 12, 32, 41–47, 54, 60–70, 107–14, 146, 148, 168–69, 171–78, 181–87, 229–30, 233
Spivak, Gayatri, 70n1

Suharto, 242
Sukarno, 13, 68, 168, 232
Sun Yat Sen, 202
Swift, George, 201

Tang Yen-lu, 220n12
Tarde, Gabriel, 26
Taylor, Charles, 118, 120, 122
telescope, inverted, 13–15, 68, 168, 176, 183, 232–33, 241
Tetsuro, Watsuji, 176, 184, 188
Thailand, 16, 243
Thompson, E. P., 165
Toer, Pramoedya Ananta, 11–12, 58–59, 69, 148, 162

United States, 18, 114, 120, 134, 145–59, 173–74, 235, 238–39
universality, viii, 9, 12, 14, 75–76, 122,

124–25, 127, 163, 168–69, 179, 192–93, 213

Vargas Llosa, Mario, 8, 17–18, 32, 41–47, 60–67, 108–14, 125, 229–30
Veyne, Paul, 116
Victoria, Queen, 202
Vilar, Pierre, 179
Vitoria, Francisco de, 215–17

Wachirawut, Prince, 243
Weber, Max, 2
Weber, Samuel, 88
Wheaton, Henry, 210
Wittgenstein, Ludwig, 120, 130, 132–33

Zentella, Ana Celia, 132
Zhang Zhidong, 205, 206, 20, 211–12, 221n17